STOCK
TRADER'S
ALMANAC
2 0 2 4

Jeffrey A. Hirsch & Christopher Mistal

WILEY

www.stocktradersalmanac.com

Editor-in-Chief	Jeffrey A. Hirsch
Director of Research	Christopher Mistal
Graphic Design	Darlene Dion Design
Publisher 1966–2000 & Editor 1966–2003	Yale Hirsch (1923-2021)

ISBN: 978-1-394-20316-1 (paper)
ISBN: 978-139-420323-9 (ePDF)
ISBN: 978-139-420322-2 (ePub)

SKY10058743_103123

THE 2024 STOCK TRADER'S ALMANAC

CONTENTS

DIRECTORY OF TRADING PATTERNS & DATABANK

STRATEGY PLANNING AND RECORD SECTION

INTRODUCTION TO THE FIFTY-SEVENTH EDITION

We are honored to present the 57th annual edition of the S*tock Trader's Almanac*. The *Almanac* provides you with the necessary tools and data to invest and trade successfully in the twenty-first century.

J.P. Morgan's classic retort "Stocks will fluctuate" is often quoted with a wink-of-the-eye implication that the only prediction one can make about the stock market is that it will go up, down, or sideways. Many investors and traders agree that no one ever really knows which way the market will move. Nothing could be further from the truth.

We discovered many years ago that while stocks do indeed fluctuate, they do so in well-defined, often predictable patterns. These patterns recur too frequently to be the result of chance or coincidence. How else do we explain that since 1950 the Dow has gained 26249.55 points during November through April compared to just 7634.28 May through October? (See page 54.)

The *Almanac* is a practical investment tool. It alerts you to those little-known market patterns and tendencies on which shrewd professionals enhance profit potential. You will be able to forecast market trends with accuracy and confidence when you use the *Almanac* to help you understand:

- How our presidential elections affect the economy and the stock market—just as the moon affects the tides. Many investors have made fortunes following the political cycle. You can be sure that money managers who control billions of dollars are also political cycle watchers. Astute people do not ignore a pattern that has been working effectively throughout most of our economic history.

- How the passage of the Twentieth Amendment to the Constitution fathered the January Barometer. This barometer has an outstanding record for predicting the general course of the stock market each year with only 12 major errors since 1950 for an 83.6% accuracy ratio. (See page 18.)

- Why there is a significant market bias at certain times of the day, week, month and year.

Even if you are an investor who pays scant attention to cycles, indicators and patterns, your investment survival could hinge on your interpretation of one of the recurring patterns found within these pages. One of the most intriguing and important patterns is the symbiotic relationship between Washington and Wall Street. Aside from the potential profitability in seasonal patterns, there's the pure joy of seeing the market very often do just what you expected.

The *Stock Trader's Almanac* is also an organizer. Its wealth of information is presented on a calendar basis. The *Almanac* puts investing in a business framework and makes investing easier because it:

- Updates investment knowledge and informs you of new techniques and tools.

- Is a monthly reminder and refresher course.

- Alerts you to both seasonal opportunities and dangers.

- Furnishes a historical viewpoint by providing pertinent statistics on past market performance.

- Supplies forms necessary for portfolio planning, record keeping and tax preparation.

 The WITCH Icon signifies THIRD FRIDAY OF THE MONTH on calendar pages and alerts you to extraordinary volatility due to expiration of monthly equity and index options and index futures contracts. "Triple-Witching" days appear during March, June, September, and December. Some readers have questioned why we do not use the term "Quadruple Witching" as some in the business do. As we point out on page 108 the market for single-stock and ETF futures remains small and their impact on the market is virtually nonexistent. If and when single-stock futures trading volume expands and exerts influence on the market, we will reconsider. Until such time we do not believe the term "quadruple witching" is applicable.

 The BULL Icon on calendar pages signifies favorable trading days based on the S&P 500 rising 60% or more of the time on a particular trading day during the 21-year period January 2002 to December 2022.

 A BEAR Icon on calendar pages signifies unfavorable trading days based on the S&P falling 60% or more of the time for the same 21-year period.

Clusters of two or more BULLs or BEARs can be especially helpful in identifying periods of strength or weakness throughout the year. Clusters can also be three out of four days or three out of five days. An example of three BULLs in four days can be observed on page 41 during the first week of April.

On pages 123–130 you will find complete Market Probability Calendars both long term and the recent 21-year period for the Dow, S&P and NASDAQ, as well as for the Russell 1000 and Russell 2000 indices. To give you even greater perspective we have listed next to the date every day that the market is open the Market Probability numbers for the same 21-year period for the Dow (D), S&P 500 (S) and NASDAQ (N). You will see a "D," "S" and "N" followed by a number signifying the actual Market Probability number for that trading day based on the recent 21-year period.

Other seasonalities near the ends, beginnings and middles of months; options expirations, around holidays and other times are noted for *Almanac* investors' convenience on the weekly planner pages. All other important economic releases are provided in the Strategy Calendar every month in our newsletter, *Almanac Investor*, available at our website *www.stocktradersalmanac.com*. Please see the insert for a special offer for new subscribers.

One-year seasonal pattern charts for Dow, S&P 500, NASDAQ, Russell 1000, and Russell 2000 appear on pages 42, 44 and 46. There are three charts each for Dow and S&P 500 spanning our entire database starting in 1901 and one each for the younger indices. As 2024 is a presidential election year, each chart contains typical election year performance compared to all years.

The Russell 2000 is an excellent proxy for small- and mid-caps and the Russell 1000 provides a broader view of large caps. Annual highs and lows for all five indices covered in the *Almanac* appear on pages 151–155. Top 10 Best & Worst days, weeks, months, quarters and years for all five indices are listed on pages 174–183.

We have converted many of the paper forms in our Record Keeping section into spreadsheets for our own internal use. As a service to our faithful readers, we are making these forms available at our website *www.stocktradersalmanac.com*. Look for a link titled "Forms."

Presidential election years have historically been the second-best year of the four-year cycle. Election-year performance has improved the last three cycles after an undecided election in 2000 and the Great Financial Crisis in 2008 generated losses. You can find all the market charts of election years since the Depression on page 28, "2024 Presidential Election Year Perspectives" on page 26, "How the Government Manipulates the Economy to Stay in Power" on page 32, "Incumbent Party Wins & Losses" on page 34 and "Only Two Losses Last 7 Months of Election Years" on page 80.

This year we feature two brand new pages. "Bulls Win When Market Hits the January Trifecta" on page 20 shows a new indicator we built in 2013 that combines our Santa Claus Rally (page 118) and January Barometer (page 18) with the First Five Days (page 16), creating a more powerful indicator. On page 104 is a new trading strategy, "Traders Feast on Small Stocks Thanksgiving through Santa Claus Rally."

Our 2024 Outlook on pages 10–11 foresees the continuation of the bull market in 2024 with market gains in line with historical election year averages. "How To Trade Best Months Switching Strategies" appears on page 38. How "Summer Market Volume Doldrums Drives Worst Six Months" is updated on page 50. Revised sector seasonalities including several consistent shorting opportunities, appear on pages 94–98.

We are constantly searching for new insights and nuances about the stock market and welcome any suggestions from our readers.

Have a healthy and prosperous 2024!

2024 OUTLOOK

The power of the 4-Year Presidential Election Cycle is evident in the graph at the bottom of this page. The performance of the current cycle from 2021 to June 2023 for the Dow, S&P 500 and NASDAQ is overlaid on the average cycles for the three main U.S. stock market indexes. At the midpoint of 2023 the stock market has been tracking the historical 4-Year Cycle trend rather closely. Understanding this impactful recurring pattern, and recognizing when it's in play, enabled us to anticipate the 2022 midterm-year bear market and guide our *Almanac Investor* members to safety early on.

October 2022 once again delivered a quintessential midterm-year bear market bottom, setting up the "Sweet Spot" of the 4-Year Cycle, which runs from Q4 midterm year through Q2 pre-election year. In the face of overly bearish sentiment and naysayers—and partially due to them—we made our bullish call early in October 2022. At the time our reading of seasonality, cycles, sentiment, monetary policy, technical analysis, market internals, fundamentals, and economic data indicated to us that the bear was over, and it was time to get bullish again.

As of mid-June 2023, the Sweet Spot has delivered. Since 1949, over the three-quarter period, the Dow has gained an average of 19.3% while the S&P 500 produced 20.0% on average. NASDAQ has jumped 29.3% on average during this period since 1971. This time around from the September 2022 closing prices to the closes on June 16: Dow is up 19.4%, S&P is up 23.0%, and NASDAQ is up 29.4%. U.S. equity markets will likely move sideways with a pullback or correction over the weak summer months, especially after mid-July into the worst two months of the year August and September. We expect the 4-Year Cycle trend to continue through 2023, pushing the indexes near all-time highs at yearend 2023.

While many economists and market prognosticators are still expecting a recession, we contend the U.S. had its recession with the two consecutive negative quarters of GDP in 2022 Q1 and Q2. This was the traditional definition of recession from time immemorial until it was changed during the Covid-19 shutdown in 2020, and it is the one still being used in the rest of the world. Recession proponents argue that an inverted yield curve always precedes a recession. The Federal Reserve's Federal Open Market Committee (FOMC) sets the Fed Funds Rate at its eight regular meetings each year. FOMC interest rate policy drives the rest of the interest rate yield curve.

But the Fed and the FOMC operate much differently today than they have in the past. We dug through the old minutes of the FOMC meeting and found that back in the 1970s and 1980s interest rates were set by the bond market and it was at the FOMC meetings that the Fed would adjust their rates to match the bond market. This is the exact opposite of what is happening today.

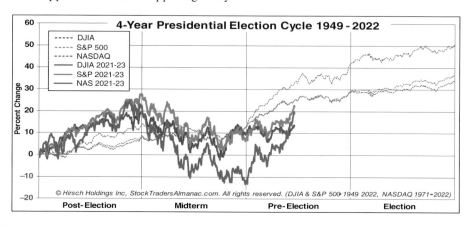

The stock market is likely to benefit greatly from the power of a sitting president running for reelection in 2024. To gain reelection, presidents tend to take care of their least savory initiatives in the first half of their term and "prime the pump" in the second half so the electorate is most prosperous when they enter the voting booths. Sitting presidents also have the capacity to control the narrative from the bully pulpit. "How the Government Manipulates the Economy to Stay in Power" on page 32 dives into deeper detail.

As you can see in the chart at the bottom of this page, comparing the average market gains in an election year when a sitting president is running for reelection to an open field when there is no sitting president in office running the gains are substantially better averaging 12.8% for the S&P 500 since 1949 versus poor performance all year long when there is an open field, culminating in a loss of –1.5% for the year. The market hates uncertainty, and with a sitting president running, there is a good chance market, economic, and civic conditions will likely remain unchanged, whereas with an open field there are a great deal of unknowns. 2024 has that power of incumbency going for it.

Sitting presidents have won reelection 15 times and lost 6 in the past 21 occurrences since 1900. Years incumbents won reelection were stronger early in the year. Years incumbent presidents lost suffered weak starts, but finished strong as unpopular administrations were removed (see page 34 for more). Since 1900 the Dow averages a gain of 8.8% in election years with a sitting president running and 9.9% since 1950.

One of the more impressive election cycle phenomena is that there have "Only Been Two Losses in the Last Seven Months of Election Years:" in 2000 with the undecided election and in 2008 during the Great Financial Crisis (page 80). For more "2024 Presidential Election Year Perspectives" see page 26.

Expect a continuation of the current four-year cycle tracking the historical pattern with rather typical solid election year performance in 2024—save any geopolitical, political, or exogenous event. Look for some sideways action during the spring and summer months of 2024 during Q2 and Q3 as you can see in the chart. S&P and NASDAQ will likely deliver somewhat greater gains in both 2023 and 2024.

Average election year gains for the Dow of approximately 7–8% from today's levels around 34000 would put the Dow at about 36500 by the end of 2024. A similar move from 36000 at yearend 2023 would put the Dow over 38000 near our forecasted "Super Boom" level of 38820. This would be on or ahead of the schedule we projected in our book *Super Boom*, a forecast originally made in May of 2010 in *Almanac Investor* near Dow 10000. After that we will be updating our long-term forecast beyond 2024–2025 for what looks like a range-bound, stock picker's, seasonal trader's market for several years.

Jeffrey A. Hirsch, June 21, 2023

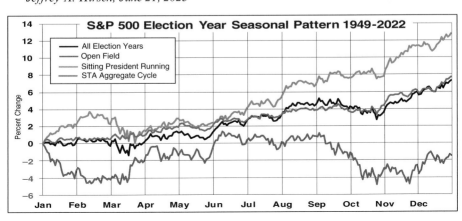

2024 STRATEGY CALENDAR
(Option expiration dates circled)

	MONDAY	TUESDAY	WEDNESDAY	THURSDAY	FRIDAY	SATURDAY	SUNDAY
JANUARY	1 JANUARY New Year's Day	2	3	4	5	6	7
	8	9	10	11	12	13	14
	15 Martin Luther King Jr. Day	16	17	18	(19)	20	21
	22	23	24	25	26	27	28
	29	30	31	1 FEBRUARY	2	3	4
FEBRUARY	5	6	7	8	9	10	11
	12	13	14 ♥ Ash Wednesday	15	(16)	17	18
	19 Presidents' Day	20	21	22	23	24	25
	26	27	28	29	1 MARCH	2	3
MARCH	4	5	6	7	8	9	10 Daylight Saving Time Begins
	11	12	13	14	(15)	16	17 ♣ St. Patrick's Day
	18	19	20	21	22	23	24
	25	26	27	28	29 Good Friday	30	31 Easter
APRIL	1 APRIL	2	3	4	5	6	7
	8	9	10	11	12	13	14
	15 Tax Deadline	16	17	18	(19)	20	21
	22	23 Passover	24	25	26	27	28
	29	30	1 MAY	2	3	4	5
MAY	6	7	8	9	10	11	12 Mother's Day
	13	14	15	16	(17)	18	19
	20	21	22	23	24	25	26
	27 Memorial Day	28	29	30	31	1 JUNE	2
JUNE	3	4	5	6	7	8	9
	10	11	12	13	14	15	16 Father's Day
	17	18	19 Juneteenth	20	(21)	22	23
	24	25	26	27	28	29	30

Market closed on shaded weekdays; closes early when half-shaded.

2024 STRATEGY CALENDAR

(Option expiration dates circled)

MONDAY	TUESDAY	WEDNESDAY	THURSDAY	FRIDAY	SATURDAY	SUNDAY	
1 JULY	2	3	4 Independence Day	5	6	7	
8	9	10	11	12	13	14	JULY
15	16	17	18	(19)	20	21	
22	23	24	25	26	27	28	
29	30	31	1 AUGUST	2	3	4	
5	6	7	8	9	10	11	
12	13	14	15	(16)	17	18	AUGUST
19	20	21	22	23	24	25	
26	27	28	29	30	31	1 SEPTEMBER	
2 Labor Day	3	4	5	6	7	8	SEPTEMBER
9	10	11	12	13	14	15	
16	17	18	19	(20)	21	22	
23	24	25	26	27	28	29	
30	1 OCTOBER	2	3 Rosh Hashanah	4	5	6	
7	8	9	10	11	12 Yom Kippur	13	OCTOBER
14 Columbus Day	15	16	17	(18)	19	20	
21	22	23	24	25	26	27	
28	29	30	31 🎃	1 NOVEMBER	2	3 Daylight Saving Time Ends	
4	5 Election Day	6	7	8	9	10	NOVEMBER
11 Veterans' Day	12	13	14	(15)	16	17	
18	19	20	21	22	23	24	
25	26	27	28 Thanksgiving Day	29	30	1 DECEMBER	
2	3	4	5	6	7	8	DECEMBER
9	10	11	12	13	14	15	
16	17	18	19	(20)	21	22	
23	24	25 Christmas	26 Chanukah	27	28	29	
30	31	1 JANUARY New Year's Day	2	3	4	5	

JANUARY ALMANAC

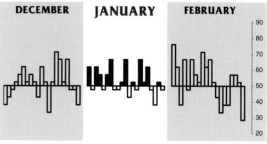

Market Probability Chart above is a graphic representation of the S&P 500 Recent Market Probability Calendar on page 126.

◆ January Barometer predicts year's course with .726 batting average (page 18) ◆ 12 of last 18 presidential-election years followed January's direction ◆ Every down January on the S&P since 1950, *without exception*, preceded a new or extended bear market, a flat market, or a 10% correction (page 24) ◆ S&P gains January's first five days preceded full-year gains 83.0% of the time, 15 of last 18 presidential-election years followed first five day's direction (page 16) ◆ November, December, and January constitute the year's best three-month span, a 4.2% S&P gain (pages 52 & 149) ◆ January NASDAQ powerful 2.7% since 1971 (pages 60 & 150) ◆ "January Effect" now starts in mid-December and favors small-cap stocks (pages 112 & 114) ◆ 2009 has the dubious honor of the worst S&P 500 January on record ◆ Dow gained more than 1000 points in 2018 & 2019 ◆ See January Indicator Trifecta (page 20)

January Vital Statistics

	DJIA	S&P 500	NASDAQ	Russell 1K	Russell 2K
Rank	6	6	1	5	3
Up	46	44	35	27	25
Down	28	30	18	18	20
Average % Change	0.9%	1.1%	2.7%	1.1%	1.5%
Election Year	−0.1%	0.1%	1.7%	0.1%	0.8%

			Best & Worst January						
	% Change		% Change		% Change		% Change		% Change
Best	1976	14.4	1987	13.2	1975	16.6	1987	12.7	1985	13.1
Worst	2009	−8.8	2009	−8.6	2008	−9.9	2009	−8.3	2009	−11.2

			Best & Worst January Weeks						
Best	1/9/76	6.1	1/2/09	6.8	1/12/01	9.1	1/2/09	6.8	1/9/87	7.0
Worst	1/8/16	−6.2	1/8/16	−6.0	1/28/00	−8.2	1/8/16	−6.0	1/8/16	−7.9

			Best & Worst January Days						
Best	1/17/91	4.6	1/3/01	5.0	1/3/01	14.2	1/3/01	5.3	1/21/09	5.3
Worst	1/8/88	−6.9	1/8/88	−6.8	1/2/01	−7.2	1/8/88	−6.1	1/20/09	−7.0

	First Trading Day of Expiration Week: 1980–2023				
Record (#Up – #Down)	27–15	24–20	23–21	22–22	22–22
Current streak	D2	D2	U1	D2	D2
Avg % Change	0.02	0.02	0.03	0.001	−0.04

	Options Expiration Day: 1980–2023				
Record (#Up – #Down)	25–19	25–19	26–18	25–19	26–18
Current streak	U1	U1	U1	U1	U1
Avg % Change	0.01	0.05	0.01	0.04	0.08

	Options Expiration Week: 1980–2023				
Record (#Up – #Down)	24–20	20–22	26–18	27–17	29–15
Current streak	D2	D2	U2	U2	U1
Avg % Change	−0.16	−0.03	0.29	−0.04	0.10

	Week After Options Expiration: 1980–2023				
Record (#Up – #Down)	25–19	25–17	26–18	25–17	29–15
Current streak	U2	U2	U2	U2	U1
Avg % Change	0.07	0.23	0.21	0.21	0.10

	First Trading Day Performance				
% of Time Up	59.5	50.0	56.6	46.7	46.7
Avg % Change	0.24	0.15	0.20	0.14	0.04

	Last Trading Day Performance				
% of Time Up	55.4	60.8	64.2	57.8	71.1
Avg % Change	0.17	0.24	0.32	0.30	0.30

Dow & S&P 1950—June 9, 2023, NASDAQ 1971—June 9, 2023, Russell 1K & 2K 1979—June 9, 2023.

20th Amendment made "lame ducks" disappear.
Now, "As January goes, so goes the year."

New Year's Day

MONDAY

1

Don't worry about people stealing your ideas. If the ideas are any good, you'll have to ram them down people's throats.
— Howard Aiken (U.S. computer scientist, 1900–1973)

First Trading Day of Year NASDAQ Up 18 of Last 26

TUESDAY

D 71.4
S 61.9
N 71.4

2

Governments last as long as the under-taxed can defend themselves against the over-taxed.
— Bernard Berenson (American art critic, 1865–1959)

Second Trading Day of the Year, Dow Up 21 of Last 30
Santa Claus Rally Ends (Page 118)

WEDNESDAY

D 61.9
S 47.6
N 42.9

3

Industrial capitalism has generated the greatest productive power in human history. To date, no other socioeconomic system has been able to generate comparable productive power.
— Peter L. Berger (Author, *The Capitalist Revolution*)

THURSDAY

D 52.4
S 61.9
N 57.1

4

The government would not look fondly on Caesar's Palace if it opened a table for wagering on corporate failure. It should not give greater encouragement for Goldman Sachs [et al] to do so.
— Roger Lowenstein (Financial journalist and author, *End of Wall Street, N Y Times* OpEd 4/20/2010, b. 1954)

FRIDAY

D 52.4
S 57.1
N 57.1

5

I've learned that only through focus can you do world-class things, no matter how capable you are.
— William H. Gates (Microsoft founder, *Fortune*, July 8, 2002)

SATURDAY

6

January Almanac Investor Sector Seasonalities: See Pages 94, 96 and 98

SUNDAY

7

JANUARY'S FIRST FIVE DAYS: AN EARLY WARNING SYSTEM

The last 47 up First Five Days were followed by full-year gains 39 times for an 83.0% accuracy ratio and a 14.0% average gain in all 47 years. The eight exceptions include flat years 1994, 2011, 2015, four related to war and 2018. Vietnam military spending delayed start of 1966 bear market. Ceasefire imminence early in 1973 raised stocks temporarily. Saddam Hussein turned 1990 into a bear. The war on terrorism, instability in the Mideast and corporate malfeasance shaped 2002 into one of the worst years on record. In 2018 a partially inverted yield curve and trade tensions triggered a fourth quarter selloff. The 26 down First Five Days were followed by 14 up years and 12 down (46.2% accurate) and an average gain of 0.3%.

In presidential election years this indicator has a respectable record. In the last 18 presidential election years 15 full years followed the direction of the First Five Days. See January Indicator Trifecta (page 20).

THE FIRST-FIVE-DAYS-IN-JANUARY INDICATOR

	Chronological Data				Ranked by Performance		
	Previous Year's Close	January 5th Day	5-Day Change	Year Change	Rank	5-Day Change	Year Change
1950	16.76	17.09	2.0%	21.8%	1	1987	6.2%	2.0%
1951	20.41	20.88	2.3	16.5	2	1976	4.9	19.1
1952	23.77	23.91	0.6	11.8	3	1999	3.7	19.5
1953	26.57	26.33	-0.9	-6.6	4	2003	3.4	26.4
1954	24.81	24.93	0.5	45.0	5	2006	3.4	13.6
1955	35.98	35.33	-1.8	26.4	6	1983	3.3	17.3
1956	45.48	44.51	-2.1	2.6	7	1967	3.1	20.1
1957	46.67	46.25	-0.9	-14.3	8	1979	2.8	12.3
1958	39.99	40.99	2.5	38.1	9	2018	2.8	-6.2
1959	55.21	55.40	0.3	8.5	10	2019	2.7	28.9
1960	59.89	59.50	-0.7	-3.0	11	2010	2.7	12.8
1961	58.11	58.81	1.2	23.1	12	1963	2.6	18.9
1962	71.55	69.12	-3.4	-11.8	13	1958	2.5	38.1
1963	63.10	64.74	2.6	18.9	14	1984	2.4	1.4
1964	75.02	76.00	1.3	13.0	15	1951	2.3	16.5
1965	84.75	85.37	0.7	9.1	16	2013	2.2	29.6
1966	92.43	93.14	0.8	-13.1	17	1975	2.2	31.5
1967	80.33	82.81	3.1	20.1	18	1950	2.0	21.8
1968	96.47	96.62	0.2	7.7	19	2012	1.8	13.4
1969	103.86	100.80	-2.9	-11.4	20	2021	1.8	26.9
1970	92.06	92.68	0.7	0.1	21	2004	1.8	9.0
1971	92.15	92.19	0.04	10.8	22	1973	1.5	-17.4
1972	102.09	103.47	1.4	15.6	23	2023	1.4	??
1973	118.05	119.85	1.5	-17.4	24	1972	1.4	15.6
1974	97.55	96.12	-1.5	-29.7	25	1964	1.3	13.0
1975	68.56	70.04	2.2	31.5	26	2017	1.3	19.4
1976	90.19	94.58	4.9	19.1	27	1961	1.2	23.1
1977	107.46	105.01	-2.3	-11.5	28	1989	1.2	27.3
1978	95.10	90.64	-4.7	1.1	29	2011	1.1	-0.003
1979	96.11	98.80	2.8	12.3	30	2002	1.1	-23.4
1980	107.94	108.95	0.9	25.8	31	1997	1.0	31.0
1981	135.76	133.06	-2.0	-9.7	32	1980	0.9	25.8
1982	122.55	119.55	-2.4	14.8	33	1966	0.8	-13.1
1983	140.64	145.23	3.3	17.3	34	1994	0.7	-1.5
1984	164.93	168.90	2.4	1.4	35	1965	0.7	9.1
1985	167.24	163.99	-1.9	26.3	36	2009	0.7	23.5
1986	211.28	207.97	-1.6	14.6	37	2020	0.7	16.3
1987	242.17	257.28	6.2	2.0	38	1970	0.7	0.1
1988	247.08	243.40	-1.5	12.4	39	1952	0.6	11.8
1989	277.72	280.98	1.2	27.3	40	1954	0.5	45.0
1990	353.40	353.79	0.1	-6.6	41	1996	0.4	20.3
1991	330.22	314.90	-4.6	26.3	42	1959	0.3	8.5
1992	417.09	418.10	0.2	4.5	43	1995	0.3	34.1
1993	435.71	429.05	-1.5	7.1	44	1992	0.2	4.5
1994	466.45	469.90	0.7	-1.5	45	1968	0.2	7.7
1995	459.27	460.83	0.3	34.1	46	2015	0.2	-0.7
1996	615.93	618.46	0.4	20.3	47	1990	0.1	-6.6
1997	740.74	748.41	1.0	31.0	48	1971	0.04	10.8
1998	970.43	956.04	-1.5	26.7	49	2007	-0.4	3.5
1999	1229.23	1275.09	3.7	19.5	50	2014	-0.6	11.4
2000	1469.25	1441.46	-1.9	-10.1	51	1960	-0.7	-3.0
2001	1320.28	1295.86	-1.8	-13.0	52	1957	-0.9	-14.3
2002	1148.08	1160.71	1.1	-23.4	53	1953	-0.9	-6.6
2003	879.82	909.93	3.4	26.4	54	1974	-1.5	-29.7
2004	1111.92	1131.91	1.8	9.0	55	1998	-1.5	26.7
2005	1211.92	1186.19	-2.1	3.0	56	1988	-1.5	12.4
2006	1248.29	1290.15	3.4	13.6	57	1993	-1.5	7.1
2007	1418.30	1412.11	-0.4	3.5	58	1986	-1.6	14.6
2008	1468.36	1390.19	-5.3	-38.5	59	2001	-1.8	-13.0
2009	903.25	909.73	0.7	23.5	60	1955	-1.8	26.4
2010	1115.10	1144.98	2.7	12.8	61	2022	-1.9	-19.4
2011	1257.64	1271.50	1.1	-0.003	62	2000	-1.9	-10.1
2012	1257.60	1280.70	1.8	13.4	63	1985	-1.9	26.3
2013	1426.19	1457.15	2.2	29.6	64	1981	-2.0	-9.7
2014	1848.36	1837.49	-0.6	11.4	65	1956	-2.1	2.6
2015	2058.90	2062.14	0.2	-0.7	66	2005	-2.1	3.0
2016	2043.94	1922.03	-6.0	9.5	67	1977	-2.3	-11.5
2017	2238.83	2268.90	1.3	19.4	68	1982	-2.4	14.8
2018	2673.61	2747.71	2.8	-6.2	69	1969	-2.9	-11.4
2019	2506.85	2574.41	2.7	28.9	70	1962	-3.4	-11.8
2020	3230.78	3253.05	0.7	16.3	71	1991	-4.6	26.3
2021	3756.07	3824.68	1.8	26.9	72	1978	-4.7	1.1
2022	4766.18	4667.03	-1.9	-19.4	73	2008	-5.3	-38.5
2023	3839.50	3892.09	1.4	??	74	2016	-6.0	9.5

Based on S&P 500

JANUARY 2024

January's First Five Days Act as an "Early Warning" (Page 16)

MONDAY

D 38.1
S 47.6
N 66.7

8

Mankind is divided into three classes: Those that are immovable, those that are movable, and those that move.
— Arabian proverb (also attributed to Benjamin Franklin)

TUESDAY

D 52.4
S 57.1
N 61.9

9

*The only way to even begin to manage this new world is by focusing on...nation building—
helping others restructure their economies and put in place decent non-corrupt government.*
— Thomas L. Friedman (*NY Times* foreign affairs columnist)

WEDNESDAY

D 57.1
S 66.7
N 71.4

10

I don't know where speculation got such a bad name, since I know of no forward leap which was not fathered by speculation.
— John Steinbeck

January Ends "Best Three-Month Span" (Pages 52, 60, 149, and 150)

THURSDAY

D 47.6
S 47.6
N 52.4

11

The thing you do obsessively between age 13 and 18, that's the thing you have the most chance of being world-class at.
— William H. Gates (Microsoft founder, "Charlie Rose" interview 2/22/2016, b. 1955)

FRIDAY

D 47.6
S 47.6
N 42.9

12

Taxes are what we pay for civilized society.
— Oliver Wendell Holmes Jr. (U.S. Supreme Court Justice 1902–1932,
"The Great Dissenter," inscribed above IRS HQ entrance, 1841–1935)

SATURDAY

13

SUNDAY

14

THE INCREDIBLE JANUARY BAROMETER (DEVISED 1972): ONLY 12 SIGNIFICANT ERRORS IN 73 YEARS

Devised by Yale Hirsch in 1972, our January Barometer states that as the S&P 500 goes in January, so goes the year. The indicator has registered **twelve major errors since 1950 for an 83.6% accuracy ratio.** Vietnam affected 1966 and 1968; major bull market started in August 1982; two January rate cuts and 9/11 affected 2001; anticipation of military action in Iraq held stocks down in January 2003; new bull market began in 2009; the Fed saved 2010 with QE2; QE3 likely staved off declines in 2014; global growth fears sparked selling in January 2016; a partially inverted yield curve and trade tensions fueled Q4 selling in 2018; and Covid-19 disrupted 2020 and 2021. (*Almanac Investor* subscribers receive full analysis of each reading as well as its potential implications for the full year.)

Including the eight flat-year errors (less than +/- 5%) yields a 72.6% accuracy ratio. A full comparison of all monthly barometers for the Dow, S&P and NASDAQ can be seen at *www.stocktradersalmanac.com* in the January 5, 2023 issue. Full years followed January's direction in 12 of the last 18 presidential election years. See pages 20 and 24 for more.

AS JANUARY GOES, SO GOES THE YEAR

Market Performance in January

	Previous Year's Close	January Close	January Change	Year Change	
1950	16.76	17.05	1.7%	21.8%	
1951	20.41	21.66	6.1	16.5	
1952	23.77	24.14	1.6	11.8	
1953	26.57	26.38	-0.7	-6.6	
1954	24.81	26.08	5.1	45.0	
1955	35.98	36.63	1.8	26.4	
1956	45.48	43.82	-3.6	2.6	flat
1957	46.67	44.72	-4.2	-14.3	
1958	39.99	41.70	4.3	38.1	
1959	55.21	55.42	0.4	8.5	
1960	59.89	55.61	-7.1	-3.0	flat
1961	58.11	61.78	6.3	23.1	
1962	71.55	68.84	-3.8	-11.8	
1963	63.10	66.20	4.9	18.9	
1964	75.02	77.04	2.7	13.0	
1965	84.75	87.56	3.3	9.1	
1966	92.43	92.88	0.5	-13.1	X
1967	80.33	86.61	7.8	20.1	
1968	96.47	92.24	-4.4	7.7	X
1969	103.86	103.01	-0.8	-11.4	
1970	92.06	85.02	-7.6	0.1	flat
1971	92.15	95.88	4.0	10.8	
1972	102.09	103.94	1.8	15.6	
1973	118.05	116.03	-1.7	-17.4	
1974	97.55	96.57	-1.0	-29.7	
1975	68.56	76.98	12.3	31.5	
1976	90.19	100.86	11.8	19.1	
1977	107.46	102.03	-5.1	-11.5	
1978	95.10	89.25	-6.2	1.1	flat
1979	96.11	99.93	4.0	12.3	
1980	107.94	114.16	5.8	25.8	
1981	135.76	129.55	-4.6	-9.7	
1982	122.55	120.40	-1.8	14.8	X
1983	140.64	145.30	3.3	17.3	
1984	164.93	163.41	-0.9	1.4	flat
1985	167.24	179.63	7.4	26.3	
1986	211.28	211.78	0.2	14.6	
1987	242.17	274.08	13.2	2.0	flat
1988	247.08	257.07	4.0	12.4	
1989	277.72	297.47	7.1	27.3	
1990	353.40	329.08	-6.9	-6.6	
1991	330.22	343.93	4.2	26.3	
1992	417.09	408.79	-2.0	4.5	flat
1993	435.71	438.78	0.7	7.1	
1994	466.45	481.61	3.3	-1.5	flat
1995	459.27	470.42	2.4	34.1	
1996	615.93	636.02	3.3	20.3	
1997	740.74	786.16	6.1	31.0	
1998	970.43	980.28	1.0	26.7	
1999	1229.23	1279.64	4.1	19.5	
2000	1469.25	1394.46	-5.1	-10.1	
2001	1320.28	1366.01	3.5	-13.0	X
2002	1148.08	1130.20	-1.6	-23.4	
2003	879.82	855.70	-2.7	26.4	X
2004	1111.92	1131.13	1.7	9.0	
2005	1211.92	1181.27	-2.5	3.0	flat
2006	1248.29	1280.08	2.5	13.6	
2007	1418.30	1438.24	1.4	3.5	flat
2008	1468.36	1378.55	-6.1	-38.5	
2009	903.25	825.88	-8.6	23.5	X
2010	1115.10	1073.87	-3.7	12.8	X
2011	1257.64	1286.12	2.3	-0.003	flat
2012	1257.60	1312.41	4.4	13.4	
2013	1426.19	1498.11	5.0	29.6	
2014	1848.36	1782.59	-3.6	11.4	X
2015	2058.90	1994.99	-3.1	-0.7	flat
2016	2043.94	1940.24	-5.1	9.5	X
2017	2238.83	2278.87	1.8	19.4	
2018	2673.61	2823.81	5.6	-6.2	X
2019	2506.85	2704.10	7.9	28.9	
2020	3230.78	3225.52	-0.2	16.3	X
2021	3756.07	3714.24	-1.1	26.9	X
2022	4766.18	4515.55	-5.3	-19.4	
2023	3839.50	4076.60	6.2	??	

January Performance by Rank

Rank		January Change	Year Change	
1	1987	13.2%	2.0%	flat
2	1975	12.3	31.5	
3	1976	11.8	19.1	
4	2019	7.9	28.9	
5	1967	7.8	20.1	
6	1985	7.4	26.3	
7	1989	7.1	27.3	
8	1961	6.3	23.1	
9	2023	6.2	??	
10	1997	6.1	31.0	
11	1951	6.1	16.5	
12	1980	5.8	25.8	
13	2018	5.6	-6.2	X
14	1954	5.1	45.0	
15	2013	5.0	29.6	
16	1963	4.9	18.9	
17	2012	4.4	13.4	
18	1958	4.3	38.1	
19	1991	4.2	26.3	
20	1999	4.1	19.5	
21	1971	4.0	10.8	
22	1988	4.0	12.4	
23	1979	4.0	12.3	
24	2001	3.5	-13.0	X
25	1965	3.3	9.1	
26	1983	3.3	17.3	
27	1996	3.3	20.3	
28	1994	3.3	-1.5	flat
29	1964	2.7	13.0	
30	2006	2.5	13.6	
31	1995	2.4	34.1	
32	2011	2.3	-0.003	flat
33	1972	1.8	15.6	
34	1955	1.8	26.4	
35	2017	1.8	19.4	
36	1950	1.7	21.8	
37	2004	1.7	9.0	
38	1952	1.6	11.8	
39	2007	1.4	3.5	flat
40	1998	1.0	26.7	
41	1993	0.7	7.1	
42	1966	0.5	-13.1	X
43	1959	0.4	8.5	
44	1986	0.2	14.6	
45	2020	-0.2	16.3	X
46	1953	-0.7	-6.6	
47	1969	-0.8	-11.4	
48	1984	-0.9	1.4	flat
49	1974	-1.0	-29.7	
50	2021	-1.1	26.9	X
51	2002	-1.6	-23.4	
52	1973	-1.7	-17.4	
53	1982	-1.8	14.8	X
54	1992	-2.0	4.5	flat
55	2005	-2.5	3.0	flat
56	2003	-2.7	26.4	X
57	2015	-3.1	-0.7	flat
58	2014	-3.6	11.4	X
59	1956	-3.6	2.6	flat
60	2010	-3.7	12.8	X
61	1962	-3.8	-11.8	
62	1957	-4.2	-14.3	
63	1968	-4.4	7.7	X
64	1981	-4.6	-9.7	
65	1977	-5.1	-11.5	
66	2000	-5.1	-10.1	
67	2016	-5.1	9.5	X
68	2022	-5.3	-19.4	
69	2008	-6.1	-38.5	
70	1978	-6.2	1.1	flat
71	1990	-6.9	-6.6	
72	1960	-7.1	-3.0	flat
73	1970	-7.6	0.1	flat
74	2009	-8.6	23.5	X

18

X = major error Based on S&P 500

Martin Luther King Jr. Day *(Market Closed)*

MONDAY
15

Keep me away from the wisdom which does not cry, the philosophy which does not laugh
and the greatness which does not bow before children.
— Kahlil Gibran (Lebanese-born American mystic, poet and artist, 1883–1931)

First Trading Day of January Expiration Week, Dow Up 19 of Last 31,
But Down 7 of Last 10

TUESDAY

D 47.6
S 52.4
N 42.9
16

In Washington people tell the truth off the record and lie on the record.
In the Middle East they lie off the record and tell the truth on the record.
— Thomas L. Friedman (*NY Times* foreign affairs columnist, "Meet the Press" 12/17/06)

January Expiration Week, Dow Down 13 of Last 25, But Up 9 of Last 13

WEDNESDAY

D 57.1
S 66.7
N 66.7
17

Fight until death over taxes? Oh, no. Women, country, God, things like that. Taxes? No.
— Daniel Patrick Moynihan (U.S. Senator New York 1977–2001, "Meet The Press" 5/23/1993, 1927–2003)

THURSDAY

D 42.9
S 42.9
N 47.6
18

The only thing I do know is that from chaos comes opportunity.
— Daniel S. Loeb (American investor, hedge fund manager & philanthropist, founder CEO CIO Third Point, b. 1961)

January Expiration Day Improving Since 2011, Dow Up 11 of Last 13

FRIDAY

D 42.9
S 52.4
N 38.1
19

Bear markets don't act like a medicine ball rolling down a smooth hill. Instead, they behave like a basketball
bouncing down a rock-strewn mountainside; there's lots of movement up and sideways before the bottom is reached.
— Daniel Turov (*Turov on Timing, Barron's* May 21, 2001, b. 1947)

SATURDAY
20

SUNDAY
21

BULLS WIN WHEN MARKET HITS THE JANUARY TRIFECTA

We invented our January Indicator Trifecta in 2013 by combining our Santa Claus Rally (page 118) and January Barometer (page 18), both invented by our late founder Yale Hirsch in 1972 published in the *1973 Almanac*, with the age-old First Five Days Early Warning System (page 16).

The predicative power of the three is considerably greater than any of them alone; we have been rather impressed by its forecasting prowess. When the market hits this trifecta, the bulls win. Since 1950 when our January Barometer, Santa Claus Rally and First Five Days indicators are all positive for the S&P 500 the odds of the rest of the year—and the year as a whole—being up increase dramatically.

When all three are up the S&P 500 has been up 90.3% of the time, 28 of 31 years, with an average gain of 17.5%, and the next 11 months are up 87.1% of the time, 27 of 31 years, with an average gain of 12.3%. When any of them are down the year's results are reduced with S&P up 59.5% of the time, 25 of 42 years, with an average gain of 2.9%. When all three are down the S&P was down 3 of 8 years with an average loss of -3.6% with bear markets in 1969 (-11.4%), 2000 (-10.1%) and 2008 (-38.5%), flat years in 1956 (2.6%), 1978 (1.1%) and 2005 (3.0%). Down Trifecta's were followed by gains in 1982 (14.8%) and 2016 (9.5%).

When the January Indicator Trifecta was preceded by a bear market in the year prior the results were even more striking. Next 11-months and full-year performance were always positive, up 13-0, with average gains of 16.8% and 22.1% respectively. We hit this trifecta in 2023 and as our *Almanac Investor* subscribers and followers know our analysis is that we are currently in a new bull market off the October 2022 low. At midyear 2023 this trifecta continues to support our bullish outlook for pre-election year 2023.

S&P 500 JANUARY INDICATOR TRIFECTA — THREE POSITIVE

Year	SC Rally	FFD	JB	Feb	Feb-Dec	Full Year
1950	1.3%	2.0%	1.7%	1.0%	19.7%	21.8
1951	3.1	2.3	6.1	0.6	9.7	16.5
1952	1.4	0.6	1.6	−3.6	10.1	11.8
1954	1.7	0.5	5.1	0.3	38.0	45.0
1958	3.5	2.5	4.3	−2.1	32.4	38.1
1959	3.6	0.3	0.4	−0.02	8.1	8.5
1961	1.7	1.2	6.3	2.7	15.8	23.1
1963	1.7	2.6	4.9	−2.9	13.3	18.9
1964	2.3	1.3	2.7	1.0	10.0	13.0
1965	0.6	0.7	3.3	−0.1	5.6	9.1
1966	0.1	0.8	0.5	−1.8	−13.5	−13.1
1971	1.9	0.04	4.0	0.9	6.5	10.8
1972	1.3	1.4	1.8	2.5	13.6	15.6
1975	7.2	2.2	12.3	6.0	17.2	31.5
1976	4.3	4.9	11.8	−1.1	6.5	19.1
1979	3.3	2.8	4.0	−3.7	8.0	12.3
1983	1.2	3.2	3.3	1.9	13.5	17.3
1987	2.4	6.2	13.2	3.7	−9.9	2.0
1989	0.9	1.2	7.1	−2.9	18.8	27.3
1995	0.2	0.3	2.4	3.6	30.9	34.1
1996	1.8	0.4	3.3	0.7	16.5	20.3
1997	0.1	1.0	6.1	0.6	23.4	31.0
1999	1.3	3.7	4.1	−3.2	14.8	19.5
2004	2.4	1.8	1.7	1.2	7.1	9.0
2006	0.4	3.4	2.5	0.05	10.8	13.6
2011	1.1	1.1	2.3	3.2	−2.2	−0.003
2012	1.9	1.8	4.2	4.1	8.7	13.4
2013	2.0	2.2	4.8	1.1	23.4	29.6
2017	0.4	1.3	1.8	3.7	17.3	19.4
2018	1.1	2.8	5.6	−3.9	−11.2	−6.2
2019	1.3	2.7	7.9	3.0	19.5	28.9
2023	0.8	1.4	6.2	−2.6	—	—
Average				0.4%	12.3%	17.5%
# Up				20	27	28
#Down				12	4	3

JANUARY 2024

MONDAY
D 33.3
S 47.6
N 42.9
22

In nature there are no rewards or punishments; there are consequences.
— Horace Annesley Vachell (English writer, *The Face of Clay*, 1861–1955)

TUESDAY
D 47.6
S 66.7
N 57.1
23

Things may come to those who wait, but only the things left by those who hustle.
— Abraham Lincoln (16th U.S. President, 1809–1865)

WEDNESDAY
D 47.6
S 52.4
N 66.7
24

Nothing has a stronger influence psychologically on their environment and especially on their children than the unlived life of the parent.
— C.G. Jung (Swiss psychiatrist)

THURSDAY
D 52.4
S 61.9
N 52.4
25

If you are not willing to study, if you are not sufficiently interested to investigate and analyze the stock market yourself, then I beg of you to become an outright long-pull investor, to buy good stocks, and hold on to them; for otherwise your chances of success as a trader will be nil.
— Humphrey B. Neill (Investor, analyst, author, *Tape Reading and Market Tactics*, 1931, 1895–1977)

FRIDAY
D 57.1
S 47.6
N 66.7
26

The most important lesson in investing is humility.
— Sir John Templeton (Founder Templeton Funds, philanthropist, 1912–2008)

SATURDAY
27

February Almanac Investor Sector Seasonalities: See Pages 94, 96 and 98

SUNDAY
28

FEBRUARY ALMANAC

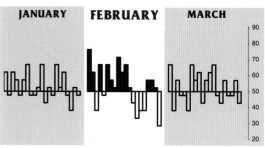

FEBRUARY						
S	M	T	W	T	F	S
					1	2	3
4	5	6	7	8	9	10
11	12	13	14	15	16	17
18	19	20	21	22	23	24
25	26	27	28	29		

MARCH						
S	M	T	W	T	F	S
					1	2
3	4	5	6	7	8	9
10	11	12	13	14	15	16
17	18	19	20	21	22	23
24	25	26	27	28	29	30
31						

Market Probability Chart above is a graphic representation of the S&P 500 Recent Market Probability Calendar on page 126.

◆ February is the weak link in "Best Six Months" (pages 52, 54 & 149) ◆ RECENT RECORD: S&P up 9, down 6, average change +0.1% last 15 years ◆ #3 NASDAQ month in presidential election years average gain 1.8%, up 7 down 6 (page 166), #11 Dow, up 10 down 8 and #11 S&P, up 9, down 9 (pages 156 & 162) ◆ Day before Presidents' Day weekend S&P down 19 of 32, 11 straight 1992–2002, day after up 8 of last 14 (see page 100 & 135) ◆ Many technicians modify market predictions based on January's market in February

February Vital Statistics

	DJIA	S&P 500	NASDAQ	Russell 1K	Russell 2K
Rank	8	11	9	11	6
Up	43	40	28	26	26
Down	31	34	25	19	19
Average % Change	0.1%	−0.08%	0.5%	0.1%	1.0%
Election Year	−0.7%	−0.4%	1.8%	−0.5%	1.2%
Best & Worst February					
	% Change	% Change	% Change	% Change	% Change
Best	1986 8.8	1986 7.1	2000 19.2	1986 7.2	2000 16.4
Worst	2009 −11.7	2009 −11.0	2001 −22.4	2009 −10.7	2009 −12.3
Best & Worst February Weeks					
Best	2/1/08 4.4	2/6/09 5.2	2/4/00 9.2	2/6/09 5.3	2/1/91 7.7
Worst	2/28/20 −12.4	2/28/20 −11.5	2/28/20 −10.5	2/28/20 −11.6	2/28/20 −12.0
Best & Worst February Days					
Best	2/24/09 3.3	2/24/09 4.0	2/11/99 4.2	2/24/09 4.1	2/24/09 4.5
Worst	2/10/09 −4.6	2/10/09 −4.9	2/16/01 −5.0	2/10/09 −4.8	2/10/09 −4.7
First Trading Day of Expiration Week: 1980–2023					
Record (#Up – #Down)	26–18	30–14	26–18	30–14	26–18
Current Streak	U1	U1	U1	U1	U1
Avg % Change	0.30	0.28	0.15	0.25	0.16
Options Expiration Day: 1980–2023					
Record (#Up – #Down)	23–21	18–26	18–26	19–25	22–22
Current Streak	U1	D4	D2	D4	U1
Avg % Change	−0.02	−0.13	−0.27	−0.12	−0.004
Options Expiration Week: 1980–2023					
Record (#Up – #Down)	26–18	23–21	24–20	23–21	28–16
Current Streak	D2	D4	U1	D4	U1
Avg % Change	0.46	0.27	0.21	0.33	0.44
Week After Options Expiration: 1980–2023					
Record (#Up – #Down)	20–24	21–23	25–19	21–23	23–21
Current Streak	D4	D1	D1	D1	D1
Avg % Change	−0.57	−0.47	−0.48	−0.45	−0.37
First Trading Day Performance					
% of Time Up	64.9	63.5	71.7	68.9	68.9
Avg % Change	0.16	0.19	0.41	0.26	0.42
Last Trading Day Performance					
% of Time Up	44.6	50.0	49.1	48.7	53.3
Avg % Change	−0.08	−0.06	−0.08	−0.13	−0.03

Dow & S&P 1950–June 9, 2023, NASDAQ 1971–June 9, 2023, Russell 1K & 2K 1979–June 9, 2023.

Either go short or stay away the day before Presidents' Day.

JANUARY/FEBRUARY 2024

MONDAY
D 47.6
S 38.1
N 52.4
29

Those that forget the past are condemned to repeat its mistakes, and those that mis-state the past should be condemned.
— Eugene D. Cohen (Letter to the Editor, *Financial Times* 10/30/06)

TUESDAY
D 47.6
S 52.4
N 47.6
30

The first panacea for a mismanaged nation is inflation of the currency; the second is war. Both bring a temporary prosperity; both bring a permanent ruin. But both are the refuge of political and economic opportunists.
— Ernest Hemingway (American writer, 1954 Nobel Prize, 1899–1961)

"January Barometer"83.6% Accurate (Page 18)
Almanac Investor Subscribers Emailed Official Results (See Insert)
FOMC Meeting (2 Days)

WEDNESDAY
D 42.9
S 47.6
N 52.4
31

Beware of inside information…all inside information.
— Jesse Livermore (Early 20th century stock trader and speculator, *How to Trade in Stocks*, 1877–1940)

First Trading Day in February, Dow Up 18 of Last 21

THURSDAY
D 81.0
S 76.2
N 76.2
1

I am sorry to say that there is too much point to the wisecrack that life is extinct on other planets because their scientists were more advanced than ours.
— John F. Kennedy (35th U.S. President, 1917–1963)

FRIDAY
D 52.4
S 61.9
N 57.1
2

A "tired businessman" is one whose business is usually not a successful one.
— Joseph R. Grundy (U.S. Senator Pennsylvania 1929–1930, businessman, 1863–1961)

SATURDAY
3

SUNDAY
4

DOWN JANUARYS: A REMARKABLE RECORD

In the first third of the 20th century there was no correlation between January markets and the year as a whole. Then in 1972 Yale Hirsch discovered that the 1933 "Lame Duck" Amendment to the Constitution changed the political calendar and the January Barometer was born—its record has been quite accurate (page 18).

Down Januarys are harbingers of trouble ahead, in the economic, political, or military arenas. Eisenhower's heart attack in 1955 cast doubt on whether he could run in 1956—a flat year. Two other election years with down Januarys were also flat (1984 & 1992). Sixteen bear markets began and 10 continued into second years with poor Januarys. 1968 started down as we were mired in Vietnam, but Johnson's "bombing halt" changed the climate. Imminent military action in Iraq held January 2003 down before the market triple-bottomed in March. After Baghdad fell pre-election and recovery forces fueled 2003 into a banner year. 2005 was flat, registering the narrowest Dow trading range on record. 2008 was the worst January on record and preceded the worst bear market since the Great Depression. A negative reading in 2015 and 2016 preceded an official Dow bear market declaration in February 2016. In 2020 the shortest bear market in history began after the close on February 19. ZIRP and QE fueled a banner 2021 however, NASDAQ did correct 10.5% during February and March. Aggressive interest rate hikes triggered a bear in 2022.

Unfortunately, bull and bear markets do not start conveniently at the beginnings and ends of months or years. Though some years ended higher, **every down January since 1950 was followed by a new or continuing bear market, a 10% correction or a flat year. Down Januarys were followed by substantial declines averaging** *minus* **13.3%**, providing excellent buying opportunities later in most years.

FROM DOWN JANUARY S&P CLOSES TO LOW NEXT 11 MONTHS

Year	January Close	% Change	11-Month Low	Date of Low	Jan Close to Low %	% Feb to Dec	Year % Change	
1953	26.38	−0.7%	22.71	14-Sep	−13.9%	−6.0%	−6.6%	bear
1956	43.82	−3.6	43.42	14-Feb	−0.9	6.5	2.6	bear/FLAT
1957	44.72	−4.2	38.98	22-Oct	−12.8	−10.6	−14.3	Cont. bear
1960	55.61	−7.1	52.30	25-Oct	−6.0	4.5	−3.0	bear
1962	68.84	−3.8	52.32	26-Jun	−24.0	−8.3	−11.8	bear
1968	92.24	−4.4	87.72	5-Mar	−4.9	12.6	7.7	−10%/bear
1969	103.01	−0.8	89.20	17-Dec	−13.4	−10.6	−11.4	Cont. bear
1970	85.02	−7.6	69.20	26-May	−18.6	8.4	0.1	Cont. bear
1973	116.03	−1.7	92.16	5-Dec	−20.6	−15.9	−17.4	bear
1974	96.57	−1.0	62.28	3-Oct	−35.5	−29.0	−29.7	Cont. bear
1977	102.03	−5.1	90.71	2-Nov	−11.1	−6.8	−11.5	bear
1978	89.25	−6.2	86.90	6-Mar	−2.6	7.7	1.1	Cont. bear/bear
1981	129.55	−4.6	112.77	25-Sep	−13.0	−5.4	−9.7	bear
1982	120.40	−1.8	102.42	12-Aug	−14.9	16.8	14.8	Cont. bear
1984	163.42	−0.9	147.82	24-Jul	−9.5	2.3	1.4	Cont. bear/FLAT
1990	329.07	−6.9	295.46	11-Oct	−10.2	0.4	−6.6	bear
1992	408.79	−2.0	394.50	8-Apr	−3.5	6.6	4.5	FLAT
2000	1394.46	−5.1	1264.74	20-Dec	−9.3	−5.3	−10.1	bear
2002	1130.20	−1.6	776.76	9-Oct	−31.3	−22.2	−23.4	bear
2003	855.70	−2.7	800.73	11-Mar	−6.4	29.9	26.4	Cont. bear
2005	1181.27	−2.5	1137.50	20-Apr	−3.7	5.7	3.0	FLAT
2008	1378.55	−6.1	752.44	20-Nov	−45.4	−34.5	−38.5	bear
2009	825.88	−8.6	676.53	9-Mar	−18.1	35.0	23.5	Cont. bear
2010	1073.87	−3.7	1022.58	2-Jul	−4.8	17.1	12.8	−10%/no bear
2014	1782.59	−3.6	1741.89	3-Feb	−2.3	15.5	11.4	−10% intraday
2015	1994.99	−3.1	1867.61	25-Aug	−6.4	2.5	−0.7	bear
2016	1940.24	−5.1	1829.08	11-Feb	−5.7	15.4	9.5	Cont. bear
2020	3225.52	−0.2	2237.40	23-Mar	−30.6	16.4	16.3	bear
2021	3714.24	−1.1	3768.47	4-Mar	1.5	28.3	26.9	−10% NAS
2022	4515.55	−5.3	3577.03	12-Oct	−20.8	15.0	−19.4	bear
				Totals	**−398.7%**	**92.0%**	**−52.2%**	
				Average	**−13.3%**	**3.1%**	**−1.7%**	

FEBRUARY 2024

MONDAY
5

D 47.6
S 38.1
N 33.3

Those who cast the votes decide nothing. Those who count the votes decide everything.
— Joseph Stalin (Ruler USSR 1929–1953, 1879–1953)

TUESDAY
6

D 61.9
S 66.7
N 61.9

Remember to look up at the stars and not down at your feet.
— Professsor Stephen Hawking (English theoretical physicist, cosmologist, and author, 1942–2018)

Week Before February Expiration Week, NASDAQ Down 12 of Last 22, But Up 9 of Last 13

WEDNESDAY
7

D 52.4
S 47.6
N 47.6

You know you're right when the other side starts to shout.
— I. A. O'Shaughnessy (American oilman, 1885–1973)

THURSDAY
8

D 52.4
S 66.7
N 66.7

It is wise to remember that too much success [in the stock market] is in itself an excellent warning.
— Gerald M. Loeb (E.F. Hutton, *The Battle for Investment Survival*, predicted 1929 Crash, 1900–1974)

FRIDAY
9

D 57.1
S 57.1
N 61.9

Q. What kind of grad students do you take? A. I never take a straight-A student.
A real scientist tends to be critical, and somewhere along the line, they had to rebel against their teachers.
— Lynn Margulis (U. Mass science professor, *The Scientist*, 6/30/03)

SATURDAY
10

SUNDAY
11

2024 PRESIDENTIAL ELECTION YEAR PERPECTIVES

First Five Months Better When Party Retains White House
Since 1901 there have been 30 presidential elections. When the Party in power retained the White House 17 times, the Dow was up 1.5% on average for the first five months, compared to a 4.5% loss the 13 times the Party was ousted. Since 1950, retaining the White House 8 times brought an average gain of 1.9% compared to -1.0% the 10 times the Party in power was ousted.

War Can Be a Major Factor in Presidential Races
Democrats used to lose the White House on foreign shores (1920 WW1, 1952 Korea, 1968 Vietnam, 1980 Iran Crisis). Republicans on the other hand lost it here at home (1912 Party split, 1932 Depression, 1960 Economy, 1976 Watergate). Homeland issues have dominated since with the Republican loss in 1992 (economy), the Democratic loss in 2000 (scandal), and the Republican loss in 2008 (economy). Covid-19 and controversy cost Republicans the White House in 2020. The Russia-Ukraine war is a factor for 2024 as well domestic affairs.

Market Bottoms Two Years After a Presidential Election
A takeover of the White House by the opposing party in the past eight decades (1960, 1968, 1976, 1980, 1992, 2000, 2008, 2016 and 2020) has resulted in a bottom within two years, except 1994, a flat year. When incumbent parties retained power (1964, 1972, 1984, 1988, 1996, 2004, 2012) stocks often bottomed within two years as well, except 1984 (three years, 1987), 2004 (one year, flat 2005) and 2012 (no bottom, QE). Look for the next major market bottom in 2025 or 2026.

Only Six Election Year Declines Greater Than 5% Since 1896
Presidential election years are the second best performing year of the four-year cycle, producing losses of greater than 5% in only six of those thirty-two years. Incumbent parties lost power in five of those years. Five losses occurred at the end of the second term. FDR defeated Hoover in 1932 and was re-elected to an unprecedented third term as WWII ravaged Europe. *Page 132.*

Market Better When Sitting President Runs for Reelection
Politics and parties aside, stocks have performed better in election years when a sitting president is running for reelection. Since 1900 the Dow has gained 8.8% on average in election years when incumbents run for reelection vs. just 5.1% when it's an open field. When they win the Dow averages 10.5% compared to 4.8% when they lose. Since 1950 the Dow averages 9.9% during incumbent reelection bids vs. –1.6% when no sitting president is running.

August-October Market Performance Presidential Predictor
Our good friend and colleague Sam Stovall, Chief Investment Strategist at CFRA, tracks a rather reliable "Presidential Predictor" indicator. When the S&P 500 is up from July 31 to October 31 during presidential election years the incumbent party retains power 11 of the 13 election years or 85% of the time since 1936. Losses for the S&P 500 over this 3-month span, just before the election, have seen a shift in party control in 8 of the 9 years for an 89% success rate. Two misses were due to significant third-party candidates in 1968 (Wallace) and 1980 (Anderson). Eisenhower's was reelected in 1956 despite a bear market, the Suez Crisis/Sinai War in October-November and Soviet tanks rolling into Hungary October.

Market Charts of Presidential Election Years
Market behavior for the last 21 elections including candidates and winners. *Page 28.*

How the Government Manipulates the Economy to Stay in Power
Money faucets get turned on, if possible, in years divisible by 4. *Page 32.*

Incumbent Party Wins & Losses
Markets tend to be stronger when party in power wins. *Page 34.*

Only Two Losses in Last Seven Months of Election Years
Regardless which party is victorious, the last seven months have seen gains on the S&P in 16 of the 18 presidential election years since 1950. One loss was in 2000 when the election's outcome was delayed for 36 tumultuous days, though the Dow did end higher. Financial crisis and the worst bear market since the Great Depression impacted 2008. *Page 80.*

FEBRUARY 2024

First Trading Day of February Expiration Week Dow Down 10 of Last 19

MONDAY
D 52.4
S 52.4
N 57.1
12

There is no great mystery to satisfying your customers. Build them a quality product and treat them with respect. It's that simple.
— Lee Iacocca (American industrialist, Former Chrysler CEO, 1924–2019)

TUESDAY
D 57.1
S 71.4
N 71.4
13

I have a simple philosophy. Fill what's empty. Empty what's full. And scratch where it itches.
— Alice Roosevelt Longworth (American writer, socialite, daughter of Teddy, 1884–1980)

Valentine's Day ♥
Ash Wednesday

WEDNESDAY
D 52.4
S 61.9
N 76.2
14

Savor the joy of others. It is abundant and free and it will lift your spirits and boost your wellbeing even as you add positive energy to the world.
— Phil Pearlman (Founder, Pearl Institute, b. 1967)

THURSDAY
D 66.7
S 66.7
N 66.7
15

Thank God for recording. It's the best thing that's happened to us since writing.
— Keith Richards (Rolling Stones, *Life*, b. 1943)

February Expiration Day, NASDAQ Down 13 of Last 20
Day Before Presidents' Day Weekend, S&P Up 10 of Last 13

FRIDAY
D 61.9
S 52.4
N 42.9
16

In a bear market everyone loses. And the winner is the one who loses the least.
— Richard Russell (*Dow Theory Letters*, 1924–2015)

SATURDAY
17

SUNDAY
18

MARKET CHARTS OF PRESIDENTIAL ELECTION YEARS

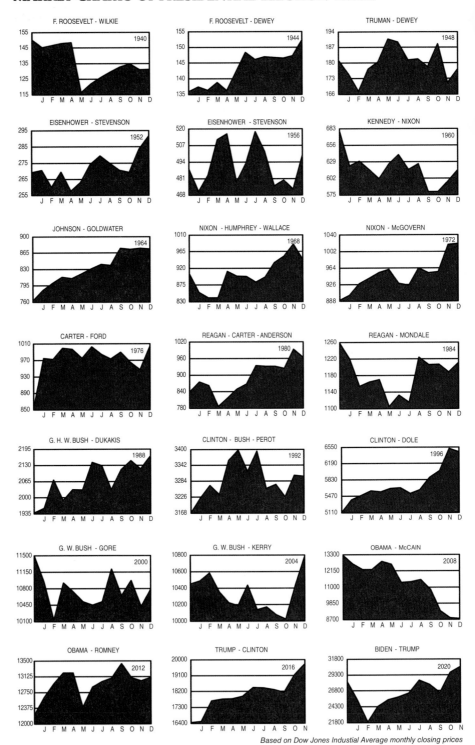

Based on Dow Jones Industial Average monthly closing prices

FEBRUARY 2024

Presidents' Day *(Market Closed)*

MONDAY
19

Change is the law of life. And those who look only to the past or present are certain to miss the future.
— John F. Kennedy (35th U.S. President, 1917–1963)

Day After Presidents Day, NASDAQ Down 18 of Last 29, But Up 7 of Last 11

TUESDAY

D 42.9
S 42.9
N 42.9

20

You are your own Promised Land, your own new frontier.
— Julia Margaret Cameron (19th century English photographer)

Week After February Expiration Week, Dow Down 15 of Last 25,
But Up 7 of Last 12, 2020 Down 12.4% 5th Worst Week Since 1950

WEDNESDAY

D 38.1
S 33.3
N 38.1

21

Learn from the mistakes of others; you can't live long enough to make them all yourself.
— Eleanor Roosevelt (First Lady, 1884–1962)

THURSDAY

D 42.9
S 38.1
N 42.9

22

A bull market tends to bail you out of all your mistakes. Conversely, bear markets make you PAY for your mistakes.
— Richard Russell (*Dow Theory Letters*, 1924–2015)

End of February Miserable in Recent Years (Pages 22 and 135)

FRIDAY

D 47.6
S 38.1
N 42.9

23

We will have to pay more and more attention to what the funds are doing.
They are the ones who have been contributing to the activity, especially in the high-fliers.
— Humphrey B. Neill (Investor, analyst, author, *NY Times* 6/11/1966, 1895–1977)

SATURDAY
24

March Almanac Investor Sector Seasonalities: See Pages 94, 96 and 98

SUNDAY
25

MARCH ALMANAC

MARCH						
S	M	T	W	T	F	S
					1	2
3	4	5	6	7	8	9
10	11	12	13	14	15	16
17	18	19	20	21	22	23
24	25	26	27	28	29	30
31						

APRIL						
S	M	T	W	T	F	S
	1	2	3	4	5	6
7	8	9	10	11	12	13
14	15	16	17	18	19	20
21	22	23	24	25	26	27
28	29	30				

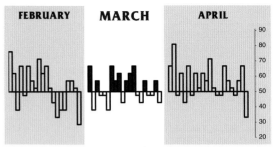

Market Probability Chart above is a graphic representation of the S&P 500 Recent Market Probability Calendar on page 126.

◆ Mid-month strength and late-month weakness are most evident above ◆ RECENT RECORD: S&P 13 up, 8 down, average gain 1.1%, fifth best ◆ Rather turbulent in recent years with wild fluctuations and large gains and losses ◆ March 2020 Dow declined 13.7%, worst March loss since 1938 ◆ March has been taking some mean end-of-quarter hits (page 136), down 1469 Dow points March 9-22, 2001 ◆ Last three or four days Dow a net loser 22 out of last 34 years ◆ NASDAQ hard hit in 2001, down 14.5% after 22.4% drop in February ◆ Second worst NASDAQ month during presidential election years average loss 1.6%, up 7, down 6 ◆ Third Dow month to gain more than 1000 points in 2016

March Vital Statistics

	DJIA		S&P 500		NASDAQ		Russell 1K		Russell 2K	
Rank	5		5		7		7		7	
Up	48		48		34		30		31	
Down	26		26		19		15		14	
Average % Change	1.0%		1.1%		0.8%		0.9%		0.7%	
Election Year	0.2%		0.4%		–1.6%		–1.1%		–3.0%	
				Best & Worst March						
	% Change		**% Change**		**% Change**		**% Change**		**% Change**	
Best	2000	7.8	2000	9.7	2009	10.9	2000	8.9	1979	9.7
Worst	2020	–13.7	2020	–12.5	1980	–17.1	2020	–13.4	2020	–21.9
				Best & Worst March Weeks						
Best	3/27/20	12.8	3/13/09	10.7	3/13/09	10.6	3/13/09	10.7	3/13/09	12.0
Worst	3/20/20	–17.3	3/20/20	–15.0	3/20/20	–12.6	3/20/20	–15.3	3/13/20	–16.5
				Best & Worst March Days						
Best	3/24/20	11.4	3/24/20	9.4	3/13/20	9.4	3/24/20	9.5	3/24/20	9.4
Worst	3/16/20	–12.9	3/16/20	–12.0	3/16/20	–12.3	3/16/20	–12.2	3/16/20	–14.3
				First Trading Day of Expiration Week: 1980–2023						
Record (#Up – #Down)	28–16		27–15		23–21		25–19		23–21	
Current Streak	D1		D2		U1		D2		D2	
Avg % Change	–0.12		–0.19		–0.45		–0.24		–0.61	
				Options Expiration Day: 1980–2023						
Record (#Up – #Down)	23–21		29–15		23–21		24–20		22–21	
Current Streak	D1		D1		D1		D1		D1	
Avg % Change	–0.04		–0.06		–0.05		–0.05		–0.10	
				Options Expiration Week: 1980–2023						
Record (#Up – #Down)	29–14		29–15		27–17		28–16		24–20	
Current Streak	D1		U2		U2		U2		D1	
Avg % Change	0.52		0.52		0.14		0.46		–0.08	
				Week After Options Expiration: 1980–2023						
Record (#Up – #Down)	20–24		16–28		21–23		16–28		19–25	
Current Streak	U4		U4		U2		U4		U1	
Avg % Change	–0.05		0.01		0.08		0.004		–0.12	
				First Trading Day Performance						
% of Time Up	67.6		65.3		62.3		60.0		66.7	
Avg % Change	0.23		0.24		0.35		0.26		0.34	
				Last Trading Day Performance						
% of Time Up	41.9		41.9		64.2		48.9		80.0	
Avg % Change	–0.10		0.0005		0.21		0.09		0.40	

Dow & S&P 1950–June 9, 2023, NASDAQ 1971–June 9, 2023, Russell 1K & 2K 1979–June 9, 2023.

March has Ides and St. Patrick's Day;
Begins bullishly, then fades away.

FEBRUARY/MARCH 2024

MONDAY

D 52.4
S 57.1
N 47.6
26

The Stone Age didn't end for lack of stone, and the oil age will end long before the world runs out of oil.
— Sheik Ahmed Zaki Yamani (Saudi oil minister 1962–1986, b. 1930)

TUESDAY

D 57.1
S 57.1
N 71.4
27

The men who can manage men manage the men who manage only things, and the men who can manage money manage all.
— Will and Ariel Durant (*The Story of Civilization*, 1885–1981, 1898–1981)

WEDNESDAY

D 47.6
S 52.4
N 61.9
28

Those who cannot remember the past are condemned to repeat it.
— George Santayana (American philosopher, poet, 1863–1952)

THURSDAY

D 28.6
S 28.6
N 33.3
29

To an imagination of any scope the most far-reaching form of power is not money, it is the command of ideas.
— Oliver Wendell Holmes Jr. (U.S. Supreme Court Justice 1902–1932, *The Mind and Faith of Justice Holmes*, edited by Max Lerner, 1841–1935)

First Trading Day in March, S&P Up 16 of Last 24

FRIDAY

D 61.9
S 66.7
N 61.9
1

Inflation is the one form of taxation that can be imposed without legislation.
— Milton Friedman (American economist, 1976 Nobel Prize, 1912–2006)

SATURDAY

2

SUNDAY

3

HOW THE GOVERNMENT MANIPULATES THE ECONOMY TO STAY IN POWER

Bull markets tend to occur in the third and fourth years of presidential terms while bear markets tend to decline in the first and second years. The "making of presidents" is accompanied by an unsubtle manipulation of the economy. Incumbent administrations are duty-bound to retain the reins of power. Subsequently, many significant bear markets began in years following presidential elections: 1929, 1937, 1957, 1969, 1973, 1977, and 1981. Our major wars also began in years following elections: Civil War (1861), WWI (1917), WWII (1941), and Vietnam (1965). 9/11 and the build-up to the Iraq War caused post-election 2001 and midterm 2002 to be the worst back-to-back years since 1973–74. The Russia-Ukraine War triggered a bear market and a technical recession in midterm 2022.

Some cold, hard facts to prove economic manipulation appeared in a book by Edward R. Tufte, *Political Control of the Economy* (Princeton University Press). Stimulative fiscal measures designed to increase per capita disposable income providing a sense of well-being to the voting public included: increases in federal budget deficits, government spending and social security benefits; interest rate reductions on government loans; and speed-ups of projected funding.

Federal Spending: During 1962–1973, the average increase was 29% higher in election years than in non-election years.

Social Security: There were nine increases during the 1952–1974 period. Half of the six election-year increases became effective in September eight weeks before Election Day. The average increase was 100% higher in presidential than in midterm election years. Annual adjustments for inflation have been the norm since then.

Real Disposable Income: Accelerated in all but one election year between 1947 and 1973 (excluding the Eisenhower years). Only one of the non-election years (1973) showed a marked acceleration.

These moves were obviously not coincidences and explain why we tend to have a political (four-year) stock market cycle. Here are more examples of Election Year "generosity":

- Nixon plans to pump about $1 billion a month more than originally planned into spending programs designed to put money into the pockets of millions of currently unhappy voters…Such openhanded spending marks Nixon's conversion from unsuccessful policies of conservatism and gradualism to the activist, pump-priming Keynesian economic theory. *Time Magazine*, January 31, 1972.

- EPA administrator Carol M. Browner today announced President Clinton's proposed fiscal year 2001 budget of $7.3 billion for the United States Environmental Protection Agency, the largest increase in the history of the Clinton/Gore administration in spending for EPA. February 7, 2000.

- Like many of its predecessors, the Bush White House has used the machinery of government to promote the re-election of the president by awarding federal grants to strategically important states. *NY Times*, May 18, 2004.

- Even some conservatives grumble that Bush's tax cuts, expanded drug benefits for seniors and increased military spending have spurred a dramatic increase in the federal budget deficit, projected to be $477 billion in fiscal 2004, according to the Congressional Budget Office. *TheStreet.com*, July 2, 2004.

- After his historic midterm losses Obama quickly introduced a compromise deal with Congressional Republicans, overcame opposition from both parties, passed the $858 billion 2010 Tax Relief Act and signed it into law on December 17, 2010, just in time for his 2012 reelection campaign that began April 4, 2011.

The United States does not have an exclusive on electoral spending manipulations:

- An executive increases spending to reward or cultivate loyalty to himself as the party or coalition leader. Evidence from South Korea and Taiwan between the 1970s and 2000 supports the theory. This strategy affects spending outcomes in election years. *Journal of East Asian Studies*, January 2006

Covid and civil unrest likely helped derail Trump's reelection bid. By the 2020 election the positive impacts of his Tax Cuts and Jobs Act of 2017 had likely worn thin. Among other spending initiatives Biden negotiated the Fiscal Responsibility Act to suspend the debt ceiling until after the election, keeping the spigot open while avoiding draconian spending cuts. You can bet the negotiator-in-chief will do everything in their power to manipulate the economy to stay in power and keep the stock market propped up by Election Day.

MARCH 2024

March Historically Strong Early in the Month (Pages 30 and 136)

MONDAY

D 33.3
S 38.1
N 42.9

4

During the first period of a man's life the greatest danger is not to take the risk.
— Soren Kierkegaard (Danish philosopher, 1813–1855)

TUESDAY

D 52.4
S 57.1
N 52.4

5

The man who can master his time can master nearly anything.
— Winston Churchill (British statesman, 1874–1965)

WEDNESDAY

D 42.9
S 47.6
N 38.1

6

It wasn't raining when Noah built the ark.
— Howard Ruff (Financial advisor and author, *The Ruff Times*, 1930–2016)

THURSDAY

D 47.6
S 47.6
N 33.3

7

The only thing that saves us from the bureaucracy is its inefficiency.
— Eugene McCarthy (U.S. Congressman and Senator Minnesota 1949–1971, 3-time presidential candidate, 1916–2005)

Dow Down 1469 Points March 9–22 in 2001

FRIDAY

D 42.9
S 38.1
N 42.9

8

Any human anywhere will blossom in a hundred unexpected talents and capacities simply by being given the opportunity to do so.
— Doris Lessing (Iranian born British writer, 2007 Nobel Prize in Literature, 1919–2013)

SATURDAY

9

Daylight Saving Time Begins

SUNDAY

10

INCUMBENT PARTY WINS & LOSSES

Since 1944 stocks tend to move up earlier when White House occupants are popular but do even better in November and December when unpopular administrations are ousted.

TREND OF S&P 500 INDEX IN ELECTION YEARS 1944-2020

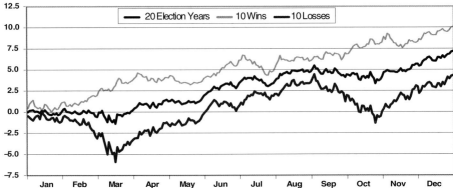

Actual percent changes reveal that March, June, October and December are best when incumbents stay in power, while July is worst. January, February, September and October are the worst when they are removed. Ironically, November is best when incumbents are ousted and third worst when they win.

Other interesting tidbits: there were no major losses in October (1984 off fractionally and 2012) and only one in June and December when incumbent parties retained the White House. Republican wins in November resulted in total gains of 27.0% (excluding no-decision 2000). Democratic victories produced total gains of 6.2% in November; however, Democrats "gained" 20.8% in December, the Republicans 9.7%.

MONTHLY % CHANGES IN S&P 500 DURING ELECTION YEARS

Incumbents Win

Year	Jan	Feb	Mar	Apr	May	Jun	Jul	Aug	Sep	Oct	Nov	Dec
1944	1.5	−0.3	1.7	−1.2	4.0	5.1	−2.1	0.9	−0.3	N/C	0.4	3.5
1948	−4.0	−4.7	7.7	2.7	7.8	0.3	−5.3	0.8	−3.0	6.8	−10.8	3.1
1956	−3.6	3.5	6.9	−0.2	−6.6	3.9	5.2	−3.8	−4.5	0.5	−1.1	3.5
1964	2.7	1.0	1.5	0.6	1.1	1.6	1.8	−1.6	2.9	0.8	−0.5	0.4
1972	1.8	2.5	0.6	0.4	1.7	−2.2	0.2	3.4	−0.5	0.9	4.6	1.2
1984	−0.9	−3.9	1.3	0.5	−5.9	1.7	−1.6	10.6	−0.3	−0.01	−1.5	2.2
1988	4.0	4.2	−3.3	0.9	0.3	4.3	−0.5	−3.9	4.0	2.6	−1.9	1.5
1996	3.3	0.7	0.8	1.3	2.3	0.2	−4.6	1.9	5.4	2.6	7.3	−2.2
2004	1.7	1.2	−1.6	−1.7	1.2	1.8	−3.4	0.2	0.9	1.4	3.9	3.2
2012	4.4	4.1	3.1	−0.7	−6.3	4.0	1.3	2.0	2.4	−2.0	0.3	0.7
Totals	**10.9**	**8.3**	**18.7**	**2.6**	**−0.4**	**20.7**	**−9.0**	**10.5**	**7.0**	**13.6**	**0.7**	**17.1**
Average	**1.1**	**0.8**	**1.9**	**0.3**	**−0.04**	**2.1**	**−0.9**	**1.1**	**0.7**	**1.4**	**0.07**	**1.7**

Incumbents Lose

Year	Jan	Feb	Mar	Apr	May	Jun	Jul	Aug	Sep	Oct	Nov	Dec
1952	1.6	−3.6	4.8	−4.3	2.3	4.6	1.8	−1.5	−2.0	−0.1	4.6	3.5
1960	−7.1	0.9	−1.4	−1.8	2.7	2.0	−2.5	2.6	−6.0	−0.2	4.0	4.6
1968	−4.4	−3.1	0.9	8.2	1.1	0.9	−1.8	1.1	3.9	0.7	4.8	−4.2
1976	11.8	−1.1	3.1	−1.1	−1.4	4.1	−0.8	−0.5	2.3	−2.2	−0.8	5.2
1980	5.8	−0.4	−10.2	4.1	4.7	2.7	6.5	0.6	2.5	1.6	10.2	−3.4
1992	−2.0	1.0	−2.2	2.8	0.1	−1.7	3.9	−2.4	0.9	0.2	3.0	1.0
2000	−5.1	−2.0	9.7	−3.1	−2.2	2.4	−1.6	6.1	−5.3	−0.5	−8.0*	0.4
2008	−6.1	−3.5	−0.6	4.8	1.1	−8.6	−1.0	1.2	−9.1	−16.9	−7.5	0.8
2016	−5.1	−0.4	6.6	0.3	1.5	0.1	3.6	−0.1	−0.1	−1.9	3.4	1.8
2020	−0.2	−8.4	−12.5	12.7	4.5	1.8	5.5	7.0	−3.9	−2.8	10.8	3.7
Totals	**−10.8**	**−20.6**	**−1.8**	**22.6**	**14.4**	**8.3**	**13.6**	**14.1**	**−16.8**	**−22.1**	**24.5**	**13.4**
Average	**−1.1**	**−2.1**	**−0.2**	**2.3**	**1.4**	**0.8**	**1.4**	**1.4**	**−1.7**	**−2.2**	**2.5**	**1.3**
20 Elections	**0.1**	**−12.3**	**16.9**	**25.2**	**14.0**	**29.0**	**4.6**	**24.6**	**−9.8**	**−8.5**	**25.2**	**30.5**
Average	**0.01**	**−0.6**	**0.8**	**1.3**	**0.7**	**1.5**	**0.2**	**1.2**	**−0.5**	**−0.5**	**1.3**	**1.5**

* Undecided election

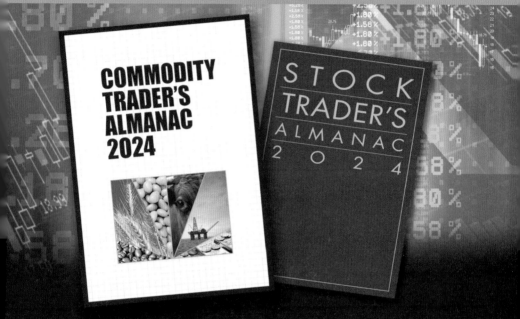

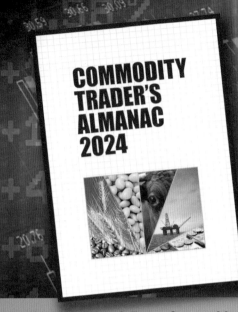

MARCH 2024

Monday Before March Triple Witching, Dow Up 25 of Last 36
In 2020 Dow Down 12.9%, 2nd Worst Dow Day Since 1901

MONDAY
D 66.7
S 66.7
N 57.1

11

Friendship renders prosperity more brilliant, while it lightens adversity by sharing it and making its burden common.
— Marcus Tullius Cicero (Great Roman Orator, Politician, 106–43 BCE)

TUESDAY
D 52.4
S 57.1
N 42.9

12

If I had eight hours to chop down a tree, I'd spend six sharpening my axe.
— Abraham Lincoln (16th U.S. President, 1809–1865)

WEDNESDAY
D 52.4
S 61.9
N 61.9

13

When Amercia sneezes, the rest of the world catches cold.
— Anonymous (circa 1929)

THURSDAY
D 71.4
S 42.9
N 42.9

14

When you get to the end of your rope, tie a knot and hang on.
— Franklin D. Roosevelt (32nd U.S. President, 1882–1945)

March Triple Witching Day Mixed Last 30 Years,
But NASDAQ Up 7 of Last 9

FRIDAY
D 71.4
S 57.1
N 52.4

15

People have difficulty cutting losses, admitting an error, and moving on. I am rather frequently—and on occasion, quite spectacularly—wrong. However, if we expect to be wrong, then there should be no ego tied up in admitting the error, honoring the stop loss, selling the loser—and preserving your capital.
— Barry L. Ritholtz (Founder/CIO Ritholtz Wealth Management, *Bailout Nation*, The Big Picture blog, 8/12/2010, b. 1961)

SATURDAY

16

St. Patrick's Day ♣

SUNDAY

17

THE DECEMBER LOW INDICATOR: A USEFUL PROGNOSTICATING TOOL

When the Dow closes below its December closing low in the first quarter, it is frequently an excellent warning sign. Jeffrey Saut brought this to our attention years ago. The December Low Indicator was originated by Lucien Hooper, a *Forbes* columnist and Wall Street analyst back in the 1970s. Hooper dismissed the importance of January and January's first week as reliable indicators. He noted that the trend could be random or even manipulated during a holiday-shortened week. Instead, said Hooper, "Pay much more attention to the December low. If that low is violated during the first quarter of the New Year, watch out!"

Twenty-one of the 37 occurrences were followed by gains for the rest of the year—and 19 full-year gains—after the low for the year was reached. For perspective we've included the January Barometer readings for the selected years. Hooper's "Watch Out" warning was absolutely correct, though. All but two of the instances since 1952 experienced further declines, as the Dow fell an additional 11.1% on average when December's low was breached in Q1. At press time, Dow's subsequent decline is below average.

Only three significant drops occurred (not shown) when December's low was not breached in Q1 (1974, 1981 and 1987). Both indicators were wrong eight times and nine years ended flat. If the December low is not crossed, turn to our January Barometer (page 18) and January Indicator Trifecta (page 20) for guidance.

YEARS DOW FELL BELOW DECEMBER LOW IN FIRST QUARTER

Year	Previous Dec Low	Date Crossed	Crossing Price	Subseq. Low	% Change Cross-Low	Rest of Year % Change	Full Year % Change	Jan Bar
1952	262.29	2/19/52	261.37	256.35	−1.9%	11.7%	8.4%	1.6%[2]
1953	281.63	2/11/53	281.57	255.49	−9.3	−0.2	−3.8	−0.7[3]
1956	480.72	1/9/56	479.74	462.35	−3.6	4.1	2.3	−3.6[1,2,3]
1957	480.61	1/18/57	477.46	419.79	−12.1	−8.7	−12.8	−4.2
1960	661.29	1/12/60	660.43	566.05	−14.3	−6.7	−9.3	−7.1
1962	720.10	1/5/62	714.84	535.76	−25.1	−8.8	−10.8	−3.8
1966	939.53	3/1/66	938.19	744.32	−20.7	−16.3	−18.9	0.5[1]
1968	879.16	1/22/68	871.71	825.13	−5.3	8.3	4.3	−4.4[1,2,3]
1969	943.75	1/6/69	936.66	769.93	−17.8	−14.6	−15.2	−0.8
1970	769.93	1/26/70	768.88	631.16	−17.9	9.1	4.8	−7.6[2,3]
1973	1000.00	1/29/73	996.46	788.31	−20.9	−14.6	−16.6	−1.7
1977	946.64	2/7/77	946.31	800.85	−15.4	−12.2	−17.3	−5.1
1978	806.22	1/5/78	804.92	742.12	−7.8	0.01	−3.1	−6.2[3]
1980	819.62	3/10/80	818.94	759.13	−7.3	17.7	14.9	5.8[2]
1982	868.25	1/5/82	865.30	776.92	−10.2	20.9	19.6	−1.8[1,2]
1984	1236.79	1/25/84	1231.89	1086.57	−11.8	−1.6	−3.7	−0.9[3]
1990	2687.93	1/15/90	2669.37	2365.10	−11.4	−1.3	−4.3	−6.9[3]
1991	2565.59	1/7/91	2522.77	2470.30	−2.1	25.6	20.3	4.2[2]
1993	3255.18	1/8/93	3251.67	3241.95	−0.3	15.5	13.7	0.7[2]
1994	3697.08	3/30/94	3626.75	3593.35	−0.9	5.7	2.1	3.3[2,3]
1996	5059.32	1/10/96	5032.94	5032.94	NC	28.1	26.0	3.3[2]
1998	7660.13	1/9/98	7580.42	7539.07	−0.5	21.1	16.1	1.0[2]
2000	10998.39	1/4/00	10997.93	9796.03	−10.9	−1.9	−6.2	−5.1
2001	10318.93	3/12/01	10208.25	8235.81	−19.3	−1.8	−7.1	3.5[1]
2002	9763.96	1/16/02	9712.27	7286.27	−25.0	−14.1	−16.8	−1.6
2003	8303.78	1/24/03	8131.01	7524.06	−7.5	28.6	25.3	−2.7[1,2]
2005	10440.58	1/21/05	10392.99	10012.36	−3.7	3.1	−0.6	−2.5[3]
2006	10717.50	1/20/06	10667.39	10667.39	NC	16.8	16.3	2.5[2]
2007	12194.13	3/2/07	12114.10	12050.41	−0.5	9.5	6.4	1.4[2]
2008	13167.20	1/2/08	13043.96	7552.29	−42.1	−32.7	−33.8	−6.1
2009	8149.09	1/20/09	7949.09	6547.05	−17.6	31.2	18.8	−8.6[1,2]
2010	10285.97	1/22/10	10172.98	9686.48	−4.8	13.8	11.0	−3.7[1,2]
2014	15739.43	1/29/14	15738.79	15372.80	−2.3	13.2	7.5	−3.6[1,2]
2016	17128.55	1/6/16	16906.51	15660.18	−7.4	16.9	13.4	−5.1[1,2]
2018	24140.91	2/8/18	23860.46	21792.20	−8.7	−2.2	−5.6	5.6[1]
2020	27502.81	2/25/20	27081.36	18591.93	−31.3	13.0	7.2	−0.2[1,2]
2022	34022.04	2/22/22	33596.61	28725.51	−14.5	−1.3	−8.8	−5.3
2023	32757.54	2/28/23	32656.70	31819.14	−2.6	*As of June 6, 2023		6.2
			Average Drop		−11.1%			

[1]January Barometer wrong. [2]December Low Indicator wrong. [3]Year Flat.

Week After Triple Witching, Dow Down 22 of Last 36, 2000 Up 4.9%, 2009 Up 6.8%, 2020 Up 12.8% Best Week Since 1931

MONDAY
D 57.1
S 61.9
N 71.4
18

Knowing others is intelligence; knowing yourself is true wisdom.
Mastering others is strength; mastering yourself is true power.
— Lao Tzu (Chinese philosopher, Shaolin monk, founder of Taoism, 6th century BCE)

TUESDAY
D 66.7
S 66.7
N 71.4
19

Small business has been the first rung on the ladder upward for every minority group in the nation's history.
— S. I. Hayakawa (U.S. Senator California 1977-1983, 1906–1992)

Dow Lost 4012 Points (17.3%) on the Week Ending 3/20/2020
Worst Dow Weekly Point Loss and 2nd Worst Percent Loss Overall
FOMC Meeting (2 Days)

WEDNESDAY
D 57.1
S 47.6
N 71.4
20

I never won a fight in the ring; I always won in preparation.
— Muhammad Ali (American boxer, activist, "The Greatest," 1942–2016)

THURSDAY
D 33.3
S 42.9
N 47.6
21

Leadership is the ability to hide your panic from others
— Lao Tzu (Chinese philosopher, Shaolin monk, founder of Taoism, 6th century BCE)

March Historically Weak Later in the Month (Pages 32 and 136)

FRIDAY
D 61.9
S 57.1
N 66.7
22

Tell me and I'll forget; show me and I may remember; involve me and I'll understand.
— Confucius (Chinese philosopher, 551–478 BCE)

SATURDAY
23

SUNDAY
24

HOW TO TRADE BEST MONTHS SWITCHING STRATEGIES

Our Best Months Switching Strategies found on pages 54, 56, 62 and 64 are simple and reliable, with a proven 73-year track record. Thus far we have failed to find a similar trading strategy that even comes close over the past six decades. And to top it off, the strategy has only been improving since we first discovered it in 1986.

Exogenous factors and cultural shifts must be considered. "Backward" tests that go back to 1925 or even 1896 and conclude that the pattern does not work are best ignored. They do not take into account these factors. Farming made August the best month from 1900–1951. Since 1988 it is the worst month of the year for Dow and second worst for S&P. Panic caused by financial crisis in 2007–08 caused every asset class aside from U.S. Treasuries to decline substantially. But the bulk of the major decline in equities in the worst months of 2008 was sidestepped using these strategies. Again in 2022 we avoided most of the bear from May to October.

Our Best Months Switching Strategy will not make you an instant millionaire as other strategies claim they can do. What it will do is steadily build wealth over time with possibly less risk of a "buy and hold" approach.

A sampling of tradable funds for the Best and Worst Months appears in the table below. These are just a starting point and only skim the surface of possible trading vehicles currently available to take advantage of these strategies. Your specific situation and risk tolerance will dictate a suitable choice. If you are trading in a tax-advantaged account such as a company sponsored 401(k) or Individual Retirement Account (IRA), your investment options may be limited to what has been selected by your employer or IRA administrator. But if you are a self-directed trader with a brokerage account, then you likely have unlimited choices (perhaps too many).

TRADABLE BEST AND WORST MONTHS SWITCHING STRATEGY FUNDS

Best Months Exchange Traded Funds (ETF)		Worst Months Exchange Traded Funds (ETF)	
Symbol	Name	Symbol	Name
DIA	SPDR Dow Jones Industrial Average	SHY	iShares 1–3 Year Treasury Bond
SPY	SPDR S&P 500	IEI	iShares 3–7 Year Treasury Bond
QQQ	Invesco QQQ	IEF	iShares 7–10 Year Treasury Bond
IWM	iShares Russell 2000	TLT	iShares 20+ Year Treasury Bond

Mutual Funds		Mutual Funds	
Symbol	Name	Symbol	Name
VWNDX	Vanguard Windsor Fund	VFSTX	Vanguard Short-Term Investment-Grade Bond Fund
FMAGX	Fidelity Magellan Fund	FBNDX	Fidelity Investment Grade Bond Fund
AMCPX	American Funds AMCAP Fund	ABNDX	American Funds Bond Fund of America
FCGAX	Franklin Growth Fund	FKFSX	Franklin U.S. Government Securities Fund
SECEX	Guggenheim Large Cap Core Fund	SIUSX	Guggenheim Investment Grade Bond Fund

Generally speaking, during the Best Months you want to be invested in equities that offer similar exposure to the companies that constitute Dow, S&P 500, and NASDAQ indices. These would typically be large-cap growth and value stocks as well as technology concerns. Reviewing the holdings of a particular ETF or mutual fund and comparing them to the index members is an excellent way to correlate.

During the Worst Months switch into Treasury bonds, money market funds or a bear/short fund. **Grizzly Short** (GRZZX) and **AdvisorShares Ranger Equity Bear** (HDGE) are two possible choices. Money market funds will be the safest, but are likely to offer the smallest return, while bear/short funds offer potentially greater returns, but more risk. If the market moves sideways or higher during the Worst Months, a bear/short fund is likely to lose money. Treasuries can offer a combination of fair returns with limited risk.

Additional Worst Month possibilities include precious metals and the companies that mine them. **SPDR Gold Shares** (GLD), **VanEck Vectors Gold Miners** (GDX) and **Aberdeen Standard Gold** (SGOL) are a few well recognized names available from the ETF universe.

BECOME AN ALMANAC INVESTOR

Almanac Investor subscribers receive specific buy and sell trade ideas based upon the Best Months Switching Strategies online and via email. Sector Index Seasonalities, found on page 94, are also put into action throughout the year with corresponding ETF trades. Buy limits, stop losses, and auto-sell price points for the majority of seasonal trades are delivered directly to your inbox. Visit *www.stocktradersalmanac.com* or see the insert for details and a special offer for new subscribers.

MONDAY
D 47.6
S 47.6
N 38.1
25

The fear of capitalism has compelled socialism to widen freedom, and the fear of socialism has compelled capitalism to increase equality.
— Will and Ariel Durant (*The Lessons of History*, 1885–1981, 1898–1981)

Start Looking for Dow and S&P MACD SELL Signal on April 1 (Pages 56 & 64)
Almanac Investor Subscribers Emailed When It Triggers (See Insert)

TUESDAY
D 47.6
S 47.6
N 47.6
26

There are ways for the individual investor to make money in the securities markets. Buying value and holding long term while collecting dividends has been proven over and over again.
— Robert M. Sharp (Author, T*he Lore and Legends of Wall Street*)

WEDNESDAY
D 61.9
S 57.1
N 66.7
27

Our firm conviction is that, sooner or later, capitalism will give way to socialism... We will bury you.
— Nikita Khrushchev (Soviet leader 1953–1964, 1894–1971)

Last Day of March, Dow Down 21 of Last 33, Russell 2000 Up 25 of Last 34
NASDAQ Up 21 of Last 23 Days Before Good Friday

THURSDAY
D 38.1
S 42.9
N 52.4
28

An autobiography must be such that one can sue oneself for libel.
— Thomas Hoving (Museum Director)

Good Friday *(Market Closed)*

FRIDAY
29

Absorb what is useful, discard what is useless, and add what is specifically your own.
— Bruce Lee (American martial artist, actor, philosopher and filmmaker, founder of Jeet Kune Do, 1940–1973)

SATURDAY
30

Easter
April Almanac Investor Sector Seasonalities: See Pages 94, 96 and 98

SUNDAY
31

APRIL
ALMANAC

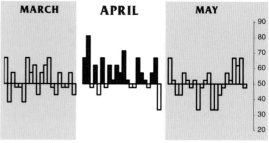

APRIL						
S	M	T	W	T	F	S
		1	2	3	4	5
6	7	8	9	10	11	12
13	14	15	16	17	18	19
20	21	22	23	24	25	26
27	28	29	30			

MAY						
S	M	T	W	T	F	S
				1	2	3
4	5	6	7	8	9	10
11	12	13	14	15	16	17
18	19	20	21	22	23	24
25	26	27	28	29	30	31

Market Probability Chart above is a graphic representation of the S&P 500 Recent Market Probability Calendar on page 126.

◆ April is still the best Dow month (average 1.9%) since 1950 (page 52) ◆ April 1999 first month ever to gain 1000 Dow points, 856 in 2001, knocked off its high horse in 2002 down 458, 2003 up 488 ◆ Up sixteen straight, 2006 to 2021 ◆ April 2020 Dow +11.1%, best April since 1938 ◆ Exhibits strength after tax deadline recent years ◆ Stocks anticipate great first quarter earnings by rising sharply before earnings are reported, rather than after ◆ Rarely a dangerous month, recent exceptions are 2002, 2004, 2005, and 2022 ◆ "Best Six Months" of the year end with April (page 54) ◆ Presidential election year Aprils since 1950, Dow 1.5%, S&P 1.3%, NASDAQ 0.9% ◆ End of April NASDAQ strength fading (pages 127 & 128)

April Vital Statistics

	DJIA		S&P 500		NASDAQ		Russell 1K		Russell 2K	
Rank	1		2		4		2		4	
Up	51		53		35		32		28	
Down	23		21		18		13		175	
Average % Change	1.9%		1.5%		1.4%		1.6%		1.4%	
Election Year	1.5%		1.3%		0.9%		2.0%		1.4%	
	Best & Worst April									
	% Change		% Change		% Change		% Change		% Change	
Best	2020	11.1	2020	12.7	2020	15.4	2020	13.1	2009	15.3
Worst	1970	–6.3	1970	–9.0	2000	–15.6	2002	–9.0	2000	–10.0
	Best & Worst April Weeks									
Best	4/9/20	12.7	4/9/20	12.1	4/12/01	14.0	4/9/20	12.6	4/9/20	18.5
Worst	4/14/00	–7.3	4/14/00	–10.5	4/14/00	–25.3	4/14/00	–11.2	4/14/00	–16.4
	Best & Worst April Days									
Best	4/6/20	7.7	4/6/20	7.0	4/5/01	8.9	4/6/20	7.1	4/6/20	8.2
Worst	4/14/00	–5.7	4/14/00	–5.8	4/14/00	–9.7	4/14/00	–6.0	4/14/00	–7.3
	First Trading Day of Expiration Week: 1980–2023									
Record (#Up – #Down)	25–19		23–21		23–21		23–21		19–25	
Current Streak	U1		U1		U1		U1		U1	
Avg % Change	0.13		0.07		0.07		0.06		–0.05	
	Options Expiration Day: 1980–2023									
Record (#Up – #Down)	28–16		28–16		25–19		28–16		27–17	
Current Streak	U1		U1		U1		U1		U1	
Avg % Change	0.21		0.16		–0.07		0.16		0.23	
	Options Expiration Week: 1980–2023									
Record (#Up – #Down)	34–10		30–14		25–15		28–16		32–12	
Current Streak	D2		D2		D2		D2		U3	
Avg % Change	0.99		0.81		0.91		0.80		0.73	
	Week After Options Expiration: 1980–2023									
Record (#Up – #Down)	27–17		28–16		29–15		28–16		29–15	
Current Streak	U1		U1		U1		U1		D2	
Avg % Change	0.32		0.35		0.59		0.35		0.69	
	First Trading Day Performance									
% of Time Up	59.5		62.2		47.2		60.0		48.9	
Avg % Change	0.12		0.09		–0.15		0.07		–0.19	
	Last Trading Day Performance									
% of Time Up	48.6		52.7		58.5		51.1		57.8	
Avg % Change	0.01		–0.01		–0.004		–0.08		–0.15	

Dow & S&P 1950–June 9, 2023, NASDAQ 1971–June 9, 2023, Russell 1K & 2K 1979–June 9, 2023.

April "Best Month" for Dow since 1950;
Day-before-Good Friday gains are nifty.

40

APRIL 2024

Day After Easter, Second Worst Post-Holiday (Page 100)
First Trading Day in April, Dow and S&P Up 21 of Last 29

MONDAY

D 66.7
S 66.7
N 66.7

1

More people and increased income cause resources to become scarcer in the short run. Heightened scarcity causes prices to rise. The higher prices present opportunity and prompt investors to search for solutions. These solutions eventually lead to prices dropping lower than before the scarcity occurred.
— Julian Simon (Businessman, Professor of Business Administration, *The Ultimate Resource*, 1996, 1932–1998)

TUESDAY

D 76.2
S 81.0
N 76.2

2

The punishment of wise men who refuse to take part in the affairs of government is to live under the government of unwise men.
— Plato (Greek philosopher, 427–347 BCE)

April Is the Best Month for the Dow, Average 1.9% Gain Since 1950

WEDNESDAY

D 42.9
S 47.6
N 52.4

3

The word "crisis" in Chinese is composed of two characters: the first, the symbol of danger; the second, opportunity.
— Anonymous

THURSDAY

D 61.9
S 61.9
N 52.4

4

A gold mine is a hole in the ground with a liar on top.
— Mark Twain (1835–1910, pen name of Samuel Longhorne Clemens, American novelist and satirist)

FRIDAY

D 47.6
S 42.9
N 33.3

5

The only things that evolve by themselves in an organization are disorder, friction and malperformance.
— Peter Drucker (Austrian-born pioneer management theorist, 1909–2005)

SATURDAY

6

SUNDAY

7

DOW JONES INDUSTRIALS ONE-YEAR SEASONAL PATTERN CHARTS SINCE 1901

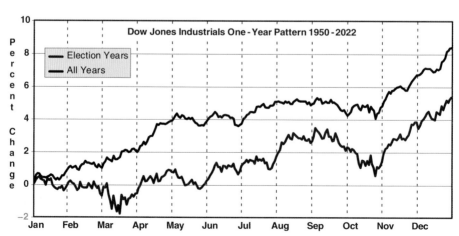

APRIL 2024

MONDAY

D 61.9
S 66.7
N 66.7

8

The greatest safety lies in putting all your eggs in one basket and watching the basket.
— Gerald M. Loeb (E.F. Hutton, *The Battle for Investment Survival*, predicted 1929 Crash, 1900–1974)

TUESDAY

D 47.6
S 47.6
N 42.9

9

If you could kick the person in the pants responsible for most of your trouble, you wouldn't sit for a month.
— Theodore Roosevelt (26th U.S. President, 1858–1919)

April Is 2nd Best Month for S&P, 4th Best for NASDAQ (Since 1971)

WEDNESDAY

D 52.4
S 61.9
N 66.7

10

My best shorts come from research reports where there are recommendations to buy stocks on weakness; also, where a brokerage firm changes its recommendation from a buy to a hold.
— Marc Howard (Hedge fund manager, *New York Magazine* 1976, b. 1941)

THURSDAY

D 52.4
S 52.4
N 42.9

11

I'm a great believer in luck, and I find the harder I work the more I have of it.
— Thomas Jefferson (3rd U.S. President, 1743–7/4/1826)

FRIDAY

D 66.7
S 61.9
N 47.6

12

If a man can see both sides of a problem, you know that none of his money is tied up in it.
— Verda Ross

SATURDAY

13

SUNDAY

14

S&P 500 ONE-YEAR
SEASONAL PATTERN CHARTS SINCE 1901

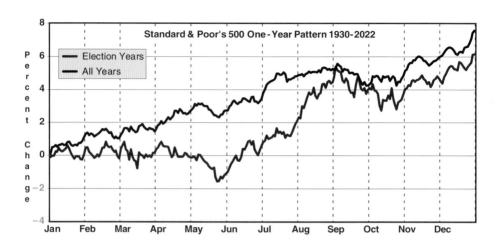

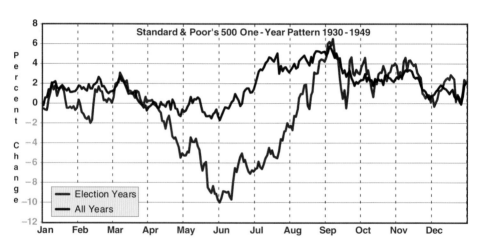

APRIL 2024

Income Tax Deadline
Monday Before April Expiration, Dow Up 21 of Last 35, Down 11 of Last 19

MONDAY
D 57.1
S 57.1
N 47.6
15

There are very few instances in history when any government has ever paid off debt.
— Walter Wriston (Retired CEO of Citicorp and Citibank)

TUESDAY
D 61.9
S 71.4
N 71.4
16

The stock market is that creation of man which humbles him the most.
— Anonymous

April Exhibits Strength After Tax Deadline Recent Years (Pages 40 and 136)

WEDNESDAY
D 52.4
S 52.4
N 38.1
17

The key to long-term profits on Wall Street is not making big killings, it's not getting killed.
— Daniel Turov (*Turov on Timing*)

April 1999 First Month Ever to Gain 1000 Dow Points

THURSDAY
D 57.1
S 47.6
N 52.4
18

Victory goes to the player who makes the next-to-last mistake.
— Savielly Grigorievitch Tartakower (Chess master, 1887–1956)

April Expiration Day Dow Up 18 of Last 27, But Down 6 of Last 10

FRIDAY
D 61.9
S 47.6
N 61.9
19

Of 120 companies from 1987 to 1992 that relied primarily on cost cutting to improve the bottom line, 68 percent failed to achieve profitable growth during the next five years.
— Mercer Management Consulting (*Smart Money Magazine*, August 2001)

SATURDAY
20

SUNDAY
21

NASDAQ, RUSSELL 1000 & 2000 ONE-YEAR SEASONAL PATTERN CHARTS SINCE 1971

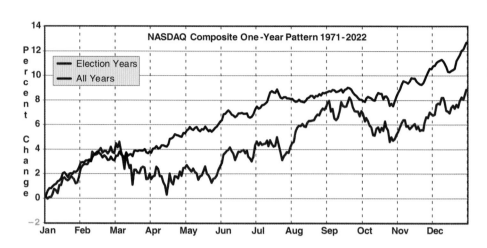

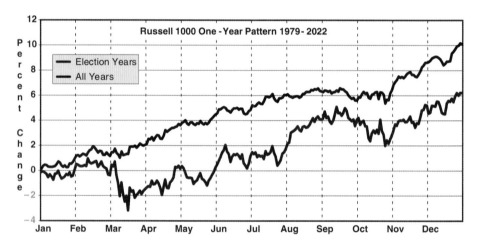

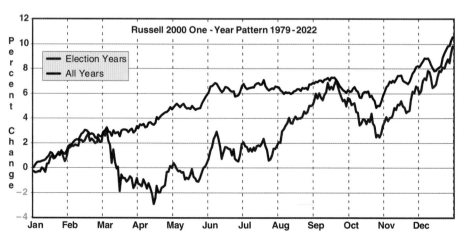

APRIL 2024

MONDAY

D 61.9
S 66.7
N 61.9

22

Imagination is more important than knowledge.
— Albert Einstein (German/American physicist, 1921 Nobel Prize, 1879–1955)

Passover

TUESDAY

D 61.9
S 57.1
N 47.6

23

When the public buys toilet paper, I buy stocks.
— Larry Williams (Legendary trader, author, politician, 3/16/2020, b. 1942)

WEDNESDAY

D 47.6
S 52.4
N 57.1

24

Whoso neglects learning in his youth, loses the past and is dead for the future.
— Euripides (Greek tragedian, *Medea*, 485–406 BCE)

End of "Best Six Months" of the Year (Pages 54, 56, 64 and 149)

THURSDAY

D 57.1
S 47.6
N 38.1

25

In Wall Street, the man who does not change his mind will soon have no change to mind.
— William D. Gann (Trader, technical analyst, author, publisher, 1878–1955)

FRIDAY

D 66.7
S 57.1
N 47.6

26

I always keep these seasonal patterns in the back of my mind. My antennae start to purr at certain times of the year.
— Kenneth Ward (VP Hayden Stone, *General Technical Survey*, 1899–1976)

SATURDAY

27

May Almanac Investor Sector Seasonalities: See Pages 94, 96 and 98

SUNDAY

28

MAY ALMANAC

MAY							JUNE						
S	M	T	W	T	F	S	S	M	T	W	T	F	S
		1	2	3	4								1
5	6	7	8	9	10	11	2	3	4	5	6	7	8
12	13	14	15	16	17	18	9	10	11	12	13	14	15
19	20	21	22	23	24	25	16	17	18	19	20	21	22
26	27	28	29	30	31		23	24	25	26	27	28	29
							30						

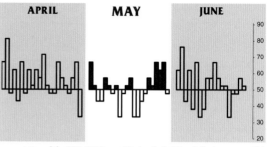

Market Probability Chart above is a graphic representation of the S&P 500 Recent Market Probability Calendar on page 126.

◆ "May/June disaster area" between 1965 and 1984 with S&P down 15 out of 20 Mays ◆ Between 1985 and 1997 May was the best month with 13 straight gains, gaining 3.3% per year on average, up 17, down 9 since ◆ Worst six months of the year begin with May (page 54) ◆ A $10,000 investment compounded to $1,180,836 gain for November-April in 73 years compared to a $3,323 gain for May-October ◆ Dow Memorial Day week record: up 12 years in a row (1984-1995), down 16 of the last 28 years ◆ Since 1950 presidential election year Mays rank, #9 Dow, #9 S&P and #8 NASDAQ

May Vital Statistics

	DJIA		S&P 500		NASDAQ		Russell 1K		Russell 2K	
Rank	9		8		5		8		5	
Up	40		45		32		31		28	
Down	34		29		21		14		17	
Average % Change	−0.05%		0.2%		1.0%		0.9%		1.2%	
Election Year	−0.4%		−0.1%		−0.2%		0.2%		0.6%	
	Best & Worst May									
	% Change		% Change		% Change		% Change		% Change	
Best	1990	8.3	1990	9.2	1997	11.1	1990	8.9	1997	11.0
Worst	2010	−7.9	1962	−8.6	2000	−11.9	2010	−8.1	2019	−7.9
	Best & Worst May Weeks									
Best	5/29/70	6.2	5/2/97	6.6	5/17/02	8.8	5/2/97	6.6	5/22/20	7.8
Worst	5/25/62	−6.0	5/25/62	−6.8	5/7/10	−8.0	5/7/10	−6.6	5/7/10	−8.9
	Best & Worst May Days									
Best	5/27/70	5.1	5/27/70	5.0	5/30/00	7.9	5/10/10	4.4	5/18/20	6.1
Worst	5/28/62	−5.7	5/28/62	−6.7	5/23/00	−5.9	5/20/10	−4.0	5/20/10	−5.1
	First Trading Day of Expiration Week: 1980–2023									
Record (#Up − #Down)	27–17		28–16		24–20		26–18		22–22	
Current Streak	U2		U1		U1		U1		U1	
Avg % Change	0.11		0.10		0.08		0.08		−0.04	
	Options Expiration Day: 1980–2023									
Record (#Up − #Down)	23–21		24–20		20–24		24–20		22–22	
Current Streak	D1		D1		D3		D1		D2	
Avg % Change	−0.06		−0.07		−0.10		−0.06		0.03	
	Options Expiration Week: 1980–2023									
Record (#Up − #Down)	20–24		20–24		22–22		19–25		22–22	
Current Streak	U1		U1		U1		U4		U1	
Avg % Change	−0.11		−0.10		0.08		−0.10		−0.26	
	Week After Options Expiration: 1980–2023									
Record (#Up − #Down)	25–19		29–15		31–13		29–15		32–12	
Current Streak	D1		U4		U4		U4		D1	
Avg % Change	0.25		0.41		0.57		0.44		0.69	
	First Trading Day Performance									
% of Time Up	55.4		58.1		60.4		57.8		62.2	
Avg % Change	0.16		0.19		0.27		0.18		0.18	
	Last Trading Day Performance									
% of Time Up	55.4		58.1		62.3		51.1		55.6	
Avg % Change	0.11		0.20		0.14		0.11		0.15	

Dow & S&P 1950–June 9, 2023, NASDAQ 1971–June 9, 2023, Russell 1K & 2K 1979–June 9, 2023.

Better to reposition in May
Than to sell in May and go away.

APRIL/MAY 2024

MONDAY
D 66.7
S 66.7
N 76.2
29

Lack of money is the root of all evil.
— George Bernard Shaw (Irish dramatist, 1856–1950)

TUESDAY
D 28.6
S 33.3
N 28.6
30

Some traders are born with an innate discipline. Most have to learn it the hard way.
— J. Welles Wilder Jr. (Creator of several technical indicators including Relative Strength Index (RSI) 1935– 2021)

First Trading Day in May, S&P Up 18 of Last 26
FOMC Meeting (2 Days)

WEDNESDAY
D 57.1
S 66.7
N 66.7
1

Liberties voluntarily forfeited are not easily retrieved. All the more so for those that are removed surreptitiously.
— Ted Koppel (Newsman and anchor *NY Times* 11/6/06, b. 1940)

THURSDAY
D 71.4
S 52.4
N 57.1
2

I am glad that I paid so little attention to good advice; had I abided by it I might have been saved from my most valuable mistakes.
— Gene Fowler (Journalist, screenwriter, film director, biographer, 1890–1960)

FRIDAY
D 47.6
S 42.9
N 42.9
3

In business, the competition will bite you if you keep running; if you stand still, they will swallow you.
— William Knudsen (Former President of GM)

SATURDAY
4

SUNDAY
5

SUMMER MARKET VOLUME DOLDRUMS DRIVE WORST SIX MONTHS

In recent years, Memorial Day weekend has become the unofficial start of summer. Not long afterwards trading activity typically begins to slowly decline (barring any external event triggers) towards a later summer low. We refer to this summertime slowdown in trading as the doldrums due to the anemic volume and uninspired trading on Wall Street. The individual trader, if they are looking to sell a stock, is generally met with disinterest from The Street. It becomes difficult to sell a stock at a good price. That is also why many summer rallies tend to be short lived and are quickly followed by a pullback or correction.

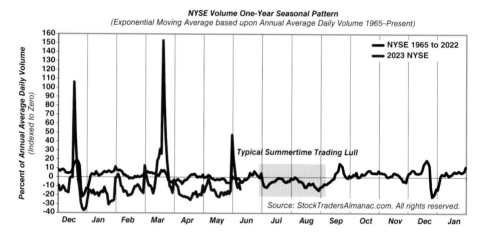

NYSE Volume One-Year Seasonal Pattern
(Exponential Moving Average based upon Annual Average Daily Volume 1965–Present)

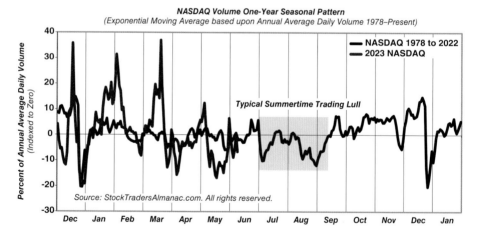

NASDAQ Volume One-Year Seasonal Pattern
(Exponential Moving Average based upon Annual Average Daily Volume 1978–Present)

Above are plotted the one-year seasonal volume patterns since 1965 for the NYSE and since 1978 for NASDAQ against the annual average daily volume moving average for 2023 as of the close on June 9, 2023. The typical summer lull is highlighted in red. A prolonged surge in volume during the typically quiet summer months, especially when accompanied by gains, can be an encouraging sign that the bull market will continue. However, should traders lose their conviction and participate in the annual summer exodus from The Street, a market pullback or correction could quickly unfold.

MAY 2024

MONDAY

D 38.1
S 42.9
N 47.6

6

We are all born originals; why is it so many die copies?
— Edward Young (English poet, 1683–1765)

TUESDAY

D 61.9
S 57.1
N 52.4

7

The price of a stock varies inversely with the thickness of its research file.
— Martin Sosnoff (Atalanta Sosnoff Capital, *Silent Investor, Silent Loser*)

WEDNESDAY

D 66.7
S 52.4
N 66.7

8

Market risk tends to be poorly rewarded when market valuations are rich and interest rates are rising.
— John P. Hussman, Ph.D. (Hussman Funds, 5/22/06)

THURSDAY

D 38.1
S 47.6
N 52.4

9

Towering genius disdains a beaten path. It scorns to tread in the footsteps of any predecessor, however illustrious. It thirsts for distinction.
— Abraham Lincoln (16th U.S. President, 1809–1865)

Friday Before Mother's Day, Dow Up 19 of Last 29

FRIDAY

D 57.1
S 52.4
N 42.9

10

The greatest discovery of my generation is that human beings can alter their lives by altering their attitudes.
— William James (Philosopher, psychologist, 1842–1910)

SATURDAY

11

Mother's Day

SUNDAY

12

TOP-PERFORMING MONTHS:
STANDARD & POOR'S 500 AND DOW JONES INDUSTRIALS

Monthly performance of the S&P and the Dow are ranked over the past 73 1/3 years. NASDAQ monthly performance is shown on page 60.

April, November and December still hold the top three positions in both the Dow and S&P. Disastrous Januarys in 2008, 2009, 2016 and 2022 knocked January into sixth. This, in part, led to our discovery in 1986 of the market's most consistent seasonal pattern. You can divide the year into two sections and have practically all the gains in one six-month section and very little in the other. September is the worst month on both lists. (See "Best Six Months" on page 54.)

MONTHLY % CHANGES (JANUARY 1950–APRIL 2023)

	Standard & Poor's 500					Dow Jones Industrials			
Month	Total % Change	Avg. % Change	# Up	# Down	Month	Total % Change	Avg. % Change	# Up	# Down
Jan	77.7%	1.1%	44	30	Jan	67.7%	0.9%	46	28
Feb	−5.6	−0.08	40	34	Feb	3.7	0.1	43	31
Mar	81.3	1.1	48	26	Mar	70.4	1.0	48	26
Apr	114.5	1.5	53	21	Apr	143.1	1.9	51	23
May	16.3	0.2	44	29	May	− 0.6	− 0.01	40	33
Jun	1.4	0.02	40	33	Jun	− 18.0	− 0.2	34	39
Jul	91.8	1.3	43	30	Jul	97.3	1.3	48	25
Aug	0.9	0.01	40	33	Aug	− 6.7	− 0.09	41	32
Sep*	−48.3	−0.7	32	40	Sep	− 60.1	− 0.8	29	44
Oct	69.8	1.0	44	29	Oct	57.3	0.8	44	29
Nov	125.8	1.7	50	23	Nov	127.5	1.7	50	23
Dec	105.4	1.4	54	19	Dec	110.4	1.5	51	22
%					**%**				
Rank					**Rank**				
Apr	125.8%	1.7%	50	23	Apr	143.1%	1.9%	51	23
Nov	114.5	1.5	53	21	Nov	127.5	1.7	50	23
Dec	105.4	1.4	54	19	Dec	110.4	1.5	51	22
Jul	91.8	1.3	43	30	Jul	97.3	1.3	48	25
Jan	81.3	1.1	48	26	Jan	70.4	1.0	48	26
Mar	77.7	1.1	44	30	Mar	67.7	0.9	46	28
Oct	69.8	1.0	44	29	Oct	57.3	0.8	44	29
May	16.3	0.2	44	29	Feb	3.7	0.1	43	31
Jun	1.4	0.02	40	33	May	− 0.6	− 0.01	40	33
Aug	0.9	0.01	40	33	Aug	− 6.7	− 0.09	41	32
Feb	−5.6	−0.08	40	34	Jun	− 18.0	− 0.2	34	39
Sep*	−48.3	−0.7	32	40	Sep	− 60.1	− 0.8	29	44
Totals	**631.0%**	**8.6%**			**Totals**	**592.0%**	**8.1%**		
Average		**0.71%**			**Average**		**0.68%**		

*No change 1979

Anticipators, shifts in cultural behavior and faster information flow have altered seasonality in recent years. Here is how the months ranked over the past 15 1/3 years (184 months) using total percentage gains on the S&P 500: July 45.2, April 37.1, November 30.0, March 23.9, October 16.2, December 9.6, May –1.0, February –2.5, August –2.5, January –3.6, June –9.9, and September –16.8.

January has declined in 13 of the last 24 years. Sizeable turnarounds in "bear killing" October were a common occurrence from 1999 to 2007 and 2022. Recent big Dow losses in the period were: September 2001 (9/11 attack), off 11.1%; September 2002 (Iraq war drums), off 12.4%; June 2008, off 10.2%, October 2008, off 14.1%, February 2009, off 11.7% (financial crisis) and March 2020, off 13.7% (Covid-19 shutdown).

MAY 2024

MONDAY

D 33.3
S 33.3
N 47.6

13

A loss never bothers me after I take it. I forget it overnight. But being wrong—not taking the loss—that is what does damage to the pocketbook and to the soul.
— Jesse Livermore (Early 20th century stock trader and speculator, *How to Trade in Stocks*, 1877–1940)

TUESDAY

D 57.1
S 47.6
N 57.1

14

I have but one lamp by which my feet [or "investments"] are guided, and that is the lamp of experience. I know of no way of judging the future but by the past.
— Patrick Henry (U.S. Founding Father, twice Governor of VA, 1736–1799, March 23, 1775 speech)

WEDNESDAY

D 61.9
S 52.4
N 47.6

15

The soul is dyed the color of its thoughts. Think only on those things that are in line with your principles and can bear the light of day. The content of your character is your choice. Day by day, what you do is who you become.
— Heraclitus (Greek philosopher, 535–475 BCE)

THURSDAY

D 52.4
S 57.1
N 61.9

16

A day will come when all nations on our continent will form a European brotherhood…A day will come when we shall see…the United States of Europe…reaching out for each other across the seas.
— Victor Hugo (French novelist, playwright, *Hunchback of Notre Dame* and *Les Misérables*, 1802–1885)

May Expiration Day, Dow Up 15 of Last 23

FRIDAY

D 33.3
S 33.3
N 38.1

17

Every successful enterprise requires three people—a dreamer, a businessman, and a son-of-a-bitch.
— Peter McArthur (1904)

SATURDAY

18

SUNDAY

19

"BEST SIX MONTHS": STILL AN EYE-POPPING STRATEGY

Our Best Six Months Switching Strategy consistently delivers. Investing in the Dow Jones Industrial Average between November 1st and April 30th each year and then switching into fixed income for the other six months has produced reliable returns with reduced risk since 1950.

The chart on page 149 shows November, December, January, March and April to be the top months since 1950. Add February, and an excellent strategy is born! These six consecutive months gained 26249.55 Dow points in 73 years, while the remaining May through October months gained 7634.28 points. The S&P gained 3018.83 points in the same best six months versus 1132.58 points in the worst six.

Percentage changes are shown along with a compounding $10,000 investment. The November-April $1,180,836 gain overshadows May-October's $3,323 gain. (S&P results were $977,443 to $13,335.) Just four November-April losses were double-digit: April 1970 (Cambodian invasion), 1973 (OPEC oil embargo), 2008 (financial crisis) and 2019 (Covid-19 shutdown). Similarly, Iraq muted the Best Six and inflated the Worst Six in 2003. When we discovered this strategy in 1986, November-April outperformed May-October by $88,163 to minus $1,522. Results improved substantially these past 37 years, $1,092,673 to $4,845. A simple timing indicator nearly triples results (page 56).

	SIX-MONTH SWITCHING STRATEGY			
	DJIA % Change May 1–Oct 31	Investing $10,000	DJIA % Change Nov 1–Apr 30	Investing $10,000
1950	5.0%	$10,500	15.2%	$11,520
1951	1.2	10,626	−1.8	11,313
1952	4.5	11,104	2.1	11,551
1953	0.4	11,148	15.8	13,376
1954	10.3	12,296	20.9	16,172
1955	6.9	13,144	13.5	18,355
1956	−7.0	12,224	3.0	18,906
1957	−10.8	10,904	3.4	19,549
1958	19.2	12,998	14.8	22,442
1959	3.7	13,479	−6.9	20,894
1960	−3.5	13,007	16.9	24,425
1961	3.7	13,488	−5.5	23,082
1962	−11.4	11,950	21.7	28,091
1963	5.2	12,571	7.4	30,170
1964	7.7	13,539	5.6	31,860
1965	4.2	14,108	−2.8	30,968
1966	−13.6	12,189	11.1	34,405
1967	−1.9	11,957	3.7	35,678
1968	4.4	12,483	−0.2	35,607
1969	−9.9	11,247	−14.0	30,622
1970	2.7	11,551	24.6	38,155
1971	−10.9	10,292	13.7	43,382
1972	0.1	10,302	−3.6	41,820
1973	3.8	10,693	−12.5	36,593
1974	−20.5	8,501	23.4	45,156
1975	1.8	8,654	19.2	53,826
1976	−3.2	8,377	−3.9	51,727
1977	−11.7	7,397	2.3	52,917
1978	−5.4	6,998	7.9	57,097
1979	−4.6	6,676	0.2	57,211
1980	13.1	7,551	7.9	61,731
1981	−14.6	6,449	−0.5	61,422
1982	16.9	7,539	23.6	75,918
1983	−0.1	7,531	−4.4	72,578
1984	3.1	7,764	4.2	75,626
1985	9.2	8,478	29.8	98,163
1986	5.3	8,927	21.8	119,563
1987	−12.8	7,784	1.9	121,835
1988	5.7	8,228	12.6	137,186
1989	9.4	9,001	0.4	137,735
1990	−8.1	8,272	18.2	162,803
1991	6.3	8,793	9.4	178,106
1992	−4.0	8,441	6.2	189,149
1993	7.4	9,066	0.03	189,206
1994	6.2	9,628	10.6	209,262
1995	10.0	10,591	17.1	245,046
1996	8.3	11,470	16.2	284,743
1997	6.2	12,181	21.8	346,817
1998	−5.2	11,548	25.6	435,602
1999	−0.5	11,490	0.04	435,776
2000	2.2	11,743	−2.2	426,189
2001	−15.5	9,923	9.6	467,103
2002	−15.6	8,375	1.0	471,774
2003	15.6	9,682	4.3	492,060
2004	−1.9	9,498	1.6	499,933
2005	2.4	9,726	8.9	544,427
2006	6.3	10,339	8.1	588,526
2007	6.6	11,021	−8.0	541,444
2008	−27.3	8,012	−12.4	474,305
2009	18.9	9,526	13.3	537,388
2010	1.0	9,621	15.2	619,071
2011	−6.7	8,976	10.5	684,073
2012	−0.9	8,895	13.3	775,055
2013	4.8	9,322	6.7	826,984
2014	4.9	9,779	2.6	848,486
2015	−1.0	9,681	0.6	853,577
2016	2.1	$9,884	15.4	$985,223
2017	11.6	$11,031	3.4	$1,018,721
2018	3.9	$11,461	5.9	$1,078,826
2019	1.7	$11,656	−10.0	$970,943
2020	8.9	$12,693	27.8	$1,240,086
2021	5.7	$13,417	−7.9	$1,142,837
2022	−0.7	$13,323	4.2	$1,190,836
Average/Gain	0.8%	$3,323	7.3%	$1,180,836
# Up/Down	45/28		57/16	

54

MAY 2024

The reasonable man adapts himself to the world; the unreasonable one persists in trying to adapt the world to himself. Therefore, all progress depends on the unreasonable man.
— George Bernard Shaw (Irish dramatist, 1856–1950)

TUESDAY
D 42.9
S 42.9
N 52.4
21

Corporate guidance has become something of an art. The CFO has refined and perfected his art, gracefully leading on the bulls with the calculating grace and cunning of a great matador.
— Joe Kalinowski (I/B/E/S)

WEDNESDAY
D 38.1
S 47.6
N 42.9
22

Those heroes of finance are like beads on a string, when one slips off, the rest follow.
— Henrik Ibsen (Norwegian playwright, 1828–1906)

THURSDAY
D 57.1
S 57.1
N 57.1
23

Most people can bear adversity. But if you wish to know what a man really is, give him power.
— Robert G. Ingersoll (American lawyer, politician and orator, "The Great Agnostic," 1833–1899)

Friday Before Memorial Day Tends to Be Lackluster with Light Trading, Dow Mixed, Up 12 Down 12, Average –0.03%

FRIDAY
D 47.6
S 52.4
N 47.6
24

Genius, that power which dazzles mortal eyes, is often perseverance in disguise.
— Henry Willard Austin (American writer, *Perseverance Conquers All*, 1858–1916)

SATURDAY
25

June Almanac Investor Sector Seasonalities: See Pages 94, 96 and 98

SUNDAY
26

MACD-TIMING TRIPLES "BEST SIX MONTHS" RESULTS

Using the simple MACD (Moving Average Convergence Divergence) indicator developed by our friend Gerald Appel to better time entries and exits into and out of the Best Six Months (page 54) period nearly triples the results. Sy Harding enhanced our Best Six Months Switching Strategy with MACD triggers, dubbing it the "best mechanical system ever." In 2006 we improved it even more, achieving improved results with just four trades every four years (page 64).

Our *Almanac Investor* (see insert) implements this system with quite a degree of success. Starting on the first trading day of October we look to catch the market's first hint of an uptrend after the summer doldrums, and beginning on the first trading day of April we prepare to exit these seasonal positions as soon as the market falters.

In up-trending markets MACD signals get you in earlier and keep you in longer. But if the market is trending down, entries are delayed until the market turns up and exit points can come a month earlier.

The results are astounding applying the simple MACD signals. Instead of $10,000 gaining $1,180,836 over the 73 recent years when invested only during the Best Six Months (page 54), the gain nearly tripled to $3,392,617. The $3,323 gain during the worst six months became a loss of $5,376.

Impressive results for being invested during only 6.3 months of the year on average! For the rest of the year consider money markets, bonds, puts, bear funds, covered calls or credit call spreads.

Updated signals are emailed to our *Almanac Investor* subscribers as soon as they are triggered. Visit *www.stocktradersalmanac.com* or see the insert for details and a special offer for new subscribers.

BEST SIX-MONTH SWITCHING STRATEGY+TIMING

	DJIA % Change May 1–Oct 31*	Investing $10,000	DJIA % Change Nov 1–Apr 30*	Investing $10,000
1950	7.3%	$10,730	13.3%	$11,330
1951	0.1	10,741	1.9	11,545
1952	1.4	10,891	2.1	11,787
1953	0.2	10,913	17.1	13,803
1954	13.5	12,386	16.3	16,053
1955	7.7	13,340	13.1	18,156
1956	−6.8	12,433	2.8	18,664
1957	−12.3	10,904	4.9	19,579
1958	17.3	12,790	16.7	22,849
1959	1.6	12,995	−3.1	22,141
1960	−4.9	12,358	16.9	25,883
1961	2.9	12,716	−1.5	25,495
1962	−15.3	10,770	22.4	31,206
1963	4.3	11,233	9.6	34,202
1964	6.7	11,986	6.2	36,323
1965	2.6	12,298	−2.5	35,415
1966	−16.4	10,281	14.3	40,479
1967	−2.1	10,065	5.5	42,705
1968	3.4	10,407	0.2	42,790
1969	−11.9	9,169	−6.7	39,923
1970	−1.4	9,041	20.8	48,227
1971	−11.0	8,046	15.4	55,654
1972	−0.6	7,998	−1.4	54,875
1973	−11.0	7,118	0.1	54,930
1974	−22.4	5,524	28.2	70,420
1975	0.1	5,530	18.5	83,448
1976	−3.4	5,342	−3.0	80,945
1977	−11.4	4,733	0.5	81,350
1978	−4.5	4,520	9.3	88,916
1979	−5.3	4,280	7.0	95,140
1980	9.3	4,678	4.7	99,612
1981	−14.6	3,995	0.4	100,010
1982	15.5	4,614	23.5	123,512
1983	2.5	4,729	−7.3	114,496
1984	3.3	4,885	3.9	118,961
1985	7.0	5,227	38.1	164,285
1986	−2.8	5,081	28.2	210,613
1987	−14.9	4,324	3.0	216,931
1988	6.1	4,588	11.8	242,509
1989	9.8	5,038	3.3	250,532
1990	−6.7	4,700	15.8	290,116
1991	4.8	4,926	11.3	322,899
1992	−6.2	4,621	6.6	344,210
1993	5.5	4,875	5.6	363,486
1994	3.7	5,055	13.1	411,103
1995	7.2	5,419	16.7	479,757
1996	9.2	5,918	21.9	584,824
1997	3.6	6,131	18.5	693,016
1998	−12.4	5,371	39.9	969,529
1999	−6.4	5,027	5.1	1,018,975
2000	−6.0	4,725	5.4	1,074,000
2001	−17.3	3,908	15.8	1,243,692
2002	−25.2	2,923	6.0	1,318,314
2003	16.4	3,402	7.8	1,421,142
2004	−0.9	3,371	1.8	1,446,723
2005	−0.5	3,354	7.7	1,558,121
2006	4.7	3,512	14.4	1,782,490
2007	5.6	3,709	−12.7	1,556,114
2008	−24.7	2,793	−14.0	1,338,258
2009	23.8	3,458	10.8	1,482,790
2010	4.6	3,617	7.3	1,591,034
2011	−9.4	3,277	18.7	1,888,557
2012	0.3	3,287	10.0	2,077,413
2013	4.1	3,422	7.1	2,224,909
2014	2.3	3,501	7.4	2,389,552
2015	−6.0	3,291	4.9	2,506,640
2016	3.5	3,406	13.1	2,835,010
2017	15.7	3,941	0.4	2,846,350
2018	5.0	4,138	5.2	2,994,360
2019	1.5	4,200	−13.3	2,596,110
2020	22.1	5,128	19.1	3,091,967
2021	2.8	5,272	−0.5	3,076,507
2022	−12.3	4,624	10.6	3,402,617
Average	**−0.5%**		**8.8%**	
# Up	**41**		**62**	
# Down	**32**		**11**	
73-Year Gain (Loss)		**($5,376)**		**$3,392,617**

*MACD generated entry and exit points (earlier or later) can lengthen or shorten six-month periods.

56

MAY/JUNE 2024

Memorial Day *(Market Closed)*

MONDAY

27

The test of success is not what you do when you are on top. Success is how high you bounce when you hit bottom.
— General George S. Patton, Jr. (U.S. Army field commander WWII, 1885–1945)

Day After Memorial Day, Dow Up 23 of Last 38, But Down 7 of Last 9

TUESDAY

D 61.9
S 66.7
N 66.7

28

Your chances for success in any undertaking can be measured by your belief in yourself.
— Robert Collier (Direct marketing copywriter & author, 1885–1950)

Memorial Day Week Dow Down 16 of Last 28, Up 12 Straight 1984-1995

WEDNESDAY

D 52.4
S 61.9
N 66.7

29

At the extremes sentiment works real well but in the middle of a trend sentiment is not as valuable.
— Larry Williams (Legendary trader, author, politician, 3/16/2020, b. 1942)

Start Looking for NASDAQ MACD Sell Signal on June 1 (Page 62)
Almanac Investor Subscribers Emailed When It Triggers (See Insert)

THURSDAY

D 66.7
S 66.7
N 71.4

30

The ability to foretell what is going to happen tomorrow, next week, next month, and next year.
And to have the ability afterwards to explain why it didn't happen.
— Winston Churchill (British statesman, 1874–1965, when asked what qualities a politician required)

FRIDAY

D 33.3
S 47.6
N 47.6

31

If you can buy all you want of a new issue, you do not want any; if you cannot obtain any, you want all you can buy.
— Rod Fadem (Stifel Nicolaus & Co., *Barron's* 1989)

SATURDAY

1

SUNDAY

2

JUNE ALMANAC

JUNE						
S	M	T	W	T	F	S
						1
2	3	4	5	6	7	8
9	10	11	12	13	14	15
16	17	18	19	20	21	22
23	24	25	26	27	28	29
30						

JULY						
S	M	T	W	T	F	S
		1	2	3	4	5	6
7	8	9	10	11	12	13
14	15	16	17	18	19	20
21	22	23	24	25	26	27
28	29	30	31			

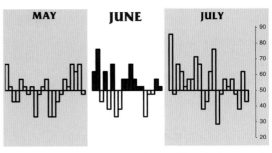

Market Probability Chart above is a graphic representation of the S&P 500 Recent Market Probability Calendar on page 126.

◆ The "summer rally" in most years is the weakest rally of all four seasons (page 74) ◆ Week after June Triple-Witching Day Dow down 26 of last 32 (page 108) ◆ RECENT RECORD: S&P up 12, down 9, average loss 0.8%, ranks eleventh ◆ Summer doldrums can begin in late June (page 50) ◆ Watch out for end-of-quarter "portfolio pumping" on last day of June, Dow down 18 of last 32, NASDAQ up 9 of last 12 ◆ Presidential election year Junes: #4 S&P, #5 Dow, #2 NASDAQ ◆ June ends NASDAQ's Best Eight Months (page 62)

June Vital Statistics

	DJIA		S&P 500		NASDAQ		Russell 1K		Russell 2K	
Rank	11		9		9		10		8	
Up	34		40		28		27		28	
Down	39		32		23		17		16	
Average % Change	−0.2%		0.02%		0.8%		0.2%		0.6%	
Election Year	0.9%		1.3%		1.9%		0.9%		1.6%	
Best & Worst June										
		% Change		% Change		% Change		% Change		% Change
Best	2019	7.2	1955	8.2	2000	16.6	2019	6.9	2000	8.6
Worst	2008	−10.2	2008	−8.6	2002	−9.4	2008	−8.5	2010	−8.4
Best & Worst June Weeks										
Best	6/5/20	6.8	6/2/00	7.2	6/2/00	19.0	6/2/00	8.0	6/2/00	12.2
Worst	6/30/50	−6.8	6/30/50	−7.6	6/15/01	−8.4	6/12/20	−5.9	6/12/20	−7.9
Best & Worst June Days										
Best	6/28/62	3.8	6/28/62	3.4	6/2/00	6.4	6/10/10	3.1	6/2/00	4.2
Worst	6/11/20	−6.9	6/11/20	−5.9	6/11/20	−5.3	6/11/20	−5.9	6/11/20	−7.6
First Trading Day of Expiration Week: 1980–2023										
Record (#Up – #Down)	22–21		25–18		20–23		23–20		17–25	
Current Streak	D2		D1		D1		D1		D2	
Avg % Change	−0.09		−0.16		−0.28		−0.18		−0.35	
Options Expiration Day: 1980–2023										
Record (#Up – #Down)	23–20		25–18		22–21		25–18		22–21	
Current Streak	D5		U1		U1		U1		U1	
Avg % Change	−0.11		−0.02		−0.03		−0.04		−0.06	
Options Expiration Week: 1980–2023										
Record (#Up – #Down)	24–19		23–20		19–24		21–22		20–23	
Current Streak	D2		D2		D2		D2		D2	
Avg % Change	−0.19		−0.18		−0.23		−0.23		−0.41	
Week After Options Expiration: 1980–2023										
Record (#Up – #Down)	14–29		20–23		24–19		20–23		23–20	
Current Streak	U2		U2		U2		U2		U2	
Avg % Change	−0.33		−0.04		0.29		−0.01		0.12	
First Trading Day Performance										
% of Time Up	58.1		54.1		58.5		60.0		66.7	
Avg % Change	0.15		0.13		0.13		0.10		0.23	
Last Trading Day Performance										
% of Time Up	56.2		53.4		67.3		56.8		65.9	
Avg % Change	0.07		0.12		0.32		0.08		0.41	

Dow & S&P 1950–June 9, 2023, NASDAQ 1971–June 9, 2023, Russell 1K & 2K 1979–June 9, 2023.

Last Day of June not hot for the Dow;
Down 18 of 32, WOW!

JUNE 2024

First Trading Day in June, Dow Up 28 of Last 36, Down 4 of 5 2008–2012

🐾 **MONDAY**
D 71.4
S 61.9
N 52.4

3

There is only one corner of the universe you can be certain of improving, and that's yourself.
— Aldous Huxley (English author, *Brave New World*, 1894–1963)

June Ends NASDAQ's "Best Eight Months" (Pages 60, 62 and 150

🐾 **TUESDAY**
D 61.9
S 76.2
N 71.4

4

The principles of successful stock speculation are based on the supposition that people will continue in the future to make the mistakes that they have made in the past.
— Thomas F. Woodlock (*Wall Street Journal* editor & columnist, quoted in *Reminiscences of a Stock Operator*, 1866–1945)

WEDNESDAY
D 38.1
S 42.9
N 47.6

5

Men, it has been well said, think in herds; it will be seen that they go mad in herds, while they only recover their senses slowly, and one by one.
— Charles Mackay (Scottish poet, journalist, author, anthologist, novelist, and songwriter, *Extraordinary Popular Delusions and the Madness of Crowds*, 1814–1889)

🐾 **THURSDAY**
D 66.7
S 61.9
N 61.9

6

The less a man knows about the past and the present the more insecure must be his judgment of the future.
— Sigmund Freud (Austrian neurologist, psychiatrist, father of psychoanalysis, 1856–1939)

🐾 **FRIDAY**
D 61.9
S 38.1
N 42.9

7

The four most expensive words in the English language, "This time it's different."
— Sir John Templeton (Founder Templeton Funds, philanthropist, 1912–2008)

SATURDAY

8

SUNDAY

9

TOP-PERFORMING NASDAQ MONTHS

NASDAQ stocks continue to run away during three consecutive months, November, December and January, with an average gain of 6.1% despite the slaughter of November 2000, down 22.9%, December 2000, –4.9%, December 2002, –9.7%, November 2007, –6.9%, January 2008, –9.9%, November 2008, –10.8%, January 2009, –6.4%, January 2010, –5.4% January 2016, –7.9%, December 2018, –9.5%, January 2022, –9.0%, and December 2022 –8.7%. Solid gains in November and December 2004 offset January 2005's 5.2% Iraq-turmoil-fueled drop.

You can see the months graphically on page 150. January by itself is impressive, up 2.7% on average. April, May and June also shine, creating our NASDAQ Best Eight Months strategy. What appears as a Death Valley abyss occurs during NASDAQ's leanest months: August and September. NASDAQ's Best Eight Months seasonal strategy using MACD timing is displayed on page 62.

MONTHLY % CHANGES (JANUARY 1971–APRIL 2023)

NASDAQ Composite*					Dow Jones Industrials				
Month	Total % Change	Avg. % Change	# Up	# Down	Month	Total % Change	Avg. % Change	# Up	# Down
Jan	142.1%	2.7%	35	18	Jan	58.0%	1.1%	32	21
Feb	25.9	0.5	28	25	Feb	9.3	0.2	31	22
Mar	42.8	0.8	34	19	Mar	49.2	0.9	35	18
Apr	76.5	1.4	35	18	Apr	112.1	2.1	36	17
May	46.5	0.9	31	21	May	12.8	0.2	30	22
Jun	41.3	0.8	29	23	Jun	– 0.8	– 0.01	26	26
Jul	44.1	0.8	30	22	Jul	53.8	1.0	32	20
Aug	18.8	0.4	29	23	Aug	– 9.4	– 0.2	29	23
Sep	– 44.6	– 0.9	27	25	Sep	– 56.2	– 1.1	19	33
Oct	41.4	0.8	29	23	Oct	45.9	0.9	32	20
Nov	98.0	1.9	37	15	Nov	83.5	1.6	36	16
Dec	76.9	1.5	31	21	Dec	74.1	1.4	36	16
% Rank					**% Rank**				
Jan	142.1%	2.7%	35	18	Apr	112.1%	2.1%	36	17
Apr	98.0	1.9	37	15	Nov	83.5	1.6	36	16
Nov	76.9	1.5	31	21	Dec	74.1	1.4	36	16
Dec	76.5	1.4	35	18	Jan	58.0	1.1	32	21
May	46.5	0.9	31	21	Jul	53.8	1.0	32	20
Jun	44.1	0.8	30	22	Mar	49.2	0.9	35	18
Oct	42.8	0.8	34	19	Oct	45.9	0.9	32	20
Mar	41.4	0.8	29	23	Feb	12.8	0.2	30	22
Feb	41.3	0.8	29	23	May	9.3	0.2	31	22
Jul	25.9	0.5	28	25	Jun	– 0.8	– 0.01	26	26
Aug	18.8	0.4	29	23	Aug	– 9.4	– 0.2	29	23
Sep	– 44.6	– 0.9	27	25	Sep	– 56.2	– 1.1	19	33
Totals	609.7%	11.6%			**Totals**	432.3%	8.1%		
Average		0.97%			**Average**		0.67%		

*Based on NASDAQ composite, prior to Feb. 5, 1971 based on National Quotation Bureau indices.

For comparison, Dow figures are shown. During this period NASDAQ averaged a 0.97% gain per month, 43.0% more than the Dow's 0.67% per month. Between January 1971 and January 1982 NASDAQ's composite index doubled in twelve years, while the Dow stayed flat. But while NASDAQ plummeted 77.9% from its 2000 highs to the 2002 bottom, the Dow only lost 37.8%. The Great Recession and bear market of 2007-2009 spread its carnage equally across Dow and NASDAQ. Recent market moves are increasingly more correlated, but NASDAQ still has a sizable advantage.

JUNE 2024

Of a stock's move, 31% can be attributed to the general stock market, 12% to the industry influence, 37% to the influence of other groupings, and the remaining 20% is peculiar to the one stock.
— Benjamin F. King ("Market and Industry Factors in Stock Price Behavior," Journal of Business, January 1966)

2008 Second Worst June Ever, Dow -10.2%, S&P -8.6%,
Only 1930 Was Worse, NASDAQ June 2008 -9.1%, June 2002 -9.4%

🐂 TUESDAY
D 38.1
S 33.3
N 33.3
11

Successful innovation is not a feat of intellect, but of will.
— Joseph A. Schumpeter (Austrian-American economist, *Theory of Economic Development*, 1883–1950)

🐻 WEDNESDAY
D 38.1
S 38.1
N 42.9
12

To me, the "tape" is the final arbiter of any investment decision. I have a cardinal rule: Never fight the tape!
— Martin Zweig (Fund manager, *Winning on Wall Street*, 1943–2013)

THURSDAY
D 57.1
S 57.1
N 52.4
13

No profession requires more hard work, intelligence, patience, and mental discipline than successful speculation.
— Robert Rhea (Economist, trader, *The Dow Theory*, 1887–1952)

FRIDAY
D 52.4
S 57.1
N 66.7
14

When an old man dies, a library burns down.
— African proverb

SATURDAY
15

Father's Day

SUNDAY
16

GET MORE OUT OF NASDAQ'S "BEST EIGHT MONTHS" WITH MACD TIMING

NASDAQ's amazing eight-month run from November through June is hard to miss on pages 60 and 150. A $10,000 investment in these eight months since 1971 gained $1,054,544 versus $1,567 during the void that is the four-month period July-October (as of June 9, 2023).

Using the same MACD timing indicators on the NASDAQ as is done for the Dow (page 56) has enabled us to capture much of October's improved performance, pumping up NASDAQ's results considerably. Over the 52 years since NASDAQ began, the gain on the same $10,000 more than doubles to $2,633,972 and the gain during the four-month void becomes a loss of $5,431. Only five sizeable losses occurred during the favorable period and the bulk of NASDAQ's bear markets were avoided including the worst of the 2000–2002 bear.

Updated signals are emailed to *Almanac Investor* subscribers as soon as they are triggered. Visit *www.stocktradersalmanac.com*, or see insert for details and a special offer for new subscribers.

BEST EIGHT MONTHS STRATEGY + TIMING

MACD Signal Date	Worst 4 Months July 1–Oct 31* NASDAQ	% Change	Investing $10,000	MACD Signal Date	Best 8 Months Nov 1–June 30* NASDAQ	% Change	Investing $10,000
22-Jul-71	109.54	–3.6	$9,640	4-Nov-71	105.56	24.1	$12,410
7-Jun-72	131.00	–1.8	9,466	23-Oct-72	128.66	–22.7	9,593
25-Jun-73	99.43	–7.2	8,784	7-Dec-73	92.32	–20.2	7,655
3-Jul-74	73.66	–23.2	6,746	7-Oct-74	56.57	47.8	11,314
11-Jun-75	83.60	–9.2	6,125	7-Oct-75	75.88	20.8	13,667
22-Jul-76	91.66	–2.4	5,978	19-Oct-76	89.45	13.2	15,471
27-Jul-77	101.25	–4.0	5,739	4-Nov-77	97.21	26.6	19,586
7-Jun-78	123.10	–6.5	5,366	6-Nov-78	115.08	19.1	23,327
3-Jul-79	137.03	–1.1	5,307	30-Oct-79	135.48	15.5	26,943
20-Jun-80	156.51	26.2	6,697	9-Oct-80	197.53	11.2	29,961
4-Jun-81	219.68	–17.6	5,518	1-Oct-81	181.09	–4.0	28,763
7-Jun-82	173.84	12.5	6,208	7-Oct-82	195.59	57.4	45,273
1-Jun-83	307.95	–10.7	5,544	3-Nov-83	274.86	–14.2	38,844
1-Jun-84	235.90	5.0	5,821	15-Oct-84	247.67	17.3	45,564
3-Jun-85	290.59	–3.0	5,646	1-Oct-85	281.77	39.4	63,516
10-Jun-86	392.83	–10.3	5,064	1-Oct-86	352.34	20.5	76,537
30-Jun-87	424.67	–22.7	3,914	2-Nov-87	328.33	20.1	91,921
8-Jul-88	394.33	–6.6	3,656	29-Nov-88	368.15	22.4	112,511
13-Jun-89	450.73	0.7	3,682	9-Nov-89	454.07	1.9	114,649
11-Jun-90	462.79	–23.0	2,835	2-Oct-90	356.39	39.3	159,706
11-Jun-91	496.62	6.4	3,016	1-Oct-91	528.51	7.4	171,524
11-Jun-92	567.68	1.5	3,061	14-Oct-92	576.22	20.5	206,686
7-Jun-93	694.61	9.9	3,364	1-Oct-93	763.23	–4.4	197,592
17-Jun-94	729.35	5.0	3,532	11-Oct-94	765.57	13.5	224,267
1-Jun-95	868.82	17.2	4,140	13-Oct-95	1018.38	21.6	272,709
3-Jun-96	1238.73	1.0	4,181	7-Oct-96	1250.87	10.3	300,798
4-Jun-97	1379.67	24.4	5,201	3-Oct-97	1715.87	1.8	306,212
1-Jun-98	1746.82	–7.8	4,795	15-Oct-98	1611.01	49.7	458,399
1-Jun-99	2412.03	18.5	5,682	6-Oct-99	2857.21	35.7	622,047
29-Jun-00	3877.23	–18.2	4,648	18-Oct-00	3171.56	–32.2	421,748
1-Jun-01	2149.44	–31.1	3,202	1-Oct-01	1480.46	5.5	444,944
3-Jun-02	1562.56	–24.0	2,434	2-Oct-02	1187.30	38.5	616,247
20-Jun-03	1644.72	15.1	2,802	6-Oct-03	1893.46	4.3	642,746
21-Jun-04	1974.38	–1.6	2,757	1-Oct-04	1942.20	6.1	681,954
8-Jun-05	2060.18	1.5	2,798	19-Oct-05	2091.76	6.1	723,553
1-Jun-06	2219.86	3.9	2,907	5-Oct-06	2306.34	9.5	792,291
7-Jun-07	2541.38	7.9	3,137	1-Oct-07	2740.99	–9.1	724,796
2-Jun-08	2491.53	–31.3	2,155	17-Oct-08	1711.29	6.1	769,009
15-Jun-09	1816.38	17.8	2,539	9-Oct-09	2139.28	1.6	781,313
7-Jun-10	2173.90	18.6	3,011	4-Nov-10	2577.34	7.4	839,130
1-Jun-11	2769.19	–10.5	2,695	7-Oct-11	2479.35	10.8	929,756
1-Jun-12	2747.48	9.6	2,954	6-Nov-12	3011.93	16.2	1,080,376
4-Jun-13	3445.26	10.1	3,252	15-Oct-13	3794.01	15.4	1,227,442
26-Jun-14	4379.05	0.9	3,281	21-Oct-14	4419.48	14.5	1,405,421
4-Jun-15	5059.12	–5.5	3,101	5-Oct-15	4781.26	1.4	1,425,097
13-Jun-16	4848.44	9.5	3,396	24-Oct-16	5309.83	18.8	1,693,015
9-Jun-17	6207.92	11.3	3,780	28-Nov-17	6912.36	11.6	1,859,187
21-Jun-18	7712.95	–5.3	3,580	31-Oct-18	7305.90	7.9	2,006,063
19-Jul-19	8146.49	–1.1	3,541	11-Oct-19	8057.04	17.8	2,441,987
11-Jun-20	9492.73	25.3	4,437	5-Nov-20	11890.93	18.3	2,888,871
14-Jul-21	14644.95	– 0.4	4,419	8-Oct-21	14579.54	– 25.9	2,343,643
13-Jun-22	10809.23	3.4	4,569	4-Oct-22	11176.41	18.6**	2,643,972**
9-Jun-23**	13259.14						
	52-Year Loss	**($5,431)**			**52-Year Gain $2,633,972**		

** As of 6/9/2023 – NASDAQ Seasonal Sell NOT triggered yet
* MACD-generated entry and exit points (earlier or later) can lengthen or shorten eight-month periods.

JUNE 2024

Monday of Triple Witching Week, Dow Down 15 of Last 27

MONDAY
D 57.1
S 66.7
N 66.7
17

He who knows how will always work for he who knows why.
— David Lee Roth (Lead singer of Van Halen, b. 1954)

Triple Witching Week Often Up in Bull Markets and Down in Bears (Page 108)

TUESDAY
D 57.1
S 57.1
N 52.4
18

Foolish consistency is the hobgoblin of little minds.
— Ralph Waldo Emerson (American author, poet and philosopher, *Self-Reliance*, 1803–1882)

Juneteenth National Independence Day *(Market Closed)*

WEDNESDAY
19

Keep away from people who try to belittle your ambitions. Small people always do that, but the really great make you feel that you, too, can become great.
— Mark Twain (1835–1910, pen name of Samuel Longhorne Clemens, American novelist and satirist)

THURSDAY
D 47.6
S 52.4
N 66.7
20

I went to a restaurant that serves "breakfast at any time." So I ordered French toast during the Renaissance.
— Steven Wright (Comedian, b. 1955)

June Triple Witching Day Dow Mixed, But Down 7 of Last 8

FRIDAY
D 47.6
S 52.4
N 47.6
21

The worst mistake investors make is taking their profits too soon, and their losses too long.
— Michael Price (Mutual Shares Fund)

SATURDAY
22

SUNDAY
23

TRIPLE RETURNS, FEWER TRADES: BEST 6 + 4–YEAR CYCLE

We first introduced this strategy to *Almanac Investor* subscribers in October 2006. Recurring seasonal stock market patterns and the Four-Year Presidential Election/Stock Market Cycle (page 132) have been integral to our research since the first *Almanac* over 50 years ago. Yale Hirsch discovered the Best Six Months in 1986 (page 54) and it has been a cornerstone of our seasonal investment analysis and strategies ever since.

Most of the market's gains have occurred during the Best Six Months and the market generally hits a low point every four years in the first (post-election) or second (midterm) year and exhibits the greatest gains in the third (pre-election) year. This strategy combines the best of these two market phenomena, the Best Six Months and the 4-Year Cycle, timing entries and exits with MACD (pages 56 and 62).

We've gone back to 1949 to include the full four-year cycle that began with post-election year 1949. Only four trades every four years are needed to triple the results of the Best Six Months. Buy and sell during the post-election and midterm years and then hold from the midterm MACD seasonal buy signal sometime after October 1 until the post-election MACD seasonal sell signal sometime after April 1, approximately 2.5 years. Solid returns, less effort, lower transaction fees and fewer taxable events.

BEST SIX MONTHS+TIMING+4-YEAR CYCLE STRATEGY				
	DJIA % Change May 1–Oct 31*	Investing $10,000	DJIA % Change Nov 1–Apr 30*	Investing $10,000
1949	3.0%	$10,300	17.5%	$11,750
1950	7.3	11,052	19.7	14,065
1951		11,052		14,065
1952		11,052		14,065
1953	0.2	11,074	17.1	16,470
1954	13.5	12,569	35.7	22,350
1955		12,569		22,350
1956		12,569		22,350
1957	−12.3	11,023	4.9	23,445
1958	17.3	12,930	27.8	29,963
1959		12,930		29,963
1960		12,930		29,963
1961	2.9	13,305	−1.5	29,514
1962	−15.3	11,269	58.5	46,780
1963		11,269		46,780
1964		11,269		46,780
1965	2.6	11,562	−2.5	45,611
1966	−16.4	9,666	22.2	55,737
1967		9,666		55,737
1968		9,666		55,737
1969	−11.9	8,516	−6.7	52,003
1970	−1.4	8,397	21.5	63,184
1971		8,397		63,184
1972		8,397		63,184
1973	−11.0	7,473	0.1	63,247
1974	−22.4	5,799	42.5	90,127
1975		5,799		90,127
1976		5,799		90,127
1977	−11.4	5,138	0.5	90,578
1978	−4.5	4,907	26.8	114,853
1979		4,907		114,853
1980		4,907		114,853
1981	−14.6	4,191	0.4	115,312
1982	15.5	4,841	25.9	145,178
1983		4,841		145,178
1984		4,841		145,178
1985	7.0	5,180	38.1	200,491
1986	−2.8	5,035	33.2	267,054
1987		5,035		267,054
1988		5,035		267,054
1989	9.8	5,528	3.3	275,867
1990	−6.7	5,158	35.1	372,696
1991		5,158		372,696
1992		5,158		372,696
1993	5.5	5,442	5.6	393,455
1994	3.7	5,643	88.2	740,482
1995		5,643		740,482
1996		5,643		740,482
1997	3.6	5,846	18.5	877,471
1998	−12.4	5,121	36.3	1,195,993
1999		5,121		1,195,993
2000		5,121		1,195,993
2001	−17.3	4,235	15.8	1,384,960
2002	−25.2	3,168	34.2	1,858,616
2003		3,168		1,858,616
2004		3,168		1,858,616
2005	−0.5	3,152	7.7	2,001,729
2006	4.7	3,300	−31.7	1,367,181
2007		3,300		1,367,181
2008		3,300		1,367,181
2009	23.8	4,085	10.8	1,514,738
2010	4.6	4,273	27.4	1,929,777
2011		4,273		1,929,777
2012		4,273		1,929,777
2013	4.1	4,448	7.1	2,066,791
2014	2.3	4,550	24.0	2,562,820
2015		4,550		2,562,820
2016		4,550		2,562,820
2017	15.7	$5,265	0.4	$2,573,072
2018	5.0	$5,528	34.6	$3,463,354
2019		$5,528		$3,463,354
2020		$5,528		$3,463,354
2021	2.8	$5,683	−0.5	$3,446,038
2022**	−12.3	$4,984	11.0	$3,825,102
Average	−0.6%		9.6%	
# Up	21		33	
# Down	17		5	
74-Year Gain (Loss)	($5,016)			$3,453,354

MACD and 2.5-year hold lengthen and shorten six-month periods.
** As of June 7, 2023 close.*

FOUR TRADES EVERY FOUR YEARS		
Year	Worst Six Months May–Oct	Best Six Months Nov–April
Post-election	Sell	Buy
Midterm	Sell	Buy
Pre-election	Hold	Hold
Election	Hold	Hold

JUNE 2024

Week After June Triple Witching, Dow Down 27 of Last 33
Average Loss Since 1990, 0.8%

MONDAY
D 33.3
S 33.3
N 23.8
24

*Don't be the last bear or last bull standing, let history guide you, be contrary to the crowd,
and let the tape tell you when to act.*
— Jeffrey A. Hirsch (Editor, S*tock Trader's Almanac*, b. 1966)

TUESDAY
D 42.9
S 47.6
N 47.6
25

Success is going from failure to failure without loss of enthusiasm.
— Winston Churchill (British statesman, 1874–1965)

WEDNESDAY
D 47.6
S 47.6
N 61.9
26

Liberal institutions straightaway cease from being liberal the moment they are firmly established.
— Friedrich Nietzsche (German philosopher, 1844–1900)

THURSDAY
D 57.1
S 57.1
N 61.9
27

What lies behind us and what lies before us are tiny matters, compared to what lies within us.
— Ralph Waldo Emerson (American author, poet and philosopher, *Self-Reliance*, 1803–1882)

Last Day of Q2 Bearish for Dow, Down 18 of Last 32, But Up 9 of Last 12,
Bullish for NASDAQ, Up 21 of 31

FRIDAY
D 52.4
S 52.4
N 52.4
28

*Over the last 25 years, computer processing capacity has risen more than a millionfold,
while communication capacity has risen over a thousandfold.*
— Richard Worzel (Futurist, *Facing the Future*, b. 1950)

SATURDAY
29

July Almanac Investor Sector Seasonalities: See Pages 94, 96 and 98

SUNDAY
30

JULY ALMANAC

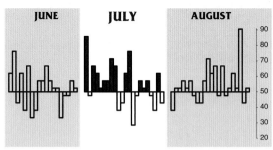

JULY							AUGUST						
S	M	T	W	T	F	S	S	M	T	W	T	F	S
	1	2	3	4	5	6					1	2	3
7	8	9	10	11	12	13	4	5	6	7	8	9	10
14	15	16	17	18	19	20	11	12	13	14	15	16	17
21	22	23	24	25	26	27	18	19	20	21	22	23	24
28	29	30	31				25	26	27	28	29	30	31

Market Probability Chart above is a graphic representation of the S&P 500 Recent Market Probability Calendar on page 126.

◆ July is the best month of the third quarter (page 68) ◆ Start of 2nd half brings an inflow of retirement funds ◆ First trading day Dow up 28 of last 34 ◆ Graph above shows strength in the first half of July ◆ Huge gain in July usually provides better buying opportunity over next four months ◆ Start of NASDAQ's worst four months of the year (page 60) ◆ Presidential election Julys are ranked #6 Dow (up 10, down 8), #6 S&P (up 9, down 9), and #9 NASDAQ (up 7, down 6)

July Vital Statistics

	DJIA		S&P 500		NASDAQ		Russell 1K		Russell 2K	
Rank	4		4		6		4		10	
Up	48		43		30		24		23	
Down	25		30		22		20		21	
Average % Change	1.3%		1.3%		0.7%		1.1%		−0.01%	
Election Year	0.6%		0.7%		−0.1%		0.6%		−0.03%	
Best & Worst July										
	% Change		% Change		% Change		% Change		% Change	
Best	1989	9.0	2022	9.1	2022	12.3	2022	9.2	1980	11.0
Worst	1969	−6.6	2002	−7.9	2002	−9.2	2002	−7.5	2002	−15.2
Best & Worst July Weeks										
Best	7/17/09	7.3	7/17/09	7.0	7/17/09	7.4	7/17/09	7.0	7/17/09	8.0
Worst	7/19/02	−7.7	7/19/02	−8.0	7/28/00	−10.5	7/19/02	−7.4	7/2/10	−7.2
Best & Worst July Days										
Best	7/24/02	6.4	7/24/02	5.7	7/29/02	5.8	7/24/02	5.6	7/29/02	4.9
Worst	7/19/02	−4.6	7/19/02	−3.8	7/28/00	−4.7	7/19/02	−3.6	7/23/02	−4.1
First Trading Day of Expiration Week: 1980–2023										
Record (#Up – #Down)	27–16		26–17		28–15		26–17		23–20	
Current Streak	D1		D1		D1		D1		D1	
Avg % Change	0.11		0.01		−0.04		−0.02		−0.11	
Options Expiration Day: 1980–2023										
Record (#Up – #Down)	18–23		21–22		18–25		21–22		17–26	
Current Streak	U1		U1		U1		U1		U1	
Avg % Change	−0.19		−0.22		−0.34		−0.23		−0.38	
Options Expiration Week: 1980–2023										
Record (#Up – #Down)	26–17		24–19		21–22		24–19		23–20	
Current Streak	D2		D2		D5		D2		D2	
Avg % Change	0.45		0.13		0.004		0.08		−0.12	
Week After Options Expiration: 1980–2023										
Record (#Up – #Down)	24–19		22–21		20–23		23–20		17–26	
Current Streak	U2		U2		U2		U2		U2	
Avg % Change	0.07		0.003		−0.22		−0.002		−0.21	
First Trading Day Performance										
% of Time Up	67.1		74.0		65.4		77.3		68.2	
Avg % Change	0.28		0.28		0.18		0.35		0.15	
Last Trading Day Performance										
% of Time Up	50.7		60.3		50.0		56.8		61.4	
Avg % Change	0.02		0.07		0.0002		−0.004		−0.03	

Dow & S&P 1950–June 9, 2023, NASDAQ 1971–June 9, 2023, Russell 1K & 2K 1979–June 9, 2023.

When Dow and S&P in July are inferior,
NASDAQ days tend to be even drearier.

Understanding Market History Can Produce Gains

Those who understand market history are bound to profit from it!

"I'm a mechanical engineer, and an investment advisor, and been in this business for over 30 years. Throughout the years I subscribed to the most expensive newsletters in the country, and never made a profit because of the momentum stocks they all recommend, and most of their recommendations made a round trip no exception. In 8 weeks I followed your recommendations regarding the seasonality trends and I made over $135,000.00.' – Sam C. from Mississippi

ACT NOW! Visit www.STOCKTRADERSALMANAC.com
CALL 914-750-5860. <u>TWO WAYS TO SAVE</u>:

◆ **1-Year @ $179** – 45% Off vs. Quarterly – Use promo code **1YRSTA24**

◆ **2-Years @ $299** – BEST DEAL, over 54% Off – Use promo code **2YRSTA24**

Now you can find out which seasonal trends are on schedule and which are not, and how to take advantage of them. You will be kept abreast of upcoming market-moving events and what our indicators are saying about the next major market move. Every week you will receive timely dispatches about bullish and bearish seasonal patterns.

Our digital subscription service, *Almanac Investor*, provides all this plus unusual investing opportunities – exciting small-, mid- and large-cap stocks; seasoned, undervalued equities; timely sector ETF trades and more. Our **Data-Rich and Data-Driven Market Cycle Analysis** is the only investment tool of its kind that helps traders and investors forecast market trends with accuracy and confidence.

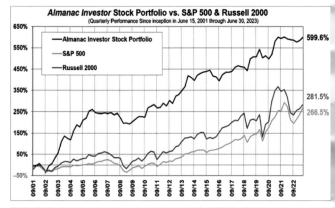

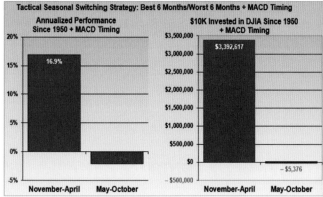

YOU RECEIVE WEEKLY EMAILS CONTAINING:	◆ Opportune ETF and Stock Trading Ideas with Specific Buy and Sell Price Limits ◆ Timely Data-Rich and Data-Driven Market Analysis ◆ Access to Webinars, Videos, Tools and Resources ◆ Market-Tested and Time-Proven Short- and Long-term Trading Strategies ◆ Best Six-Months Switching Strategy MACD Timing Signals.

JULY 2024

First Trading Day in July, S&P Up 30 of Last 34, Average Gain 0.5%

MONDAY

D 76.2
S 85.7
N 81.0

1

Ignorance is not knowing something; stupidity is not admitting your ignorance.
— Daniel Turov (*Turov on Timing*)

TUESDAY

D 38.1
S 47.6
N 47.6

2

If you can buy more of your best idea, why put [the money] into your 10th-best idea or your 20th-best idea?
The more positions you have, the more average you are.
— Bruce Berkowitz (Fairholme Fund, *Barron's* 3/17/08)

(Shortened Trading Day)
July is the Best Performing Dow and S&P Month of the Third Quarter (Page 68)

WEDNESDAY

D 61.9
S 66.7
N 66.7

3

There's no such thing as a loss, it's just an unmonetized lesson.
— Ted Weschler (Investment Manager at Berkshire Hathaway, b. 1962)

Independence Day *(Market Closed)*

THURSDAY

4

If a political party does not have its foundation in the determination to advance a cause that is right and
that is moral, then it is not a political party; it is merely a conspiracy to seize power.
— Dwight D. Eisenhower (34th U.S. President, 1890–1969)

Market Subject to Elevated Volatility After July 4th

FRIDAY

D 61.9
S 61.9
N 66.7

5

Every man is the architect of his own fortune.
— Appius Claudius

SATURDAY

6

SUNDAY

7

FIRST MONTH OF QUARTERS IS THE MOST BULLISH

We have observed over the years that the investment calendar reflects the annual, semi-annual and quarterly operations of institutions during January, April and July. The opening month of the first three quarters produces the greatest gains in the Dow Jones Industrials, S&P 500 and NASDAQ.

The fourth quarter had behaved quite differently since it is affected by year-end portfolio adjustments and Presidential and Congressional elections in even-numbered years. Since 1991 major turnarounds have helped October join the ranks of bullish first months of quarters. October transformed into a bear-killing-turnaround month, posting Dow gains in 18 of the last 25 years, 2008 was a significant exception (See pages 156–173.)

After experiencing the most powerful bull market of all time during the 1990s, followed by two ferocious bear markets early in the millennium, we divided the monthly average percent changes into two groups: before 1991 and after. Comparing the month-by-month quarterly behavior of the three major U.S. averages in the table, you'll see that first months of the first three quarters perform best overall. Nasty selloffs in April 2000, 2002, 2004, 2005 and 2022 and July 2000–2002 and 2004, hit the NASDAQ hardest. The bear market of October 2007-March 2009, which more than cut the markets in half, took a toll on every first month except April. October 2008 was the worst month in a decade. January was also a difficult month in 13 of the last 24 years pulling its performance lower. (See pages 156–173.)

Between 1950 and 1990, the S&P 500 gained 1.3% (Dow, 1.4%) on average in first months of the first three quarters. Second months barely eked out any gain, while third months, thanks to March, moved up 0.23% (Dow, 0.07%) on average. NASDAQ's first month of the first three quarters averages 1.67% from 1971–1990 with July being a negative drag.

DOW JONES INDUSTRIALS, S&P 500 AND NASDAQ
AVERAGE MONTHLY % CHANGES BY QUARTER

	DJIA 1950–1990			S&P 500 1950–1990			NASDAQ 1971–1990		
	1st Mo	2nd Mo	3rd Mo	1st Mo	2nd Mo	3rd Mo	1st Mo	2nd Mo	3rd Mo
1Q	1.5%	−0.01%	1.0%	1.5%	−0.1%	1.1%	3.8%	1.2%	0.9%
2Q	1.6	−0.4	0.1	1.3	−0.1	0.3	1.7	0.8	1.1
3Q	1.1	0.3	−0.9	1.1	0.3	−0.7	−0.5	0.1	−1.6
Tot	4.2%	−0.1%	0.2%	3.9%	0.1%	0.7%	5.0%	2.1%	0.4%
Avg	1.40%	−0.04%	0.07%	1.30%	0.03%	0.23%	1.67%	0.70%	0.13%
4Q	−0.1%	1.4%	1.7%	0.4%	1.7%	1.6%	−1.4%	1.6%	1.4%
	DJIA 1991-April 2023			S&P 500 1991-April 2023			NASDAQ 1991-April 2023		
1Q	0.2%	0.1%	0.8%	0.5%	−0.07%	1.1%	2.0%	0.04%	0.8%
2Q	2.3	0.5	−0.6	1.9	0.7	−0.3	1.3	0.9	0.6
3Q	1.6	−0.6	−0.8	1.5	−0.3	−0.7	1.7	0.5	−0.4
Tot	4.2%	0.02%	−0.6%	3.9%	0.3%	0.1%	5.0%	1.4%	1.0%
Avg	1.37%	0.01%	−0.20%	1.30%	0.11%	0.04%	1.67%	0.48%	0.33%
4Q	1.9%	2.2%	1.3%	1.7%	1.8%	1.3%	2.1%	2.1%	1.5%
	DJIA 1950-April 2023			S&P 500 1950-April 2023			NASDAQ 1971-April 2023		
1Q	0.9%	0.1%	1.0%	1.1%	−0.08%	1.1%	2.7%	0.5%	0.8%
2Q	1.9	−0.01	−0.3	1.5	0.2	0.02	1.4	0.9	0.8
3Q	1.3	−0.1	−0.8	1.3	0.01	−0.7	0.9	0.4	−0.9
Tot	4.1%	0.002%	−0.1%	3.9%	0.1%	0.4%	5.0%	1.8%	0.7%
Avg	1.37%	0.001%	−0.04%	1.30%	0.05%	0.14%	1.65%	0.59%	0.23%
4Q	0.8%	1.7%	1.5%	1.0%	1.7%	1.4%	0.8%	1.9%	1.5%

JULY 2024

Moses Shapiro (of General Instrument) told me, "Son, this is Talmudic wisdom. Always ask the question 'If not?'
Few people have good strategies for when their assumptions are wrong." That's the best business advice I ever got.
— John Malone (CEO of cable giant TCI, *Fortune*, 2/16/98)

TUESDAY

D 57.1
S 57.1
N 71.4

9

Writing a book is an adventure. To begin with it is a toy, an amusement; then it is a mistress,
and then a master, and then a tyrant.
— Winston Churchill (British statesman, 1874–1965)

Beware the "Summer Rally" Hype
Historically the Weakest Rally of All Seasons (Page 74)

WEDNESDAY

D 47.6
S 57.1
N 57.1

10

As for it being different this time, it is different every time. The question is in what way, and to what extent.
— Tom McClellan (*The McClellan Market Report*)

🐂 THURSDAY

D 71.4
S 71.4
N 57.1

11

All you need is to look over the earnings forecasts publicly made a year ago to see how much care you need
to give those being made now for next year.
— Gerald M. Loeb (E.F. Hutton, *The Battle for Investment Survival*, predicted 1929 Crash, 1900–1974)

🐂 FRIDAY

D 71.4
S 66.7
N 71.4

12

If all the economists in the world were laid end to end, they still wouldn't reach a conclusion.
— George Bernard Shaw (Irish dramatist, 1856–1950)

SATURDAY

13

SUNDAY

14

2022 DAILY DOW POINT CHANGES (DOW JONES INDUSTRIAL AVERAGE)

Week #		Monday**	Tuesday	Wednsday	Thursday	Friday**	Weekly Dow Close	Net Point Change
1						2021 Close	36338.30	
2		246.76	214.59	-392.54	-170.64	-4.81	36231.66	-106.64
3	J	-162.79	183.15	38.30	-176.70	-201.81	35911.81	-319.85
4	A	Holiday	-543.34	-339.82	-313.26	-450.02	34265.37	-1646.44
5	N	99.13	-66.77	-129.64	-7.31	564.69	34725.47	460.10
6		406.39	273.38	224.09	-518.17	-21.42	35089.74	364.27
7		1.39	371.65	305.28	-526.47	-503.53	34738.06	-351.68
8	F	-171.89	422.67	-54.57	-622.24	-232.85	34079.18	-658.88
9	E B	Holiday	-482.57	-464.85	92.07	834.92	34058.75	-20.43
10		-166.15	-597.65	596.40	-96.69	-179.86	33614.80	-443.95
11	M	-797.42	-184.74	653.61	-112.18	-229.88	32944.19	-670.61
12	A	1.05	599.10	518.76	417.66	274.17	34754.93	1810.74
13	R	-201.94	254.47	-448.96	349.44	153.30	34861.24	106.31
14		94.65	338.30	-65.38	-550.46	139.92	34818.27	-42.97
15	A	103.61	-280.70	-144.67	87.06	137.55	34721.12	-97.15
16	P	-413.04	-87.72	344.23	-113.36	Holiday	34451.23	-269.89
17	R	-39.54	499.51	249.59	-368.03	-981.36	33811.40	-639.83
18		238.06	-809.28	61.75	614.46	-939.18	32977.21	-834.19
19		84.29	67.29	932.27	-1063.09	-98.60	32899.37	-77.84
20	M	-653.67	-84.96	-326.63	-103.81	466.36	32196.66	-702.71
21	A	26.76	431.17	-1164.52	-236.94	8.77	31261.90	-934.76
22	Y	618.34	58.38	181.66	516.91	575.77	33212.96	1951.06
23		Holiday	-222.84	-176.89	435.05	-348.58	32899.70	-313.26
24		16.08	264.36	-269.24	-638.11	-880.00	31392.79	-1506.91
25	J	-876.05	-151.91	303.70	-741.46	-38.29	29888.78	-1504.01
26	U	Holiday	641.47	-47.12	194.23	823.32	31500.68	1611.90
27	N	-62.42	-491.27	82.32	-253.88	321.83	31097.26	-403.42
28	J	Holiday	-129.44	69.86	346.87	-46.40	31338.15	240.89
29	U	-164.31	-192.51	-208.54	-142.62	658.09	31288.26	-49.89
30	L	-215.65	754.44	47.79	162.06	-137.61	31899.29	611.03
31		90.75	-228.50	436.05	332.04	315.50	32845.13	945.84
32		-46.73	-402.23	416.33	-85.68	76.65	32803.47	-41.66
33	A	29.07	-58.13	535.10	27.16	424.38	33761.05	957.58
34	U	151.39	239.57	-171.69	18.72	-292.30	33706.74	-54.31
35	G	-643.13	-154.02	59.64	322.55	-1008.38	32283.40	-1423.34
36		-184.41	-308.12	-280.44	145.99	-337.98	31318.44	-964.96
37	S	Holiday	-173.14	435.98	193.24	377.19	32151.71	833.27
38	E	229.63	-1276.37	30.12	-173.27	-139.40	30822.42	-1329.29
39	P	197.26	-313.45	-522.45	-107.10	-486.27	29590.41	-1232.01
40		-329.60	-125.82	548.75	-458.13	-500.10	28725.51	-864.90
41		765.38	825.43	-42.45	-346.93	-630.15	29296.79	571.28
42	O	-93.91	36.31	-28.34	827.87	-403.89	29634.83	338.04
43	C	550.99	337.98	-99.99	-90.22	748.97	31082.56	1447.73
44	T	417.06	337.12	2.37	194.17	828.52	32861.80	1779.24
45		-128.85	-79.75	-505.44	-146.51	401.97	32403.22	-458.58
46	N	423.78	333.83	-646.89	1201.43	32.49	33747.86	1344.64
47	O	-211.16	56.22	-39.09	-7.51	199.37	33745.69	-2.17
48	V	-45.41	397.82	95.96	Holiday	152.97	34347.03	601.34
49		-497.57	3.07	737.24	-194.76	34.87*	34429.88	82.85
50		-482.78	-350.76	1.58	183.56	-305.02	33476.46	-953.42
51	D	528.58	103.60	-142.29	-764.13	-281.76	32920.46	-556.00
52	E	-162.92	92.20	526.74	-348.99	176.44	33203.93	283.47
53	C	Holiday	37.63	-365.85	345.09	-73.55	33147.25	-56.68
TOTALS		-2303.17	1250.95	1357.18	-2357.66	-1138.35		-3191.05

Outline Bold Color: Down Friday, Down Monday   *Shortened trading day: Nov 25
** Monday denotes first trading day of week, Friday denotes last trading day of week

JULY 2024

Monday Before July Expiration, Dow Up 15 of Last 20

🐻 **MONDAY**

D 61.9
S 38.1
N 52.4

15

The problem with the world is that the intelligent people are full of doubts, while the stupid ones are full of confidence.
— Charles Bukowski (American poet, novelist & writer, *Barfly*, 1920–1994)

TUESDAY

D 42.9
S 42.9
N 47.6

16

Based on my own personal experience—both as an investor in recent years and an expert witness in years past—rarely do more than three or four variables really count. Everything else is noise.
— Martin J. Whitman (Founder Third Avenue Funds, 1924–2018)

🐂 **WEDNESDAY**

D 61.9
S 61.9
N 66.7

17

Most people can stay excited for two or three months. A few people can stay excited for two or three years. But a winner will stay excited for 20 to 30 years—or as long as it takes to win.
— A.L. Williams (Motivational speaker)

🐂 **THURSDAY**

D 76.2
S 76.2
N 76.2

18

We pay the debts of the last generation by issuing bonds payable by the next generation.
— Lawrence J. Peter

July Expiration Day, Dow Down 15 of Last 23, -4.6% 2002, -2.5% 2010

🐻 🧙 **FRIDAY**

D 23.8
S 28.6
N 19.0

19

Regardless of current economic conditions, it's always best to remember that the stock market is a barometer and not a thermometer.
— Yale Hirsch (Creator of *Stock Trader's Almanac*, 1923–2021)

SATURDAY

20

SUNDAY

21

DON'T SELL STOCKS ON MONDAY OR FRIDAY

Since 1989, Monday*, Tuesday and Wednesday have been the most consistently bullish days of the week for the Dow, Thursday and Friday* the least bullish, as traders have become reluctant to stay long going into the weekend. Since 1989 Mondays and Tuesdays gained 18375.19 Dow points, while Thursdays and Fridays have gained 6143.70 points. Note Monday's and Friday's poor performance in bear market years 2001–2002, 2008–2009 and 2022. See pages 70, 78 and 143–146 for more.

ANNUAL DOW POINT CHANGES FOR DAYS OF THE WEEK SINCE 1953

Year	Monday*	Tuesday	Wednesday	Thursday	Friday*	DJIA YR Close	Yr Point Change
1953	−36.16	−7.93	19.63	5.76	7.70	280.90	−11.00
1954	15.68	3.27	24.31	33.96	46.27	404.39	123.49
1955	−48.36	26.38	46.03	−0.66	60.62	488.40	84.01
1956	−27.15	−9.36	−15.41	8.43	64.56	499.47	11.07
1957	−109.50	−7.71	64.12	3.32	−14.01	435.69	−63.78
1958	17.50	23.59	29.10	22.67	55.10	583.65	147.96
1959	−44.48	29.04	4.11	13.60	93.44	679.36	95.71
1960	−111.04	−3.75	−5.62	6.74	50.20	615.89	−63.47
1961	−23.65	10.18	87.51	−5.96	47.17	731.14	115.25
1962	−101.60	26.19	9.97	−7.70	−5.90	652.10	−79.04
1963	−8.88	47.12	16.23	22.39	33.99	762.95	110.85
1964	−0.29	−17.94	39.84	5.52	84.05	874.13	111.18
1965	−73.23	39.65	57.03	3.20	68.48	969.26	95.13
1966	−153.24	−27.73	56.13	−46.19	−12.54	785.69	−183.57
1967	−68.65	31.50	25.42	92.25	38.90	905.11	119.42
1968†	6.41	34.94	25.16	−72.06	44.19	943.75	38.64
1969	−164.17	−36.70	18.33	23.79	15.36	800.36	−143.39
1970	−100.05	−46.09	116.07	−3.48	72.11	838.92	38.56
1971	−2.99	9.56	13.66	8.04	23.01	890.20	51.28
1972	−87.40	−1.23	65.24	8.46	144.75	1020.02	129.82
1973	−174.11	10.52	−5.94	36.67	−36.30	850.86	−169.16
1974	−149.37	47.51	−20.31	−13.70	−98.75	616.24	−234.62
1975	39.46	−109.62	56.93	124.00	125.40	852.41	236.17
1976	70.72	71.76	50.88	−33.70	−7.42	1004.65	152.24
1977	−65.15	−44.89	−79.61	−5.62	21.79	831.17	−173.48
1978	−31.29	−70.84	71.33	−64.67	69.31	805.01	−26.16
1979	−32.52	9.52	−18.84	75.18	0.39	838.74	33.73
1980	−86.51	135.13	137.67	−122.00	60.96	963.99	125.25
1981	−45.68	−49.51	−13.95	−14.67	34.82	875.00	−88.99
1982	5.71	86.20	28.37	−1.47	52.73	1046.54	171.54
1983	30.51	−30.92	149.68	61.16	1.67	1258.64	212.10
1984	−73.80	78.02	−139.24	92.79	−4.84	1211.57	−47.07
1985	80.36	52.70	51.26	46.32	104.46	1546.67	335.10
1986	−39.94	97.63	178.65	29.31	83.63	1895.95	349.28
1987	−559.15	235.83	392.03	139.73	−165.56	1938.83	42.88
1988	268.12	166.44	−60.48	−230.84	86.50	2168.57	229.74
1989	−53.31	143.33	233.25	90.25	171.11	2753.20	584.63
Subtotal	*−1937.20*	*941.79*	*1708.54*	*330.82*	*1417.35*		*2461.30*
1990	219.90	−25.22	47.96	−352.55	−9.63	2633.66	−119.54
1991	191.13	47.97	174.53	254.79	−133.25	3168.83	535.17
1992	237.80	−49.67	3.12	108.74	−167.71	3301.11	132.28
1993	322.82	−37.03	243.87	4.97	−81.65	3754.09	452.98
1994	206.41	−95.33	29.98	−168.87	108.16	3834.44	80.35
1995	262.97	210.06	357.02	140.07	312.56	5117.12	1282.68
1996	626.41	155.55	−34.24	268.52	314.91	6448.27	1331.15
1997	1136.04	1989.17	−590.17	−949.80	−125.26	7908.25	1459.98
1998	649.10	679.95	591.63	−1579.43	931.93	9181.43	1273.18
1999	980.49	−1587.23	826.68	735.94	1359.81	11497.12	2315.69
2000	2265.45	306.47	−1978.34	238.21	−1542.06	10786.85	−710.27
Subtotal	*7098.52*	*1594.69*	*−327.96*	*−1299.41*	*967.81*		*8033.65*
2001	−389.33	336.86	−396.53	976.41	−1292.76	10021.50	−765.35
2002	−1404.94	−823.76	1443.69	−428.12	−466.74	8341.63	−1679.87
2003	978.87	482.11	−425.46	566.22	510.55	10453.92	2112.09
2004	201.12	523.28	358.76	−409.72	−344.35	10783.01	329.09
2005	316.23	−305.62	27.67	−128.75	24.96	10717.50	−65.51
2006	95.74	573.98	1283.87	193.34	−401.28	12463.15	1745.65
2007	278.23	−157.93	1316.74	−766.63	131.26	13264.82	801.67
2008	−1387.20	1704.51	−3073.72	−940.88	−791.14	8776.39	−4488.43
2009	−45.22	161.76	617.56	932.68	−15.12	10428.05	1651.66
2010	1236.88	−421.80	1019.66	−76.73	−608.55	11577.51	1149.46
2011	−571.02	1423.66	−776.05	246.27	317.19	12217.56	640.05
2012	254.59	−49.28	−456.37	847.34	299.30	13104.14	886.58
2013	−79.63	1091.75	170.93	653.64	1635.83	16576.66	3472.52
2014	−171.63	817.56	265.07	−337.48	672.89	17823.07	1246.41
2015	308.28	−879.14	926.70	982.16	−1736.04	17425.03	−398.04
2016	602.00	594.09	636.92	678.40	−173.84	19762.60	2337.57
2017	1341.29	1184.32	882.40	445.43	1103.18	24719.22	4956.62
2018	−1694.23	252.29	754.24	−47.39	−656.67	23327.46	−1391.76
2019	−1723.31	1364.93	656.12	1156.52	3756.72	28538.44	5210.98
2020	1126.98	3852.74	1067.54	−4418.94	439.72	30606.48	2068.00
2021	1119.75	−586.19	708.55	2795.04	1694.67	36338.30	5731.82
2022 ‡	−2303.17	1250.95	1357.18	−2357.66	−1138.35	33147.25	−3191.05
2023 ‡	71.94	−871.31	−1537.84	128.59	2824.13		
Subtotal	*−1837.78*	*11519.76*	*6827.63*	*689.74*	*5785.56*		*22360.40*
Totals	*3323.54*	*14056.24*	*8208.21*	*−278.85*	*8170.72*		*32855.35*

* Monday denotes first trading day of week, Friday denotes last trading day of week
† Most Wednesdays closed last 7 months of 1968   ‡ Partial year through June 2, 2023

JULY 2024

MONDAY
D 47.6
S 47.6
N 57.1
22

I keep hearing "Should I buy? Should I buy?" When I start hearing "Should I sell?" that's the bottom.
— Nick Moore (Portfolio manager, Jurika & Voyles, TheStreet.com Mar. 12, 2001)

TUESDAY
D 52.4
S 57.1
N 57.1
23

*When a falling stock becomes a screaming buy because it cannot conceivably drop further,
try to buy it 30 percent lower.*
— Al Rizzo (Investment Advisor, Dynamic Growth Letter, 1986)

Week After July Expiration Prone to Wild Swings, Dow Up 15 of Last 25
1998 -4.3%, 2002 +3.1%, 2006 +3.2%, 2007 -4.2%, 2009 +4.0%, 2010 +3.2

WEDNESDAY
D 38.1
S 52.4
N 47.6
24

With enough inside information and a million dollars, you can go broke in a year.
— Warren Buffett (CEO Berkshire Hathaway, investor and philanthropist, b. 1930)

THURSDAY
D 61.9
S 57.1
N 52.4
25

Companies which do well generally tend to report (their quarterly earnings) earlier than those which do poorly.
— Alan Abelson (Financial journalist and editor, Barron's, 1925-2013)

FRIDAY
D 47.6
S 47.6
N 52.4
26

*What people in the Middle East tell you in private is irrelevant. All that matters is what they will defend
in public in their language.*
— Thomas L. Friedman (NY Times foreign affairs columnist, "Meet the Press" 12/17/06)

SATURDAY
27

August Almanac Investor Sector Seasonalities: See Pages 94, 96 and 98

SUNDAY
28

A RALLY FOR ALL SEASONS

Most years, especially when the market sells off during the first half, prospects for the perennial summer rally become the buzz on the street. Parameters for this "rally" were defined by the late Ralph Rotnem as the lowest close in the Dow Jones Industrials in May or June to the highest close in July, August, or September. Such a big deal is made of the "summer rally" that one might get the impression the market puts on its best performance in the summertime. Nothing could be further from the truth! Not only does the market "rally" in every season of the year, but it does so with more gusto in the winter, spring, and fall than in the summer.

Winters in 60 years averaged a 12.9% gain as measured from the low in November or December to the first quarter closing high. Spring rose 11.8% followed by fall with 11.1%. Last and least was the average 9.4% "summer rally." Even 2020's impressive 25.2% "summer rally" was outmatched by spring. Nevertheless, no matter how thick the gloom or grim the outlook, don't despair! There's always a rally for all seasons, statistically.

SEASONAL GAINS IN DOW JONES INDUSTRIALS

	WINTER RALLY Nov/Dec Low to Q1 High	SPRING RALLY Feb/Mar Low to Q2 High	SUMMER RALLY May/Jun Low to Q3 High	FALL RALLY Aug/Sep Low to Q4 High
1964	15.3%	6.2%	9.4%	8.3%
1965	5.7	6.6	11.6	10.3
1966	5.9	4.8	3.5	7.0
1967	11.6	8.7	11.2	4.4
1968	7.0	11.5	5.2	13.3
1969	0.9	7.7	1.9	6.7
1970	5.4	6.2	22.5	19.0
1971	21.6	9.4	5.5	7.4
1972	19.1	7.7	5.2	11.4
1973	8.6	4.8	9.7	15.9
1974	13.1	8.2	1.4	11.0
1975	36.2	24.2	8.2	8.7
1976	23.3	6.4	5.9	4.6
1977	8.2	3.1	2.8	2.1
1978	2.1	16.8	11.8	5.2
1979	11.0	8.9	8.9	6.1
1980	13.5	16.8	21.0	8.5
1981	11.8	9.9	0.4	8.3
1982	4.6	9.3	18.5	37.8
1983	15.7	17.8	6.3	10.7
1984	5.9	4.6	14.1	9.7
1985	11.7	7.1	9.5	19.7
1986	31.1	18.8	9.2	11.4
1987	30.6	13.6	22.9	5.9
1988	18.1	13.5	11.2	9.8
1989	15.1	12.9	16.1	5.7
1990	8.8	14.5	12.4	8.6
1991	21.8	11.2	6.6	9.3
1992	14.9	6.4	3.7	3.3
1993	8.9	7.7	6.3	7.3
1994	9.7	5.2	9.1	5.0
1995	13.6	19.3	11.3	13.9
1996	19.2	7.5	8.7	17.3
1997	17.7	18.4	18.4	7.3
1998	20.3	13.6	8.2	24.3
1999	15.1	21.6	8.2	12.6
2000	10.8	15.2	9.8	3.5
2001	6.4	20.8	1.7	23.1
2002	14.8	7.9	2.8	17.6
2003	6.5	23.9	14.3	15.7
2004	11.6	5.2	4.4	10.6
2005	9.0	2.1	5.6	5.3
2006	8.8	8.3	9.5	13.0
2007	6.7	13.5	6.6	10.3
2008	2.5	11.2	3.8	4.5
2009	19.6	34.4	19.7	15.5
2010	11.6	13.1	11.1	16.0
2011	12.6	10.3	7.0	14.7
2012	18.0	4.5	12.4	5.7
2013	16.2	11.8	6.9	12.2
2014	6.0	10.2	5.5	10.3
2015	7.1	5.5	3.0	14.4
2016	3.4	15.6	8.7	10.8
2017	18.0	8.3	8.8	14.6
2018	14.4	7.6	11.8	6.6
2019	19.7	6.8	10.3	12.4
2020	8.1	48.3	25.2	14.8
2021	23.2	15.1	7.0	7.8
2022	8.2	7.7	14.3	20.4
2023	7.2	7.2*		
Totals	**773.5%**	**705.4%**	**557.0%**	**657.6%**
Average	**12.9%**	**11.8%**	**9.4%**	**11.1%**

*As of 6/2/2023

JULY/AUGUST 2024

Explosive growth of shadow banking was about the invisible hand having a party, a non-regulated drinking party, with rating agencies handing out fake IDs.
— Paul McCulley (Economist, bond investor, PIMCO, coined "shadow banking" in 2007, *NY Times* 4/26/2010, b. 1957)

TUESDAY
D 42.9
S 61.9
N 71.4
30

When the market goes against the trend, go with the market.
— Wayne Whaley (Commodity Trading Advisor, Witter & Lester Inc.)

Last Trading Day in July, NASDAQ and S&P Down 12 of Last 18, Dow Down 13 of Last 18
FOMC Meeting (2 Days)

WEDNESDAY
D 38.1
S 42.9
N 38.1
31

Nobody can be a great economist who is only an economist—and I am even tempted to add that the economist who is only an economist is likely to become a nuisance if not a positive danger.
— Friedrich Hayek (Austrian-British economist & philosopher, 1899–1992)

First Trading Day in August, Dow Down 18 of Last 26

THURSDAY
D 33.3
S 38.1
N 52.4
1

The facts are unimportant! It's what they are perceived to be that determines the course of events.
— R. Earl Hadady (*Bullish Consensus, Contrary Opinion*)

First Nine Trading Days of August Are Historically Weak (Pages 76 and 126)

FRIDAY
D 47.6
S 52.4
N 42.9
2

If the market does not rally, as it should during bullish seasonal periods, it is a sign that other forces are stronger and that when the seasonal period ends those forces will really have their say.
— Edson Gould (Stock market analyst, *Findings & Forecasts*, 1902–1987)

SATURDAY
3

SUNDAY
4

AUGUST ALMANAC

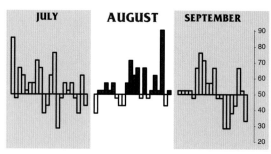

AUGUST							SEPTEMBER					
S	M	T	W	T	F	S	S	M	T	W	T	F	S
					1	2	3		1	2	3	4	5	6	7
4	5	6	7	8	9	10	8	9	10	11	12	13	14
11	12	13	14	15	16	17	15	16	17	18	19	20	21
18	19	20	21	22	23	24	22	23	24	25	26	27	28
25	26	27	28	29	30	31	29	30					

Market Probability Chart above is a graphic representation of the S&P 500 Recent Market Probability Calendar on page 126.

◆ Harvesting made August the best stock market month 1901–1951 ◆ Now that about 2% farm, August is the worst Dow and second worst S&P and NASDAQ (2000 up 11.7%, 2001 down 10.9%) month since 1988 ◆ Second shortest bear in history (45 days) caused by turmoil in Russia, currency crisis and hedge fund debacle ended here in 1998, 1344.22-point drop in the Dow, twelfth worst point loss, off 15.1% second worst percent loss since 1941 ◆ Saddam Hussein triggered a 10.0% slide in 1990 ◆ Best Dow gains: 1982 (11.5%) and 1984 (9.8%) as bear markets ended ◆ Next to last day S&P up only nine times last 27 years ◆ Presidential election year Augusts' rankings #5 S&P, #4 Dow, and #1 NASDAQ (+3.2%, up 9, down 4)

August Vital Statistics

	DJIA	S&P 500	NASDAQ	Russell 1K	Russell 2K
Rank	10	10	11	9	9
Up	41	40	29	27	25
Down	32	33	23	17	19
Average % Change	–0.09%	0.01%	0.4%	0.3%	0.3%
Election Year	1.1%	1.3%	3.2%	2.4%	3.5%
Best & Worst August					
	% Change	% Change	% Change	% Change	% Change
Best	1982 11.5	1982 11.6	2000 11.7	1982 11.3	1984 11.5
Worst	1998 –15.1	1998 –14.6	1998 –19.9	1998 –15.1	1998 –19.5
Best & Worst August Weeks					
Best	8/20/82 10.3	8/20/82 8.8	8/3/84 7.4	8/20/82 8.5	8/3/84 7.0
Worst	8/23/74 –6.1	8/5/11 –7.2	8/28/98 –8.8	8/5/11 –7.7	8/5/11 –10.3
Best & Worst August Days					
Best	8/17/82 4.9	8/17/82 4.8	8/9/11 5.3	8/9/11 5.0	8/9/11 6.9
Worst	8/31/98 –6.4	8/31/98 –6.8	8/31/98 –8.6	8/8/11 –6.9	8/8/11 –8.9
First Trading Day of Expiration Week: 1980–2023					
Record (#Up - #Down)	27–16	31–12	31–12	31–12	27–16
Current streak	U2	U3	U1	U3	U1
Avg % Change	0.22	0.25	0.32	0.23	0.24
Options Expiration Day: 1980–2023					
Record (#Up - #Down)	22–21	23–20	24–21	24–19	24–19
Current streak	D1	D1	D1	D1	D1
Avg % Change	–0.09	–0.04	–0.10	–0.04	0.09
Options Expiration Week: 1980–2023					
Record (#Up - #Down)	19–24	23–20	22–21	23–20	24–19
Current streak	D4	D2	D2	D2	D4
Avg % Change	–0.03	0.13	0.26	0.14	0.19
Week After Options Expiration: 1980–2023					
Record (#Up - #Down)	27–16	28–15	27–16	28–15	28–15
Current streak	D1	D1	D1	U1	D1
Avg % Change	0.23	0.30	0.51	0.31	0.20
First Trading Day Performance					
% of Time Up	45.2	47.9	53.8	43.2	45.5
Avg % Change	0.01	0.04	–0.03	0.08	–0.01
Last Trading Day Performance					
% of Time Up	57.5	61.6	63.5	56.8	65.9
Avg % Change	0.09	0.10	0.05	–0.05	0.03

Dow & S&P 1950–June 9, 2023, NASDAQ 1971–June 9, 2023, Russell 1K & 2K 1979–June 9, 2023.

August's a good month to go on vacation;
Trading stocks will likely lead to frustration.

AUGUST 2024

D 57.1
S 52.4
N 57.1

5

Whom the gods would destroy, they first put on the cover of Business Week.
— Paul Krugman (*Economist, NY Times* 8/17/2001, referring to Enron CEO, cover 2/12, scandal 6/23, quits 8/16)

TUESDAY

D 52.4
S 57.1
N 57.1

6

The finest thought runs the risk of being irrevocably forgotten if we do not write it down.
— Arthur Schopenhauer (German philosopher, 1788–1860)

August Worst Dow and Second Worst S&P Month 1988–2022
Harvesting Made August Best Dow Month 1901–1951

WEDNESDAY

D 57.1
S 52.4
N 38.1

7

A statistician is someone who can draw a straight line from an unwarranted assumption to a foregone conclusion.
— Anonymous

THURSDAY

D 57.1
S 57.1
N 47.6

8

A fanatic is one who can't change his mind and won't change the subject.
— Winston Churchill (British statesman, 1874–1965)

FRIDAY

D 42.9
S 47.6
N 42.9

9

The most valuable executive is one who is training somebody to be a better man than he is.
— Robert G. Ingersoll (American lawyer, politician and orator, "The Great Agnostic," 1833–1899)

SATURDAY

10

SUNDAY

11

TAKE ADVANTAGE OF DOWN FRIDAY/ DOWN MONDAY WARNING

Fridays* and Mondays* are the most important days of the week. Friday* is the day for squaring positions—trimming longs or covering shorts before taking off for the weekend. Traders want to limit their exposure (particularly to stocks that are not acting well) since there could be unfavorable developments before trading resumes two or more days later.

Monday* is important because the market then has the chance to reflect any weekend news, plus what traders think after digesting the previous week's action and the many Monday* morning research and strategy comments.

For over 30 years a down Friday* followed by down Monday* has frequently corresponded with important market inflection points that exhibit a clearly negative bias, often coinciding with market tops and on a few climactic occasions, such as in October 2002, March 2009, March 2020 and August–October 2022 near major market bottoms.

One simple way to get a quick reading on which way the market may be heading is to keep track of the performance of the Dow Jones Industrial Average on Fridays* and the following Mondays*. Since 1995 there have been 286 occurrences of Down Friday/Down Monday* (DF/DM) with 92 falling in the bear market years of 2001, 2002, 2008, 2011, 2015, 2020 and 2022 producing an average decline of 12.5% (shaded).

To illustrate how DF/DM* can telegraph market infection points we created the chart below of the Dow Jones Industrials from November 2021 to June 2, 2023, with arrows pointing to occurrences of DF/DM*. Use DF/DM* as a warning to examine market conditions carefully.

DOWN FRIDAY/DOWN MONDAY

Year	Total Number Down Friday/ Down Monday	Subsequent Average % Dow Loss*	Average Number of Days it took
1995	8	−1.2%	18
1996	9	−3.0%	28
1997	6	−5.1%	45
1998	9	−6.4%	47
1999	9	−6.4%	39
2000	11	−6.6%	32
2001	13	−13.5%	53
2002	18	−11.9%	54
2003	9	−3.0%	17
2004	9	−3.7%	51
2005	10	−3.0%	37
2006	11	−2.0%	14
2007	8	−6.0%	33
2008	15	−17.0%	53
2009	10	−8.7%	15
2010	7	−3.1%	10
2011	11	−9.0%	53
2012	11	−4.0%	38
2013	7	−2.4%	15
2014	7	−2.5%	8
2015	12	−9.2%	44
2016	10	−2.7%	25
2017	11	−1.2%	18
2018	14	−5.8%	45
2019	7	−4.3%	32
2020	8	−19.0%	27
2021	7	−4.4%	38
2022	15	−7.8%	46
2023**	4	−3.9%	24
Average	10	−6.1%	33

* Over next 3 months, ** Ending June 2, 2023

DOW JONES INDUSTRIALS (November 2021 - June 2, 2023)

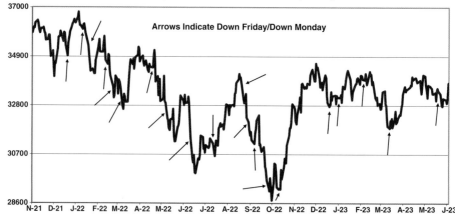

* Monday denotes first trading day of week, Friday denotes last trading day of week.

AUGUST 2024

Monday Before August Expiration, Dow Up 18 of Last 28, Average Gain 0.2%

MONDAY
D 33.3
S 42.9
N 42.9
12

By the law of nature the father continues master of his child no longer than the child stands in need of his assistance; after that term they become equal, and then the son entirely independent of the father, owes him no obedience, but only respect.
— Jean-Jacques Rousseau (Swiss philosopher, *The Social Contract*, 1712–1778)

TUESDAY
D 52.4
S 42.9
N 52.4
13

To know values is to know the meaning of the market.
— Charles Dow (Co-founder Dow Jones & Co, 1851–1902)

Mid-August Stronger Than Beginning and End

WEDNESDAY
D 66.7
S 57.1
N 61.9
14

A committee is a cul-de-sac down which ideas are lured and then quietly strangled.
— Sir Barnett Cocks (Member of Parliament, 1907–1989)

THURSDAY
D 61.9
S 71.4
N 61.9
15

The best time to be wrong is with money in one's pocket.
— George Brooks (60-year market veteran, hired by Yale Hirsch in 1974, mentor, confidant, *Investors First Read*, b. 1937)

August Expiration Day Less Bullish Lately, Dow Down 8 of Last 13 Down 531 Points (3.1%) in 2015

FRIDAY
D 52.4
S 61.9
N 57.1
16

The first rule is not to lose. The second rule is not to forget the first rule.
— Warren Buffett (CEO Berkshire Hathaway, investor and philanthropist, b. 1930)

SATURDAY
17

SUNDAY
18

ONLY TWO LOSSES LAST 7 MONTHS OF ELECTION YEARS

Election years are traditionally up years. Incumbent administrations shamelessly attempt to massage the economy so voters will keep them in power. But sometimes overpowering events occur and the market crumbles, usually resulting in a change of political control. The Republicans won in 1920 as the post-war economy contracted and President Wilson ailed. The Democrats came back during the 1932 Depression when the Dow hit its lowest level of the 20th century. A world at war and the fall of France jolted the market in 1940, but Roosevelt won an unprecedented third term. Cold War confrontations and Truman's historic upset of Dewey held markets down through the end of 1948.

Since 1948, investors have barely been bruised during election years, except for a brief span early in the year—until 2000 (undecided election) and then again in 2008 (Global Financial Crisis). In both years a bubble burst: technology and internet stocks in 2000 and credit in 2008. Global pandemic impacted Q1 of 2020, but unprecedented stimulus quickly erased market declines. Barring another massive regulatory failure, financial crisis, political miscalculation or exogenous event, this is unlikely to occur again in 2024.

The table below presents a very positive picture for the last seven or eight months of election years.

- Since 1952, January through April losses occurred in 9 of 18 election years. Incumbent parties were ousted on 7 of these 9 losses. Ironically, bear markets commenced following 4 of 9 gainers in 1956, 1968, 1973 and 1976.

- Comparing month-end June with month-end April reveals gains in 1952, 1960, 1968, 1988, 2000 and 2016 for the 60-day period, when no sitting president ran for reelection.

- Of the 18 Julys since 1952, nine were losers (1960, 1968, 1976, 1984, 1988, 1996, 2000, 2004, and 2008). Five were years when, at convention time, no strong incumbent was running for reelection. Note that April through July periods had seven losers, five in a row (1996-2012): 1972 by a small margin, 1984 as the market was turning around, 1996 and 2000 as the bubble began to work off its excesses, 2004 and 2008 as the credit bubble burst, and 2012 as the Fed moved from Operation Twist to QE3.

- For a longer perspective, we extended the table to December. Just three losing eight-month periods in an election year are revealed and **only two losses in the last seven months of all these election years.**

S&P 500 DURING ELECTION YEARS

Election Year	% Change First 4 Months	April	May	June	July	Dec	% Change Last 8 Months	Last 7 Months
1952*	– 1.9%	**23.32**	23.86	24.96	25.40	26.57	13.9%	11.4%
1956	6.4	**48.38**	**45.20**	46.97	49.39	46.67	– 3.5	3.3
1960*	– 9.2	**54.37**	55.83	56.92	**55.51**	58.11	6.9	4.1
1964	5.9	79.46	80.37	81.69	83.18	84.75	6.7	5.4
1968*	1.2	97.59	98.68	99.58	**97.74**	**103.86**	6.4	5.2
1972	5.5	107.67	109.53	**107.14**	107.39	118.05	9.6	7.8
1976*	12.7	**101.64**	**100.18**	104.28	**103.44**	107.46	5.7	7.3
1980*	– 1.5	106.29	111.24	114.24	121.67	135.76	27.7	22.0
1984	– 3.0	160.05	**150.55**	153.18	**150.66**	167.24	4.5	11.1
1988	5.8	261.33	262.16	273.50	**272.02**	277.72	6.3	5.9
1992*	– 0.5	414.95	415.35	**408.14**	424.21	435.71	5.0	4.9
1996	6.2	654.17	669.12	670.63	**639.95**	**740.74**	13.2	10.7
2000**	– 1.1	**1452.43**	**1420.60**	1454.60	**1430.83**	1320.28	– 9.1	– 7.1
2004	– 0.4	**1107.30**	1120.68	1140.84	**1101.72**	1211.92	9.4	8.1
2008*	– 5.6	1385.59	1400.38	**1280.00**	**1267.38**	903.25	– 34.8	– 35.5
2012	11.2	1397.91	1310.33	1362.16	1379.32	1426.19	2.0	8.8
2016*	1.0	2065.30	2096.96	2098.86	2173.60	2238.83	8.4	6.8
2020*	– 9.9	2912.43	3044.31	3100.29	3271.12	3756.07	29.0	23.4
Totals	**22.8%**						**107.3%**	**103.6%**
Average	**1.3%**						**6.0%**	**5.8%**

* Incumbents ousted, ** Incumbent ousted & undecided Election. Down months are bold.

AUGUST 2024

MONDAY
D 66.7
S 66.7
N 61.9
19

Excellent firms don't believe in excellence—only in constant improvement and constant change.
— Tom Peters (*In Search of Excellence*, b. 1942)

TUESDAY
D 47.6
S 47.6
N 47.6
20

The critical ingredient is getting off your butt and doing something. It's as simple as that. A lot of people have ideas, but there are few who decide to do something about them now. Not tomorrow. Not next week. But today. The true entrepreneur is a doer, not a dreamer.
— Nolan Bushnell (Founder Atari & Chuck E. Cheese's, b. 1943)

Week After August Expiration Mixed, Dow Up 9 of Last 18, Down 4.2% in 2022 **WEDNESDAY**
D 57.1
S 66.7
N 76.2
21

Anyone who believes that exponential growth can go on forever in a finite world is either a madman or an economist.
— Kenneth Ewart Boulding (Economist, activist, poet, scientist, philosopher, cofounder General Systems Theory, 1910–1993)

THURSDAY
D 52.4
S 47.6
N 47.6
22

If banking institutions are protected by the taxpayer and they are given free reign to speculate, I may not live long enough to see the crisis, but my soul is going to come back and haunt you.
— Paul A. Volcker (Fed Chairman 1979–1987, Chair Economic Recovery Advisory Board, 2/2/2010, 1927–2019)

FRIDAY
D 57.1
S 52.4
N 52.4
23

Banking establishments are more dangerous than standing armies; and that the principle of spending money to be paid by posterity, under the name of funding, is but swindling futurity on a large scale.
— Thomas Jefferson (3rd U.S. President, 1743–7/4/1826, 1816 letter to John Taylor of Caroline)

SATURDAY
24

September Almanac Investor Sector Seasonalities: See Pages 94, 96 and 98

SUNDAY
25

FOURTH QUARTER MARKET MAGIC

Examining market performance on a quarterly basis reveals several intriguing and helpful patterns. Fourth quarter market gains have been magical, providing the greatest and most consistent gains over the years. First quarter performance runs a respectable second. This should not be surprising as cash inflows, trading volume and buying bias are generally elevated during these two quarters.

Positive market psychology hits a fever pitch as the holiday season approaches and does not begin to wane until spring. Professionals drive the market higher as they make portfolio adjustments to maximize yearend numbers. Bonuses are paid and invested around the turn of the year.

The market's sweet spot of the Four-Year Cycle begins in the fourth quarter of the midterm year. The best two-quarter span runs from the fourth quarter of the midterm year through the first quarter of the pre-election year, averaging 13.8% for the Dow, 14.4% for the S&P 500 and an amazing 19.5% for NASDAQ. Pre-election Q2 is smoking too, the third best quarter of the cycle, creating a three-quarter sweet spot from midterm Q4 to pre-election Q2.

Quarterly strength fades in the latter half of the pre-election year, but stays impressively positive through the election year. Losses dominate the first quarter of post-election years and the second and third quarters of midterm years.

QUARTERLY % CHANGES

	Q1	Q2	Q3	Q4	Year	Q2–Q3	Q4–Q1
Dow Jones Industrials (1949–March 2023)							
Average	1.9%	1.6%	0.6%	4.1%	8.5%	2.3%	6.3%
Post Election	0.3%	1.9%	0.4%	4.3%	7.4%	2.3%	5.4%
Midterm	0.9%	−1.9%	−0.2%	6.6%	5.2%	−2.0%	13.8%
Pre-Election	6.9%	4.8%	1.0%	2.7%	16.2%	5.8%	2.3%
Election	−0.5%	1.9%	1.1%	2.8%	5.4%	3.2%	3.3%
S&P 500 (1949–March 2023)							
Average	2.1%	1.8%	0.8%	4.2%	9.1%	3.0%	6.4%
Post Election	0.1%	2.5%	0.8%	4.0%	8.0%	3.5%	4.8%
Midterm	0.6%	−2.8%	0.2%	6.6%	4.6%	−1.5%	14.4%
Pre-Election	7.4%	4.9%	0.6%	3.5%	16.8%	5.5%	3.7%
Election	0.2%	2.8%	1.5%	2.5%	7.3%	4.4%	2.9%
NASDAQ Composite (1971–March 2023)							
Average	4.1%	3.3%	0.5%	4.4%	12.7%	4.1%	8.6%
Post Election	−0.9%	6.6%	2.2%	5.2%	13.2%	8.8%	6.3%
Midterm	1.1%	−3.5%	−3.6%	5.8%	−0.5%	−6.6%	19.5%
Pre-Election	13.4%	7.2%	0.9%	5.9%	29.3%	8.1%	8.3%
Election	2.0%	3.0%	2.5%	0.6%	8.9%	6.0%	0.3%

AUGUST/SEPTEMBER 2024

D 52.4
S 61.9
N 61.9 **26**

Big money is made in the stock market by being on the right side of major moves. I don't believe in swimming against the tide.
— Martin Zweig (Fund manager, *Winning on Wall Street*, 1943–2013)

TUESDAY
D 42.9
S 52.4
N 52.4 **27**

Bad days are good days in disguise.
— Christopher Reeves (Actor, on Johnson & Johnson commercial)

August's Third-to-Last Trading Day, S&P Up 19 Years In A Row 2003–2021, 🐂 WEDNESDAY
Down 0.7% in 2022
D 85.7
S 90.5
N 81.0 **28**

When I have to depend upon hope in a trade, I get out of it.
— Jesse Livermore (Early 20th century stock trader and speculator, *How to Trade in Stocks*, 1877–1940)

August's Next-to-Last Trading Day, S&P Down 18 of Last 27 Years
THURSDAY
D 38.1
S 42.9
N 61.9 **29**

What is conservatism? Is it not adherence to the old and tried, against the new and untried?
— Abraham Lincoln (16th U.S. President, 1809–1865)

Last Trading Day in August, S&P Up 13 of Last 23 Years, But Down 5 of Last 8
FRIDAY
D 47.6
S 52.4
N 47.6 **30**

The whole problem with the world is that fools and fanatics are always so certain of themselves,
but wiser people so full of doubts.
— Bertrand Russell (British mathematician and philosopher, 1872–1970)

SATURDAY
31

SUNDAY
1

SEPTEMBER ALMANAC

SEPTEMBER							OCTOBER						
S	M	T	W	T	F	S	S	M	T	W	T	F	S
1	2	3	4	5	6	7			1	2	3	4	5
8	9	10	11	12	13	14	6	7	8	9	10	11	12
15	16	17	18	19	20	21	13	14	15	16	17	18	19
22	23	24	25	26	27	28	20	21	22	23	24	25	26
29	30						27	28	29	30	31		

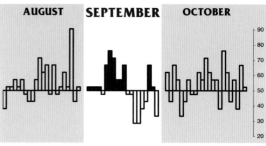

Market Probability Chart above is a graphic representation of the S&P 500 Recent Market Probability Calendar on page 126.

◆ Portfolio managers back after Labor Day tend to clean house in September ◆ Biggest % loser on the S&P, Dow and NASDAQ since 1950 (pages 52 & 60) ◆ Streak of four great Dow Septembers averaging 4.2% gains ended in 1999 with six losers in a row averaging –5.9% (page 156), up three straight 2005–2007, down 6% in 2008 and 2011, up 7.7% in 2010, down big last three years ◆ Day after Labor Day Dow down 11 of last 15 ◆ S&P opened strong 17 of last 28 years but tends to close weak due to end-of-quarter mutual fund portfolio restructuring, last trading day: S&P down 19 of past 30 ◆ September Triple-Witching Week can be dangerous, week after is pitiful (page 108)

September Vital Statistics

	DJIA	S&P 500	NASDAQ	Russell 1K	Russell 2K
Rank	12	12	12	12	12
Up	29	32	27	21	23
Down	44	40	25	23	21
Average % Change	–0.8%	–0.7%	–0.9%	–0.9%	–0.7%
Election Year	–0.5%	–0.4%	–0.4%	–0.2%	0.4%
Best & Worst September					
	% Change	% Change	% Change	% Change	% Change
Best	2010 7.7	2010 8.8	1998 13.0	2010 9.0	2010 12.3
Worst	2002 –12.4	1974 –11.9	2001 –17.0	2002 –10.9	2001 –13.6
Best & Worst September Weeks					
Best	9/28/01 7.4	9/28/01 7.8	9/16/11 6.3	9/28/01 7.6	9/28/01 6.9
Worst	9/21/01 –14.3	9/21/01 –11.6	9/21/01 –16.1	9/21/01 –11.7	9/21/01 –14.0
Best & Worst September Days					
Best	9/8/98 5.0	9/30/08 5.4	9/8/98 6.0	9/30/08 5.3	9/18/08 7.0
Worst	9/17/01 –7.1	9/29/08 –8.8	9/29/08 –9.1	9/29/08 –8.7	9/29/08 –6.7
First Trading Day of Expiration Week: 1980–2023					
Record (#Up - #Down)	28–15	24–19	17–26	24–19	20–23
Current streak	U3	U3	U1	U3	U4
Avg % Change	0.03	–0.01	–0.19	–0.03	–0.06
Options Expiration Day: 1980–2023					
Record (#Up - #Down)	20–23	20–23	24–19	21–22	25–18
Current streak	D4	D5	D5	D5	D1
Avg % Change	–0.08	–0.002	0.0002	–0.02	0.06
Options Expiration Week: 1980–2023					
Record (#Up - #Down)	22–21	24–19	23–20	24–19	23–20
Current streak	D4	D4	D5	D4	D1
Avg % Change	–0.20	–0.06	–0.05	–0.06	0.09
Week After Options Expiration: 1980–2023					
Record (#Up - #Down)	15–28	13–30	19–24	13–29	15–28
Current streak	D1	D1	D1	D1	D1
Avg % Change	–0.75	–0.79	–0.88	–0.81	–1.42
First Trading Day Performance					
% of Time Up	58.9	60.3	55.8	54.5	50.0
Avg % Change	–0.002	–0.01	–0.03	–0.06	–0.03
Last Trading Day Performance					
% of Time Up	41.1	42.5	50.0	50.0	61.4
Avg % Change	–0.12	–0.06	0.01	0.02	0.22

Dow & S&P 1950–June 9, 2023, NASDAQ 1971–June 9, 2023, Russell 1K & 2K 1979–June 9, 2023.

September is when leaves and stocks tend to fall;
On Wall Street it's the worst month of all.

SEPTEMBER 2024

Labor Day *(Market Closed)*

MONDAY

2

Take care of your employees and they'll take care of your customers.
— John W. Marriott (Founder Marriott International, 1900–1985)

Day After Labor Day, Dow Up 16 of Last 29, But Down 10 of Last 13
First Trading Day in September, S&P Up 17 of Last 28, But Down 9 of Last 15

TUESDAY

D 42.9
S 52.4
N 57.1

3

When I stand before God at the end of my life, I would hope that I would not have a single bit of talent left, and could say, 'I used everything you gave me.'
— Erma Bombeck (American humorist, columnist & writer, 1927–1996)

WEDNESDAY

D 71.4
S 52.4
N 52.4

4

We like what's familiar, and we dislike change. So, we push the familiar until it starts working against us big-time—a crisis. Then, MAYBE we can accept change.
— Kevin Cameron (Journalist, *Cycle World,* April 2013)

THURSDAY

D 57.1
S 52.4
N 52.4

5

When someone told me "We're going with you guys because no one ever got fired for buying Cisco (products)." That's what they used to say in IBM's golden age.
— Mark Dickey (Former Cisco sales exec, then at SmartPipes, *Fortune* 5/15/00).

FRIDAY

D 47.6
S 52.4
N 57.1

6

The biggest change we made was the move to a boundary-less company. We got rid of the corner offices, the bureaucracy, and the not-invented-here syndrome. Instead we got every mind in the game, got the best out of all our people.
— Jack Welch (retiring CEO of General Electric, *Business Week,* September 10, 2001, 1935–2020)

SATURDAY

7

SUNDAY

8

MARKET GAINS MORE ON SUPER-8 DAYS EACH MONTH THAN ON ALL 13 REMAINING DAYS COMBINED

For many years the last day plus the first four days were the best days of the month. The market currently exhibits greater bullish bias from the last three trading days of the previous month through the first two days of the current month, and now shows significant bullishness during the middle three trading days, nine to eleven, due to 401(k) cash inflows (see pages 147 and 148). This pattern was not as pronounced during the boom years of the 1990s, with market strength all month long. Since the 2009 market bottom, the "Super Eight" advantage has been sporadic. So far in 2023 the "Super Eight" have a clear advantage. The "Super Eight" were destroyed in 2020 through the end of June. When compared to the last 24 and third-year record (at the bottom of the page), the "Super Eight" edge has dulled recently.

SUPER-8 DAYS* DOW % CHANGES VS. REST OF MONTH

	Super 8 Days	Rest of Month		Super 8 Days	Rest of Month		Super 8 Days	Rest of Month
	2015			**2016**			**2017**	
Jan	− 3.64%	− 0.07%		− 2.95%	− 4.93%		− 0.44%	1.24%
Feb	2.65	2.00		1.69	0.30		0.62	2.90
Mar	1.91	− 4.78		4.02	2.21		1.16	− 1.66
Apr	1.20	0.83		2.14	0.43		− 0.39	1.83
May	1.31	− 1.28		− 1.33	0.57		− 0.03	0.45
Jun	− 1.32	0.49		− 1.33	− 2.68		1.18	− 0.09
Jul	− 0.11	− 1.31		4.97	2.66		0.89	0.98
Aug	0.37	− 8.02		− 0.11	− 0.30		2.12	− 1.65
Sep	2.27	− 2.04		0.84	− 1.72		0.53	1.65
Oct	1.03	6.57		− 0.65	0.49		1.97	2.96
Nov	0.68	0.68		− 0.71	5.93		− 0.15	0.93
Dec	− 0.74	− 0.86		0.38	3.73		3.61	1.27
Totals	**5.61%**	**− 7.79%**		**6.96%**	**6.69%**		**11.07%**	**10.81%**
Average	**0.47%**	**− 0.65%**		**0.58%**	**0.56%**		**0.92%**	**0.90%**
	2018			**2019**			**2020**	
Jan	2.83%	4.54%		0.04%	7.10%		1.40%	− 1.01%
Feb	− 1.68	− 3.17		4.70	1.54		− 0.78	− 4.78
Mar	− 4.26	− 0.09		0.11	− 1.77		− 18.59	2.59
Apr	0.89	− 1.34		2.90	0.21		− 4.42	11.77
May	− 0.79	3.59		− 1.71	− 2.56		− 1.92	5.59
Jun	− 0.67	− 1.17		0.35	4.32		− 1.56	4.78
Jul	0.33	4.72		1.81	0.60		2.81	− 0.33
Aug	− 1.39	3.53		− 3.87	− 1.41		1.23	6.03
Sep	0.05	1.59		1.98	2.62		4.04	− 7.99
Oct	− 0.30	− 6.62		− 1.32	1.85		0.68	0.55
Nov	1.97	− 1.68		2.50	1.05		1.94	7.30
Dec	− 2.63	− 5.08		− 0.85	2.85		0.13	1.06
Totals	**− 5.65%**	**− 1.18%**		**6.64%**	**16.40%**		**− 15.04%**	**25.56%**
Average	**− 0.47%**	**− 0.10%**		**0.55%**	**1.37%**		**− 1.25%**	**2.13%**
	2021			**2022**			**2023**	
Jan	− 0.46%	2.22%		− 1.44%	− 4.78%		− 2.53%	4.72%
Feb	− 0.54	2.49		3.56	− 6.40		1.07	− 3.40
Mar	1.57	3.25		3.41	2.09		− 0.56	− 1.69
Apr	2.92	− 0.18		0.46	− 5.41		2.95	0.57
May	2.64	− 1.64		0.88	− 4.23		− 0.08	− 2.21
Jun	0.36	0.004		1.20	− 3.07			
Jul	0.44	1.36		− 0.53	1.59			
Aug	0.57	− 0.11		3.81	− 1.99			
Sep	0.32	− 1.28		− 3.90	− 6.16			
Oct	0.19	2.41		7.39	1.83			
Nov	0.85	− 0.71		0.61	7.12			
Dec	− 3.37	5.15		− 2.12	− 1.12			
Totals	**5.49%**	**12.96%**		**13.33%**	**− 20.53%**		**0.85%**	**− 2.01%**
Average	**0.46%**	**1.08%**		**1.11%**	**− 1.71%**		**0.17%**	**− 0.40%**

	Super Eight Days		Rest of Month (13 days)	
293	Net % Changes	134.39%	Net % Changes	26.19%
Month	Average Period	0.46%	Average Period	0.09%
Totals	Average Day	0.06%	Average Day	0.01%

* Super 8 Days = Last 3 + First 2 + Middle 3

SEPTEMBER 2024

MONDAY

D 57.1
S 47.6
N 52.4

9

When a company reports higher earnings for its first quarter (over its previous year's first quarter), chances are almost five to one it will also have increased earnings in its second quarter.
— Niederhoffer, Cross & Zeckhauser

TUESDAY

D 61.9
S 66.7
N 61.9

10

Small volume is usually accompanied by a fall in price; large volume by a rise in price.
— Charles C. Ying ("Stock Market Prices and Volumes of Sales," *Econometrica*, July 1966)

2001 4-Day Closing, Longest Since 9-Day Banking Moratorium in March 1933

WEDNESDAY

D 76.2
S 76.2
N 66.7

11

A good trader has to have three things: a chronic inability to accept things at face value, to feel continuously unsettled, and to have humility.
— Michael Steinhardt (Financier, philanthropist, political activist, chairman WisdomTree Investments, b. 1940

THURSDAY

D 66.7
S 71.4
N 61.9

12

I am not a member of any organized party—I am a Democrat.
— Will Rogers (American humorist and showman, 1879–1935)

FRIDAY

D 57.1
S 57.1
N 66.7

13

An inventor fails 999 times, and if he succeeds once, he's in. He treats his failures simply as practice shots.
— Charles Kettering (Inventor of electric ignition, founded Delco in 1909, 1876–1958)

SATURDAY

14

SUNDAY

15

A CORRECTION FOR ALL SEASONS

While there's a rally for every season (page 74), almost always there's a decline or correction, too. Fortunately, corrections tend to be smaller than rallies, and that's what gives the stock market its long-term upward bias. In each season the average bounce outdoes the average setback. On average the net gain between the rally and the correction is smallest in summer and fall.

The summer setback tends to be slightly outdone by the average correction in the fall. Tax selling and portfolio cleaning are the usual explanations—individuals sell to register a tax loss and institutions like to get rid of their losers before preparing year-end statements. The October jinx also plays a major part. Since 1964, there have been 20 fall declines of over 10%, and in 12 of them (1966, 1974, 1978, 1979, 1987, 1990, 1997, 2000, 2002, 2008, 2018 and 2022) much damage was done in October, where so many bear markets end. Recent October lows were also seen in 1998, 1999, 2004, 2005 and 2011. Most often, it has paid to buy after fourth quarter or late third quarter "waterfall declines" for a rally that may continue into January or even beyond. Covid-19 pandemic economic shutdown in late Q1/early Q2 of 2020 caused the worst Winter and Spring slumps since 1932. Easy monetary policy and strong corporate earnings spared Q1 2011 and 2012 from a seasonal slump. Tax cut expectations lifted the market in Q4 2017.

SEASONAL CORRECTIONS IN DOW JONES INDUSTRIALS

	WINTER SLUMP Nov/Dec High to Q1 Low	SPRING SLUMP Feb/Mar High to Q2 Low	SUMMER SLUMP May/Jun High to Q3 Low	FALL SLUMP Aug/Sep High to Q4 Low
1964	−0.1%	−2.4%	−1.0%	−2.1%
1965	−2.5	−7.3	−8.3	−0.9
1966	−6.0	−13.2	−17.7	−12.7
1967	−4.2	−3.9	−5.5	−9.9
1968	−8.8	−0.3	−5.5	+0.4
1969	−8.7	−8.7	−17.2	−8.1
1970	−13.8	−20.2	−8.8	−2.5
1971	−1.4	−4.8	−10.7	−13.4
1972	−0.5	−2.6	−6.3	−5.3
1973	−11.0	−12.8	−10.9	−17.3
1974	−15.3	−10.8	−29.8	−27.6
1975	−6.3	−5.5	−9.9	−6.7
1976	−0.2	−5.1	−4.7	−8.9
1977	−8.5	−7.2	−11.5	−10.2
1978	−12.3	−4.0	−7.0	−13.5
1979	−2.5	−5.8	−3.7	−10.9
1980	−10.0	−16.0	−1.7	−6.8
1981	−6.9	−5.1	−18.6	−12.9
1982	−10.9	−7.5	−10.6	−3.3
1983	−4.1	−2.8	−6.8	−3.6
1984	−11.9	−10.5	−8.4	−6.2
1985	−4.8	−4.4	−2.8	−2.3
1986	−3.3	−4.7	−7.3	−7.6
1987	−1.4	−6.6	−1.7	−36.1
1988	−6.7	−7.0	−7.6	−4.5
1989	−1.7	−2.4	−3.1	−6.6
1990	−7.9	−4.0	−17.3	−18.4
1991	−6.3	−3.6	−4.5	−6.3
1992	+0.1	−3.3	−5.4	−7.6
1993	−2.7	−3.1	−3.0	−2.0
1994	−4.4	−9.6	−4.4	−7.1
1995	−0.8	−0.1	−0.2	−2.0
1996	−3.5	−4.6	−7.5	+0.2
1997	−1.8	−9.8	−2.2	−13.3
1998	−7.0	−3.1	−18.2	−13.1
1999	−2.7	−1.7	−8.0	−11.5
2000	−14.8	−7.4	−4.1	−11.8
2001	−14.5	−13.6	−27.4	−16.2
2002	−5.1	−14.2	−26.7	−19.5
2003	−15.8	−5.3	−3.1	−2.1
2004	−3.9	−7.7	−6.3	−5.7
2005	−4.5	−8.5	−3.3	−4.5
2006	−2.4	−5.4	−7.8	−0.4
2007	−3.7	−3.2	−6.1	−8.4
2008	−14.5	−11.0	−20.6	−35.9
2009	−32.0	−6.3	−7.4	−3.5
2010	−6.1	−10.4	−13.1	−1.0
2011	+0.2	−4.0	−16.3	−12.2
2012	+0.5	−8.7	−5.3	−7.8
2013	−0.2	−0.3	−4.1	−5.7
2014	−7.3	−2.6	−3.4	−6.7
2015	−4.9	−3.8	−14.4	−7.6
2016	−12.6	−3.3	−0.9	−4.0
2017	−1.2	−3.4	−1.0	+0.6
2018	−5.3	−9.7	−4.5	−18.5
2019	−13.4	−4.9	−4.8	−4.2
2020	−35.1	−29.1	−6.8	−8.9
2021	−2.0	−0.1	−2.7	−4.6
2022	−10.6	−16.4	−15.7	−14.5
2023*	−8.0	−4.3*		
Totals	**−418.0%**	**−408.1%**	**−503.6%**	**−523.6%**
Average	**−7.0%**	**−6.8%**	**−8.5%**	**−8.9%**

* As of 6/9/23

SEPTEMBER 2024

Monday Before September Triple Witching, NASDAQ Down 14 of Last 24

MONDAY

D 61.9
S 57.1
N 42.9

16

Price is profoundly important. It is the only measurement we have of all other factors known and unknown for the foreseeable future.
— Christopher N. Mistal (Director of Research, *Stock Trader's Almanac*, b. 1975)

TUESDAY

D 76.2
S 66.7
N 76.2

17

One machine can do the work of fifty ordinary men. No machine can do the work of one extraordinary man.
— Elbert Hubbard (American author, *A Message To Garcia*, 1856–1915)

Expiration Week 2001, Dow Lost 1370 Points (14.3%)
9th Worst Weekly Point Loss Ever, 6th Worst Week Overall
FOMC Meeting (2 Days)

WEDNESDAY

D 47.6
S 47.6
N 42.9

18

It's not that I am so smart; it's just that I stay with problems longer.
— Albert Einstein (German-American physicist, 1921 Nobel Prize, 1879–1955)

THURSDAY

D 52.4
S 47.6
N 47.6

19

When September doth soar, you are promised much more. The stronger the defiance of September's traditional weakness, the more robust is the market's gallop into the yearend.
— Wayne Whaley (Commodity Trading Advisor, Witter & Lester Inc.)

September Triple Witching, Dow Up 11 of Last 19, Down 8 of Last 11

FRIDAY

D 42.9
S 28.6
N 42.9

20

If you don't make bold moves, you don't get f***ing anywhere. You've got to push the limits.
— Keith Richards (Rolling Stones, *Life*, b. 1943)

SATURDAY

21

SUNDAY

22

FIRST-TRADING-DAY-OF-THE-MONTH PHENOMENON

Dow Jones Industrial Average has gained 26254.36 points between September 2, 1997 (7622.42) and June 9, 2023 (33876.78), it is incredible that 10080.13 points were gained on the first trading days of these 310 months. The remaining 6176 trading days combined gained 16174.23 points during the period. This averages out to gains of 32.52 points on first days, in contrast to just 2.62 points on all others.

Note September 1997 through October 2000 racked up a total gain of 2632.39 Dow points on the first trading days of these 38 months (winners except for seven occasions). But between November 2000 and September 2002, when the 2000–2002 bear markets did the bulk of their damage, frightened investors switched from pouring money into the market on that day to pulling it out, 14 months out of 23, netting a 404.80 Dow point loss. The 2007–2009 bear market lopped off 964.14 Dow points on first days in 17 months November 2007–March 2009. First days had their worst year in 2014, declining nine times for a total loss of 820.86 Dow points.

First days of August have performed worst, declining 17 times in the last 25 years. July's first trading day is third best by points but best based upon frequency of gains with only six declines in the last 34 years. In rising market trends first days tend to perform much better as institutions are likely anticipating strong performance at each month's outset. S&P 500 and NASDAQ first days differ slightly from Dow's pattern. August's first trading day is worst for S&P 500. April is worst for NASDAQ while December is also a net decliner.

DOW POINTS GAINED FIRST DAY OF MONTH
SEPTEMBER 1997–JUNE 9, 2023

	Jan	Feb	Mar	Apr	May	Jun	Jul	Aug	Sep	Oct	Nov	Dec	Totals
1997									257.36	70.24	232.31	189.98	749.89
1998	56.79	201.28	4.73	68.51	83.70	22.42	96.65	−96.55	288.36	−210.09	114.05	16.99	646.64
1999	2.84	−13.13	18.20	46.35	225.65	36.52	95.62	−9.19	108.60	−63.95	−81.35	120.58	486.74
2000	−139.61	100.52	9.62	300.01	77.87	129.87	112.78	84.97	23.68	49.21	−71.67	−40.95	636.30
2001	−140.70	96.27	−45.14	−100.85	163.37	78.47	91.32	−12.80	47.74	−10.73	188.76	−87.60	268.11
2002	51.90	−12.74	262.73	−41.24	113.41	−215.46	−133.47	−229.97	−355.45	346.86	120.61	−33.52	−126.34
2003	265.89	56.01	−53.22	77.73	−25.84	47.55	55.51	−79.83	107.45	194.14	57.34	116.59	819.32
2004	−44.07	11.11	94.22	15.63	88.43	14.20	−101.32	39.45	−5.46	112.38	26.92	162.20	413.69
2005	−53.58	62.00	63.77	−99.46	59.19	82.39	28.47	−17.76	−21.97	−33.22	−33.30	106.70	143.23
2006	129.91	89.09	60.12	35.62	−23.85	91.97	77.80	−59.95	83.00	−8.72	−49.71	−27.80	397.48
2007	11.37	51.99	−34.29	27.95	73.23	40.47	126.81	150.38	91.12	191.92	−362.14	−57.15	311.66
2008	−220.86	92.83	−7.49	391.47	189.87	−134.50	32.25	−51.70	−26.63	−19.59	−5.18	−679.95	−439.48
2009	258.30	−64.03	−299.64	152.68	44.29	221.11	57.06	114.95	−185.68	−203.00	76.71	126.74	299.49
2010	155.91	118.20	78.53	70.44	143.22	−112.61	−41.49	208.44	254.75	41.63	6.13	249.76	1172.91
2011	93.24	148.23	−168.32	56.99	−3.18	−279.65	168.43	−10.75	−119.96	−258.08	−297.05	−25.65	−695.75
2012	179.82	83.55	28.23	52.45	65.69	−274.88	−8.70	−37.62	−54.90	77.98	136.16	−59.98	187.80
2013	308.41	149.21	35.17	−5.69	−138.85	138.46	65.36	128.48	23.65	62.03	69.80	−77.64	758.39
2014	−135.31	−326.05	−153.68	74.95	−21.97	26.46	129.47	−69.93	−30.89	−238.19	−24.28	−51.44	−820.86
2015	9.92	196.09	155.93	−77.94	185.54	29.69	138.40	−91.66	−469.68	−11.99	165.22	168.43	395.95
2016	−276.09	−17.12	348.58	107.66	117.52	2.47	19.38	−27.73	18.42	−54.30	−105.32	68.35	201.82
2017	119.16	26.85	303.31	−13.01	−27.05	135.53	129.64	72.80	39.46	152.51	57.77	−40.76	956.21
2018	104.79	37.32	−420.22	−458.92	−64.10	219.37	35.77	−81.37	−12.34	192.90	264.98	287.97	106.15
2019	18.78	64.22	110.32	329.74	−162.77	4.74	117.47	−280.85	−285.26	−343.79	301.13	−268.37	−394.64
2020	330.36	143.78	1293.96	−973.65	−622.03	91.91	−77.91	236.08	215.61	35.20	423.45	185.28	1282.04
2021	−382.59	229.29	603.14	171.66	238.38	45.86	131.02	−97.31	−48.20	482.54	94.28	−461.68	1006.39
2022	246.76	273.38	−597.65	139.92	84.29	−176.89	321.83	−46.73	145.99	765.38	−79.75	−194.76	881.77
2023	−10.88	6.92	5.14	327.00	−46.46	153.30							435.02
Totals	940.46	1805.07	1696.05	676.00	815.55	418.77	1668.15	−266.15	88.77	1319.27	1225.87	−307.68	10080.13

SUMMARY FIRST DAYS VS. OTHER DAYS OF MONTH

	# of Days	Total Points Gained	Average Daily Point Gain
First days	310	10080.13	32.52
Other days	6176	16174.23	2.62

SEPTEMBER 2024

MONDAY
D 28.6
S 28.6
N 38.1
23

The years teach much which the days never know.
— Ralph Waldo Emerson (American author, poet and philosopher, *Self-Reliance*, 1803–1882)

Week After September Triple Witching Dow Down 25 of Last 33, Average Loss Since 1990, 1.1%

TUESDAY
D 38.1
S 38.1
N 42.9
24

I'm not better than the next trader, just quicker at admitting my mistakes and moving on to the next opportunity.
— George Soros (Financier, philanthropist, political activist, author and philosopher, b. 1930)

WEDNESDAY
D 52.4
S 42.9
N 52.4
25

A.I. (artificial intelligence) is the science of how to get machines to do the things they do in the movies.
— Professor Astro Teller (Carnegie Mellon University)

End of September Prone to Weakness From End-of-Q3 Institutional Portfolio Restructuring

THURSDAY
D 66.7
S 66.7
N 52.4
26

Capitalism works because it encourages and rewards those who successfully take risks, adapt to change, and develop profitable opportunities.
— Henry Blodget (Former stock analyst, *NY Times* Op-Ed 12/20/06, *The Wall Street Self-Defense Manual*)

FRIDAY
D 52.4
S 52.4
N 38.1
27

Success isn't measured by the position you reach in life; it's measured by the obstacles you overcome.
— Booker T. Washington (Founder of Tuskegee Institute, 1856–1915)

SATURDAY
28

October Almanac Investor Sector Seasonalities: See Pages 94, 96 and 98

SUNDAY
29

OCTOBER ALMANAC

OCTOBER							NOVEMBER					
S	M	T	W	T	F	S	S	M	T	W	T	F	S
		1	2	3	4	5						1	2
6	7	8	9	10	11	12	3	4	5	6	7	8	9
13	14	15	16	17	18	19	10	11	12	13	14	15	16
20	21	22	23	24	25	26	17	18	19	20	21	22	23
27	28	29	30	31			24	25	26	27	28	29	30

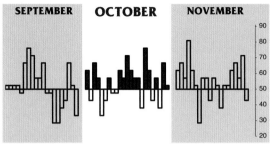

Market Probability Chart above is a graphic representation of the S&P 500 Recent Market Probability Calendar on page 126.

◆ Beware "Octoberphobia" from crashes in 1929, 1987, 554-point drop October 27, 1997, back-to-back massacres 1978 and 1979, Friday the 13th 1989 and the 2008 meltdown ◆ Yet October is a "Bear Killer" and turned the tide in 13 post-WWII bear markets: 1946, 1957, 1960, 1962, 1966, 1974, 1987, 1990, 1998, 2001, 2002, 2011 and 2022 ◆ First October Dow top in 2007, ◆ Worst six months of the year ends with October (page 54) ◆ No longer worst month (pages 52 & 60) ◆ Best Dow, S&P and NASDAQ month from 1993 to 2007 ◆ Presidential election year Octobers since 1950, #12 Dow (–1.0), #12 S&P (–0.9%) and #12 NASDAQ (–2.2%) ◆ October is a great time to buy ◆ Big October Dow gains five years 1999-2003 after atrocious Septembers ◆ Enter Best Six Months earlier using MACD (page 56) ◆ October 2022, best Dow month by points, up over 4000 (+14.0%)

October Vital Statistics

	DJIA	S&P 500	NASDAQ	Russell 1K	Russell 2K
Rank	7	7	8	6	11
Up	44	44	29	28	26
Down	29	29	23	16	18
Average % Change	0.8%	1.0%	0.8%	1.1%	–0.03%
Election Year	–1.0%	–0.9%	–2.2%	–1.6%	–2.4%
Best & Worst October					
	% Change	% Change	% Change	% Change	% Change
Best	2022 14.0	1974 16.3	1974 17.2	1982 11.3	2011 15.0
Worst	1987 –23.2	1987 –21.8	1987 –27.2	1987 –21.9	1987 –30.8
Best & Worst October Weeks					
Best	10/11/74 12.6	10/11/74 14.1	10/31/08 10.9	10/31/08 10.8	10/31/08 14.1
Worst	10/10/08 –18.2	10/10/08 –18.2	10/23/87 –19.2	10/10/08 –18.2	10/23/87 –20.4
Best & Worst October Days					
Best	10/13/08 11.1	10/13/08 11.6	10/13/08 11.8	10/13/08 11.7	10/13/08 9.3
Worst	10/19/87 –22.6	10/19/87 –20.5	10/19/87 –11.4	10/19/87 –19.0	10/19/87 –12.5
First Trading Day of Expiration Week: 1980–2021					
Record (#Up - #Down)	32–11	30–15	28–15	31–12	30–13
Current streak	U1	U1	U1	U1	U1
Avg % Change	0.66	0.65	0.57	0.63	0.41
Options Expiration Day: 1980–2021					
Record (#Up - #Down)	22–21	23–20	24–19	22–21	17–26
Current streak	U3	U3	U2	U2	U1
Avg % Change	–0.04	–0.11	–0.05	–0.10	–0.15
Options Expiration Week: 1980–2021					
Record (#Up - #Down)	31–12	32–11	26–17	31–12	26–17
Current streak	U3	U8	U4	U4	U2
Avg % Change	0.71	0.75	0.80	0.75	0.50
Week After Options Expiration: 1980–2021					
Record (#Up - #Down)	22–21	20–23	23–20	20–23	21–22
Current streak	U2	U2	U2	U2	U4
Avg % Change	–0.17	–0.22	–0.24	–0.24	–0.40
First Trading Day Performance					
% of Time Up	50.7	52.1	50.0	56.8	50.0
Avg % Change	0.11	0.09	–0.06	0.26	–0.14
Last Trading Day Performance					
% of Time Up	52.1	53.4	61.5	61.4	65.9
Avg % Change	0.06	0.12	0.41	0.26	0.49

Dow & S&P 1950–June 9, 2023, NASDAQ 1971–June 9, 2023, Russell 1K & 2K 1979–June 9, 2023.

October has killed many a bear;
Buy techs and small caps and soon wear a grin ear to ear.

SEPTEMBER/OCTOBER 2024

Last Day of Q3, S&P Down 17 of Last 26, But Up 5 of Last 8,
Massive 5.4% Rally in 2008

MONDAY

D 38.1
S 33.3
N 42.9

30

Central Bankers are brought up pulling the legs off ants.
— Paul A. Volcker (Fed Chairman 1979–1987, Quoted by William Grieder, Secrets of the Temple)

First Trading Day in October Mixed, Dow Up 9 of Last 18, Up 2.7% in 2022

TUESDAY

D 57.1
S 61.9
N 57.1

1

It's a buy when the 10-week moving average crosses the 30-week moving average and the slope of both averages is up.
— Victor Sperandeo (Trader Vic—Methods of a Wall Street Master)

Start Looking for MACD BUY Signals on October 1 (Pages 56, 62 and 64)
Almanac Investor Subscribers Emailed When It Triggers (See Insert)

WEDNESDAY

D 38.1
S 42.9
N 47.6

2

If the market prefers a system that looks inefficient that's a good sign that its more efficient than it looks.
— Matt Levine (Bloomberg View columnist, former investment banker, lawyer & high-school Latin teacher)

Rosh Hashanah

THURSDAY

D 66.7
S 66.7
N 71.4

3

The knowledge of past times… is both an ornament and nutriment to the human mind.
— Leonardo da Vinci (Italian Renaissance polymath, 1452–1519)

October Ends Dow and S&P "Worst Six Months"(Pages 52, 54, 56, 64 and 149)
And NASDAQ "Worst Four Months" (Pages 60, 62 and 150)

FRIDAY

D 61.9
S 57.1
N 52.4

4

Short-term volatility is greatest at turning points and diminishes as a trend becomes established.
— George Soros (Financier, philanthropist, political activist, author and philosopher, b. 1930)

SATURDAY

5

SUNDAY

6

SECTOR SEASONALITY: SELECTED PERCENTAGE PLAYS

Sector seasonality was featured in the first 1968 *Almanac*. A Merrill Lynch study showed that buying seven sectors around September or October and selling in the first few months of 1954–1964 tripled the gains of holding them for 10 years. Over the years we have honed this strategy significantly and now devote a significant portion of our time and resources to investing and trading during positive and negative seasonal periods for the different sector indexes below with highly correlated exchange-traded funds (ETFs).

Updated seasonalities appear in the table below. We specify whether the seasonality starts or finishes in the beginning third (B), middle third (M) or last third (E) of the month. These Selected Percentage Plays are geared to take advantage of the bulk of seasonal sector strength or weakness.

By design entry points are in advance of the major seasonal moves, providing traders ample opportunity to accumulate positions at favorable prices. Conversely, exit points have been selected to capture the majority of the move.

From the major seasonalities in the table below we created the Sector Index Seasonality Strategy Calendar on pages 96 and 98. Note the concentration of bullish sector seasonalities during the Best Six Months, November–April, and bearish sector seasonalities during the Worst Six Months, May–October.

Almanac Investor subscribers receive specific entry and exit points for highly correlated ETFs and detailed analysis in our *ETF Trades* report. Visit *www.stocktradersalmanac.com* or see the insert for additional details and a special offer for new subscribers.

SECTOR INDEX SEASONALITY TABLE

Ticker	Sector Index	Type	Seasonality Start		Finish		Average % Return[†] 15-Year	10-Year	5-Year
XCI	Computer Tech	Short	January	B	March	B	−5.05	−1.05	−3.58
XNG	Natural Gas	Long	February	E	June	B	17.57	18.73	21.81
S5INFT	InfoTech	Long	March	M	July	B	9.22	10.81	15.65
UTY	Utilities	Long	March	M	October	B	9.29	7.20	11.22
XCI	Computer Tech	Long	April	M	July	M	9.42	9.89	10.50
BKX	Banking	Short	May	B	July	B	−6.42	−3.35	−7.05
XAU	Gold & Silver	Short	May	M	June	E	−7.12	−6.38	−4.54
S5MATR	Materials	Short	May	M	October	M	−6.73	−2.47	−2.74
XOI	Oil	Short	June	B	August	E	−6.65	−9.73	−13.04
XNG	Natural Gas	Short	June	M	July	E	−7.83	−7.44	−9.22
XAU	Gold & Silver	Long	July	E	December	E	8.74	−1.86	7.35
S5INDU	Industrials	Short	July	M	October	B	−4.70	−2.24	−1.06
DJT	Transports	Short	July	M	October	M	−6.25	−1.23	−0.47
BTK	Biotech	Long	August	B	March	B	21.81	11.18	4.41
S5INFT	InfoTech	Long	August	M	January	M	11.78	8.85	7.24
SOX	Semiconductor	Short	August	M	October	E	−7.51	−2.05	−7.07
BKX	Banking	Long	October	B	May	B	14.08	12.28	10.56
XBD	Broker/Dealer	Long	October	B	April	M	26.77	17.55	16.03
XCI	Computer Tech	Long	October	B	January	B	14.72	9.53	9.65
S5COND	Consumer Discretionary	Long	October	B	June	B	15.34	11.87	8.41
S5CONS	Consumer Staples	Long	October	B	June	B	8.78	8.33	5.00
S5HLTH	Healthcare	Long	October	B	May	B	9.90	10.09	7.31
S5INDU	Industrials	Long	October	E	May	M	11.63	9.08	6.09
S5MATR	Materials	Long	October	B	May	B	15.74	11.70	8.86
DRG	Pharmaceutical	Long	October	M	January	B	7.40	7.89	10.44
RMZ	Real Estate	Long	October	E	May	B	10.15	5.75	2.53
SOX	Semiconductor	Long	October	E	December	B	15.00	12.56	17.28
XTC	Telecom	Long	October	B	December	B	7.29	2.66	1.63
DJT	Transports	Long	October	B	May	B	16.88	11.71	8.50
XOI	Oil	Long	December	M	July	B	11.79	11.15	15.70

[†] *Average % Return based on full seasonality completion through April 14, 2023*

OCTOBER 2024

D 33.3
S 33.3
N 42.9

7

Today's Ponzi-style acute fragility and speculative dynamics dictate that he who panics first panics best.
— Doug Noland (Prudent Bear Funds, *Credit Bubble Bulletin*, 10/26/07)

October 2011, Second Dow Month to Gain 1000 Points

TUESDAY
D 47.6
S 42.9
N 47.6

8

Get to the Point! Blurt it out! Tell me plainly what's in it for me!
— Roy H. Williams (*The Wizard of Ads*, A reader's mental response to a poorly constructed advertisement.
Quoted in *Your Company*, 12/98)

WEDNESDAY
D 61.9
S 57.1
N 57.1

9

If there is something you really want to do, make your plan and do it. Otherwise, you'll just regret it forever.
— Richard Rocco (PostNet franchisee, *Entrepreneur* magazine 12/2006, b. 1946)

Dow Lost 18.2% (1874 points) on the Week Ending 10/10/2008 Worst Dow Week in the History of Wall Street

THURSDAY
D 47.6
S 47.6
N 52.4

10

First-rate people hire first-rate people; second-rate people hire third-rate people.
— Leo Rosten (American author, 1908–1997)

FRIDAY
D 38.1
S 47.6
N 57.1

11

People become attached to their burdens sometimes more than the burdens are attached to them.
— George Bernard Shaw (Irish dramatist, 1856–1950)

Yom Kippur

SATURDAY

12

SUNDAY

13

SECTOR INDEX SEASONALITY STRATEGY CALENDAR*

Index		Jan	Feb	Mar	Apr	May	Jun	Jul	Aug	Sep	Oct	Nov	Dec
BKX	L / S												
BTK	L / S												
S5COND & S5CONS	L / S												
S5INDU	L / S												
DJT	L / S												
DRG	S												
S5HLTH	L / S												
S5INFT	L / S												
RMZ	L / S												

* Graphic representation of the Sector Index Seasonality Percentage Plays on page 94.
L = Long Trade, S = Short Trade, ➞ = Start of Trade

(continued on page 98)

OCTOBER 2024

Columbus Day *(Bond Market Closed)*
Monday Before October Expiration, Dow Up 31 of 41

🎃 MONDAY

D 61.9
S 61.9
N 61.9

14

Complexity is the enemy of execution.
— Anthony Robbins (American author, coach, speaker, and philanthropist, b. 1960)

TUESDAY

D 52.4
S 57.1
N 57.1

15

Life is like riding a bicycle. You don't fall off unless you stop peddling.
— Claude D. Pepper (U.S. Senator Florida 1936–1951, 1900–1989)

Crash of October 19, 1987, Dow down 22.6% in One Day

🎃 WEDNESDAY

D 57.1
S 71.4
N 61.9

16

If you develop the absolute sense of certainty that powerful beliefs provide, then you can get yourself to accomplish virtually anything, including those things that other people are certain are impossible.
— Anthony Robbins (American author, coach, speaker, and philanthropist, b. 1960)

🎃 THURSDAY

D 52.4
S 61.9
N 57.1

17

At a time of war, we need you to work for peace. At a time of inequality, we need you to work for opportunity. At a time of so much cynicism and so much doubt, we need you to make us believe again.
— Barack H. Obama (44th U.S. President, Commencement Wesleyan University 5/28/2008, b. 1961)

October Expiration Day, Dow Down 6 Straight 2005–2010,
But Up 9 of Last 12

🦅 FRIDAY

D 52.4
S 57.1
N 47.6

18

Institutions tend to dump stock in a single transaction and buy, if possible, in smaller lots, gradually accumulating a position. Therefore, many more big blocks are traded on downticks than on upticks.
— Justin Mamis (Technical analyst and author, *The Mamis Letter, When To Sell*, 1929–2019)

SATURDAY

19

SUNDAY

20

(continued from page 96)

SECTOR INDEX SEASONALITY STRATEGY CALENDAR*

Index		Jan	Feb	Mar	Apr	May	Jun	Jul	Aug	Sep	Oct	Nov	Dec
S5MATR	L												
	S												
SOX	L												
	S												
UTY	L												
	S												
XAU	L												
	S												
XBD	L												
	S												
XCI	L												
	S												
XNG	L												
	S												
XOI	L												
	S												
XTC	L												
	S												

* Graphic representation of the Sector Index Seasonality Percentage Plays on page 94.
L = Long Trade, S = Short Trade, ⟶ = Start of Trade

OCTOBER 2024

Between two evils, I always pick the one I never tried before.
— Mae West (American actress and playwright, 1893–1980)

🐻 **TUESDAY**
D 28.6
S 38.1
N 33.3
22

I invest in people, not ideas; I want to see fire in the belly and intellect.
— Arthur Rock (First venture capitalist)

Late October is Time to Buy Depressed Stocks
Especially Techs and Small Caps

🐂 **WEDNESDAY**
D 61.9
S 76.2
N 71.4
23

There are many people who think they want to be matadors [or money managers or traders] only to find themselves in the ring with two thousand pounds of bull bearing down on them, and then discover that what they really wanted was to wear tight pants and hear the crowd roar.
— Terry Pearce (Founder and President of Leadership Communication, b. 1941)

🐂 **THURSDAY**
D 52.4
S 61.9
N 57.1
24

Price is a fact. Earnings are an estimate.
— Ralph Acampora (Godfather of Technical Analysis, co-founder CMT Association, Altaira Wealth Management, b. 1941)

FRIDAY
D 47.6
S 42.9
N 52.4
25

How a minority, Reaching majority, Seizing authority, Hates a minority.
— Leonard H. Robbins

SATURDAY
26

November Almanac Investor Sector Seasonalities: See Pages 94, 96 and 98

SUNDAY
27

MARKET BEHAVIOR THREE DAYS BEFORE AND THREE DAYS AFTER HOLIDAYS

The *Stock Trader's Almanac* has tracked holiday seasonality annually since the first edition in 1968. Stocks used to rise on the day before holidays and sell off the day after, but nowadays each holiday moves to its own rhythm. Eight holidays are separated into six groups. Average percent changes for the Dow, S&P 500, NASDAQ and Russell 2000 are shown.

The Dow and S&P consist of blue chips and the largest cap stocks, whereas NASDAQ represents tech stocks and the Russell 2000 would be more representative of smaller cap stocks. This is evident on the last day of the year with NASDAQ and the Russell 2000 having a field day, while their larger brethren in the Dow and S&P are showing losses on average.

Thanks to the Santa Claus Rally the three days before and after New Year's Day and Christmas are best. NASDAQ and the Russell 2000 average gains of 1.0% to 1.6% over the six-day spans. However, trading around the first day of the year has been mixed recently. Traders have been selling more the first trading day of the year, pushing gains and losses into the New Year.

Bullishness before Labor Day and after Memorial Day is often affected by strength the first day of September and June. The second worst day after a holiday is the day after Easter. Surprisingly, the following day is the best second day after a holiday, eclipsing the second day after New Year's Day.

Presidents' Day is the least bullish of all the holidays, bearish the day before and three days after. NASDAQ has dropped 22 of the last 34 days before Presidents' Day (Dow, 18 of 34; S&P 20 of 34; Russell 2000, 16 of 34).

HOLIDAYS: 3 DAYS BEFORE, 3 DAYS AFTER (Average % change 1980–May 2023)

	−3	−2	−1		+1	+2	+3
S&P 500	0.01	0.19	− 0.10	Mixed Before &	0.18	0.22	0.03
DJIA	0.004	0.13	− 0.14	Positive After	0.28	0.20	0.16
NASDAQ	0.04	0.25	0.12	New Year's Day	0.21	0.42	0.09
Russell 2K	− 0.02	0.39	0.32	1/1/24	0.03	0.22	0.10
S&P 500	0.35	− 0.04	− 0.10	Negative Before & After	− 0.21	− 0.08	− 0.09
DJIA	0.32	− 0.06	− 0.03	Presidents'	− 0.17	− 0.09	− 0.12
NASDAQ	0.54	0.18	− 0.26	Day	− 0.47	− 0.07	− 0.03
Russell 2K	0.42	0.11	− 0.01	2/19/24	− 0.38	− 0.16	− 0.03
S&P 500	0.08	0.04	0.38	Positive Before &	− 0.18	0.42	0.05
DJIA	0.06	0.02	0.30	Negative After	− 0.13	0.39	0.07
NASDAQ	0.24	0.26	0.46	Good Friday	− 0.25	0.49	0.12
Russell 2K	0.15	0.15	0.55	3/29/24	− 0.34	0.39	0.01
S&P 500	0.10	0.08	0.10	Positive Before	0.22	0.12	0.27
DJIA	0.07	0.02	0.02	& After	0.27	0.13	0.15
NASDAQ	0.18	0.26	0.19	Memorial Day	0.20	− 0.02	0.47
Russell 2K	0.09	0.27	0.21	5/27/24	0.25	0.09	0.37
S&P 500	0.20	0.13	0.12	Negative After	− 0.08	0.03	0.10
DJIA	0.17	0.10	0.12	Independence	− 0.05	0.04	0.08
NASDAQ	0.32	0.14	0.10	Day	− 0.02	− 0.10	0.28
Russell 2K	0.29	0.03	0.04	7/4/24	− 0.20	− 0.13	0.10
S&P 500	0.23	− 0.21	0.08	Positive Before	− 0.02	0.16	− 0.08
DJIA	0.20	− 0.24	0.08	& Mixed After	− 0.01	0.19	− 0.13
NASDAQ	0.43	− 0.07	0.08	Labor Day	− 0.11	0.05	0.05
Russell 2K	0.51	0.01	0.08	9/2/24	− 0.05	0.18	0.04
S&P 500	0.11	0.06	0.25	Positive Before	0.10	− 0.38	0.26
DJIA	0.14	0.07	0.21	& After	0.07	− 0.34	0.26
NASDAQ	0.01	− 0.12	0.43	Thanksgiving	0.33	− 0.36	0.10
Russell 2K	0.20	− 0.02	0.38	11/28/24	0.18	− 0.52	0.22
S&P 500	0.21	0.13	0.15	Christmas	0.29	− 0.01	0.25
DJIA	0.25	0.18	0.18	12/25/24	0.32	0.01	0.21
NASDAQ	0.03	0.26	0.32		0.27	− 0.01	0.31
Russell 2K	0.31	0.27	0.29		0.28	− 0.06	0.46

OCTOBER/NOVEMBER 2024

94th Anniversary of 1929 Crash, Dow Down 23.0% in Two Days,
October 28 and 29

The real difference between men is energy. A strong will, a settled purpose, an invincible determination,
can accomplish almost anything; and in this lies the distinction between great men and little men.
— Buckminster Fuller (American architect, author, 1895–1983)

In the end, we will remember not the words of our enemies, but the silence of our friends.
— Martin Luther King Jr. (Civil rights leader, 1964 Nobel Peace Prize, 1929–1968)

November Begins Dow and S&P "Best Six Months"
(Pages 52, 54, 56, 64 and 149)
And NASDAQ "Best Eight Months" (Pages 60, 62 and 150)

When investment decisions need to consider the speed of light, something is seriously wrong.
— Frank M. Bifulco (Senior Portfolio Manager Alcott Capital Management, *Barron's Letters to the Editor*, 5/24/2010)

Halloween

There are three principal means of acquiring knowledge…observation of nature, reflection, and
experimentation. Observation collects facts; reflection combines them; experimentation verifies the result
of that combination.
— Denis Diderot (French philosopher, edited first modern Encyclopedia in 1745, 1713–1784)

First Trading Day in November, Dow Up 10 of Last 14

In the realm of ideas, everything depends on enthusiasm; in the real world, all rests on perseverance.
— Johann Wolfgang von Goethe (German poet and polymath, 1749–1832)

Daylight Saving Time Ends

NOVEMBER ALMANAC

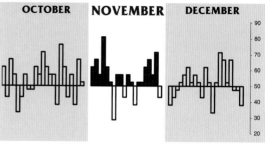

NOVEMBER							DECEMBER						
S	M	T	W	T	F	S	S	M	T	W	T	F	S
					1	2		1	2	3	4	5	6	7
3	4	5	6	7	8	9	8	9	10	11	12	13	14
10	11	12	13	14	15	16	15	16	17	18	19	20	21
17	18	19	20	21	22	23	22	23	24	25	26	27	28
24	25	26	27	28	29	30	29	30	31				

Market Probability Chart above is a graphic representation of the S&P 500 Recent Market Probability Calendar on page 126.

◆ #1 S&P and #2 Dow month since 1950, #2 on NASDAQ since 1971 (pages 52 & 60) ◆ Start of the "Best Six Months" of the year (page 54), NASDAQ's Best Eight Months and Best Three (pages 149 & 150) ◆ Simple MACD timing indicator almost triples "Best Six Months" strategy (page 56), doubles NASDAQ's Best Eight (page 62) ◆ Day before and after Thanksgiving Day combined, only 19 losses in 71 years (page 106) ◆ Week before Thanksgiving Dow up 19 of last 30, down last six ◆ Presidential election year Novembers rank #1 Dow (+2.3%), #1 S&P (+2.0%), NASDAQ #7 (+0.6%) ◆ NASDAQ down 22.9% in November 2000 (undecided election, tech bubble burst) (page 167)

November Vital Statistics

	DJIA		S&P 500		NASDAQ		Russell 1K		Russell 2K	
Rank	2		1		2		1		1	
Up	50		50		37		33		30	
Down	23		23		15		11		14	
Average % Change	1.7%		1.7%		1.9%		2.0%		2.3%	
Election Year	2.3%		2.0%		0.6%		1.8%		2.5%	
Best & Worst November										
	% Change		% Change		% Change		% Change		% Change	
Best	2020	11.8	2020	10.8	2001	14.2	2020	11.6	2020	18.3
Worst	1973	−14.0	1973	−11.4	2000	−22.9	2000	−9.3	2008	−12.0
Best & Worst November Weeks										
Best	11/28/08	9.7	11/28/08	12.0	11/28/08	10.9	11/28/08	12.5	11/28/08	16.4
Worst	11/21/08	−5.3	11/21/08	−8.4	11/10/00	−12.2	11/21/08	−8.8	11/21/08	−11.0
Best & Worst November Days										
Best	11/13/08	6.7	11/13/08	6.9	11/10/22	7.4	11/13/08	7.0	11/13/08	8.5
Worst	11/20/08	−5.6	11/20/08	−6.7	11/19/08	−6.5	11/20/08	−6.9	11/19/08	−7.9
First Trading Day of Expiration Week: 1980–2023										
Record (#Up – #Down)	23–20		19–24		16–27		21–22		18–25	
Current streak	D2		D2		D2		D2		D2	
Avg % Change	−0.03		−0.07		−0.19		−0.08		−0.08	
Options Expiration Day: 1980–2023										
Record (#Up – #Down)	27–16		25–18		23–20		25–18		25–17	
Current streak	U1		U1		U2		U1		U1	
Avg % Change	0.20		0.16		0.04		0.15		0.15	
Options Expiration Week: 1980–2023										
Record (#Up – #Down)	26–17		25–18		24–19		24–19		21–22	
Current streak	D3		D1		D1		D1		D2	
Avg % Change	0.22		0.07		0.06		0.06		−0.19	
Week After Options Expiration: 1980–2023										
Record (#Up – #Down)	25–18		27–16		28–15		27–16		26–17	
Current streak	U1		U1		U1		U1		U1	
Avg % Change	0.55		0.55		0.62		0.56		0.72	
First Trading Day Performance										
% of Time Up	64.4		64.4		65.4		72.7		63.6	
Avg % Change	0.30		0.31		0.31		0.40		0.35	
Last Trading Day Performance										
% of Time Up	54.8		52.1		61.5		45.5		63.6	
Avg % Change	0.11		0.14		−0.01		0.04		0.09	

Dow & S&P 1950–June 9, 2023, NASDAQ 1971–June 9, 2023, Russell 1K & 2K 1979–June 9, 2023.

Astute investors always smile and remember,
When stocks seasonally start soaring, and salute November.

NOVEMBER 2024

MONDAY

D 61.9
S 66.7
N 61.9

4

The future now belongs to societies that organize themselves for learning.
What we know and can do holds the key to economic progress.
— Ray Marshall (b. 1928) and Marc Tucker (b. 1939) (Thinking for a Living: Education and the Wealth of Nations, 1992)

Election Day

TUESDAY

D 61.9
S 57.1
N 57.1

5

A president is elected and tries to get rid of the dirty stuff in the economy as quickly as possible,
so that by the time the next election comes around, he looks like a hero.
The stock market is reacting to what the politicians are doing.
— Yale Hirsch (Creator of Stock Trader's Almanac, NY Times 10/10/2010, 1923–2021)

Week Before November Options Expiration, S&P 500 Up 9 of Last 14

WEDNESDAY

D 71.4
S 81.0
N 71.4

6

That's the American way. If little kids don't aspire to make money like I did, what the hell good is this country?
— Lee Iacocca (American industrialist, Former Chrysler CEO, 1924–2019)

FOMC Meeting (2 Days)

THURSDAY

D 71.4
S 61.9
N 66.7

7

New indicator: CFO Magazine gave Excellence awards to WorldCom's Scott Sullivan (1998),
Enron's Andrew Fastow (1999), and to Tyco's Mark Swartz (2000). All were subsequently indicted.
— Roger Lowenstein (Financial journalist and author, Origins Of The Crash, b. 1954)

FRIDAY

D 61.9
S 52.4
N 57.1

8

In most admired companies, key priorities are teamwork, customer focus, fair treatment of employees,
initiative, and innovation. In average companies the top priorities are minimizing risk, respecting the chain
of command, supporting the boss, and making budget.
— Bruce Pfau (Fortune)

SATURDAY

9

SUNDAY

10

TRADERS FEAST ON SMALL STOCKS THANKSGIVING THROUGH SANTA CLAUS RALLY

Welcome to the annual stock market feast and the perennial yearend rally. Thanksgiving kicks off a run of solid bullish seasonal patterns. November–January is the year's best consecutive 3-month span (Page 149). Then there's the January Effect (pages 112 & 114) of small caps outperforming large caps in January, which nowadays begins in mid-December.

And of course, the "Santa Claus Rally," (page 118) invented and named by our late founder Yale Hirsch in 1972 in the *Almanac* and often misunderstood, is the short, sweet rally that runs from the last 5 trading days of the year to the first two trading days of the New Year. Pop also coined the phrase: *"If Santa Claus should fail to call, bears may come to Broad and Wall."*

We have combined these seasonal occurrences into one trade: Buy the Tuesday before Thanksgiving and hold until the second trading day of the New Year. Our good friend and renowned technician and options guru Larry McMillan of the *Options Strategist* opened our eyes to this trade and runs it with options on iShares Russell 2000 (IWM) starting on the day before Thanksgiving.

We feature the Russell 2000 here as this trade produces a higher magnitude of returns for the small cap index with practically the same plurality of gains as the S&P. Since 1979 the Russell 2000 is up 77.3% of the time, 34 of 44 years, with an average gain of 3.2% from the Tuesday before Thanksgiving to the second trading day of the year. For comparison S&P 500 is up 79.5% of the time, 58 of 73 years, average gain 2.6% and NASDAQ is up 75.0% of the time, 39 of 52 years, average gain 2.9%.

THANKSGIVING-SANTA CLAUS RALLY TRADE

Year	Tuesday B4 Thanksgiving	Russell 2000 2nd Trading Day New Year	% Change
1979	50.00	54.11	8.22%
1980	76.92	76.28	−0.83
1981	73.94	72.78	−1.57
1982	85.36	89.08	4.36
1983	113.40	113.66	0.23
1984	101.01	101.27	0.26
1985	123.42	130.88	6.04
1986	138.49	140.76	1.64
1987	115.58	126.13	9.13
1988	139.87	148.39	6.09
1989	166.62	170.79	2.50
1990	124.13	130.35	5.01
1991	175.50	192.09	9.45
1992	210.79	220.08	4.41
1993	248.12	256.97	3.57
1994	242.26	247.65	2.22
1995	301.12	315.21	4.68
1996	351.37	361.85	2.98
1997	426.91	437.06	2.38
1998	396.60	422.09	6.43
1999	454.45	478.38	5.27
2000	466.79	484.39	3.77
2001	453.90	495.51	9.17
2002	398.32	390.31	−2.01
2003	543.18	568.92	4.74
2004	624.53	628.54	0.64
2005	682.55	689.25	0.98
2006	792.17	789.95	−0.28
2007	749.33	745.01	−0.58
2008	443.18	505.03	13.96
2009	592.58	638.49	7.75
2010	719.92	785.83	9.16
2011	696.26	747.28	7.33
2012	793.81	872.60	9.93
2013	1134.53	1156.09	1.90
2014	1186.33	1181.35	−0.42
2015	1188.81	1110.44	−6.59
2016	1334.34	1387.95	4.02
2017	1518.89	1552.58	2.22
2018	1469.01	1330.83	−9.41
2019	1624.23	1660.87	2.26
2020	1853.53	1979.11	6.78
2021	2327.86	2268.87	−2.53
2022	1860.44	1772.54	−4.72
		Average	3.19%
		Median	3.27%
		Up	34
		Down	10
		Win %	77.27%
		Avg Win	4.98%
		Avg Loss	−2.89%

Veterans' Day *(Bond Market Closed)*
Monday Before November Expiration, Dow Up 12 of Last 19, 2008 –2.6%,
2018 –2.3%

🐻 MONDAY

D 42.9
S 28.6
N 28.6

11

Never tell people how to do things. Tell them what to do and they will surprise you with their ingenuity.
— General George S. Patton, Jr. (U.S. Army field commander WWII, 1885–1945)

TUESDAY

D 42.9
S 57.1
N 61.9

12

The game is lost only when we stop trying.
— Mario Cuomo (Former NY Governor, C-Span)

Week Before Thanksgiving, Dow Up 19 of Last 30, Down Last 6
2003 –1.4%, 2004 –0.8%, 2008 –5.3%, 2011 –2.9%, 2012 –1.8%, 2018 –2.2%

WEDNESDAY

D 61.9
S 57.1
N 66.7

13

It's a lot of fun finding a country nobody knows about. The only thing better is finding a country
everybody's bullish on and shorting it.
— Jim Rogers (Financier, *Investment Biker*, b. 1942)

THURSDAY

D 42.9
S 42.9
N 38.1

14

Doubt is the father of invention.
— Galileo Galilei (Italian physicist and astronomer, 1564–1642)

November Expiration Day, Dow Up 15 of Last 21
Dow Surged in 2008, Up 494 Points (6.5%)

🐂 FRIDAY

D 66.7
S 57.1
N 52.4

15

We are humans, and as humans, we have a tendency of agreeing with each other and of trying to find further supporting
evidence for something that is thought to be correct.
— Thomas C. Südhof (German-American biochemist, 2013 Nobel Prize in Physiology or Medicine, b. 1955)

SATURDAY

16

SUNDAY

17

TRADING THE THANKSGIVING MARKET

For 35 years the "holiday spirit" gave Wednesday before Thanksgiving and Friday after a great track record, except for two occasions. Publishing it in the 1987 *Almanac* was the "kiss of death." Since 1988 Wednesday–Friday gained 19 of 35 times with a total Dow point-loss of 270.35. The best strategy appears to be coming into the week long and exiting into strength before the holiday. Omicron Covid-19 variant cancelled Thanksgiving in 2021.

DOW JONES INDUSTRIALS BEFORE AND AFTER THANKSGIVING

	Tuesday Before	Wednesday Before		Friday After	Total Gain Dow Points	Dow Close	Next Monday
1952	-0.18	1.54		1.22	2.76	283.66	0.04
1953	1.71	0.65		2.45	3.10	280.23	1.14
1954	3.27	1.89		3.16	5.05	387.79	0.72
1955	4.61	0.71		0.26	0.97	482.88	-1.92
1956	-4.49	-2.16		4.65	2.49	472.56	-2.27
1957	-9.04	10.69		3.84	14.53	449.87	-2.96
1958	-4.37	8.63		8.31	16.94	557.46	2.61
1959	2.94	1.41		1.42	2.83	652.52	6.66
1960	-3.44	1.37		4.00	5.37	606.47	-1.04
1961	-0.77	1.10		2.18	3.28	732.60	-0.61
1962	6.73	4.31		7.62	11.93	644.87	-2.81
1963	32.03	-2.52		9.52	7.00	750.52	1.39
1964	-1.68	-5.21		-0.28	-5.49	882.12	-6.69
1965	2.56	N/C		-0.78	-0.78	948.16	-1.23
1966	-3.18	1.84		6.52	8.36	803.34	-2.18
1967	13.17	3.07		3.58	6.65	877.60	4.51
1968	8.14	-3.17	**T**	8.76	5.59	985.08	-1.74
1969	-5.61	3.23	**H**	1.78	5.01	812.30	-7.26
1970	5.21	1.98		6.64	8.62	781.35	12.74
1971	-5.18	0.66	**A**	17.96	18.62	816.59	13.14
1972	8.21	7.29		4.67	11.96	1025.21	-7.45
1973	-17.76	10.08	**N**	-0.98	9.10	854.00	-29.05
1974	5.32	2.03		-0.63	1.40	618.66	-15.64
1975	9.76	3.15	**K**	2.12	5.27	860.67	-4.33
1976	-6.57	1.66		5.66	7.32	956.62	-6.57
1977	6.41	0.78	**S**	1.12	1.90	844.42	-4.85
1978	-1.56	2.95		3.12	6.07	810.12	3.72
1979	-6.05	-1.80		4.35	2.55	811.77	16.98
1980	3.93	7.00	**G**	3.66	10.66	993.34	-23.89
1981	18.45	7.90		7.80	15.70	885.94	3.04
1982	-9.01	9.01	**I**	7.36	16.37	1007.36	-4.51
1983	7.01	-0.20		1.83	1.63	1277.44	-7.62
1984	9.83	6.40		18.78	25.18	1220.30	-7.95
1985	0.12	18.92	**V**	-3.56	15.36	1472.13	-14.22
1986	6.05	4.64		-2.53	2.11	1914.23	-1.55
1987	40.45	-16.58	**I**	-36.47	-53.05	1910.48	-76.93
1988	11.73	14.58		-17.60	-3.02	2074.68	6.76
1989	7.25	17.49	**N**	18.77	36.26	2675.55	19.42
1990	-35.15	9.16		-12.13	-2.97	2527.23	5.94
1991	14.08	-16.10	**G**	-5.36	-21.46	2894.68	40.70
1992	25.66	17.56		15.94	33.50	3282.20	22.96
1993	3.92	13.41		-3.63	9.78	3683.95	-6.15
1994	-91.52	-3.36		33.64	30.28	3708.27	31.29
1995	40.46	18.06		7.23*	25.29	5048.84	22.04
1996	-19.38	-29.07		22.36*	-6.71	6521.70	N/C
1997	41.03	-14.17		28.35*	14.18	7823.13	189.98
1998	-73.12	13.13		18.80*	31.93	9333.08	-216.53
1999	-93.89	12.54		-19.26*	-6.72	10988.91	-40.99
2000	31.85	-95.18		70.91*	-24.27	10470.23	75.84
2001	-75.08	-66.70	**D**	125.03*	58.33	9959.71	23.04
2002	-172.98	255.26		-35.59*	219.67	8896.09	-33.52
2003	16.15	15.63	**A**	2.89*	18.52	9782.46	116.59
2004	3.18	27.71		1.92*	29.63	10522.23	-46.33
2005	51.15	44.66	**Y**	15.53*	60.19	10931.62	-40.90
2006	5.05	5.36		-46.78*	-41.42	12280.17	-158.46
2007	51.70	-211.10		181.84*	-29.26	12980.88	-237.44
2008	36.08	247.14		102.43*	349.57	8829.04	-679.95
2009	-17.24	30.69		-154.48*	-123.79	10309.92	34.92
2010	-142.21	150.91		-95.28*	55.63	11092.00	-39.51
2011	-53.59	-236.17		-25.77*	-261.94	11231.78	291.23
2012	-7.45	48.38		172.79*	221.17	13009.68	-42.31
2013	0.26	24.53		-10.92*	13.61	16086.41	-77.64
2014	-2.96	-2.69		15.99*	13.30	17828.24	-51.44
2015	19.51	1.20		-14.90*	-13.70	17798.49	-78.57
2016	67.18	59.31		68.96*	128.27	19152.14	-54.24
2017	160.50	-64.65		31.81*	-32.84	23557.99	22.79
2018	-551.80	-0.95		-178.74*	-179.69	24285.95	354.29
2019	55.21	42.32		-112.59*	-70.27	28051.41	-268.37
2020	454.97	-173.77		37.90*	-135.87	29910.37	-271.73
2021	194.55	-9.42		-905.04*	-914.46	34899.34	236.60
2022	397.82	95.96		152.97*	248.93	34347.03	-497.57

*Shortened trading day

NOVEMBER 2024

MONDAY
D 57.1
S 52.4
N 57.1
18

People's spending habits depend more on how wealthy they feel than with the actual amount of their current income.
— A.C. Pigou (English economist, *The Theory of Unemployment*, 1877–1959)

TUESDAY
D 33.3
S 38.1
N 38.1
19

Those who are of the opinion that money will do everything may very well be suspected to do everything for money.
— Sir George Savile (British statesman and author, 1633–1695)

Trading Thanksgiving Market: Long into Weakness Prior,
Exit into Strength (Page 106)

WEDNESDAY
D 47.6
S 52.4
N 57.1
20

A good general [or trader] plans in two ways: for an absolute victory and for absolute defeat. The one enables him to squeeze the last ounce of success out of a triumph; the other keeps a failure from turning into a catastrophe.
— Frederick Schiller Faust (AKA Max Brand, American author, *Way of the Lawless*, 1892–1944)

THURSDAY
D 57.1
S 52.4
N 61.9
21

Even being right 3 or 4 times out of 10 should yield a person a fortune, if he has the sense to cut his losses quickly on the ventures where he has been wrong.
— Bernard Baruch (Financier, speculator, statesman, presidential adviser, 1870–1965)

FRIDAY
D 66.7
S 61.9
N 61.9
22

If you are ready to give up everything else to study the whole history of the market as carefully as a medical student studies anatomy and you have the cool nerves of a great gambler, the sixth sense of a clairvoyant, and the courage of a lion, you have a ghost of a chance.
— Bernard Baruch (Financier, speculator, statesman, presidential adviser, 1870–1965)

SATURDAY
23

December Almanac Investor Sector Seasonalities: See Pages 94, 96 and 98

SUNDAY
24

AURA OF THE TRIPLE WITCH—4TH QUARTER MOST BULLISH: DOWN WEEKS TRIGGER MORE WEAKNESS WEEK AFTER

Options expire the third Friday of every month but in March, June, September and December a powerful coven gathers. Since the S&P index futures began trading on April 21, 1982, stock options, index options as well as index futures all expire at the same time four times each year—known as Triple Witching. Traders have long sought to understand and master the magic of this quarterly phenomenon.

The impact of single-stock and ETF futures on the market has thus far been subdued. Until their influence broadens, we do not believe the term "quadruple witching" is applicable just yet.

We have analyzed what the market does prior, during and following Triple Witching expirations in search of consistent trading patterns. Here are some of our findings of how the Dow Jones Industrials perform around Triple-Witching Week (TWW).

- Since 1990, TWW is most bullish in Q1 and Q4.
- Following weeks became more bearish. Since Q1 2000 only 39 of 92 were up, and 18 occurred in December, 11 in March, 6 in September, 4 in June.
- TWWs have tended to be down in flat periods and dramatically so during bear markets.
- DOWN WEEKS TEND TO FOLLOW DOWN TWWs is an interesting pattern. Since 1991, of 48 down TWWs, 29 following weeks were also down. This is surprising inasmuch as the previous decade had an exactly opposite pattern: There were 13 down TWWs then, but 12 up weeks followed them.
- TWWs in Q2 and Q3 (Worst Six Months May–October) are much weaker and the weeks following, horrendous. But in the Q1 and Q4 (Best Six Months November–April) only the week after Q1 expiration is negative.

Throughout the *Almanac* you will see notations on the performance of Mondays and Fridays of TWW as we place considerable significance on the beginnings and ends of weeks (pages 72, 78 and 143–146).

TRIPLE-WITCHING WEEK AND WEEK AFTER DOW POINT CHANGES

	Expiration Week Q1	Week After	Expiration Week Q2	Week After	Expiration Week Q3	Week After	Expiration Week Q4	Week After
1991	−6.93	−89.36	−34.98	−58.81	33.54	−13.19	20.12	167.04
1992	40.48	−44.95	−69.01	−2.94	21.35	−76.73	9.19	12.97
1993	43.76	−31.60	−10.24	−3.88	−8.38	−70.14	10.90	6.15
1994	32.95	−120.92	3.33	−139.84	58.54	−101.60	116.08	26.24
1995	38.04	65.02	86.80	75.05	96.85	−33.42	19.87	−78.76
1996	114.52	51.67	55.78	−50.60	49.94	−15.54	179.53	76.51
1997	−130.67	−64.20	14.47	−108.79	174.30	4.91	−82.01	−76.98
1998	303.91	−110.35	−122.07	231.67	100.16	133.11	81.87	314.36
1999	27.20	−81.31	365.05	−303.00	−224.80	−524.30	32.73	148.33
2000	666.41	517.49	−164.76	−44.55	−293.65	−79.63	−277.95	200.60
2001	−821.21	−318.63	−353.36	−19.05	−1369.70	611.75	224.19	101.65
2002	34.74	−179.56	−220.42	−10.53	−326.67	−284.57	77.61	−207.54
2003	662.26	−376.20	83.63	−211.70	173.27	−331.74	236.06	46.45
2004	−53.48	26.37	6.31	−44.57	−28.61	−237.22	106.70	177.20
2005	−144.69	−186.80	110.44	−325.23	−36.62	−222.35	97.01	7.68
2006	203.31	0.32	122.63	−25.46	168.66	−52.67	138.03	−102.30
2007	−165.91	370.60	215.09	−279.22	377.67	75.44	110.80	−84.78
2008	410.23	−144.92	−464.66	−496.18	−33.55	−245.31	−50.57	−63.56
2009	54.40	497.80	−259.53	−101.34	214.79	−155.01	−142.61	191.21
2010	117.29	108.38	239.57	−306.83	145.08	252.41	81.59	81.58
2011	−185.88	362.07	52.45	−69.78	516.96	−737.61	−317.87	427.61
2012	310.60	−151.89	212.97	−126.39	−13.90	−142.34	55.83	−252.73
2013	117.04	−2.08	−270.78	110.20	75.03	−192.85	465.78	257.27
2014	237.10	20.29	171.34	−95.24	292.23	−166.59	523.97	248.91
2015	378.34	−414.99	117.11	−69.27	−48.51	−69.91	−136.66	423.62
2016	388.99	−86.57	−190.18	−274.41	38.35	137.65	86.56	90.40
2017	11.64	−317.90	112.31	10.48	470.55	81.25	322.58	102.32
2018	−389.23	−1413.31	−226.05	−509.59	588.83	−285.19	−1655.14	617.03
2019	398.63	−346.55	629.52	−119.17	−284.45	−114.82	319.71	190.17
2020	−4011.64	2462.80	265.92	−855.91	−8.22	−483.46	132.68	20.82
2021	−150.67	444.91	−1189.52	1143.76	−22.84	213.12	−605.55	585.12
2022	1810.74	106.31	−1504.01	1611.90	−1329.29	−1232.01	−556.00	283.47
2023	−47.66	375.55						
Up	**22**	**14**	**18**	**6**	**18**	**8**	**23**	**25**
Down	**11**	**19**	**14**	**26**	**14**	**24**	**9**	**7**

NOVEMBER/DECEMBER 2024

MONDAY
D 76.2
S 66.7
N 71.4
25

New issues: The closest thing to a "Sure Thing" Wall Street has to offer.
— Norm Fosback (Stock Market Logic, Fosback's Fund Forecaster, New Issues Newsletter)

TUESDAY
D 61.9
S 57.1
N 57.1
26

Get inside information from the president and you will probably lose half your money.
If you get it from the chairman of the board, you will lose all your money.
— Jim Rogers (Financier, b. 1942)

WEDNESDAY
D 66.7
S 71.4
N 66.7
27

If everyone's waiting for a pullback to buy, either the market doesn't have a pullback or, if it does, you shouldn't buy into it.
— Robert J. Farrell (Farrell Advisory, Chief Market Analyst Merrill Lynch 1957–1992, b. 1932

Thanksgiving *(Market Closed)*

THURSDAY
28

For want of a nail, the shoe was lost. For want of a shoe, the horse was lost. For want of a horse, the rider was lost.
For want of a rider, the battle was lost. For want of a battle, the kingdom was lost. And all for the want of a nail!
— English proverb

(Shortened Trading Day)
Last Trading Day of November, S&P Down 16 of Last 25

FRIDAY
D 52.4
S 42.9
N 47.6
29

A generation from now, Americans may marvel at the complacency that assumed the dollar's dominance would never end.
— Floyd Norris (Chief financial correspondent, N Y Times, 2/2/07)

SATURDAY
30

SUNDAY
1

DECEMBER ALMANAC

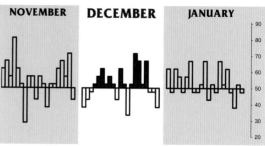

DECEMBER						
S	M	T	W	T	F	S
1	2	3	4	5	6	7
8	9	10	11	12	13	14
15	16	17	18	19	20	21
22	23	24	25	26	27	28
29	30	31				

JANUARY						
S	M	T	W	T	F	S
			1	2	3	4
5	6	7	8	9	10	11
12	13	14	15	16	17	18
19	20	21	22	23	24	25
26	27	28	29	30	31	

Market Probability Chart above is a graphic representation of the S&P 500 Recent Market Probability Calendar on page 126.

◆ #3 S&P (+1.4%) and Dow (+1.5%) month since 1950 (page 52), #3 NASDAQ (+1.5%) since 1971 ◆ 2018 worst December since 1931, Dow –8.7%, S&P –9.2%, NASDAQ –9.5% (pages 156, 162 & 166) ◆ "Free lunch" served on Wall Street before Christmas (page 116) ◆ Small caps start to outperform larger caps near middle of month (pages 112 and 114) ◆ "Santa Claus Rally" visible in graph above and on page 118 ◆ In 1998 was part of best fourth quarter since 1928 (page 180) ◆ Fourth quarter expiration week most bullish triple witching week, Dow up 23 of last 32 (page 108) ◆ Presidential election year December rankings: #2 Dow (+1.5%), #2 S&P (+1.3%) and #5 NASDAQ (+1.7%)

December Vital Statistics

	DJIA	S&P 500	NASDAQ	Russell 1K	Russell 2K
Rank	3	3	3	3	2
Up	51	54	31	33	33
Down	22	19	21	11	11
Average % Change	1.5%	1.4%	1.5%	1.3%	2.1%
Midterm Election Year	1.5%	1.3%	1.7%	1.1%	3.5%
Best & Worst December					
	% Change	% Change	% Change	% Change	% Change
Best	1991 9.5	1991 11.2	1999 22.0	1991 11.2	1999 11.2
Worst	2018 –8.7	2018 –9.2	2002 –9.7	2018 –9.3	2018 –12.0
Best & Worst December Weeks					
Best	12/2/11 7.0	12/2/11 7.4	12/8/00 10.3	12/2/11 7.4	12/2/11 10.3
Worst	12/4/87 –7.5	12/6/74 –7.1	12/15/00 –9.1	12/21/18 –7.1	12/21/18 –8.4
Best & Worst December Days					
Best	12/26/18 5.0	12/16/08 5.1	12/5/00 10.5	12/16/08 5.2	12/16/08 6.7
Worst	12/1/08 –7.7	12/1/08 –8.9	12/1/08 –9.0	12/1/08 –9.1	12/1/08 –11.9
First Trading Day of Expiration Week: 1980–2021					
Record (#Up – #Down)	25–18	25–18	20–23	25–18	19–24
Current Streak	U1	U1	U1	U1	U1
Avg % Change	0.12	0.09	–0.07	0.06	–0.21
Options Expiration Day: 1980–2021					
Record (#Up – #Down)	25–18	28–15	27–16	28–15	26–17
Current Streak	D3	D3	D3	D3	D1
Avg % Change	0.12	0.20	0.20	0.20	0.32
Options Expiration Week: 1980–2021					
Record (#Up – #Down)	31–12	29–14	24–19	28–15	22–21
Current Streak	D2	D2	D2	D2	D2
Avg % Change	0.46	0.48	0.06	0.44	0.38
Week After Options Expiration: 1980–2021					
Record (#Up – #Down)	32–10	27–16	29–14	27–16	30–13
Current Streak	U10	D1	D1	D1	D1
Avg % Change	0.83	0.59	0.76	0.62	0.96
First Trading Day Performance					
% of Time Up	46.6	47.9	57.7	47.7	47.7
Avg % Change	–0.06	–0.03	0.08	–0.05	–0.18
Last Trading Day Performance					
% of Time Up	52.1	58.9	67.3	50.0	61.4
Avg % Change	0.07	0.09	0.25	–0.06	0.32

Dow & S&P 1950–June 9, 2023, NASDAQ 1971–June 9, 2023, Russell 1K & 2K 1979–June 9, 2023.

If Santa Claus should fail to call,
Bears may come to Broad and Wall.

DECEMBER 2024

First Trading Day in December, NASDAQ Up 23 of 36, But Down 7 of Last 11   **MONDAY**

D 42.9
S 38.1
N 52.4

2

It's no coincidence that three of the top five stock option traders in a recent trading contest were all former Marines.
— Robert Prechter, Jr. (American financial author & stock market analyst, *The Elliott Wave Theorist*, b. 1949)

TUESDAY

D 38.1
S 42.9
N 47.6

3

A bank is a place where they lend you an umbrella in fair weather and ask for it back again when it begins to rain.
— Robert Frost (American poet, 1874–1963)

WEDNESDAY

D 57.1
S 47.6
N 57.1

4

Thomas Alva Edison said, "Genius is 5% inspiration and 95% perspiration!" Unfortunately, many startup "genius" entrepreneurs mistakenly switch the two percentages around, and then wonder why they can't get their projects off the ground.
— Yale Hirsch (Creator of *Stock Trader's Almanac*, 1923–2021)

THURSDAY

D 52.4
S 52.4
N 61.9

5

In a study of 3000 companies, researchers at the University of Pennsylvania found that spending 10% of revenue on capital improvements boosts productivity by 3.9%, but a similar investment in developing human capital increases productivity by 8.5%.
— John A. Byrne (Editor-in-Chief, *Fast Company Magazine*)

FRIDAY

D 66.7
S 57.1
N 52.4

6

Whenever you see a successful business, someone once made a courageous decision.
— Peter Drucker (Austrian-born pioneer management theorist, 1909–2005)

SATURDAY

7

SUNDAY

8

MOST OF THE SO-CALLED JANUARY EFFECT TAKES PLACE IN THE LAST HALF OF DECEMBER

Over the years we reported annually on the fascinating January Effect, showing that small-cap stocks handily outperformed large-cap stocks during January 40 out of 43 years between 1953 and 1995. Readers saw that "Cats and Dogs" on average quadrupled the returns of blue chips in this period. Then, the January Effect disappeared over the next four years.

Looking at the graph on page 114, comparing the Russell 1000 index of large capitalization stocks to the Russell 2000 smaller capitalization stocks, shows small cap stocks beginning to outperform the blue chips in mid-December. Narrowing the comparison down to half-month segments was an inspiration and proved to be quite revealing, as you can see in the table below.

36-YEAR AVERAGE RATES OF RETURN (DEC 1987 – FEB 2023)

Mid-Dec*	Russell 1000		Russell 2000	
	Change	Annualized	Change	Annualized
12/15-12/31	1.5%	40.6%	2.8%	88.3%
12/15-01/15	1.9	24.1	3.4	46.7
12/15-01/31	2.1	18.4	3.4	31.2
12/15-02/15	3.3	21.5	5.3	36.3
12/15-02/28	2.3	12.1	4.6	25.4
End-Dec*				
12/31-01/15	0.4	8.7	0.6	13.4
12/31-01/31	0.6	7.4	0.7	8.7
12/31-02/15	1.8	15.1	2.5	21.5
12/31-02/28	0.8	5.1	1.8	11.9

44-YEAR AVERAGE RATES OF RETURN (DEC 1979 – FEB 2023)

Mid-Dec*	Russell 1000		Russell 2000	
	Change	Annualized	Change	Annualized
12/15-12/31	1.4%	37.5%	2.6%	80.0%
12/15-01/15	2.1	26.9	3.8	53.3
12/15-01/31	2.4	21.3	3.9	36.5
12/15-02/15	3.5	22.9	5.7	39.5
12/15-02/28	2.6	13.5	5.2	28.5
End-Dec*				
12/31-01/15	0.7	15.8	1.2	28.5
12/31-01/31	1.0	12.7	1.4	18.2
12/31-02/15	2.1	17.8	3.1	27.2
12/31-02/28	1.2	7.8	2.6	17.6

* Mid-month dates are the 11th trading day of the month, month end dates are monthly closes.

Small-cap strength in the last half of December became even more magnified after the 1987 market crash. Note the dramatic shift in gains in the last half of December during the 36-year period starting in 1987, versus the 44 years from 1979 to 2023. With all the beaten down small stocks being dumped for tax loss purposes, it generally pays to get a head start on the January Effect in mid-December. You don't have to wait until December either; the small-cap sector often begins to turn around near the beginning of November.

Small Cap Strength Starts in Mid-December (Pages 112 and 114)

MONDAY

D 61.9
S 61.9
N 66.7

9

Fortune favors the brave.
— Virgil (Roman Poet, *Aeneid*, 70–19 BCE)

TUESDAY

D 47.6
S 52.4
N 57.1

10

The average man desires to be told specifically which particular stock to buy or sell. He wants to get something for nothing. He does not wish to work.
— William LeFevre (Senior analyst Ehrenkrantz King Nussbaum, 1928–1997)

WEDNESDAY

D 57.1
S 57.1
N 52.4

11

Wall Street's graveyards are filled with men who were right too soon.
— William Peter Hamilton (Editor, *Wall Street Journal*, *The Stock Market Barometer*, 1922, 1867–1929)

THURSDAY

D 61.9
S 52.4
N 47.6

12

Major bottoms are usually made when analysts cut their earnings estimates and companies report earnings which are below expectations.
— Edward Babbitt, Jr. (Avatar Associates)

FRIDAY

D 47.6
S 42.9
N 47.6

13

I'm always turned off by an overly optimistic letter from the president in the annual report. If his letter is mildly pessimistic to me, that's a good sign.
— Philip Carret (Centenarian, Founded Pioneer Fund in 1928, 1896–1998)

SATURDAY

14

SUNDAY

15

JANUARY EFFECT NOW STARTS IN MID-DECEMBER

Small-cap stocks tend to outperform big caps in January. Known as the "January Effect," the tendency is clearly revealed by the graph below. Daily data for the Russell 2000 index of smaller companies are divided by the Russell 1000 index of largest companies since July 1, 1979, and then compressed into a single year to show an idealized yearly pattern. When the graph is descending, big blue chips are outperforming smaller companies; when the graph is rising, smaller companies are moving up faster than their larger brethren.

In a typical year the smaller fry stay on the sidelines while the big boys are on the field. Then, around early November, small stocks begin to wake up and in mid-December, they take off. Anticipated year-end dividends, payouts and bonuses could be a factor. Other major moves are quite evident just before Labor Day—possibly because individual investors are back from vacations. Small caps tend to hold the lead through mid-June, though the bulk of the move is complete by early March.

RUSSELL 2000/RUSSELL 1000 ONE-YEAR SEASONAL PATTERN

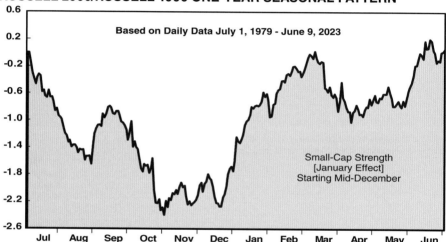

The bottom graph shows the actual ratio of the Russell 2000 divided by the Russell 1000 from 1979. Smaller companies had the upper hand for five years into 1983 as the last major bear trend wound to a close and the nascent bull market logged its first year. After falling behind for about eight years, they came back after the Persian Gulf War bottom in 1990, moving up until 1994 when big caps ruled the latter stages of the millennial bull. For six years the picture was bleak for small fry as the blue chips and tech stocks moved to stratospheric PE ratios. Small caps spiked in late 2020 and early 2021 and have been in retreat since. Note how the small cap advantage has waned during major bull moves and intensified during periods of uncertainty as traders may begin bargain hunting early.

RUSSELL 2000/RUSSELL 1000 (1979 – MAY 2023)

DECEMBER 2024

Monday Before December Triple Witching S&P Up 14 of Last 23, 2018 Down 2.1% **MONDAY**

D 61.9
S 61.9
N 61.9

16

Iron rusts from disuse; stagnant water loses its purity and in cold weather becomes frozen; even so does inaction sap the vigor of the mind.
— Leonardo da Vinci (Italian Renaissance polymath, 1452–1519)

TUESDAY

D 42.9
S 52.4
N 52.4

17

Follow the course opposite to custom and you will almost always do well.
— Jean-Jacques Rousseau (Swiss philosopher, 1712–1778)

December Triple Witching Week, S&P Up 28 of Last 39, 2018 Down 7.1% **WEDNESDAY**
FOMC Meeting (2 Days)

D 28.6
S 33.3
N 33.3

18

The difference between life and the movies is that a script has to make sense, and life doesn't.
— Joseph L. Mankiewicz (Film director, writer, producer, 1909–1993)

THURSDAY

D 52.4
S 52.4
N 47.6

19

History shows that once the United States fully recognizes an economic problem and thereby places all its efforts on solving it, the problem is about to be solved by natural forces.
— James L. Fraser (Investment counselor, writer, editor, publisher, CFA, *Contrary Investor*, 1930–2013)

December Triple Witching Day, S&P Up 26 of Last 41, 2018 -2.1% **FRIDAY**

D 71.4
S 71.4
N 71.4

20

I was in search of a one-armed economist so that the guy could never make a statement and then say: "on the other hand."
— Harry S. Truman (33rd U.S. President, 1884–1972)

The Only FREE LUNCH on Wall Street is Served (Page 116) **SATURDAY**
Almanac Investors Emailed Alert Before the Open, Monday (See Insert)

21

SUNDAY

22

WALL STREET'S ONLY "FREE LUNCH" SERVED BEFORE CHRISTMAS

Investors tend to get rid of their losers near year-end for tax purposes, often hammering these stocks down to bargain levels. Over the years, the *Almanac* has shown that NYSE stocks selling at their lows on December 15 will usually outperform the market by February 15 in the following year. Preferred stocks, closed-end funds, splits and new issues are eliminated.

BARGAIN STOCKS VS. THE MARKET*

Short Span* Late Dec–Jan/Feb	New Lows Late Dec	% Change Jan/Feb	% Change NYSE Composite	Bargain Stocks Advantage
1974–75	112	48.9%	22.1%	26.8%
1975–76	21	34.9	14.9	20.0
1976–77	2	1.3	–3.3	4.6
1977–78	15	2.8	–4.5	7.3
1978–79	43	11.8	3.9	7.9
1979–80	5	9.3	6.1	3.2
1980–81	14	7.1	–2.0	9.1
1981–82	21	–2.6	–7.4	4.8
1982–83	4	33.0	9.7	23.3
1983–84	13	–3.2	–3.8	0.6
1984–85	32	19.0	12.1	6.9
1985–86	4	–22.5	3.9	–26.4
1986–87	22	9.3	12.5	–3.2
1987–88	23	13.2	6.8	6.4
1988–89	14	30.0	6.4	23.6
1989–90	25	–3.1	–4.8	1.7
1990–91	18	18.8	12.6	6.2
1991–92	23	51.1	7.7	43.4
1992–93	9	8.7	0.6	8.1
1993–94	10	–1.4	2.0	–3.4
1994–95	25	14.6	5.7	8.9
1995–96	5	–11.3	4.5	–15.8
1996–97	16	13.9	11.2	2.7
1997–98	29	9.9	5.7	4.2
1998–99	40	–2.8	4.3	–7.1
1999–00	26	8.9	–5.4	14.3
2000–01	51	44.4	0.1	44.3
2001–02	12	31.4	–2.3	33.7
2002–03	33	28.7	3.9	24.8
2003–04	15	16.7	2.3	14.4
2004–05	36	6.8	–2.8	9.6
2005–06	71	12.0	2.6	9.4
2006–07	43	5.1	–0.5	5.6
2007–08	71	–3.2	–9.4	6.2
2008–09	88	11.4	–2.4	13.8
2009–10	25	1.8	–3.0	4.8
2010–11	20	8.3	3.4	4.9
2011–12	65	18.1	6.1	12.0
2012–13	17	20.9	3.4	17.5
2013–14	18	25.7	1.7	24.0
2014–15	17	0.2	–0.4	0.6
2015–16	38	–9.2	5.6	–14.8
2016–17	19	2.8	0.6	2.2
2017–18	18	3.3	1.2	2.1
2018–19	23	24.9	15.1	9.8
2019–20	13	–1.1	–0.3	–0.7
2020–21	3	–4.9	3.6	–8.5
2021–22	26	–1.5	–0.02	–1.5
2022–23	38	–0.3	3.7	–4.0
49-Year Totals		**542.0%**	**153.6%**	**388.3%**
Average		**11.1%**	**3.1%**	**7.9%**

* Dec 15–Feb 15 (1974–1999), Dec 1999–2023 based on actual newsletter portfolio

In response to changing market conditions we tweaked the strategy the last 24 years adding selections from NASDAQ and AMEX, and selling sooner in some years. We email the list of stocks to our *Almanac Investor* subscribers. Visit *www.stocktradersalmanac.com* or see the insert for additional details and a special offer for new subscribers.

We have come to the conclusion that the most prudent course of action is to compile our list from the stocks making new lows on Triple-Witching Friday before Christmas, capitalizing on the Santa Claus Rally (page 118). This also gives us the weekend to evaluate the issues in greater depth and weed out any glaringly problematic stocks. *Almanac Investor* subscribers will receive the list of stocks selected from the new lows made on December 15, 2023, and December 20, 2024, via email.

This "Free Lunch" strategy is an extremely short-term strategy reserved for the nimblest traders. It has performed better after market corrections and when there are more new lows to choose from. The object is to buy bargain stocks near their 52-week lows and sell any quick, generous gains, as these issues can be real dogs.

Week After December Triple Witching Dow Up 25 of Last 32, Average Gain 0.9% Since 1991

🐂 MONDAY

D 66.7
S 66.7
N 57.1

23

Never attribute to malevolence what is merely due to incompetence.
— Arthur C. Clarke (British sci-fi writer, *3001: The Final Odyssey*, 1917–2008)

(Shortened Trading Day)
Santa Claus Rally Begins December 24 *(Page 118)* Last Trading Day Before Christmas, NASDAQ Up 12 of Last 16, 2018 Down 2.2%

TUESDAY

D 47.6
S 52.4
N 66.7

24

If you can ever buy with a P/E equivalent to growth, that's a good starting point.
— Alan Lowenstein (co-portfolio manager, John Hancock Technology Fund, *TheStreet.com* 3/12/2001)

Christmas Day *(Market Closed)*

WEDNESDAY

25

There is one thing stronger than all the armies in the world, and this is an idea whose time has come.
— Victor Hugo (French novelist, playwright, *Hunchback of Notre Dame* and *Les Misérables*, 1802–1885)

Chanukah

🐂 THURSDAY

D 71.4
S 66.7
N 61.9

26

The investor who concentrated on the 50 stocks in the S&P 500 that are followed by the fewest Wall Street analysts wound up with a rousing 24.6% gain in [2006 versus] 13.6% [for] the S&P 500.
— Rich Bernstein (Chief Investment Strategist, Merrill Lynch, *Barron's* 1/8/07)

FRIDAY

D 42.9
S 47.6
N 38.1

27

It was never my thinking that made the big money for me. It was always my sitting. Got that? My sitting tight!
— Jesse Livermore (Early 20th century stock trader & speculator, *How to Trade in Stocks*, 1877–1940)

SATURDAY

28

January Almanac Investor Sector Seasonalities: See Pages 94, 96 and 98

SUNDAY

29

IF SANTA CLAUS SHOULD FAIL TO CALL, BEARS MAY COME TO BROAD AND WALL

Santa Claus tends to come to Wall Street nearly every year, bringing a short, sweet, respectable rally within the last five days of the year and the first two in January. This has been good for an average 1.3% gain since 1969 (1.3% since 1950). Santa's failure to show tends to precede bear markets, or times stocks could be purchased later in the year at much lower prices. We discovered this phenomenon in 1972. See page 20 for more.

DAILY % CHANGE IN S&P 500 AT YEAR-END

	Trading Days Before Year-End						First Days in January			Rally %
	6	5	4	3	2	1	1	2	3	Change
1969	−0.4	1.1	0.8	−0.7	0.4	0.5	1.0	0.5	−0.7	3.6
1970	0.1	0.6	0.5	1.1	0.2	−0.1	−1.1	0.7	0.6	1.9
1971	−0.4	0.2	1.0	0.3	−0.4	0.3	−0.4	0.4	1.0	1.3
1972	−0.3	−0.7	0.6	0.4	0.5	1.0	0.9	0.4	−0.1	3.1
1973	−1.1	−0.7	3.1	2.1	−0.2	0.01	0.1	2.2	−0.9	6.7
1974	−1.4	1.4	0.8	−0.4	0.03	2.1	2.4	0.7	0.5	7.2
1975	0.7	0.8	0.9	−0.1	−0.4	0.5	0.8	1.8	1.0	4.3
1976	0.1	1.2	0.7	−0.4	0.5	0.5	−0.4	−1.2	−0.9	0.8
1977	0.8	0.9	N/C	0.1	0.2	0.2	−1.3	−0.3	−0.8	−0.3
1978	0.03	1.7	1.3	−0.9	−0.4	−0.2	0.6	1.1	0.8	3.3
1979	−0.6	0.1	0.1	0.2	−0.1	0.1	−2.0	−0.5	1.2	−2.2
1980	−0.4	0.4	0.5	−1.1	0.2	0.3	0.4	1.2	0.1	2.0
1981	−0.5	0.2	−0.2	−0.5	0.5	0.2	0.2	−2.2	−0.7	−1.8
1982	0.6	1.8	−1.0	0.3	−0.7	0.2	−1.6	2.2	0.4	1.2
1983	−0.2	−0.03	0.9	0.3	−0.2	0.05	−0.5	1.7	1.2	2.1
1984	−0.5	0.8	−0.2	−0.4	0.3	0.6	−1.1	−0.5	−0.5	−0.6
1985	−1.1	−0.7	0.2	0.9	0.5	0.3	−0.8	0.6	−0.1	1.1
1986	−1.0	0.2	0.1	−0.9	−0.5	−0.5	1.8	2.3	0.2	2.4
1987	1.3	−0.5	−2.6	−0.4	1.3	−0.3	3.6	1.1	0.1	2.2
1988	−0.2	0.3	−0.4	0.1	0.8	−0.6	−0.9	1.5	0.2	0.9
1989	0.6	0.8	−0.2	0.6	0.5	0.8	1.8	−0.3	−0.9	4.1
1990	0.5	−0.6	0.3	−0.8	0.1	0.5	−1.1	−1.4	−0.3	−3.0
1991	2.5	0.6	1.4	0.4	2.1	0.5	0.04	0.5	−0.3	5.7
1992	−0.3	0.2	−0.1	−0.3	0.2	−0.7	−0.1	−0.2	0.04	−1.1
1993	0.01	0.7	0.1	−0.1	−0.4	−0.5	−0.2	0.3	0.1	−0.1
1994	0.01	0.2	0.4	−0.3	0.1	−0.4	−0.03	0.3	−0.1	0.2
1995	0.8	0.2	0.4	0.04	−0.1	0.3	0.8	0.1	−0.6	1.8
1996	−0.3	0.5	0.6	0.1	−0.4	−1.7	−0.5	1.5	−0.1	0.1
1997	−1.5	−0.7	0.4	1.8	1.8	−0.04	0.5	0.2	−1.1	4.0
1998	2.1	−0.2	−0.1	1.3	−0.8	−0.2	−0.1	1.4	2.2	1.3
1999	1.6	−0.1	0.04	0.4	0.1	0.3	−1.0	−3.8	0.2	−4.0
2000	0.8	2.4	0.7	1.0	0.4	−1.0	−2.8	5.0	−1.1	5.7
2001	0.4	−0.02	0.4	0.7	0.3	−1.1	0.6	0.9	0.6	1.8
2002	0.2	−0.5	−0.3	−1.6	0.5	0.05	3.3	−0.05	2.2	1.2
2003	0.3	−0.2	0.2	1.2	0.01	0.2	−0.3	1.2	0.1	2.4
2004	0.1	−0.4	0.7	−0.01	0.01	−0.1	−0.8	−1.2	−0.4	−1.8
2005	0.4	0.04	−1.0	0.1	−0.3	−0.5	1.6	0.4	0.002	0.4
2006	−0.4	−0.5	0.4	0.7	−0.1	−0.5	−0.1	0.1	−0.6	0.003
2007	1.7	0.8	0.1	−1.4	0.1	−0.7	−1.4	N/C	−2.5	−2.5
2008	−1.0	0.6	0.5	−0.4	2.4	1.4	3.2	−0.5	0.8	7.4
2009	0.2	0.5	0.1	−0.1	0.02	−1.0	1.6	0.3	0.05	1.4
2010	−0.2	0.1	0.1	0.1	−0.2	−0.02	1.1	−0.1	0.5	1.1
2011	0.8	0.9	0.01	−1.3	1.1	−0.4	1.6	0.02	0.3	1.9
2012	−0.9	−0.2	−0.5	−0.1	−1.1	1.7	2.5	−0.2	0.5	2.0
2013	0.5	0.3	0.5	−0.03	−0.02	0.4	−0.9	−0.03	−0.3	0.2
2014	0.2	−0.01	0.3	0.1	−0.5	−1.0	−0.03	−1.8	−0.9	−3.0
2015	1.2	−0.2	−0.2	−1.2	−1.7	−0.9	−1.5	0.2	−1.3	−2.3
2016	−0.2	0.1	0.2	−0.8	−0.03	−0.5	0.9	0.6	−0.1	0.4
2017	0.2	−0.05	−0.1	0.1	0.2	−0.5	0.8	0.6	0.4	1.1
2018	−2.1	−2.7	5.0	0.9	−0.1	0.9	0.1	−2.5	3.4	1.3
2019	0.1	−0.02	0.5	0.003	−0.6	0.3	0.8	−0.7	0.4	0.3
2020	0.1	0.4	0.9	−0.2	0.1	0.6	−1.5	0.7	0.6	1.0
2021	0.6	1.4	−0.1	0.1	−0.3	−0.3	0.6	−0.1	−1.9	1.4
2022	−1.4	0.6	−0.4	−1.2	1.7	−0.3	−0.4	0.8	−1.2	0.8
Avg	0.06	0.26	0.34	0.04	0.16	0.01	0.20	0.30	0.02	1.3

The couplet above was certainly on the mark in 1999, as the period suffered a horrendous 4.0% loss. On January 14, 2000, the Dow started its 33-month 37.8% slide to the October 2002 midterm election year bottom. NASDAQ cracked eight weeks later falling 37.3% in 10 weeks, eventually dropping 77.9% by October 2002. Energy prices and Middle East terror woes may have grounded Santa in 2004. In 2007 the fourth worst reading since 1950 was recorded as a full-blown financial crisis led to the second worst bear market in history. In 2016, the period was hit again as global growth concerns escalated and the market digested the first interest rate hike in nearly a decade.

DECEMBER/JANUARY 2025

MONDAY

D 42.9
S 47.6
N 42.9

30

It is impossible to produce superior performance unless you do something different from the majority.
— Sir John Templeton (Founder Templeton Funds, philanthropist, 1912–2008)

Last Trading Day of the Year, NASDAQ Down 17 of last 23
NASDAQ Was Up 29 Years in a Row 1971–1999

🐻 **TUESDAY**

D 42.9
S 38.1
N 28.6

31

In the realm of ideas, everything depends on enthusiasm; in the real world, all rests on perseverance.
— Johann Wolfgang von Goethe (German poet and polymath, 1749–1832)

New Year's Day *(Market Closed)*

WEDNESDAY

1

Education is our passport to the future, for tomorrow belongs only to the people who prepare for it today.
— Malcom X (Minister, human rights activist and civil rights leader, 1925–1965)

First Trading Day of Year NASDAQ Up 18 of Last 26

🐂 **THURSDAY**

D 71.4
S 61.9
N 71.4

2

The authority of a thousand is not worth the humble reasoning of a single individual.
— Galileo Galilei (Italian physicist and astronomer, 1564–1642)

Second Trading Day of the Year, Dow Up 21 of Last 30
Santa Claus Rally Ends (Page 118)

FRIDAY

D 61.9
S 47.6
N 42.9

3

Buy a stock the way you would buy a house. Understand and like it such that you'd be content to own it in the absence of any market.
— Warren Buffett (CEO Berkshire Hathaway, investor and philanthropist, b. 1930)

SATURDAY

4

SUNDAY

5

2025 STRATEGY CALENDAR

(Option expiration dates circled)

	MONDAY	TUESDAY	WEDNESDAY	THURSDAY	FRIDAY	SATURDAY	SUNDAY
JANUARY	30	31	1 JANUARY New Year's Day	2	3	4	5
	6	7	8	9	10	11	12
	13	14	15	16	(17)	18	19
	20 Martin Luther King Jr. Day	21	22	23	24	25	26
	27	28	29	30	31	1 FEBRUARY	2
FEBRUARY	3	4	5	6	7	8	9
	10	11	12	13	14 ♥	15	16
	17 Presidents' Day	18	19	20	(21)	22	23
	24	25	26	27	28	1 MARCH	2
MARCH	3	4	5 Ash Wednesday	6	7	8	9 Daylight Saving Time Begins
	10	11	12	13	14	15	16
	17 ♣ St. Patrick's Day	18	19	20	(21)	22	23
	24	25	26	27	28	29	30
	31	1 APRIL	2	3	4	5	6
APRIL	7	8	9	10	11	12	13 Passover
	14	15 Tax Deadline	16	(17)	18 Good Friday	19	20 Easter
	21	22	23	24	25	26	27
	28	29	30	1 MAY	2	3	4
MAY	5	6	7	8	9	10	11 Mother's Day
	12	13	14	15	(16)	17	18
	19	20	21	22	23	24	25
	26 Memorial Day	27	28	29	30	31	1 JUNE
JUNE	2	3	4	5	6	7	8
	9	10	11	12	13	14	15 Father's Day
	16	17	18	19 Juneteenth	(20)	21	22
	23	24	25	26	27	28	29
	30	1 JULY	2	3	4 Independence Day	5	6

Market closed on shaded weekdays; closes early when half-shaded.

2025 STRATEGY CALENDAR

(Option expiration dates circled)

MONDAY	TUESDAY	WEDNESDAY	THURSDAY	FRIDAY	SATURDAY	SUNDAY	
7	8	9	10	11	12	13	JULY
14	15	16	17	(18)	19	20	
21	22	23	24	25	26	27	
28	29	30	31	1 AUGUST	2	3	
4	5	6	7	8	9	10	AUGUST
11	12	13	14	(15)	16	17	
18	19	20	21	22	23	24	
25	26	27	28	29	30	31	
1 SEPTEMBER Labor Day	2	3	4	5	6	7	SEPTEMBER
8	9	10	11	12	13	14	
15	16	17	18	(19)	20	21	
22	23 Rosh Hashanah	24	25	26	27	28	
29	30	1 OCTOBER	2 Yom Kippur	3	4	5	OCTOBER
6	7	8	9	10	11	12	
13 Columbus Day	14	15	16	(17)	18	19	
20	21	22	23	24	25	26	
27	28	29	30	31	1 NOVEMBER	2 Daylight Saving Time Ends	
3	4 Election Day	5	6	7	8	9	NOVEMBER
10	11 Veterans' Day	12	13	14	15	16	
17	18	19	20	(21)	22	23	
24	25	26	27 Thanksgiving Day	28	29	30	
1 DECEMBER	2	3	4	5	6	7	DECEMBER
8	9	10	11	12	13	14	
15 Chanukah	16	17	18	(19)	20	21	
22	23	24	25 Christmas	26	27	28	
29	30	31	1 JANUARY New Year's Day	2	3	4	

DIRECTORY OF TRADING PATTERNS AND DATABANK

CONTENTS

DOW JONES INDUSTRIALS MARKET PROBABILITY CALENDAR 2024

THE % CHANCE OF THE MARKET RISING ON ANY TRADING DAY OF THE YEAR*

(Based on the number of times the DJIA rose on a particular trading day during **January 1954–December 2022**)

Date	Jan	Feb	Mar	Apr	May	Jun	Jul	Aug	Sep	Oct	Nov	Dec
1	H	62.3	65.2	59.4	55.1	S	66.7	42.0	S	49.3	62.3	S
2	59.4	55.1	S	62.3	63.8	S	56.5	46.4	H	55.1	S	44.9
3	71.0	S	S	50.7	53.6	60.9	60.9	S	56.5	56.5	S	52.2
4	49.3	S	59.4	59.4	S	55.1	H	S	60.9	60.9	53.6	60.9
5	56.5	43.5	58.0	50.7	S	50.7	56.5	50.7	59.4	S	66.7	58.0
6	S	56.5	47.8	S	46.4	60.9	S	52.2	43.5	S	59.4	52.2
7	S	47.8	44.9	S	49.3	55.1	S	56.5	S	43.5	52.2	S
8	46.4	43.5	52.2	62.3	53.6	S	59.4	47.8	S	50.7	63.8	S
9	49.3	47.8	S	60.9	46.4	S	56.5	44.9	47.8	44.9	S	47.8
10	49.3	S	S	59.4	50.7	47.8	52.2	S	46.4	42.0	S	52.2
11	47.8	S	62.3	56.5	S	36.2	46.4	S	60.9	49.3	52.2	59.4
12	55.1	60.9	50.7	69.6	S	52.2	68.1	46.4	60.9	S	53.6	46.4
13	S	46.4	55.1	S	44.9	58.0	S	49.3	49.3	S	49.3	49.3
14	S	50.7	53.6	S	55.1	55.1	S	65.2	S	58.0	47.8	S
15	H	58.0	62.3	62.3	56.5	S	53.6	58.0	S	52.2	59.4	S
16	53.6	44.9	S	58.0	46.4	S	44.9	52.2	55.1	53.6	S	50.7
17	60.9	S	S	53.6	49.3	50.7	50.7	S	56.5	44.9	S	53.6
18	42.0	S	60.9	53.6	S	50.7	55.1	S	42.0	59.4	52.2	46.4
19	39.1	H	58.0	56.5	S	H	40.6	47.8	49.3	S	46.4	53.6
20	S	46.4	53.6	S	43.5	49.3	S	53.6	44.9	S	49.3	59.4
21	S	47.8	36.2	S	49.3	44.9	S	58.0	S	53.6	65.2	S
22	40.6	53.6	52.2	50.7	43.5	S	49.3	49.3	S	44.9	62.3	S
23	55.1	39.1	S	53.6	37.7	S	46.4	53.6	37.7	43.5	S	53.6
24	47.8	S	S	50.7	53.6	37.7	44.9	S	47.8	50.7	S	59.4
25	56.5	S	49.3	58.0	S	47.8	60.9	S	53.6	31.9	66.7	H
26	56.5	46.4	53.6	56.5	S	44.9	52.2	50.7	52.2	S	58.0	72.5
27	S	60.9	46.4	S	H	56.5	S	44.9	49.3	S	55.1	49.3
28	S	46.4	42.0	S	46.4	55.1	S	63.8	S	55.1	H	S
29	47.8	46.4	46.4	H	52.2	46.4	S	46.4	40.6	S	52.2	S
30	59.4		S	47.8	58.0	S	56.5	58.0	42.0	60.9	S	53.6
31	55.1		S		53.6		49.3	S		52.2		52.2

* See new trends developing on pages 72, 86, 143–148

RECENT DOW JONES INDUSTRIALS MARKET PROBABILITY CALENDAR 2024

THE % CHANCE OF THE MARKET RISING ON ANY TRADING DAY OF THE YEAR*
(Based on the number of times the DJIA rose on a particular trading day during **January 2002–December 2022****)

Date	Jan	Feb	Mar	Apr	May	Jun	Jul	Aug	Sep	Oct	Nov	Dec
1	H	81.0	61.9	66.7	57.1	S	76.2	33.3	S	57.1	61.9	S
2	71.4	52.4	S	76.2	71.4	S	38.1	47.6	H	38.1	S	42.9
3	61.9	S	S	42.9	47.6	71.4	61.9	S	42.9	66.7	S	38.1
4	52.4	S	33.3	61.9	S	61.9	H	S	71.4	61.9	61.9	57.1
5	52.4	47.6	52.4	47.6	S	38.1	61.9	57.1	57.1	S	61.9	52.4
6	S	61.9	42.9	S	38.1	66.7	S	52.4	47.6	S	71.4	66.7
7	S	52.4	47.6	S	61.9	61.9	S	57.1	S	33.3	71.4	S
8	38.1	52.4	42.9	61.9	66.7	S	52.4	57.1	S	47.6	61.9	S
9	52.4	57.1	S	47.6	38.1	S	57.1	42.9	57.1	61.9	S	61.9
10	57.1	S	S	52.4	57.1	66.7	47.6	S	61.9	47.6	S	47.6
11	47.6	S	66.7	52.4	S	38.1	71.4	S	76.2	38.1	42.9	57.1
12	47.6	52.4	52.4	66.7	S	38.1	71.4	33.3	66.7	S	42.9	61.9
13	S	57.1	52.4	S	33.3	57.1	S	52.4	57.1	S	61.9	47.6
14	S	52.4	71.4	S	57.1	52.4	S	66.7	S	61.9	42.9	S
15	H	66.7	71.4	57.1	61.9	S	61.9	61.9	S	52.4	66.7	S
16	47.6	61.9	S	61.9	52.4	S	42.9	52.4	61.9	57.1	S	61.9
17	57.1	S	S	52.4	33.3	57.1	61.9	S	76.2	52.4	S	42.9
18	42.9	S	57.1	57.1	S	57.1	76.2	S	47.6	52.4	57.1	28.6
19	42.9	H	66.7	61.9	S	H	23.8	66.7	52.4	S	33.3	52.4
20	S	42.9	57.1	S	33.3	47.6	S	47.6	42.9	S	47.6	71.4
21	S	38.1	33.3	S	42.9	47.6	S	57.1	S	52.4	57.1	S
22	33.3	42.9	61.9	61.9	38.1	S	47.6	52.4	S	28.6	66.7	S
23	47.6	47.6	S	61.9	57.1	S	52.4	57.1	28.6	61.9	S	66.7
24	47.6	S	S	47.6	47.6	33.3	38.1	S	38.1	52.4	S	47.6
25	52.4	S	47.6	57.1	S	42.9	61.9	S	52.4	47.6	76.2	H
26	57.1	52.4	47.6	66.7	S	47.6	47.6	52.4	66.7	S	61.9	71.4
27	S	57.1	61.9	S	H	57.1	S	42.9	52.4	S	66.7	42.9
28	S	47.6	38.1	S	61.9	52.4	S	85.7	S	66.7	H	S
29	47.6	28.6	H	66.7	52.4	S	47.6	38.1	S	47.6	52.4	S
30	47.6		S	28.6	66.7	S	42.9	47.6	38.1	66.7	S	42.9
31	42.9		S		33.3		38.1	S		47.6		42.9

See new trends developing on pages 72, 86, 143–148   ** *Based on most recent 21-year period*

S&P 500 MARKET PROBABILITY CALENDAR 2024

THE % CHANCE OF THE MARKET RISING ON ANY TRADING DAY OF THE YEAR*

(Based on the number of times the S&P 500 rose on a particular trading day during **January 1954–December 2022**)

Date	Jan	Feb	Mar	Apr	May	Jun	Jul	Aug	Sep	Oct	Nov	Dec
1	H	62.3	62.3	63.8	58.0	S	73.9	44.9	S	50.7	62.3	S
2	50.7	59.4	S	63.8	65.2	S	56.5	46.4	H	62.3	S	44.9
3	66.7	S	S	52.2	55.1	56.5	56.5	S	59.4	58.0	S	50.7
4	53.6	S	56.5	56.5	S	63.8	H	S	53.6	60.9	58.0	58.0
5	52.2	49.3	60.9	52.2	S	52.2	59.4	50.7	58.0	S	66.7	56.5
6	S	53.6	46.4	S	43.5	58.0	S	53.6	44.9	S	59.4	46.4
7	S	49.3	46.4	S	47.8	47.8	S	56.5	S	44.9	49.3	S
8	46.4	47.8	53.6	63.8	50.7	S	59.4	46.4	S	47.8	60.9	S
9	52.2	44.9	S	60.9	49.3	S	56.5	50.7	47.8	42.0	S	52.2
10	55.1	S	S	53.6	52.2	47.8	53.6	S	53.6	46.4	S	53.6
11	53.6	S	62.3	52.2	S	39.1	52.2	S	60.9	50.7	55.1	50.7
12	56.5	60.9	50.7	60.9	S	53.6	72.5	46.4	65.2	S	56.5	47.8
13	S	55.1	62.3	S	43.5	60.9	S	47.8	50.7	S	49.3	42.0
14	S	49.3	43.5	S	52.2	56.5	S	63.8	S	53.6	49.3	S
15	H	56.5	60.9	60.9	55.1	S	52.2	63.8	S	52.2	52.2	S
16	60.9	40.6	S	60.9	50.7	S	43.5	56.5	53.6	59.4	S	50.7
17	59.4	S	S	52.2	50.7	56.5	47.8	S	55.1	44.9	S	56.5
18	50.7	S	62.3	53.6	S	49.3	55.1	S	47.8	63.8	50.7	43.5
19	49.3	H	56.5	52.2	S	H	40.6	53.6	52.2	S	49.3	46.4
20	S	49.3	50.7	S	39.1	55.1	S	53.6	44.9	S	53.6	56.5
21	S	40.6	49.3	S	46.4	44.9	S	60.9	S	53.6	60.9	S
22	47.8	46.4	44.9	55.1	50.7	S	43.5	46.4	S	46.4	62.3	S
23	60.9	40.6	S	47.8	44.9	S	47.8	52.2	34.8	44.9	S	50.7
24	59.4	S	S	49.3	53.6	36.2	46.4	S	46.4	47.8	S	59.4
25	55.1	S	50.7	56.5	S	42.0	58.0	S	49.3	34.8	66.7	H
26	50.7	42.0	53.6	50.7	S	49.3	52.2	50.7	58.0	S	58.0	71.0
27	S	58.0	40.6	S	H	59.4	S	46.4	49.3	S	59.4	53.6
28	S	49.3	42.0	S	50.7	53.6	S	63.8	S	58.0	H	S
29	42.0	52.2	H	50.7	49.3	S	46.4	46.4	S	53.6	49.3	S
30	62.3		S	53.6	58.0	S	62.3	62.3	43.5	60.9	S	59.4
31	60.9		S		56.5		59.4	S		53.6		59.4

* See new trends developing on pages 72, 86, 143–148

RECENT S&P 500 MARKET PROBABILITY CALENDAR 2024

THE % CHANCE OF THE MARKET RISING ON ANY TRADING DAY OF THE YEAR*

(Based on the number of times the S&P 500 rose on a particular trading day during **January 2002–December 2022****)

Date	Jan	Feb	Mar	Apr	May	Jun	Jul	Aug	Sep	Oct	Nov	Dec
1	H	76.2	66.7	66.7	66.7	S	85.7	38.1	S	61.9	61.9	S
2	61.9	61.9	S	81.0	52.4	S	47.6	52.4	H	42.9	S	38.1
3	47.6	S	S	47.6	42.9	61.9	66.7	S	52.4	66.7	S	42.9
4	61.9	S	38.1	61.9	S	76.2	H	S	52.4	57.1	66.7	47.6
5	57.1	38.1	57.1	42.9	S	42.9	61.9	52.4	52.4	S	57.1	52.4
6	S	66.7	47.6	S	42.9	61.9	S	57.1	52.4	S	81.0	57.1
7	S	47.6	47.6	S	57.1	38.1	S	52.4	S	33.3	61.9	S
8	47.6	66.7	38.1	66.7	52.4	S	52.4	57.1	S	42.9	52.4	S
9	57.1	57.1	S	47.6	47.6	S	57.1	47.6	47.6	57.1	S	61.9
10	66.7	S	S	61.9	52.4	66.7	57.1	S	66.7	47.6	S	52.4
11	47.6	S	66.7	52.4	S	33.3	71.4	S	76.2	47.6	28.6	57.1
12	47.6	52.4	57.1	61.9	S	38.1	66.7	42.9	71.4	S	57.1	52.4
13	S	71.4	61.9	S	33.3	57.1	S	42.9	57.1	S	57.1	42.9
14	S	61.9	42.9	S	47.6	57.1	S	57.1	S	61.9	42.9	S
15	H	66.7	57.1	57.1	52.4	S	38.1	71.4	S	57.1	57.1	S
16	52.4	52.4	S	71.4	57.1	S	42.9	61.9	57.1	71.4	S	61.9
17	66.7	S	S	52.4	33.3	66.7	61.9	S	66.7	61.9	S	52.4
18	42.9	S	61.9	47.6	S	57.1	76.2	S	47.6	57.1	52.4	33.3
19	52.4	H	66.7	47.6	S	H	28.6	66.7	47.6	S	38.1	52.4
20	S	42.9	47.6	S	33.3	52.4	S	47.6	28.6	S	52.4	71.4
21	S	33.3	42.9	S	42.9	52.4	S	66.7	S	57.1	52.4	S
22	47.6	38.1	57.1	66.7	47.6	S	47.6	47.6	S	38.1	61.9	S
23	66.7	38.1	S	57.1	57.1	S	57.1	52.4	28.6	76.2	S	66.7
24	52.4	S	S	52.4	52.4	33.3	52.4	S	38.1	61.9	S	52.4
25	61.9	S	47.6	47.6	S	47.6	57.1	S	42.9	42.9	66.7	H
26	47.6	57.1	47.6	57.1	S	47.6	47.6	61.9	66.7	S	57.1	66.7
27	S	57.1	57.1	S	H	57.1	S	52.4	52.4	S	71.4	47.6
28	S	52.4	42.9	S	66.7	52.4	S	90.5	S	57.1	H	S
29	38.1	28.6	H	66.7	61.9	S	38.1	42.9	S	38.1	42.9	S
30	52.4		S	33.3	66.7	S	61.9	52.4	33.3	66.7	S	47.6
31	47.6		S		47.6		42.9	S		52.4		38.1

See new trends developing on pages 72, 86, 143–148 ** Based on most recent 21-year period*

NASDAQ COMPOSITE MARKET PROBABILITY CALENDAR 2024

THE % CHANCE OF THE MARKET RISING ON ANY TRADING DAY OF THE YEAR*

(Based on the number of times the NASDAQ rose on a particular trading day during **January 1972–December 2022**)

Date	Jan	Feb	Mar	Apr	May	Jun	Jul	Aug	Sep	Oct	Nov	Dec
1	H	70.6	62.7	47.1	62.7	S	64.7	52.9	S	49.0	66.7	S
2	56.9	66.7	S	66.7	66.7	S	49.0	43.1	H	56.9	S	56.9
3	62.7	S	S	58.8	56.9	56.9	51.0	S	54.9	60.8	S	56.9
4	56.9	S	52.9	52.9	S	74.5	H	S	58.8	58.8	54.9	62.7
5	62.7	52.9	64.7	45.1	S	54.9	54.9	54.9	56.9	S	66.7	60.8
6	S	64.7	47.1	S	52.9	60.8	S	62.7	56.9	S	58.8	47.1
7	S	52.9	47.1	S	56.9	52.9	S	52.9	S	54.9	54.9	S
8	56.9	54.9	52.9	64.7	62.7	S	60.8	43.1	S	56.9	56.9	S
9	60.8	54.9	S	58.8	54.9	S	66.7	49.0	52.9	51.0	S	56.9
10	58.8	S	S	60.8	41.2	51.0	60.8	S	51.0	49.0	S	47.1
11	58.8	S	60.8	51.0	S	41.2	66.7	S	54.9	68.6	51.0	45.1
12	58.8	64.7	49.0	56.9	S	51.0	76.5	47.1	60.8	S	62.7	43.1
13	S	60.8	68.6	S	52.9	58.8	S	56.9	58.8	S	56.9	41.2
14	S	66.7	47.1	S	58.8	64.7	S	60.8	S	62.7	49.0	S
15	H	62.7	52.9	51.0	54.9	S	62.7	56.9	S	52.9	47.1	S
16	60.8	49.0	S	62.7	58.8	S	49.0	51.0	39.2	54.9	S	51.0
17	70.6	S	S	52.9	47.1	56.9	54.9	S	54.9	45.1	S	54.9
18	58.8	S	66.7	54.9	S	49.0	62.7	S	51.0	62.7	49.0	47.1
19	45.1	H	60.8	58.8	S	H	37.3	56.9	60.8	S	49.0	51.0
20	S	52.9	66.7	S	41.2	56.9	S	52.9	49.0	S	54.9	60.8
21	S	39.2	52.9	S	49.0	51.0	S	70.6	S	49.0	66.7	S
22	49.0	41.2	49.0	56.9	49.0	S	49.0	51.0	S	52.9	60.8	S
23	52.9	47.1	S	51.0	49.0	S	51.0	52.9	43.1	51.0	S	62.7
24	58.8	S	S	52.9	54.9	39.2	51.0	S	49.0	49.0	S	70.6
25	47.1	S	47.1	45.1	S	45.1	56.9	S	49.0	39.2	60.8	H
26	64.7	51.0	51.0	60.8	S	58.8	49.0	54.9	49.0	S	66.7	68.6
27	S	64.7	54.9	S	H	66.7	S	54.9	43.1	S	64.7	47.1
28	S	56.9	62.7	S	56.9	66.7	S	64.7	S	45.1	H	S
29	56.9	49.0	H	66.7	60.8	S	47.1	60.8	S	54.9	60.8	S
30	56.9		S	58.8	56.9	S	58.8	64.7	49.0	60.8	S	60.8
31	62.7		S		62.7		51.0	S		60.8		66.7

See new trends developing on pages 72, 86, 143–148
Based on NASDAQ composite, prior to Feb. 5, 1971 based on National Quotation Bureau indices

RECENT NASDAQ COMPOSITE MARKET PROBABILITY CALENDAR 2024

THE % CHANCE OF THE MARKET RISING ON ANY TRADING DAY OF THE YEAR*

(Based on the number of times the NASDAQ rose on a particular trading day during **January 2002–December 2022****)

Date	Jan	Feb	Mar	Apr	May	Jun	Jul	Aug	Sep	Oct	Nov	Dec
1	H	76.2	61.9	66.7	66.7	S	81.0	52.4	S	57.1	61.9	S
2	71.4	57.1	S	76.2	57.1	S	47.6	42.9	H	47.6	S	52.4
3	42.9	S	S	52.4	42.9	52.4	66.7	S	57.1	71.4	S	47.6
4	57.1	S	42.9	52.4	S	71.4	H	S	52.4	52.4	61.9	57.1
5	57.1	33.3	52.4	33.3	S	47.6	66.7	57.1	52.4	S	57.1	61.9
6	S	61.9	38.1	S	47.6	61.9	S	57.1	57.1	S	71.4	52.4
7	S	47.6	33.3	S	52.4	42.9	S	38.1	S	42.9	66.7	S
8	66.7	66.7	42.9	66.7	66.7	S	57.1	47.6	S	47.6	57.1	S
9	61.9	61.9	S	42.9	52.4	S	71.4	42.9	52.4	57.1	S	66.7
10	71.4	S	S	66.7	42.9	52.4	57.1	S	61.9	52.4	S	57.1
11	52.4	S	57.1	42.9	S	33.3	57.1	S	66.7	57.1	28.6	52.4
12	42.9	57.1	42.9	47.6	S	42.9	71.4	42.9	61.9	S	61.9	47.6
13	S	71.4	61.9	S	47.6	52.4	S	52.4	66.7	S	66.7	47.6
14	S	76.2	42.9	S	57.1	66.7	S	61.9	S	61.9	38.1	S
15	H	66.7	52.4	47.6	47.6	S	52.4	61.9	S	57.1	52.4	S
16	42.9	42.9	S	71.4	61.9	S	47.6	57.1	42.9	61.9	S	61.9
17	66.7	S	S	38.1	38.1	66.7	66.7	S	76.2	57.1	S	52.4
18	47.6	S	71.4	52.4	S	52.4	76.2	S	42.9	47.6	57.1	33.3
19	38.1	H	71.4	61.9	S	H	19.0	61.9	47.6	S	38.1	47.6
20	S	42.9	71.4	S	33.3	66.7	S	47.6	42.9	S	57.1	71.4
21	S	38.1	47.6	S	52.4	47.6	S	76.2	S	52.4	61.9	S
22	42.9	42.9	66.7	61.9	42.9	S	57.1	47.6	S	33.3	61.9	S
23	57.1	42.9	S	47.6	57.1	S	57.1	52.4	38.1	71.4	S	57.1
24	66.7	S	S	57.1	47.6	23.8	47.6	S	42.9	57.1	S	66.7
25	52.4	S	38.1	38.1	S	47.6	52.4	S	52.4	52.4	71.4	H
26	66.7	47.6	47.6	47.6	S	61.9	52.4	61.9	52.4	S	57.1	61.9
27	S	71.4	66.7	S	H	61.9	S	52.4	38.1	S	66.7	38.1
28	S	61.9	52.4	S	66.7	52.4	S	81.0	S	52.4	H	S
29	52.4	33.3	H	76.2	66.7	S	42.9	61.9	S	52.4	47.6	S
30	47.6		S	28.6	71.4	S	71.4	47.6	42.9	66.7	S	42.9
31	52.4		S		47.6		38.1	S		47.6		28.6

* See new trends developing on pages 72, 86, 143–148   ** Based on most recent 21-year period

RUSSELL 1000 INDEX MARKET PROBABILITY CALENDAR 2024
THE % CHANCE OF THE MARKET RISING ON ANY TRADING DAY OF THE YEAR*
(Based on the number of times the Russell 1000 rose on a particular trading day during **January 1980–December 2022**)

Date	Jan	Feb	Mar	Apr	May	Jun	Jul	Aug	Sep	Oct	Nov	Dec
1	H	67.4	60.5	60.5	60.5	S	79.1	41.9	S	58.1	72.1	S
2	46.5	62.8	S	65.1	60.5	S	44.2	41.9	H	53.5	S	48.8
3	55.8	S	S	51.2	51.2	58.1	48.8	S	55.8	58.1	S	51.2
4	58.1	S	46.5	58.1	S	62.8	H	S	51.2	55.8	58.1	58.1
5	53.5	58.1	58.1	46.5	S	48.8	58.1	51.2	51.2	S	60.5	44.2
6	S	55.8	41.9	S	39.5	58.1	S	51.2	41.9	S	65.1	48.8
7	S	53.5	41.9	S	48.8	41.9	S	53.5	S	39.5	51.2	S
8	53.5	53.5	51.2	69.8	53.5	S	55.8	53.5	S	51.2	58.1	S
9	62.8	46.5	S	55.8	55.8	S	53.5	44.2	46.5	39.5	S	51.2
10	58.1	S	S	51.2	51.2	48.8	60.5	S	58.1	44.2	S	51.2
11	55.8	S	60.5	51.2	S	37.2	65.1	S	65.1	60.5	44.2	48.8
12	53.5	72.1	44.2	55.8	S	46.5	79.1	46.5	67.4	S	55.8	44.2
13	S	65.1	60.5	S	51.2	55.8	S	44.2	55.8	S	58.1	37.2
14	S	51.2	41.9	S	55.8	58.1	S	60.5	S	62.8	53.5	S
15	H	65.1	58.1	62.8	55.8	S	48.8	65.1	S	58.1	53.5	S
16	65.1	44.2	S	60.5	55.8	S	51.2	62.8	53.5	58.1	S	58.1
17	67.4	S	S	48.8	46.5	58.1	51.2	S	51.2	46.5	S	58.1
18	44.2	S	60.5	51.2	S	53.5	65.1	S	48.8	67.4	48.8	46.5
19	39.5	H	55.8	48.8	S	H	37.2	60.5	44.2	S	53.5	44.2
20	S	41.9	51.2	S	44.2	60.5	S	62.8	37.2	S	51.2	67.4
21	S	37.2	44.2	S	48.8	41.9	S	67.4	S	58.1	58.1	S
22	48.8	41.9	53.5	53.5	51.2	S	41.9	48.8	S	48.8	65.1	S
23	55.8	44.2	S	53.5	44.2	S	48.8	55.8	37.2	51.2	S	60.5
24	51.2	S	S	48.8	60.5	34.9	41.9	S	39.5	46.5	S	60.5
25	53.5	S	44.2	53.5	S	41.9	72.1	S	46.5	37.2	67.4	H
26	58.1	46.5	48.8	58.1	S	48.8	48.8	48.8	62.8	S	67.4	67.4
27	S	60.5	46.5	S	H	60.5	S	53.5	53.5	S	65.1	55.8
28	S	55.8	48.8	S	60.5	55.8	S	62.8	S	53.5	H	S
29	48.8	46.5	H	60.5	58.1	S	44.2	48.8	S	48.8	46.5	S
30	60.5		S	51.2	58.1	S	62.8	55.8	51.2	65.1	S	60.5
31	58.1		S		51.2		55.8	S		62.8		48.8

* See new trends developing on pages 72, 86, 143–148

129

RUSSELL 2000 INDEX MARKET PROBABILITY CALENDAR 2024

THE % CHANCE OF THE MARKET RISING ON ANY TRADING DAY OF THE YEAR*

(Based on the number of times the Russell 2000 rose on a particular trading day during **January 1980–December 2022**)

Date	Jan	Feb	Mar	Apr	May	Jun	Jul	Aug	Sep	Oct	Nov	Dec
1	H	69.8	65.1	51.2	60.5	S	69.8	44.2	S	51.2	62.8	S
2	46.5	60.5	S	60.5	65.1	S	46.5	44.2	H	48.8	S	48.8
3	60.5	S	S	44.2	55.8	65.1	44.2	S	51.2	53.5	S	60.5
4	58.1	S	55.8	53.5	S	72.1	H	S	60.5	60.5	69.8	60.5
5	60.5	55.8	60.5	44.2	S	48.8	55.8	48.8	51.2	S	62.8	60.5
6	S	67.4	51.2	S	55.8	55.8	S	51.2	58.1	S	62.8	46.5
7	S	60.5	55.8	S	58.1	60.5	S	51.2	S	39.5	58.1	S
8	55.8	60.5	48.8	60.5	53.5	S	48.8	46.5	S	46.5	55.8	S
9	60.5	51.2	S	58.1	58.1	S	60.5	53.5	55.8	48.8	S	55.8
10	58.1	S	S	62.8	48.8	44.2	55.8	S	60.5	51.2	S	46.5
11	62.8	S	58.1	51.2	S	41.9	58.1	S	60.5	62.8	48.8	46.5
12	62.8	67.4	44.2	55.8	S	48.8	65.1	46.5	60.5	S	65.1	41.9
13	S	65.1	60.5	S	51.2	55.8	S	46.5	55.8	S	48.8	37.2
14	S	67.4	48.8	S	51.2	60.5	S	69.8	S	55.8	46.5	S
15	H	58.1	51.2	60.5	48.8	S	53.5	58.1	S	62.8	51.2	S
16	62.8	55.8	S	60.5	58.1	S	48.8	58.1	41.9	48.8	S	44.2
17	72.1	S	S	51.2	48.8	58.1	51.2	S	51.2	48.8	S	53.5
18	65.1	S	62.8	53.5	S	51.2	55.8	S	44.2	62.8	30.2	60.5
19	34.9	H	65.1	51.2	S	H	37.2	55.8	39.5	S	55.8	58.1
20	S	41.9	55.8	S	55.8	44.2	S	46.5	41.9	S	48.8	67.4
21	S	41.9	46.5	S	53.5	46.5	S	65.1	S	55.8	62.8	S
22	48.8	41.9	58.1	60.5	48.8	S	48.8	46.5	S	51.2	65.1	S
23	46.5	48.8	S	53.5	55.8	S	44.2	62.8	37.2	51.2	S	67.4
24	58.1	S	S	53.5	60.5	39.5	46.5	S	44.2	46.5	S	74.4
25	46.5	S	48.8	58.1	S	51.2	62.8	S	41.9	37.2	62.8	H
26	62.8	51.2	51.2	67.4	S	51.2	58.1	62.8	53.5	S	60.5	62.8
27	S	60.5	55.8	S	H	67.4	S	55.8	48.8	S	67.4	51.2
28	S	65.1	79.1	S	53.5	65.1	S	67.4	S	39.5	H	S
29	51.2	53.5	H	58.1	65.1	S	48.8	60.5	S	53.5	62.8	S
30	53.5		S	58.1	65.1	S	55.8	65.1	62.8	55.8	S	60.5
31	72.1		S		58.1		60.5	S		67.4		60.5

* See new trends developing on pages 72, 86, 143–148

DECENNIAL CYCLE: A MARKET PHENOMENON

By arranging each year's market gain or loss so the first and succeeding years of each decade fall into the same column, certain interesting patterns emerge—strong fifth and eighth years; weak second, seventh and zero years.

This fascinating phenomenon was first presented by Edgar Lawrence Smith in *Common Stocks and Business Cycles* (William-Frederick Press, 1959). Anthony Gaubis co-pioneered the decennial pattern with Smith.

When Smith first cut graphs of market prices into 10-year segments and placed them above one another, he observed that each decade tended to have three bull market cycles and that the longest and strongest bull markets seem to favor the middle years of a decade.

Don't place too much emphasis on the decennial cycle nowadays, other than the extraordinary fifth and zero years, as the stock market is more influenced by the quadrennial presidential election cycle, shown on page 132. Also, the last half-century, which has been the most prosperous in U.S. history, has distributed the returns among most years of the decade. Interestingly, NASDAQ suffered its worst bear market ever in a zero year.

Fourth years have performed better than average. This year is also a presidential election year which has been the second best of the four-year cycle. The last six years ending in four that were also election years (2004, 1984, 1964, 1944, 1924 and 1904) averaged 15.7% for the full year, but the most recent two were flat.

THE 10-YEAR STOCK MARKET CYCLE
Annual % Change in Dow Jones Industrial Average
Year of Decade

DECADES	1st	2nd	3rd	4th	5th	6th	7th	8th	9th	10th
1881–1890	3.0%	–2.9%	–8.5%	–18.8%	20.1%	12.4%	–8.4%	4.8%	5.5%	–14.1%
1891–1900	17.6	–6.6	–24.6	–0.6	2.3	–1.7	21.3	22.5	9.2	7.0
1901–1910	–8.7	–0.4	–23.6	41.7	38.2	–1.9	–37.7	46.6	15.0	–17.9
1911–1920	0.4	7.6	–10.3	–5.4	81.7	–4.2	–21.7	10.5	30.5	–32.9
1921–1930	12.7	21.7	–3.3	26.2	30.0	0.3	28.8	48.2	–17.2	–33.8
1931–1940	–52.7	–23.1	66.7	4.1	38.5	24.8	–32.8	28.1	–2.9	–12.7
1941–1950	–15.4	7.6	13.8	12.1	26.6	–8.1	2.2	–2.1	12.9	17.6
1951–1960	14.4	8.4	–3.8	44.0	20.8	2.3	–12.8	34.0	16.4	–9.3
1961–1970	18.7	–10.8	17.0	14.6	10.9	–18.9	15.2	4.3	–15.2	4.8
1971–1980	6.1	14.6	–16.6	–27.6	38.3	17.9	–17.3	–3.1	4.2	14.9
1981–1990	–9.2	19.6	20.3	–3.7	27.7	22.6	2.3	11.8	27.0	–4.3
1991–2000	20.3	4.2	13.7	2.1	33.5	26.0	22.6	16.1	25.2	–6.2
2001–2010	–7.1	–16.8	25.3	3.1	–0.6	16.3	6.4	–33.8	18.8	11.0
2011–2020	5.5	7.3	26.5	7.5	–2.2	13.4	25.1	–5.6	22.3	7.2
2021–2030	18.7	–8.8								
Total % Change	24.3%	21.6%	92.6%	99.3%	365.8%	101.2%	–6.8%	182.3%	151.7%	–68.7%
Avg % Change	1.6%	1.4%	6.6%	7.1%	26.1%	7.2%	–0.5%	13.0%	10.8%	–4.9%
Up Years	10	8	7	9	12	9	8	10	11	6
Down Years	5	7	7	5	2	5	6	4	3	8

Based on annual close; Cowles indices 1881–1885; 12 Mixed Stocks, 10 Rails, 2 Inds 1886–1889;
20 Mixed Stocks, 18 Rails, 2 Inds 1890–1896; Railroad average 1897 (First industrial average published May 26, 1896).

PRESIDENTIAL ELECTION/STOCK MARKET CYCLE: THE 190-YEAR SAGA CONTINUES

It is no mere coincidence that the last two years (pre-election year and election year) of the 48 presidential terms since 1833 produced a total net market gain of 772.0%, dwarfing the 336.5% gain of the first two years of these terms.

Presidential elections every four years have a profound impact on the economy and the stock market. Wars, recessions and bear markets tend to start or occur in the first half of the term (2022 Russia-Ukraine War and bear market); prosperous times and bull markets, in the latter half. After nine straight annual Dow gains during the millennial bull, the four-year election cycle reasserted its overarching domination of market behavior until 2008. Recovery from the worst recession since the Great Depression produced six straight annual gains until 2015 when Dow suffered its first pre-election year loss since 1939.

STOCK MARKET ACTION SINCE 1833
Annual % Change in Dow Jones Industrial Average[1]

4-Year Cycle Beginning	President Elected	Post-Election Year	Midterm Year	Pre-Election Year	Election Year
1833	Jackson (D)	−0.9	13.0	3.1	−11.7
1837	Van Buren (D)	−11.5	1.6	−12.3	5.5
1841*	W.H. Harrison (W)**	−13.3	−18.1	45.0	15.5
1845*	Polk (D)	8.1	−14.5	1.2	−3.6
1849*	Taylor (W)	N/C	18.7	−3.2	19.6
1853*	Pierce (D)	−12.7	−30.2	1.5	4.4
1857	Buchanan (D)	−31.0	14.3	−10.7	14.0
1861*	Lincoln (R)	−1.8	55.4	38.0	6.4
1865	Lincoln (R)**	−8.5	3.6	1.6	10.8
1869	Grant (R)	1.7	5.6	7.3	6.8
1873	Grant (R)	−12.7	2.8	−4.1	−17.9
1877	Hayes (R)	−9.4	6.1	43.0	18.7
1881	Garfield (R)**	3.0	−2.9	−8.5	−18.8
1885*	Cleveland (D)	20.1	12.4	−8.4	4.8
1889*	B. Harrison (R)	5.5	−14.1	17.6	−6.6
1893*	Cleveland (D)	−24.6	−0.6	2.3	−1.7
1897*	McKinley (R)	21.3	22.5	9.2	7.0
1901	McKinley (R)**	−8.7	−0.4	−23.6	41.7
1905	T. Roosevelt (R)	38.2	−1.9	−37.7	46.6
1909	Taft (R)	15.0	−17.9	0.4	7.6
1913*	Wilson (D)	−10.3	−5.4	81.7	−4.2
1917	Wilson (D)	−21.7	10.5	30.5	−32.9
1921*	Harding (R)**	12.7	21.7	−3.3	26.2
1925	Coolidge (R)	30.0	0.3	28.8	48.2
1929	Hoover (R)	−17.2	−33.8	−52.7	−23.1
1933*	F. Roosevelt (D)	66.7	4.1	38.5	24.8
1937	F. Roosevelt (D)	−32.8	28.1	−2.9	−12.7
1941	F. Roosevelt (D)	−15.4	7.6	13.8	12.1
1945	F. Roosevelt (D)**	26.6	−8.1	2.2	−2.1
1949	Truman (D)	12.9	17.6	14.4	8.4
1953*	Eisenhower (R)	−3.8	44.0	20.8	2.3
1957	Eisenhower (R)	−12.8	34.0	16.4	−9.3
1961*	Kennedy (D)**	18.7	−10.8	17.0	14.6
1965	Johnson (D)	10.9	−18.9	15.2	4.3
1969*	Nixon (R)	−15.2	4.8	6.1	14.6
1973	Nixon (R)***	−16.6	−27.6	38.3	17.9
1977*	Carter (D)	−17.3	−3.1	4.2	14.9
1981*	Reagan (R)	−9.2	19.6	20.3	−3.7
1985	Reagan (R)	27.7	22.6	2.3	11.8
1989	G. H. W. Bush (R)	27.0	−4.3	20.3	4.2
1993*	Clinton (D)	13.7	2.1	33.5	26.0
1997	Clinton (D)	22.6	16.1	25.2	−6.2
2001*	G. W. Bush (R)	−7.1	−16.8	25.3	3.1
2005	G. W. Bush (R)	−0.6	16.3	6.4	−33.8
2009*	Obama (D)	18.8	11.0	5.5	7.3
2013	Obama (D)	26.5	7.5	−2.2	13.4
2017*	Trump (R)	25.1	−5.6	22.3	7.2
2021*	Biden (D)	18.7	−8.8		
Total % Gain		**156.4%**	**180.1%**	**489.6%**	**282.4%**
Average % Gain		**3.3%**	**3.8%**	**10.4%**	**6.0%**
# Up		23	28	35	32
# Down		24	20	12	15

*Party in power ousted   **Died in office   ***Resigned   D–Democrat, W–Whig, R–Republican
[1] Based on annual close; prior to 1886 based on Cowles and other indices; 12 Mixed Stocks, 10 Rails, 2 Inds 1886–1889; 20 Mixed Stocks, 18 Rails, 2 Inds 1890–1896; Railroad average 1897 (First industrial average published May 26, 1896).

DOW JONES INDUSTRIALS BULL AND BEAR MARKETS SINCE 1900

Bear markets begin at the end of one bull market and end at the start of the next bull market (10/9/07 to 3/9/09 as an example). The longest bull market on record ended on 7/17/98, and the shortest bear market on record ended on 3/23/2020, when the new bull market began. The greatest bull super cycle in history that began 8/12/82 ended in 2000 after the Dow gained 1409% and NASDAQ climbed 3072%. The Dow gained only 497% in the eight-year super bull from 1921 to the top in 1929. NASDAQ suffered its worst loss ever from the 2000 top to the 2002 bottom, down 77.9%, nearly as much as the 89.2% drop in the Dow from the 1929 top to the 1932 bottom. The third longest Dow bull since 1900 that began 10/9/02 ended on its fifth anniversary. The ensuing bear market was the second worst bear market since 1900, slashing the Dow 53.8%. At press time, Dow is currently in a bull market, trading around 34,000. The mild bear market of 2022 ended on the last day of Q3. (See page 134 for S&P 500 and NASDAQ bulls and bears.)

DOW JONES INDUSTRIALS BULL AND BEAR MARKETS SINCE 1900

— Beginning —		— Ending —		Bull		Bear	
Date	DJIA	Date	DJIA	% Gain	Days	% Change	Days
9/24/00	38.80	6/17/01	57.33	47.8%	266	−46.1%	875
11/9/03	30.88	1/19/06	75.45	144.3	802	−48.5	665
11/15/07	38.83	11/19/09	73.64	89.6	735	−27.4	675
9/25/11	53.43	9/30/12	68.97	29.1	371	−24.1	668
7/30/14	52.32	11/21/16	110.15	110.5	845	−40.1	393
12/19/17	65.95	11/3/19	119.62	81.4	684	−46.6	660
8/24/21	63.90	3/20/23	105.38	64.9	573	−18.6	221
10/27/23	85.76	9/3/29	381.17	344.5	2138	−47.9	71
11/13/29	198.69	4/17/30	294.07	48.0	155	−86.0	813
7/8/32	41.22	9/7/32	79.93	93.9	61	−37.2	173
2/27/33	50.16	2/5/34	110.74	120.8	343	−22.8	171
7/26/34	85.51	3/10/37	194.40	127.3	958	−49.1	386
3/31/38	98.95	11/12/38	158.41	60.1	226	−23.3	147
4/8/39	121.44	9/12/39	155.92	28.4	157	−40.4	959
4/28/42	92.92	5/29/46	212.50	128.7	1492	−23.2	353
5/17/47	163.21	6/15/48	193.16	18.4	395	−16.3	363
6/13/49	161.60	1/5/53	293.79	81.8	1302	−13.0	252
9/14/53	255.49	4/6/56	521.05	103.9	935	−19.4	564
10/22/57	419.79	1/5/60	685.47	63.3	805	−17.4	294
10/25/60	566.05	12/13/61	734.91	29.8	414	−27.1	195
6/26/62	535.76	2/9/66	995.15	85.7	1324	−25.2	240
10/7/66	744.32	12/3/68	985.21	32.4	788	−35.9	539
5/26/70	631.16	4/28/71	950.82	50.6	337	−16.1	209
11/23/71	797.97	1/11/73	1051.70	31.8	415	−45.1	694
12/6/74	577.60	9/21/76	1014.79	75.7	655	−26.9	525
2/28/78	742.12	9/8/78	907.74	22.3	192	−16.4	591
4/21/80	759.13	4/27/81	1024.05	34.9	371	−24.1	472
8/12/82	776.92	11/29/83	1287.20	65.7	474	−15.6	238
7/24/84	1086.57	8/25/87	2722.42	150.6	1127	−36.1	55
10/19/87	1738.74	7/17/90	2999.75	72.5	1002	−21.2	86
10/11/90	2365.10	7/17/98	9337.97	294.8	2836	−19.3	45
8/31/98	7539.07	1/14/00	11722.98	55.5	501	−29.7	616
9/21/01	8235.81	3/19/02	10635.25	29.1	179	−31.5	204
10/9/02	7286.27	10/9/07	14164.53	94.4	1826	−53.8	517
3/9/09	6547.05	4/29/11	12810.54	95.7	781	−16.8	157
10/3/11	10655.30	5/19/15	18312.39	71.9	1324	−14.5	268
2/11/16	15660.18	2/12/20	29551.42	88.7	1462	−37.1	40
3/23/20	18591.93	1/4/22	36799.65	97.9	652	− 21.9	269
9/30/22	28725.51	11/30/22	34589.77	20.4*	61*		

As of May 26, 2023—not in averages

			Average	86.0%	793	−30.6%	380

Based on Dow Jones Industrial Average.
The NYSE was closed from 7/31/1914 to 12/11/1914 due to World War I.
DJIA figures were then adjusted back to reflect the composition change from 12 to 20 stocks in September 1916.

1900–2000 Data: Ned Davis Research

STANDARD & POOR'S 500 BULL AND BEAR MARKETS SINCE 1929 NASDAQ COMPOSITE SINCE 1971

A constant debate of the definition and timing of bull and bear markets permeates Wall Street like the bell that signals the open and close of every trading day. We have relied on the Ned Davis Research parameters for years to track bulls and bears on the Dow (see page 133). Standard & Poor's 500 index has been a stalwart indicator for decades and at times marched to a slightly different beat than the Dow. The moves of the S&P 500 and NASDAQ have been correlated to the bull & bear dates on page 133. Many dates line up for the three indices, but you will notice quite a lag or lead on several occasions, especially NASDAQ's independent cadence from 1975 to 1980. Interestingly, the 2022 bear market ended on different days for the three indices.

STANDARD & POOR'S 500 BULL AND BEAR MARKETS

— Beginning —		— Ending —		Bull		Bear	
Date	S&P 500	Date	S&P 500	% Gain	Days	% Change	Days
11/13/29	17.66	4/10/30	25.92	46.8%	148	−83.0%	783
6/1/32	4.40	9/7/32	9.31	111.6	98	−40.6	173
2/27/33	5.53	2/6/34	11.82	113.7	344	−31.8	401
3/14/35	8.06	3/6/37	18.68	131.8	723	−49.0	390
3/31/38	8.50	11/9/38	13.79	62.2	223	−26.2	150
4/8/39	10.18	10/25/39	13.21	29.8	200	−43.5	916
4/28/42	7.47	5/29/46	19.25	157.7	1492	−28.8	353
5/17/47	13.71	6/15/48	17.06	24.4	395	−20.6	363
6/13/49	13.55	1/5/53	26.66	96.8	1302	−14.8	252
9/14/53	22.71	8/2/56	49.74	119.0	1053	−21.6	446
10/22/57	38.98	8/3/59	60.71	55.7	650	−13.9	449
10/25/60	52.30	12/12/61	72.64	38.9	413	−28.0	196
6/26/62	52.32	2/9/66	94.06	79.8	1324	−22.2	240
10/7/66	73.20	11/29/68	108.37	48.0	784	−36.1	543
5/26/70	69.29	4/28/71	104.77	51.2	337	−13.9	209
11/23/71	90.16	1/11/73	120.24	33.4	415	−48.2	630
10/3/74	62.28	9/21/76	107.83	73.1	719	−19.4	531
3/6/78	86.90	9/12/78	106.99	23.1	190	−8.2	562
3/27/80	98.22	11/28/80	140.52	43.1	246	−27.1	622
8/12/82	102.42	10/10/83	172.65	68.6	424	−14.4	288
7/24/84	147.82	8/25/87	336.77	127.8	1127	−33.5	101
12/4/87	223.92	7/16/90	368.95	64.8	955	−19.9	87
10/11/90	295.46	7/17/98	1186.75	301.7	2836	−19.3	45
8/31/98	957.28	3/24/00	1527.46	59.6	571	−36.8	546
9/21/01	965.80	1/4/02	1172.51	21.4	105	−33.8	278
10/9/02	776.76	10/9/07	1565.15	101.5	1826	−56.8	517
3/9/09	676.53	4/29/11	1363.61	101.6	781	−19.4	157
10/3/11	1099.23	5/21/15	2130.82	93.8	1326	−14.2	266
2/11/16	1829.08	2/19/20	3386.15	85.1	1469	−33.9	33
3/23/20	2237.40	1/3/22	4796.56	114.4	651	−25.4	282
10/12/22	3577.03	5/26/23	4205.45	17.6*	226**As of May 26, 2023 — not in averages		
		Average		**82.7%**	**771**	**−29.7%**	**360**

NASDAQ COMPOSITE BULL AND BEAR MARKETS

— Beginning —		— Ending —		Bull		Bear	
Date	NASDAQ	Date	NASDAQ	% Gain	Days	% Change	Days
11/23/71	100.31	1/11/73	136.84	36.4%	415	−59.9%	630
10/3/74	54.87	7/15/75	88.00	60.4	285	−16.2	63
9/16/75	73.78	9/13/78	139.25	88.7	1093	−20.4	62
11/14/78	110.88	2/8/80	165.25	49.0	451	−24.9	48
3/27/80	124.09	5/29/81	223.47	80.1	428	−28.8	441
8/13/82	159.14	6/24/83	328.91	106.7	315	−31.5	397
7/25/84	225.30	8/26/87	455.26	102.1	1127	−35.9	63
10/28/87	291.88	10/9/89	485.73	66.4	712	−33.0	372
10/16/90	325.44	7/20/98	2014.25	518.9	2834	−29.5	80
10/8/98	1419.12	3/10/00	5048.62	255.8	519	−71.8	560
9/21/01	1423.19	1/4/02	2059.38	44.7	105	−45.9	278
10/9/02	1114.11	10/31/07	2859.12	156.6	1848	−55.6	495
3/9/09	1268.64	4/29/11	2873.54	126.5	781	−18.7	157
10/3/11	2335.83	7/20/15	5218.86	123.4	1386	−18.2	206
2/11/16	4266.84	2/19/20	9817.18	130.1	1469	−30.1	33
3/23/20	6860.67	11/19/21	16057.44	134.1	606	−36.4	404
12/28/22	10213.29	5/26/23	12975.69	27.0*	149**As of May 26, 2023 — not in averages		
		Average		**130.0%**	**898**	**−34.8%**	**268**

JANUARY DAILY POINT CHANGES DOW JONES INDUSTRIALS

	2014	2015	2016	2017	2018	2019	2020	2021	2022	2023
Previous Month Close	16576.66	17823.07	17425.03	19762.60	24719.22	23327.46	28538.44	30606.48	36338.30	33147.25
1	H	H	H	S	H	H	H	H	S	S
2	-135.31	9.92	S	H	104.79	18.78	330.36	S	S	H
3	28.64	S	S	119.16	98.67	-660.02	-233.92	S	246.76	-10.88
4	S	S	-276.09	60.40	152.45	746.94	S	-382.59	214.59	133.40
5	S	-331.34	9.72	-42.87	220.74	S	S	167.71	-392.54	-339.69
6	-44.89	-130.01	-252.15	64.51	S	S	68.50	437.80	-170.64	700.53
7	105.84	212.88	-392.41	S	S	98.19	-119.70	211.73	-4.81	S
8	-68.20	323.35	-167.65	S	-12.87	256.10	161.41	56.84	S	S
9	-17.98	-170.50	S	-76.42	102.80	91.67	211.81	S	S	-112.96
10	-7.71	S	S	-31.85	-16.67	122.80	-133.13	S	-162.79	186.45
11	S	S	52.12	98.75	205.60	-5.97	S	-89.28	183.15	268.91
12	S	-96.53	117.65	-63.28	228.46	S	S	60.00	38.30	216.96
13	-179.11	-27.16	-364.81	-5.27	S	S	83.28	-8.22	-176.70	112.64
14	115.92	-186.59	227.64	S	S	-86.11	32.62	-68.95	-201.81	S
15	108.08	-106.38	-390.97	H	H	155.75	90.55	-177.26	S	S
16	-64.93	190.86	S	H	-10.33	141.57	267.42	S	S	H
17	41.55	S	S	-58.96	322.79	162.94	50.46	S	H	-391.76
18	S	S	H	-22.05	-97.84	336.25	S	H	-543.34	-613.89
19	S	H	27.94	-72.32	53.91	S	S	116.26	-339.82	-252.40
20	H	3.66	-249.28	94.85	S	S	H	257.86	-313.26	330.93
21	-44.12	39.05	115.94	S	S	H	-152.06	-12.37	-450.02	S
22	-41.10	259.70	210.83	S	142.88	-301.87	-9.77	-179.03	S	S
23	-175.99	-141.38	S	-27.40	-3.79	171.14	-26.18	S	S	254.07
24	-318.24	S	S	112.86	41.31	-22.38	-170.36	S	99.13	104.40
25	S	S	-208.29	155.80	140.67	183.96	S	-36.98	-66.77	9.88
26	S	6.10	282.01	32.40	223.92	S	S	-22.96	-129.64	205.57
27	-41.23	-291.49	-222.77	-7.13	S	S	-453.93	-633.87	-7.31	28.67
28	90.68	-195.84	125.18	S	S	-208.98	187.05	300.19	564.69	S
29	-189.77	225.48	396.66	S	-177.23	51.74	11.60	-620.74	S	S
30	109.82	-251.90	S	-122.65	-362.59	434.90	124.99	S	S	-260.99
31	-149.76	S	S	-107.04	72.50	-15.19	-603.41	S	406.39	368.95
Close	15698.85	17164.95	16466.30	19864.09	26149.39	24999.67	28256.03	29982.62	35131.86	34086.04
Change	-877.81	-658.12	-958.73	101.49	1430.17	1672.21	-282.41	-623.86	-1206.44	938.79

FEBRUARY DAILY POINT CHANGES DOW JONES INDUSTRIALS

	2014	2015	2016	2017	2018	2019	2020	2021	2022	2023
Previous Month Close	15698.85	17164.95	16466.30	19864.09	26149.39	24999.67	28256.03	29982.62	35131.86	34086.04
1	S	S	-17.12	26.85	37.32	64.22	S	229.29	273.38	6.92
2	S	196.09	-295.64	-6.03	-665.75	S	S	475.57	224.09	-39.02
3	-326.05	305.36	183.12	186.55	S	S	143.78	36.12	-518.17	-127.93
4	72.44	6.62	79.92	S	S	175.48	407.82	332.26	-21.42	S
5	-5.01	211.86	-211.61	S	-1175.21	172.15	483.22	92.38	S	S
6	188.30	-60.59	S	-19.04	567.02	-21.22	88.92	S	S	-34.99
7	165.55	S	S	37.87	-19.42	-220.77	-277.26	S	1.39	265.67
8	S	S	-177.92	-35.95	-1032.89	-63.20	S	237.52	371.65	-207.68
9	S	-95.08	-12.67	118.06	330.44	S	S	-9.93	305.28	-249.13
10	7.71	139.55	-99.64	96.97	S	S	174.31	61.97	-526.47	169.39
11	192.98	-6.62	-254.56	S	S	-53.22	-0.48	-7.10	-503.53	S
12	-30.83	110.24	313.66	S	410.37	372.65	275.08	27.70	S	S
13	63.65	46.97	S	142.79	39.18	117.51	-128.11	S	S	376.66
14	126.80	S	S	92.25	253.04	-103.88	-25.23	S	-171.89	-156.66
15	S	S	H	107.45	306.88	443.86	S	H	422.67	38.78
16	S	H	222.57	7.91	19.01	S	S	64.35	-54.57	-431.20
17	H	28.23	257.42	4.28	S	S	H	90.27	-622.24	129.84
18	-23.99	-17.73	-40.40	S	S	H	-165.89	-119.68	-232.85	S
19	-89.84	-44.08	-21.44	S	H	8.07	115.84	0.98	S	S
20	92.67	154.67	S	H	-254.63	63.12	-128.05	S	S	H
21	-29.93	S	S	118.95	-166.97	-103.81	-227.57	S	H	-697.10
22	S	S	228.67	32.60	164.70	181.18	S	27.37	-482.57	-84.50
23	S	-23.60	-188.88	34.72	347.51	S	S	15.66	-464.85	108.82
24	103.84	92.35	53.21	11.44	S	S	-1031.61	424.51	92.07	-336.99
25	-27.48	15.38	212.30	S	S	60.14	-879.44	-559.85	834.92	S
26	18.75	-10.15	-57.32	S	399.28	-33.97	-123.77	-469.64	S	S
27	74.24	-81.72	S	15.68	-299.24	-72.82	-1190.95	S	S	72.17
28	49.06	S	S	-25.20	-380.83	-69.16	-357.28	S	-166.15	-232.39
29	—	—	-123.47	—	—	—	S	—	—	—
Close	16321.71	18132.70	16516.50	20812.24	25029.20	25916.00	25409.36	30932.37	33892.60	32656.70
Change	622.86	967.75	50.20	948.15	-1120.19	916.33	-2846.67	949.75	-1239.26	-1429.34

135

MARCH DAILY POINT CHANGES DOW JONES INDUSTRIALS

Previous Month Close	2014	2015	2016	2017	2018	2019	2020	2021	2022	2023
Close	16321.71	18132.70	16516.50	20812.24	25029.20	25916.00	25409.36	30932.37	33892.60	32656.70
1	S	S	348.58	303.31	-420.22	110.32	S	603.14	-597.65	5.14
2	S	155.93	34.24	-112.58	-70.92	S	1293.96	-143.99	596.40	341.73
3	-153.68	-85.26	44.58	2.74	S	S	-785.91	-121.43	-96.69	387.40
4	227.85	-106.47	62.87	S	S	-206.67	1173.45	-345.95	-179.86	S
5	-35.70	38.82	S	S	336.70	-13.02	-969.58	572.16	S	S
6	61.71	-278.94	S	-51.37	9.36	-133.17	-256.50	S	S	40.47
7	30.83	S	67.18	-29.58	-82.76	-200.23	S	S	-797.42	-574.98
8	S	S	-109.85	-69.03	93.85	-22.99	S	306.14	-184.74	-58.06
9	S	138.94	36.26	2.46	440.53	S	-2013.76	30.30	653.61	-543.54
10	-34.04	-332.78	-5.23	44.79	S	S	1167.14	464.28	-112.18	-345.22
11	-67.43	-27.55	218.18	S	S	200.64	-1464.94	188.57	-229.88	S
12	-11.17	259.83	S	S	-157.13	-96.22	-2352.60	293.05	S	S
13	-231.19	-145.91	S	-21.50	-171.58	148.23	1985.00	S	S	-90.50
14	-43.22	S	15.82	-44.11	-248.91	7.05	S	S	1.05	336.26
15	S	S	22.40	112.73	115.54	138.93	S	174.82	599.10	-280.83
16	S	228.11	74.23	-15.55	72.85	S	-2997.10	-127.51	518.76	371.98
17	181.55	-128.34	155.73	-19.93	S	S	1048.86	189.42	417.66	-384.57
18	88.97	227.11	120.81	S	S	65.23	-1338.46	-153.07	274.17	S
19	-114.02	-117.16	S	S	-335.60	-26.72	188.27	-234.33	S	S
20	108.88	168.62	S	-8.76	116.36	-141.71	-913.21	S	S	382.60
21	-28.28	S	21.57	-237.85	-44.96	216.84	S	S	-201.94	316.02
22	S	S	-41.30	-6.71	-724.42	-460.19	S	103.23	254.47	-530.49
23	S	-11.61	-79.98	-4.72	-424.69	S	-582.05	-308.05	-448.96	75.14
24	-26.08	-104.90	13.14	-59.86	S	S	2112.98	-3.09	349.44	132.28
25	91.19	-292.60	H	S	S	14.51	495.64	199.42	153.30	S
26	-98.89	-40.31	S	S	669.40	140.90	1351.62	453.40	S	S
27	-4.76	34.43	S	-45.74	-344.89	-32.14	-915.39	S	S	194.55
28	58.83	S	19.66	150.52	-9.29	91.87	S	S	94.65	-37.83
29	S	S	97.72	-42.18	254.69	211.22	S	98.49	338.30	323.35
30	S	263.65	83.55	69.17	H	S	690.70	-104.41	-65.38	141.43
31	134.60	-200.19	-31.57	-65.27	S	S	-410.32	-85.41	-550.46	415.12
Close	16457.66	17776.12	17685.09	20663.22	24103.11	25928.68	21917.16	32981.55	34678.35	33274.15
Change	135.95	-356.58	1168.59	-149.02	-926.09	12.68	-3492.20	2049.18	785.75	617.45

APRIL DAILY POINT CHANGES DOW JONES INDUSTRIALS

Previous Month Close	2014	2015	2016	2017	2018	2019	2020	2021	2022	2023
Close	16457.66	17776.12	17685.09	20663.22	24103.11	25928.68	21917.16	32981.55	34678.35	33274.15
1	74.95	-77.94	107.66	S	S	329.74	-973.65	171.66	139.92	S
2	40.39	65.06	S	S	-458.92	-79.29	469.93	H	S	S
3	-0.45	H	S	-13.01	389.17	39.00	-360.91	S	S	327.00
4	-159.84	S	-55.75	39.03	230.94	166.50	S	S	103.61	-198.77
5	S	S	-133.68	-41.09	240.92	40.36	S	373.98	-280.70	80.34
6	S	117.61	112.73	14.80	-572.46	S	1627.46	-96.95	-144.67	2.57
7	-166.84	-5.43	-174.09	-6.85	S	S	-26.13	16.02	87.06	H
8	10.27	27.09	35.00	S	S	-83.97	779.71	57.31	137.55	S
9	181.04	56.22	S	S	46.34	-190.44	285.80	297.03	S	S
10	-266.96	98.92	S	1.92	428.90	6.58	H	S	S	101.23
11	-143.47	S	-20.55	-6.72	-218.55	-14.11	S	S	-413.04	98.27
12	S	S	164.84	-59.44	293.60	269.25	S	-55.20	-87.72	-38.29
13	S	-80.61	187.03	-138.61	-122.91	S	-328.60	-68.13	344.23	383.19
14	146.49	59.66	18.15	H	S	S	558.99	53.62	-113.36	-143.22
15	89.32	75.91	-28.97	S	S	-27.53	-445.41	305.10	H	S
16	162.29	-6.84	S	S	212.90	67.89	33.33	164.68	S	S
17	-16.31	-279.47	S	183.67	213.59	-3.12	704.81	S	S	100.71
18	H	S	106.70	-113.64	-38.56	110.00	S	S	-39.54	-10.55
19	S	S	49.44	-118.79	-83.18	H	S	-123.04	499.51	-79.62
20	S	208.63	42.67	174.22	-201.95	S	-592.05	-256.33	249.59	-110.39
21	40.71	-85.34	-113.75	-30.95	S	S	-631.56	316.01	-368.03	22.34
22	65.12	88.68	21.23	S	S	-48.49	456.94	-321.41	-981.36	S
23	-12.72	20.42	S	S	-14.25	145.34	39.44	227.59	S	S
24	0.00	21.45	S	216.13	-424.56	-59.34	260.01	S	S	66.44
25	-140.19	S	-26.51	232.23	59.70	-134.97	S	S	238.06	-344.57
26	S	S	13.08	-21.03	238.51	81.25	S	-61.92	-809.28	-228.96
27	S	-42.17	51.23	6.24	-11.15	S	358.51	3.36	61.75	524.29
28	87.28	72.17	-210.79	-40.82	S	S	-32.23	-164.55	614.46	272.00
29	86.63	-74.61	-57.12	S	S	11.06	532.31	239.98	-939.18	S
30	45.47	-195.01	S	S	-148.04	38.52	-288.14	-185.51	S	S
Close	16580.84	17840.52	17773.64	20940.51	24163.15	26592.91	24345.72	33874.85	32977.21	34098.16
Change	123.18	64.40	88.55	277.29	60.04	664.23	2428.56	893.30	-1701.14	824.01

MAY DAILY POINT CHANGES DOW JONES INDUSTRIALS

Previous Month	2013	2014	2015	2016	2017	2018	2019	2020	2021	2022
Close	14839.80	16580.84	17840.52	17773.64	20940.51	24163.15	26592.91	24345.72	33874.85	32977.21
1	- 138.85	- 21.97	183.54	S	- 27.05	- 64.10	- 162.77	- 622.03	S	S
2	130.63	- 45.98	S	117.52	36.43	- 174.07	- 122.35	S	S	84.29
3	142.38	S	S	- 140.25	8.01	5.17	197.16	S	238.38	67.29
4	S	S	46.34	- 99.65	- 6.43	332.36	S	26.07	19.80	932.27
5	S	17.66	- 142.20	9.45	55.47	S	S	133.33	97.31	- 1063.09
6	- 5.07	- 129.53	- 86.22	79.92	S	S	- 66.47	- 218.45	318.19	- 98.60
7	87.31	117.52	82.08	S	S	94.81	- 473.39	211.25	229.23	S
8	48.92	32.43	267.05	S	5.34	2.89	2.24	455.43	S	S
9	- 22.50	32.37	S	- 34.72	- 36.50	182.33	- 138.97	S	S	- 653.67
10	35.87	S	S	222.44	- 32.67	196.99	114.01	S	- 34.94	- 84.96
11	S	S	- 85.94	- 217.23	- 23.69	91.64	S	- 109.33	- 473.66	- 326.63
12	S	112.13	- 36.94	9.38	- 22.81	S	S	- 457.21	- 681.50	- 103.81
13	- 26.81	19.97	- 7.74	- 185.18	S	S	- 617.38	- 516.81	433.79	466.36
14	123.57	- 101.47	191.75	S	S	68.24	207.06	377.37	360.68	S
15	60.44	- 167.16	20.32	S	85.33	- 193.00	115.97	60.08	S	S
16	- 42.47	44.50	S	175.39	- 2.19	62.52	214.66	S	S	26.76
17	121.18	S	S	- 180.73	- 372.82	- 54.95	- 98.68	S	- 54.34	431.17
18	S	S	26.32	- 3.36	56.09	1.11	S	911.95	- 267.13	- 1164.52
19	S	20.55	13.51	- 91.22	141.82	S	S	- 390.51	- 164.62	- 236.94
20	- 19.12	- 137.55	- 26.99	65.54	S	S	- 84.10	369.04	188.11	8.77
21	52.30	158.75	0.34	S	S	298.20	197.43	- 101.78	123.69	S
22	- 80.41	10.02	- 53.72	S	89.99	- 178.88	- 100.72	- 8.96	S	S
23	- 12.67	63.19	S	- 8.01	43.08	52.40	- 286.14	S	S	618.34
24	8.60	S	S	213.12	74.51	- 75.05	95.22	S	186.14	58.38
25	S	S	H	145.46	70.53	- 58.67	S	H	- 81.52	181.66
26	S	H	- 190.48	- 23.22	- 2.67	S	S	529.95	10.59	516.91
27	H	69.23	121.45	44.93	S	S	H	553.16	141.59	575.77
28	106.29	- 42.32	- 36.87	S	S	H	- 237.92	- 147.63	64.81	S
29	- 106.59	65.56	- 115.44	S	H	- 391.64	- 221.36	- 17.53	S	S
30	21.73	18.43	S	H	- 50.81	306.33	43.47	S	S	H
31	- 208.96	S	S	- 86.02	- 20.82	- 251.94	- 354.84	S	H	- 222.84
Close	15115.57	16717.17	18010.68	17787.20	21008.65	24415.84	24815.04	25383.11	34529.45	32990.12
Change	275.77	136.33	170.16	13.56	68.14	252.69	- 1777.87	1037.39	654.60	12.91

JUNE DAILY POINT CHANGES DOW JONES INDUSTRIALS

Previous Month	2013	2014	2015	2016	2017	2018	2019	2020	2021	2022
Close	15115.57	16717.17	18010.68	17787.20	21008.65	24415.84	24815.04	25383.11	34529.45	32990.12
1	S	S	29.69	2.47	135.53	219.37	S	91.91	45.86	- 176.89
2	S	26.46	- 28.43	48.89	62.11	S	S	267.63	25.07	435.05
3	138.46	- 21.29	64.33	- 31.50	S	S	4.74	527.24	- 23.34	- 348.58
4	- 76.49	15.19	- 170.69	S	S	178.48	512.40	11.93	179.35	S
5	- 216.95	98.58	- 56.12	S	- 22.25	- 13.71	207.39	829.16	S	S
6	80.03	88.17	S	113.27	- 47.81	346.41	181.09	S	S	16.08
7	207.50	S	S	17.95	37.46	95.02	263.28	S	- 126.15	264.36
8	S	S	- 82.91	66.77	8.84	75.12	S	461.46	- 30.42	- 269.24
9	S	18.82	- 2.51	- 19.86	89.44	S	S	- 300.14	- 152.68	- 638.11
10	- 9.53	2.82	236.36	- 119.85	S	S	78.74	- 282.31	19.10	- 880.00
11	- 116.57	- 102.04	38.97	S	S	5.78	- 14.17	- 1861.82	13.36	S
12	- 126.79	- 109.69	- 140.53	S	- 36.30	- 1.58	- 43.68	477.37	S	S
13	180.85	41.55	S	- 132.86	92.80	- 119.53	101.94	S	S	- 876.05
14	- 105.90	S	S	- 57.66	46.09	- 25.89	- 17.16	S	- 85.85	- 151.91
15	S	S	- 107.67	- 34.65	- 14.66	- 84.83	S	157.62	- 94.42	303.70
16	S	5.27	113.31	92.93	24.38	S	S	526.82	- 265.66	- 741.46
17	109.67	27.48	31.26	- 57.94	S	S	22.92	- 170.37	- 210.22	- 38.29
18	138.38	98.13	180.10	S	S	- 103.01	353.01	- 39.51	- 533.37	S
19	- 206.04	14.84	- 99.89	S	144.71	- 287.26	38.46	- 208.64	S	S
20	- 353.87	25.62	S	129.71	- 61.85	- 42.41	249.17	S	S	H
21	41.08	S	S	24.86	- 57.11	- 196.10	- 34.04	S	586.89	641.47
22	S	S	103.83	- 48.90	- 12.74	119.19	S	153.50	68.61	- 47.12
23	S	- 9.82	24.29	230.24	- 2.53	S	S	131.14	- 71.34	194.23
24	- 139.84	- 119.13	- 178.00	- 610.32	S	S	8.41	- 710.16	322.58	823.32
25	100.75	49.38	- 75.71	S	S	- 328.09	- 179.32	299.66	237.02	S
26	149.83	- 21.38	56.32	S	14.79	30.31	- 11.40	- 730.05	S	S
27	114.35	5.71	S	- 260.51	- 98.89	- 165.52	- 10.24	S	S	- 62.42
28	- 114.89	S	S	269.48	143.95	98.46	73.38	S	- 150.57	- 491.27
29	S	S	- 350.33	284.96	- 167.58	55.36	S	S	9.02	82.32
30	S	- 25.24	23.16	235.31	62.60	S	S	217.08	210.22	- 253.88
Close	14909.60	16826.60	17619.51	17929.99	21349.63	24271.41	26599.96	25812.88	34502.51	30775.43
Change	- 205.97	109.43	- 391.17	142.79	340.98	- 144.43	1784.92	429.77	- 26.94	- 2214.69

JULY DAILY POINT CHANGES DOW JONES INDUSTRIALS

Previous Month Close	2013	2014	2015	2016	2017	2018	2019	2020	2021	2022
Close	14909.60	16826.60	17619.51	17929.99	21349.63	24271.41	26599.96	25812.88	34502.51	30775.43
1	65.36	129.47	138.40	19.38	S	S	117.47	-77.91	131.02	321.83
2	-42.55	20.17	-27.80	S	S	35.77	69.25	92.39	152.82	S
3	56.14*	92.02	H	S	129.64*	-132.36*	179.32*	H	S	S
4	H	H	S	H	H	H	H	S	S	H
5	147.29	S	S	-108.75	-1.10	181.92	-43.88	S	H	-129.44
6	S	S	-46.53	78.00	-158.13	99.74	S	459.67	-208.98	69.86
7	S	-44.05	93.33	-22.74	94.30	S	S	-396.85	104.42	346.87
8	88.85	-117.59	-261.49	250.86	S	S	-115.98	177.10	-259.86	-46.40
9	75.65	78.99	33.20	S	S	320.11	-22.65	-361.19	448.23	S
10	-8.68	-70.54	211.79	S	-5.82	143.07	76.71	369.21	S	S
11	169.26	28.74	S	80.19	0.55	-219.21	227.88	S	S	-164.31
12	3.38	S	S	120.74	123.07	224.44	243.95	S	126.02	-192.51
13	S	S	217.27	24.45	20.95	94.52	S	10.50	-107.39	-208.54
14	S	111.61	75.90	134.29	84.65	S	S	556.79	44.44	-142.62
15	19.96	5.26	-3.41	10.14	S	S	27.13	227.51	53.79	658.09
16	-32.41	77.52	70.08	S	S	44.95	-23.53	-135.39	-299.17	S
17	18.67	-161.39	-33.80	S	-8.02	55.53	-115.78	-62.76	S	S
18	78.02	123.37	S	16.50	-54.99	79.40	3.12	S	S	-215.65
19	-4.80	S	S	25.96	66.02	-134.79	-68.77	S	-725.81	754.44
20	S	S	13.96	36.02	-28.97	-6.38	S	8.92	549.95	47.79
21	S	-48.45	-181.12	-77.80	-31.71	S	S	159.53	286.01	162.06
22	1.81	61.81	-68.25	53.62	S	S	17.70	165.44	25.35	-137.61
23	22.19	-26.91	-119.12	S	S	-13.83	177.29	-353.51	238.20	S
24	-25.50	-2.83	-163.39	S	-66.90	197.65	-79.22	-182.44	S	S
25	13.37	-123.23	S	-77.79	100.26	172.16	-128.99	S	S	90.75
26	3.22	S	S	-19.31	97.58	112.97	51.47	S	82.76	-228.50
27	S	S	-127.94	-1.58	85.54	-76.01	S	114.88	-85.79	436.05
28	S	22.02	189.68	-15.82	33.76	S	S	-205.49	-127.59	332.04
29	-36.86	-70.48	121.12	-24.11	S	S	28.90	160.29	153.60	315.50
30	-1.38	-31.75	-5.41	S	S	-144.23	-23.33	-225.92	-149.06	S
31	-21.05	-317.06	-56.12	S	60.81	108.36	-333.75	114.67	S	S
Close	15499.54	16563.30	17689.86	18432.24	21891.12	25415.19	26864.27	26428.32	34935.47	32845.13
Change	589.94	-263.30	70.35	502.25	541.49	1143.78	264.31	615.44	432.96	2069.70

*Shortened trading day

AUGUST DAILY POINT CHANGES DOW JONES INDUSTRIALS

Previous Month Close	2013	2014	2015	2016	2017	2018	2019	2020	2021	2022
Close	15499.54	16563.30	17689.86	18432.24	21891.12	25415.19	26864.27	26428.32	34935.47	32845.13
1	128.48	-69.93	S	-27.73	72.80	-81.37	-280.85	S	S	-46.73
2	30.34	S	S	-90.74	52.32	-7.66	-98.41	S	-97.31	-402.23
3	S	S	-91.66	41.23	9.86	136.42	S	236.08	278.24	416.33
4	S	75.91	-47.51	-2.95	66.71	S	S	164.07	-323.73	-85.68
5	-46.23	-139.81	-10.22	191.48	S	S	-767.27	373.05	271.58	76.65
6	-93.39	13.87	-120.72	S	S	39.60	311.78	185.46	144.26	S
7	-48.07	-75.07	-46.37	S	25.61	126.73	-22.45	46.50	S	S
8	27.65	185.66	S	-14.24	-33.08	-45.16	371.12	S	S	29.07
9	-72.81	S	S	3.76	-36.64	-74.52	-90.75	S	-106.66	-58.13
10	S	S	241.79	-37.39	-204.69	-196.09	S	357.96	162.82	535.10
11	S	16.05	-212.33	117.86	14.31	S	S	-104.53	220.30	27.16
12	-5.83	-9.44	-0.33	-37.05	S	S	-380.07	289.93	14.88	424.38
13	31.33	91.26	5.74	S	S	-125.44	372.54	-80.12	15.53	S
14	-113.35	61.78	69.15	S	135.39	112.22	-800.49	34.30	S	S
15	-225.47	-50.67	S	59.58	5.28	-137.51	99.97	S	S	151.39
16	-30.72	S	S	-84.03	25.88	396.32	306.62	S	110.02	239.57
17	S	S	67.78	21.92	-274.14	110.59	S	-86.11	-282.12	-171.69
18	S	175.83	-33.84	23.76	-76.22	S	S	-66.84	-382.59	18.72
19	-70.73	80.85	-162.61	-45.13	S	S	249.78	-85.19	-66.57	-292.30
20	-7.75	59.54	-358.04	S	S	89.37	-173.35	46.85	225.96	S
21	-105.44	60.36	-530.94	S	29.24	63.60	240.29	190.60	S	S
22	66.19	-38.27	S	-23.15	196.14	-88.69	49.51	S	S	-643.13
23	46.77	S	S	17.88	-87.80	-76.62	-623.34	S	215.63	-154.02
24	S	S	-588.40	-65.82	-28.69	133.37	S	378.13	30.55	59.64
25	S	75.65	-204.91	-33.07	30.27	S	S	-60.02	39.24	322.55
26	-64.09	29.83	619.07	-53.01	S	S	269.93	83.48	-192.38	-1008.38
27	-170.33	15.31	369.26	S	S	259.29	-120.93	160.35	242.68	S
28	48.38	-42.44	-11.76	S	-5.27	14.38	258.20	161.60	S	S
29	16.44	18.88	S	107.59	56.97	60.55	326.15	S	S	-184.41
30	-30.64	S	S	-48.69	27.06	-137.65	41.03	S	-55.96	-308.12
31	S	S	-114.98	-53.42	55.67	-22.10	S	-223.82	-39.11	-280.44
Close	14810.31	17098.45	16528.03	18400.88	21948.10	25964.82	26403.28	28430.05	35360.73	31510.43
Change	-689.23	535.15	-1161.83	-31.36	56.98	549.63	-460.99	2001.73	425.26	-1334.70

SEPTEMBER DAILY POINT CHANGES DOW JONES INDUSTRIALS

Previous Month	2013	2014	2015	2016	2017	2018	2019	2020	2021	2022
Close	14810.31	17098.45	16528.03	18400.88	21948.10	25964.82	26403.28	28430.05	35360.73	31510.43
1	S	H	-469.68	18.42	39.46	S	S	215.61	-48.20	145.99
2	H	-30.89	293.03	72.66	S	S	H	454.84	131.29	-337.98
3	23.65	10.72	23.38	S	S	H	-285.26	-807.77	-74.73	S
4	96.91	-8.70	-272.38	S	S	H	-12.34	237.45	-159.42	S
5	6.61	67.78	S	H	-234.25	22.51	372.68	S	S	H
6	-14.98	S	S	46.16	54.33	20.88	69.31	S	H	-173.14
7	S	S	H	-11.98	-22.86	-79.33	S	H	-269.09	435.98
8	S	-25.94	390.30	-46.23	13.01	S	S	-632.42	-68.93	193.24
9	140.62	-97.55	-239.11	-394.46	S	S	38.05	439.58	-151.69	377.19
10	127.94	54.84	76.83	S	S	-59.47	73.92	-405.89	-271.66	S
11	135.54	-19.71	102.69	S	259.58	113.99	227.61	131.06	S	S
12	-25.96	-61.49	S	239.62	61.49	27.86	45.41	S	S	229.63
13	75.42	S	S	-258.32	39.32	147.07	37.07	S	261.91	-1276.37
14	S	S	-62.13	-31.98	45.30	8.68	S	327.69	-312.06	30.12
15	S	43.63	228.89	177.71	64.86	S	S	2.27	256.82	-173.27
16	118.72	100.83	140.10	-88.68	S	S	-142.70	36.78	-63.07	-139.40
17	34.95	24.88	-65.21	S	S	-92.55	33.98	-130.40	-166.44	S
18	147.21	109.14	-290.16	S	63.01	184.84	36.28	-244.56	S	S
19	-40.39	13.75	S	-3.63	39.45	158.80	-52.29	S	S	197.26
20	-185.46	S	S	9.79	41.79	251.22	-159.72	S	-614.41	-313.45
21	S	S	125.61	163.74	-53.36	86.52	S	-509.72	-50.63	-522.45
22	S	-107.06	-179.72	98.76	-9.64	S	S	140.48	338.48	-107.10
23	-49.71	-116.81	-50.58	-131.01	S	S	14.92	-525.05	506.50	-486.27
24	-66.79	154.19	-78.57	S	S	-181.45	-142.22	52.31	33.18	S
25	-61.33	-264.26	113.35	S	-53.50	-69.84	162.94	358.52	S	S
26	55.04	167.35	S	-166.62	-11.77	-106.93	-79.59	S	S	-329.60
27	-70.06	S	S	133.47	56.39	54.65	-70.87	S	71.37	-125.82
28	S	S	-312.78	110.94	40.49	18.38	S	410.10	-569.38	548.75
29	S	-41.93	47.24	-195.79	23.89	S	S	-131.40	90.73	-458.13
30	-128.57	-28.32	234.87	164.70	S	S	96.58	329.04	-546.80	-500.10
Close	15129.67	17042.90	16284.00	18308.15	22405.09	26458.31	26916.83	27781.70	33843.92	28725.51
Change	319.36	-55.55	-244.03	-92.73	456.99	493.49	513.55	-648.35	-1516.81	-2784.92

OCTOBER DAILY POINT CHANGES DOW JONES INDUSTRIALS

Previous Month	2013	2014	2015	2016	2017	2018	2019	2020	2021	2022
Close	15129.67	17042.90	16284.00	18308.15	22405.09	26458.31	26916.83	27781.70	33843.92	28725.51
1	62.03	-238.19	-11.99	S	S	192.90	-343.79	35.20	482.54	S
2	-58.56	-3.66	200.36	S	152.51	122.73	-494.42	-134.09	S	S
3	-136.66	208.64	S	-54.30	84.07	54.45	122.42	S	S	765.38
4	76.10	S	S	-85.40	19.97	-200.91	372.68	S	-323.54	825.43
5	S	S	304.06	112.58	113.75	-180.43	S	465.83	311.75	-42.45
6	S	-17.78	13.76	-12.53	-1.72	S	S	-375.88	102.32	-346.93
7	-136.34	-272.52	122.10	-28.01	S	S	-95.70	530.70	337.95	-630.15
8	-159.71	274.83	138.46	S	S	39.73	-313.98	122.05	-8.69	S
9	26.45	-334.97	33.74	S	-12.60	-56.21	181.97	161.39	S	S
10	323.09	-115.15	S	88.55	69.61	-831.83	150.66	S	S	-93.91
11	111.04	S	S	-200.38	42.21	-545.91	319.92	S	-250.19	36.31
12	S	S	47.37	15.54	-31.88	287.16	S	250.62	-117.72	-28.34
13	S	-223.03	-49.97	-45.26	30.71	S	S	-157.71	-0.53	827.87
14	64.15	-5.88	-157.14	39.44	S	S	-29.23	-165.81	534.75	-403.89
15	-133.25	-173.45	217.00	S	S	-89.44	237.44	-19.80	382.20	S
16	205.82	-24.50	74.22	S	85.24	547.87	-22.82	112.11	S	S
17	-2.18	263.17	S	-51.98	40.48	-91.74	23.90	S	S	550.99
18	28.00	S	S	75.54	160.16	-327.23	-255.68	S	-36.15	337.98
19	S	19.26	14.57	40.68	5.44	64.89	S	-410.89	198.70	-99.99
20	S	215.14	-13.43	-40.27	165.59	S	S	113.37	152.03	-90.22
21	-7.45	S	-48.50	-16.64	S	S	57.44	-97.97	-6.26	748.97
22	75.46	-153.49	320.55	S	S	-126.93	-39.54	152.84	73.94	S
23	-54.33	216.58	157.54	S	-54.67	-125.98	45.85	-28.09	S	S
24	95.88	127.51	S	77.32	167.80	-608.01	-28.42	S	S	417.06
25	61.07	S	S	-53.76	-112.30	401.13	152.53	S	64.13	337.12
26	S	S	-23.65	30.06	71.40	-296.24	S	-650.19	15.73	2.37
27	S	12.53	-41.62	-29.65	33.33	S	S	-222.19	-266.19	194.17
28	-1.35	187.81	198.00	-8.49	S	S	132.66	-943.24	239.79	828.52
29	111.42	-31.44	-23.72	S	S	-245.39	-19.26	139.16	89.08	S
30	-61.59	221.11	-92.26	S	-85.45	431.72	115.23	-157.51	S	S
31	-73.01	195.10	S	-18.77	28.50	241.12	-140.46	S	S	-128.85
Close	15545.75	17390.52	17663.54	18142.42	23377.24	25115.76	27046.23	26501.60	35819.56	32732.95
Change	416.08	347.62	1379.54	-165.73	972.15	-1342.55	129.40	-1280.10	1975.64	4007.44

NOVEMBER DAILY POINT CHANGES DOW JONES INDUSTRIALS

Previous Month	2013	2014	2015	2016	2017	2018	2019	2020	2021	2022
Close	15545.75	17390.52	17663.54	18142.42	23377.24	25115.76	27046.23	26501.60	35819.56	32732.95
1	69.80	S	S	− 105.32	57.77	264.98	301.13	S	94.28	− 79.75
2	S	S	165.22	− 77.46	81.25	− 109.91	S	423.45	138.79	− 505.44
3	S	− 24.28	89.39	− 28.97	22.93	S	S	554.98	104.95	− 146.51
4	23.57	17.60	− 50.57	− 42.39	S	S	114.75	367.63	− 33.35	401.97
5	− 20.90	100.69	− 4.15	S	S	190.87	30.52	542.52	203.72	S
6	128.66	69.94	46.90	S	9.23	173.31	− 0.07	− 66.78	S	S
7	− 152.90	19.46	S	371.32	8.81	545.29	182.24	S	S	423.78
8	167.80	S	S	73.14	6.13	10.92	6.44	S	104.27	333.83
9	S	S	− 179.85	256.95	− 101.42	− 201.92	S	834.57	− 112.24	− 646.89
10	S	39.81	27.73	218.19	− 39.73	S	S	262.95	− 240.04	1201.43
11	21.32	1.16	− 55.99	39.78	S	S	10.25	− 23.29	− 158.71	32.49
12	− 32.43	− 2.70	− 254.15	S	S	− 602.12	0.00	− 317.46	179.08	S
13	70.96	40.59	− 202.83	S	17.49	− 100.69	92.10	399.64	S	S
14	54.59	− 18.05	S	21.03	− 30.23	− 205.99	− 1.63	S	S	− 211.16
15	85.48	S	S	54.37	− 138.19	208.77	222.93	S	− 12.86	56.22
16	S	S	237.77	− 54.92	187.08	123.95	S	470.63	54.77	− 39.09
17	S	13.01	6.49	35.68	− 100.12	S	S	− 167.09	− 211.17	− 7.51
18	14.32	40.07	247.66	− 35.89	S	S	31.33	− 344.93	− 60.10	199.37
19	− 8.99	− 2.09	− 4.41	S	S	− 395.78	− 102.20	44.81	− 268.97	S
20	− 66.21	33.27	91.06	S	72.09	− 551.80	− 112.93	− 219.75	S	S
21	109.17	91.06	S	88.76	160.50	− 0.95	− 54.80	S	S	− 45.41
22	54.78	S	S	67.18	− 64.65	H	109.33	S	17.27	397.82
23	S	S	− 31.13	59.31	H	− 178.74*	S	327.79	194.55	95.96
24	S	7.84	19.51	H	31.81*	S	S	454.97	− 9.42	H
25	7.77	− 2.96	1.20	68.96*	S	S	190.85	− 173.77	H	152.97*
26	0.26	− 2.69	H	S	S	354.29	55.21	H	− 905.04*	S
27	24.53	H	− 14.90*	S	22.79	108.49	42.32	37.90*	S	S
28	H	15.99*	S	− 54.24	255.93	617.70	H	S	S	− 497.57
29	− 10.92*	S	S	23.70	103.97	− 27.59	− 112.59*	S	236.60	3.07
30	S	S	− 78.57	1.98	331.67	199.62	S	− 271.73	− 652.22	737.24
Close	16086.41	17828.24	17719.92	19123.58	24272.35	25538.46	28051.41	29638.64	34483.72	34589.77
Change	540.66	437.72	56.38	981.16	895.11	422.70	1005.18	3137.04	− 1335.84	1856.82

*Shortened trading day

DECEMBER DAILY POINT CHANGES DOW JONES INDUSTRIALS

Previous Month	2013	2014	2015	2016	2017	2018	2019	2020	2021	2022
Close	16086.41	17828.24	17719.92	19123.58	24272.35	25538.46	28051.41	29638.64	34483.72	34589.77
1	S	− 51.44	168.43	68.35	− 40.76	S	S	185.28	− 461.68	− 194.76
2	− 77.64	102.75	− 158.67	− 21.51	S	S	− 268.37	59.87	617.75	34.87
3	− 94.15	33.07	− 252.01	S	S	287.97	− 280.23	85.73	− 59.71	S
4	− 24.85	− 12.52	369.96	S	58.46	− 799.36	146.97	248.74	S	S
5	− 68.26	58.69	S	45.82	− 109.41	H**	28.01	S	S	− 482.78
6	198.69	S	S	35.54	− 39.73	− 79.40	337.27	S	646.95	− 350.76
7	S	S	− 117.12	297.84	70.57	− 558.72	S	− 148.47	492.40	1.58
8	S	− 106.31	− 162.51	65.19	117.68	S	S	104.09	35.32	183.56
9	5.33	− 51.28	− 75.70	142.04	S	S	− 105.46	− 105.07	− 0.06	− 305.02
10	− 52.40	− 268.05	82.45	S	S	34.31	− 27.88	− 69.55	216.30	S
11	− 129.60	63.19	− 309.54	S	56.87	− 53.02	29.58	47.11	S	S
12	− 104.10	− 315.51	S	39.58	118.77	157.03	220.75	S	S	528.58
13	15.93	S	S	114.78	80.63	70.11	3.33	S	− 320.04	103.60
14	S	S	103.29	− 118.68	− 76.77	− 496.87	S	− 184.82	− 106.77	− 142.29
15	S	− 99.99	156.41	59.71	143.08	S	S	337.76	383.25	− 764.13
16	129.21	− 111.97	224.18	− 8.83	S	S	100.51	− 44.77	− 29.79	− 281.76
17	− 9.31	288.00	− 253.25	S	S	− 507.53	31.27	148.83	− 532.20	S
18	292.71	421.28	− 367.29	S	140.46	82.66	− 27.88	− 124.32	S	S
19	11.11	26.65	S	39.65	− 37.45	− 351.98	137.68	S	S	− 162.92
20	42.06	S	S	91.56	− 28.10	− 464.06	78.13	S	− 433.28	92.20
21	S	S	123.07	− 32.66	55.64	− 414.23	S	S	560.54	526.74
22	S	154.64	165.65	− 23.08	− 28.23	S	S	− 200.94	261.19	− 348.99
23	73.47	64.73	185.34	14.93	S	S	96.44	114.32	196.67	176.44
24	62.94*	6.04*	− 50.44*	S	S	− 653.17*	− 36.08*	70.04*	H	S
25	H	H	H	S	H	H	H	H	S	H
26	122.33	23.50	H	H	− 7.85	1086.25	105.94	S	S	H
27	− 1.47	S	S	11.23	28.09	260.37	23.87	S	351.82	37.63
28	S	S	− 23.90	− 111.36	63.21	− 76.42	S	204.10	95.83	− 365.85
29	S	− 15.48	192.71	− 13.90	− 118.29	S	S	− 68.30	90.42	345.09
30	25.88	− 55.16	− 117.11	− 57.18	S	S	− 183.12	73.89	− 90.55	− 73.55
31	72.37	− 160.00	− 178.84	S	S	265.00	76.30	196.92	− 59.78	S
Close	16576.66	17823.07	17425.03	19762.60	24719.22	23327.46	28538.44	30606.48	36338.30	33147.25
Change	490.25	− 5.17	− 294.89	639.02	446.87	− 2211.00	487.03	967.84	1854.58	− 1442.52

* Shortened trading day,   ** President H.W. Bush Funeral

A TYPICAL DAY IN THE MARKET

Half-hourly data became available for the Dow Jones Industrial Average starting in January 1987. The NYSE switched 10:00 a.m. openings to 9:30 a.m. in October 1985. Below is the comparison between half-hourly performance 1987–May 5, 2023, and hourly November 1963 to June 1985. Stronger closings in a more bullish climate are evident. Morning and afternoon weaknesses appear an hour earlier.

MARKET % PERFORMANCE EACH HALF-HOUR OF THE DAY
(January 1987–May 5, 2023)

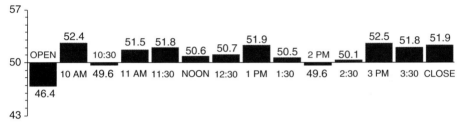

Based on the number of times the Dow Jones Industrial Average increased over the previous half-hour

MARKET % PERFORMANCE EACH HOUR OF THE DAY
(November 1963–June 1985)

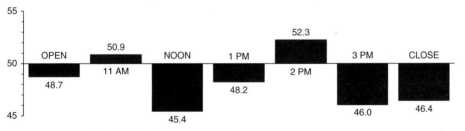

Based on the number of times the Dow Jones Industrial Average increased over the previous hour

On the next page, half-hourly movements since January 1987 are separated by day of the week. From 1953 to 1989 Monday was the worst day of the week, especially during long bear markets, but times changed. Monday was the best day of the week and on the plus side eleven years in a row from 1990 to 2000. Since the 2000 top Monday has been the worst day during bears and the best during bulls.

During the last 22 years (2001–June 2, 2023) Monday is the weakest day of the week. Tuesday is the best (page 72). On all days stocks do tend to firm up near the close with weakness early morning and from 1:30 to 2:30 frequently.

THROUGH THE WEEK ON A HALF-HOURLY BASIS

From the chart showing the percentage of times the Dow Jones Industrial Average rose over the preceding half-hour (January 1987 to May 5, 2023*), the typical week unfolds.

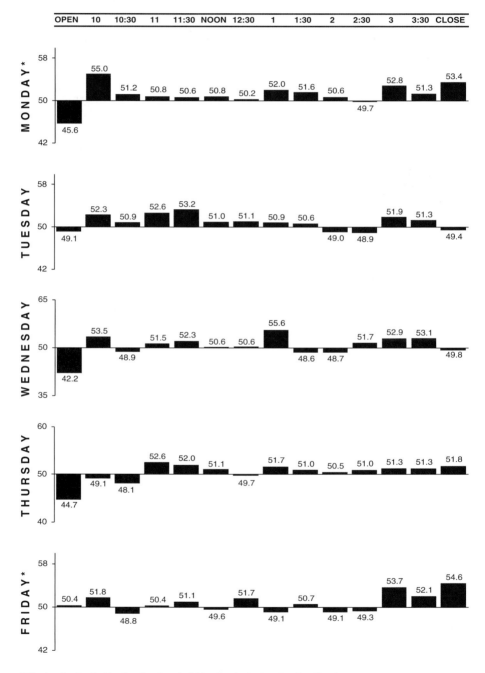

Monday denotes first trading day of week, Friday denotes last trading day of week

TUESDAY & WEDNESDAY MOST PROFITABLE DAYS OF WEEK

Between 1952 and 1989, Monday was the worst trading day of the week. The first trading day of the week (including Tuesday when Monday is a holiday) rose only 44.3% of the time, while the other trading days closed higher 54.8% of the time. (NYSE Saturday trading was discontinued in June 1952.)

MARKET % PERFORMANCE EACH DAY OF THE WEEK
(June 1952–December 1989)

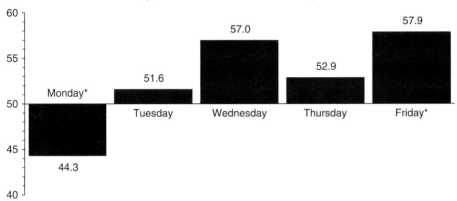

A dramatic reversal occurred in 1990—Monday became the most powerful day of the week. However, during the last 22 and a half years Tuesday has produced the most gains and Wednesday has been up the most number of times. Since the top in 2000, traders have not been inclined to stay long over the weekend nor buy up equities at the outset of the week. This is not uncommon during uncertain market times. Monday was the worst day during the 2007-2009 bear and only Tuesday was a net gainer. Since the March 2009 bottom, Tuesday is best. See pages 72 and 145.

MARKET % PERFORMANCE EACH DAY OF THE WEEK
(January 1990–May 19, 2023)

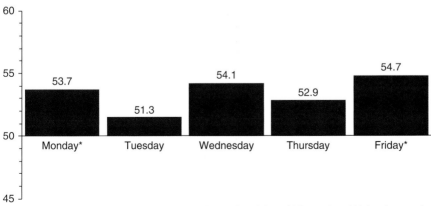

Charts based on the number of times S&P 500 closed higher than previous day
* Monday denotes first trading day of week, Friday denotes last trading day of week

NASDAQ STRONGEST LAST 3 DAYS OF WEEK

Despite 20 years less data, daily trading patterns on NASDAQ through 1989 appear to be fairly similar to the S&P on page 143 except for more bullishness on Thursdays. During the mostly flat markets of the 1970s and early 1980s, it would appear that apprehensive investors decided to throw in the towel over weekends and sell on Mondays and Tuesdays.

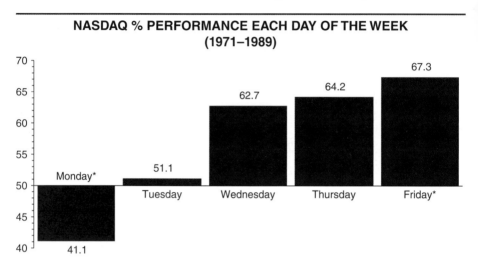

Notice the modest difference in the daily trading pattern between NASDAQ and S&P from January 1, 1990 to recent times. NASDAQ's weekly patterns are beginning to move in step with the rest of the market as technology continues to take an ever-increasing role throughout the economy. Notice the similarities to the S&P since 2001 on pages 145 and 146, Monday and Friday weakness, mid-week strength during bear markets.

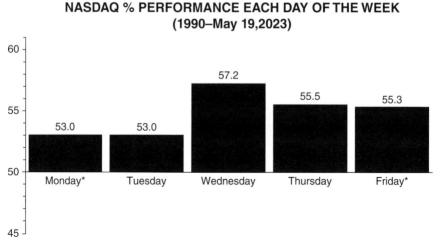

Based on NASDAQ composite, prior to Feb. 5, 1971 based on National Quotation Bureau indices
* Monday denotes first trading day of week, Friday denotes last trading day of week

S&P DAILY PERFORMANCE EACH YEAR SINCE 1952

To determine if market trend alters performance of different days of the week, we separated 24 bear years—1953, '56, '57, '60, '62, '66, '69, '70, '73, '74, '77, '78, '81, '84, '87, '90, '94, 2000, 2001, 2002, 2008, 2011, 2015 and 2022 from 47 bull market years. While Tuesdays and Thursdays did not vary much between bull and bear years, Mondays and Fridays were sharply affected. There was a swing of 10.5 percentage points in Monday's performance and 9.7 in Friday's. Tuesday is the best day of the week based on total points gained. See page 72.

PERCENTAGE OF TIMES MARKET CLOSED HIGHER THAN PREVIOUS DAY
(JUNE 1952 - MAY 19, 2023)

	Monday*	Tuesday	Wednesday	Thursday	Friday**
1952	48.4%	55.6%	58.1%	51.9%	66.7%
1953	32.7	50.0	54.9	57.5	56.6
1954	50.0	57.5	63.5	59.2	73.1
1955	50.0	45.7	63.5	60.0	78.9
1956	36.5	39.6	46.9	50.0	59.6
1957	25.0	54.0	66.7	48.9	44.2
1958	59.6	52.0	59.6	68.1	72.6
1959	42.3	53.1	55.8	48.9	69.8
1960	34.6	50.0	44.2	54.0	59.6
1961	52.9	54.4	64.7	56.0	67.3
1962	28.3	52.1	54.0	51.0	50.0
1963	46.2	63.3	51.0	57.5	69.2
1964	40.4	48.0	61.5	58.7	77.4
1965	44.2	57.5	55.8	51.0	71.2
1966	36.5	47.8	53.9	42.0	57.7
1967	38.5	50.0	60.8	64.0	69.2
1968†	49.1	57.5	64.3	42.6	54.9
1969	30.8	45.8	50.0	67.4	50.0
1970	38.5	46.0	63.5	48.9	52.8
1971	44.2	64.6	57.7	55.1	51.9
1972	38.5	60.9	57.7	51.0	67.3
1973	32.1	51.1	52.9	44.9	44.2
1974	32.7	57.1	51.0	36.7	30.8
1975	53.9	38.8	61.5	56.3	55.8
1976	55.8	55.3	55.8	40.8	58.5
1977	40.4	40.4	46.2	53.1	53.9
1978	51.9	43.5	59.6	54.0	48.1
1979	54.7	53.2	58.8	66.0	44.2
1980	55.8	54.2	71.7	35.4	59.6
1981	44.2	38.8	55.8	53.2	47.2
1982	46.2	39.6	44.2	44.9	50.0
1983	55.8	46.8	61.5	52.0	55.8
1984	39.6	63.8	31.4	46.0	44.2
1985	44.2	61.2	54.9	56.3	53.9
1986	51.9	44.9	67.3	58.3	55.8
1987	51.9	57.1	63.5	61.7	49.1
1988	51.9	61.7	51.9	48.0	59.6
1989	51.9	47.8	69.2	58.0	69.2
1990	67.9	53.2	52.9	40.0	51.9
1991	44.2	46.9	52.9	49.0	51.9
1992	51.9	49.0	53.9	56.3	45.3
1993	65.4	41.7	55.8	44.9	48.1
1994	55.8	46.8	52.9	48.0	59.6
1995	63.5	56.5	63.5	62.0	63.5
1996	54.7	44.9	51.0	57.1	63.5
1997	67.3	67.4	42.3	41.7	57.7
1998	57.7	62.5	57.7	38.3	60.4
1999	46.2	29.8	67.3	53.1	57.7
2000	51.9	43.5	40.4	56.0	46.2
2001	45.3	51.1	44.0	59.2	43.1
2002	40.4	37.5	56.9	38.8	48.1
2003	59.6	62.5	42.3	58.3	50.0
2004	51.9	61.7	59.6	52.1	52.8
2005	59.6	47.8	59.6	56.0	55.8
2006	55.8	55.6	67.3	52.0	48.1
2007	47.2	50.0	64.0	50.0	61.5
2008	42.3	50.0	41.5	60.4	55.8
2009	53.9	50.0	57.7	63.8	52.8
2010	61.5	57.5	55.8	53.1	57.7
2011	48.1	56.5	55.8	56.0	57.7
2012	52.8	48.9	50.0	58.0	53.9
2013	51.9	60.4	54.9	59.2	65.4
2014	53.9	56.3	57.7	56.3	61.5
2015	51.9	43.8	44.2	53.2	43.4
2016	50.0	58.7	55.8	50.0	46.2
2017	55.8	55.6	61.5	50.0	61.5
2018	52.8	60.9	50.0	46.0	53.9
2019	50.0	54.2	60.8	65.3	67.3
2020	63.5	54.2	61.5	52.1	54.7
2021	51.9	44.7	61.5	65.3	59.6
2022	38.5	48.9	46.2	38.0	44.2
2023‡	60.0	35.3	40.0	57.9	60.0
Average	**48.6%**	**51.7%**	**55.8%**	**52.8%**	**56.3%**
47 Bull Years	**52.1%**	**53.2%**	**58.2%**	**53.8%**	**59.6%**
24 Bear Years	**41.6%**	**48.7%**	**51.2%**	**50.8%**	**49.9%**

Based on S&P 500

† Most Wednesdays closed last 7 months of 1968   ‡ Through 5/19/2023 only, not included in averages
Monday denotes first trading day of week, Friday denotes last trading day of week.

NASDAQ DAILY PERFORMANCE EACH YEAR SINCE 1971

After dropping a hefty 77.9% from its 2000 high (versus −37.8% on the Dow and −49.1% on the S&P 500), NASDAQ tech stocks still outpace the blue chips and big caps—but not nearly by as much as they did. From January 1, 1971, through May 19, 2023, NASDAQ moved up an impressive 14026%. The Dow (up 3884%) and the S&P (up 4449%) gained less than a third as much.

Monday's performance on NASDAQ was lackluster during the three-year bear market of 2000–2002. As NASDAQ rebounded (up 50% in 2003), strength returned to Monday during 2003–2006. During the bear market from late 2007 to early 2009, weakness was most consistent on Monday and Friday. At press time, Mondays and Tuesdays have been most challenging.

PERCENTAGE OF TIMES NASDAQ CLOSED HIGHER THAN PREVIOUS DAY
(1971 - MAY 19, 2023)

	Monday*	Tuesday	Wednesday	Thursday	Friday**
1971	51.9%	52.1%	59.6%	65.3%	71.2%
1972	30.8	60.9	63.5	57.1	78.9
1973	34.0	48.9	52.9	53.1	48.1
1974	30.8	44.9	52.9	51.0	42.3
1975	44.2	42.9	63.5	64.6	63.5
1976	50.0	63.8	67.3	59.2	58.5
1977	51.9	40.4	53.9	63.3	73.1
1978	48.1	47.8	73.1	72.0	84.6
1979	45.3	53.2	64.7	86.0	82.7
1980	46.2	64.6	84.9	52.1	73.1
1981	42.3	32.7	67.3	76.6	69.8
1982	34.6	47.9	59.6	51.0	63.5
1983	42.3	44.7	67.3	68.0	73.1
1984	22.6	53.2	35.3	52.0	51.9
1985	36.5	59.2	62.8	68.8	66.0
1986	38.5	55.1	65.4	72.9	75.0
1987	42.3	49.0	65.4	68.1	66.0
1988	50.0	55.3	61.5	66.0	63.5
1989	38.5	54.4	71.2	72.0	75.0
1990	54.7	42.6	60.8	46.0	55.8
1991	51.9	59.2	66.7	65.3	51.9
1992	44.2	53.1	59.6	60.4	45.3
1993	55.8	56.3	69.2	57.1	67.3
1994	51.9	46.8	54.9	52.0	55.8
1995	50.0	52.2	63.5	64.0	63.5
1996	50.9	57.1	64.7	61.2	63.5
1997	65.4	59.2	53.9	52.1	55.8
1998	59.6	58.3	65.4	44.7	58.5
1999	61.5	40.4	63.5	57.1	65.4
2000	40.4	41.3	42.3	60.0	57.7
2001	41.5	57.8	52.0	55.1	47.1
2002	44.2	37.5	56.9	46.9	46.2
2003	57.7	60.4	40.4	60.4	46.2
2004	57.7	59.6	53.9	50.0	50.9
2005	61.5	47.8	51.9	48.0	59.6
2006	55.8	51.1	65.4	50.0	44.2
2007	47.2	63.0	66.0	56.0	57.7
2008	34.6	52.1	49.1	54.2	42.3
2009	51.9	54.2	63.5	63.8	50.9
2010	61.5	53.2	61.5	55.1	61.5
2011	50.0	56.5	50.0	64.0	53.9
2012	49.1	53.3	50.0	54.0	51.9
2013	57.7	60.4	52.9	59.2	67.3
2014	57.7	58.3	57.7	52.1	59.6
2015	55.8	39.6	53.9	59.6	49.1
2016	51.9	52.2	55.8	50.0	57.7
2017	59.6	62.2	67.3	50.0	67.3
2018	54.7	69.6	50.0	46.0	50.0
2019	50.0	58.3	62.8	59.2	59.6
2020	69.2	58.3	67.3	60.4	54.7
2021	55.8	44.7	48.1	67.4	63.5
2022	40.4	51.1	44.2	44.0	42.3
2023†	50.0	35.3	60.0	63.2	55.0
Average	**48.7%**	**52.7%**	**59.2%**	**58.5%**	**59.7%**
38 Bull Years	**51.2%**	**54.9%**	**61.6%**	**59.5%**	**62.5%**
14 Bear Years	**41.8%**	**46.7%**	**52.7%**	**55.9%**	**52.0%**

Based on NASDAQ composite; prior to Feb. 5, 1971 based on National Quotation Bureau indices
† Through 5/19/2023 only, not included in averages
*Monday denotes first trading day of week, Friday denotes last trading day of week

146

MONTHLY CASH INFLOWS INTO S&P STOCKS

For many years, the last trading day of the month, plus the first four of the following month, were the best market days of the month. This pattern is quite clear in the first chart, showing these five consecutive trading days towering above the other 16 trading days of the average month in the 1953–1981 period. The rationale was that individuals and institutions tended to operate similarly, causing a massive flow of cash into stocks near beginnings of months.

MARKET % PERFORMANCE EACH DAY OF THE MONTH
(January 1953 to December 1981)
Based on the number of times the S&P 500
closed higher than previous day.

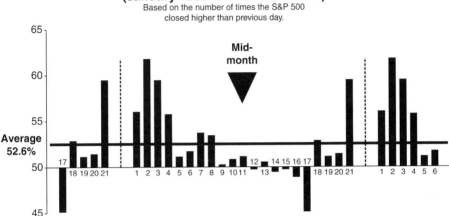

Clearly "front-running" traders took advantage of this phenomenon, drastically altering the previous pattern. The second chart from 1982 onward shows the trading shift caused by these "anticipators" to the last three trading days of the month plus the first two. Another development shows the ninth, tenth, eleventh, and twelfth trading days rising strongly as well. Growth of 401(k) retirement plans, IRAs and similar plans (participants' salaries are usually paid twice monthly) are responsible for this mid-month bulge. First trading days of the month have produced the greatest gains in recent years (see pages 90). Last trading day of the month strength has faded substantially.

MARKET % PERFORMANCE EACH DAY OF THE MONTH
(January 1982 to December 2022)

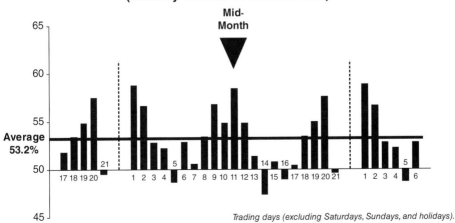

Trading days (excluding Saturdays, Sundays, and holidays).

MONTHLY CASH INFLOWS INTO NASDAQ STOCKS

NASDAQ stocks moved up 58.1% of the time through 1981 compared to 52.6% for the S&P on page 147. Ends and beginnings of the month are fairly similar, specifically the last plus the first four trading days. But notice how investors piled into NASDAQ stocks until midmonth. NASDAQ rose 118.6% from January 1, 1971, to December 31, 1981, compared to 33.0% for the S&P.

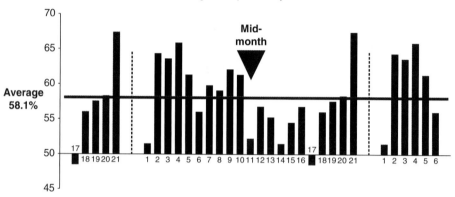

NASDAQ % PERFORMANCE EACH DAY OF THE MONTH
(January 1971 to December 1981)
Based on the number of times the NASDAQ composite closed higher than previous day.

After the air was let out of the tech market in 2000–2002, S&P's 3033% gain over the last 41 years is more evenly matched with NASDAQ's 5244% gain. Last three, first four, and middle ninth, tenth, eleventh and twelfth days rose the most. Where the S&P now has four days of the month that go down more often than up, NASDAQ has none. NASDAQ exhibits the most strength on the first trading day of the month. Over the past 21 years, last days have weakened considerably, down more frequently than not.

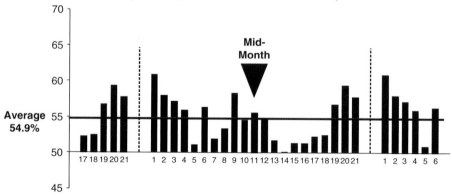

NASDAQ % PERFORMANCE EACH DAY OF THE MONTH
(January 1982 to December 2022)

Trading days (excluding Saturdays, Sundays, and holidays).
Based on NASDAQ composite, prior to February 5, 1971, based on National Quotation Bureau indices.

NOVEMBER, DECEMBER, AND JANUARY: YEAR'S BEST THREE-MONTH SPAN

The most important observation to be made from a chart showing the average monthly percent change in market prices since 1950 is that institutions (mutual funds, pension funds, banks, etc.) determine the trading patterns in today's market.

The "investment calendar" reflects the annual, semiannual, and quarterly operations of institutions during January, April, and July. October, besides being the last campaign month before elections, is also the time when most bear markets seem to end, as in 1946, 1957, 1960, 1966, 1974, 1987, 1990, 1998, 2002 and 2022. (August and September tend to combine to make the worst consecutive two-month period.)

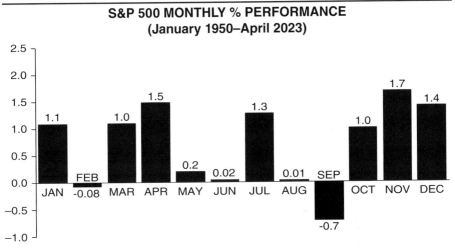

S&P 500 MONTHLY % PERFORMANCE
(January 1950–April 2023)

Average month-to-month % change in S&P 500.
(Based on monthly closing prices.)

Unusual year-end strength comes from corporate and private pension funds, producing a 4.3% gain on average between November 1 and January 31. In 2007–2008, these three months were all down for the fourth time since 1930; previously in 1931–1932, 1940–1941 and 1969–1970, also bear markets. September's dismal performance makes it the worst month of the year. However, in the last 19 years, it has been up 11 times after being down five in a row 1999–2003, but down six of the last nine.

In presidential-election years since 1950, November is the best month +2.0% (up 11, down 7). December is second best with an average 1.3% gain. March, April, May, June, July and August are also positive. January and May are flat. October is the worst month in presidential-election years, average loss –0.9% (up 9, down 9). February and September are also net decliners.

See page 52 for monthly performance tables for the S&P 500 and the Dow Jones industrials. See pages 54, 56, 62 and 64 for unique switching strategies.

On page 68, you can see how the first month of the first three quarters far outperforms the second and third months since 1950, and note the improvement in May's and October's performance since 1991.

NOVEMBER THROUGH JUNE: NASDAQ'S EIGHT-MONTH RUN

The two-and-a-half-year plunge of 77.9% in NASDAQ stocks, between March 10, 2000, and October 9, 2002, brought several horrendous monthly losses (the two greatest were November 2000, –22.9% and February 2001, –22.4%), which trimmed average monthly performance over the $52^1/_3$-year period. Ample Octobers in 17 of the last 25 years, including three huge turnarounds in 2001 (+12.8%), 2002 (+13.5%) and 2011 (+11.1%) have put bear-killing October in the number one spot since 1998. January's 2.7% average gain is still awesome, and more than twice S&P's 1.1% January average since 1971.

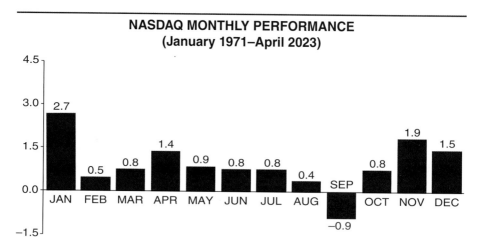

NASDAQ MONTHLY PERFORMANCE
(January 1971–April 2023)

Average month-to-month % change in NASDAQ composite,
prior to February 5, 1971, based on National Quotation Bureau indices.
(Based on monthly closing prices.)

Bear in mind, when comparing NASDAQ to the S&P on page 149, that there are 23 fewer years of data here. During this $52^1/_3$-year (1971–April 2023) period, NASDAQ gained 13544%, while the S&P and the Dow rose only 4425% and 3965%, respectively. On page 60, you can see a statistical monthly comparison between NASDAQ and the Dow.

Year-end strength is even more pronounced in NASDAQ, producing a 6.1% gain on average between November 1 and January 31—nearly 1.5 times greater than that of the S&P 500 on page 149. September is the worst month of the year for the over-the-counter index as well, posting an average loss of –0.9%. These extremes underscore NASDAQ's higher volatility—and moves of greater magnitude.

In presidential-election years since 1971, August is best with an average gain of 3.2% (up 9, down 4). January, February, April, May, June, November and December are all also positive. October is the worst month in presidential-election years, –2.2% (down 9, up 4). March, July and September also are negative on average.

DOW JONES INDUSTRIALS ANNUAL HIGHS, LOWS, & CLOSES SINCE 1901

YEAR	HIGH DATE	HIGH CLOSE	LOW DATE	LOW CLOSE	YEAR CLOSE	YEAR	HIGH DATE	HIGH CLOSE	LOW DATE	LOW CLOSE	YEAR CLOSE
1901	6/17	57.33	12/24	45.07	47.29	1933	7/18	108.67	2/27	50.16	99.90
1902	4/24	50.14	12/15	43.64	47.10	1934	2/5	110.74	7/26	85.51	104.04
1903	2/16	49.59	11/9	30.88	35.98	1935	11/19	148.44	3/14	96.71	144.13
1904	12/5	53.65	3/12	34.00	50.99	1936	11/17	184.90	1/6	143.11	179.90
1905	12/29	70.74	1/25	50.37	70.47	1937	3/10	194.40	11/24	113.64	120.85
1906	1/19	75.45	7/13	62.40	69.12	1938	11/12	158.41	3/31	98.95	154.76
1907	1/7	70.60	11/15	38.83	43.04	1939	9/12	155.92	4/8	121.44	150.24
1908	11/13	64.74	2/13	42.94	63.11	1940	1/3	152.80	6/10	111.84	131.13
1909	11/19	73.64	2/23	58.54	72.56	1941	1/10	133.59	12/23	106.34	110.96
1910	1/3	72.04	7/26	53.93	59.60	1942	12/26	119.71	4/28	92.92	119.40
1911	6/19	63.78	9/25	53.43	59.84	1943	7/14	145.82	1/8	119.26	135.89
1912	9/30	68.97	2/10	58.72	64.37	1944	12/16	152.53	2/7	134.22	152.32
1913	1/9	64.88	6/11	52.83	57.71	1945	12/11	195.82	1/24	151.35	192.91
1914	3/20	61.12	7/30	52.32	54.58	1946	5/29	212.50	10/9	163.12	177.20
1915	12/27	99.21	2/24	54.22	99.15	1947	7/24	186.85	5/17	163.21	181.16
1916	11/21	110.15	4/22	84.96	95.00	1948	6/15	193.16	3/16	165.39	177.30
1917	1/3	99.18	12/19	65.95	74.38	1949	12/30	200.52	6/13	161.60	200.13
1918	10/18	89.07	1/15	73.38	82.20	1950	11/24	235.47	1/13	196.81	235.41
1919	11/3	119.62	2/8	79.15	107.23	1951	9/13	276.37	1/3	238.99	269.23
1920	1/3	109.88	12/21	66.75	71.95	1952	12/30	292.00	5/1	256.35	291.90
1921	12/15	81.50	8/24	63.90	81.10	1953	1/5	293.79	9/14	255.49	280.90
1922	10/14	103.43	1/10	78.59	98.73	1954	12/31	404.39	1/11	279.87	404.39
1923	3/20	105.38	10/27	85.76	95.52	1955	12/30	488.40	1/17	388.20	488.40
1924	12/31	120.51	5/20	88.33	120.51	1956	4/6	521.05	1/23	462.35	499.47
1925	11/6	159.39	3/30	115.00	156.66	1957	7/12	520.77	10/22	419.79	435.69
1926	8/14	166.64	3/30	135.20	157.20	1958	12/31	583.65	2/25	436.89	583.65
1927	12/31	202.40	1/25	152.73	202.40	1959	12/31	679.36	2/9	574.46	679.36
1928	12/31	300.00	2/20	191.33	300.00	1960	1/5	685.47	10/25	566.05	615.89
1929	9/3	381.17	11/13	198.69	248.48	1961	12/13	734.91	1/3	610.25	731.14
1930	4/17	294.07	12/16	157.51	164.58	1962	1/3	726.01	6/26	535.76	652.10
1931	2/24	194.36	12/17	73.79	77.90	1963	12/18	767.21	1/2	646.79	762.95
1932	3/8	88.78	7/8	41.22	59.93	1964	11/18	891.71	1/2	766.08	874.13

continued

151

DOW JONES INDUSTRIALS ANNUAL HIGHS, LOWS, & CLOSES SINCE 1901 (continued)

YEAR	HIGH DATE	HIGH CLOSE	LOW DATE	LOW CLOSE	YEAR CLOSE	YEAR	HIGH DATE	HIGH CLOSE	LOW DATE	LOW CLOSE	YEAR CLOSE
1965	12/31	969.26	6/28	840.59	969.26	1995	12/13	5216.47	1/30	3832.08	5117.12
1966	2/9	995.15	10/7	744.32	785.69	1996	12/27	6560.91	1/10	5032.94	6448.27
1967	9/25	943.08	1/3	786.41	905.11	1997	8/6	8259.31	4/11	6391.69	7908.25
1968	12/3	985.21	3/21	825.13	943.75	1998	11/23	9374.27	8/31	7539.07	9181.43
1969	5/14	968.85	12/17	769.93	800.36	1999	12/31	11497.12	1/22	9120.67	11497.12
1970	12/29	842.00	5/26	631.16	838.92	2000	1/14	11722.98	3/7	9796.03	10786.85
1971	4/28	950.82	11/23	797.97	890.20	2001	5/21	11337.92	9/21	8235.81	10021.50
1972	12/11	1036.27	1/26	889.15	1020.02	2002	3/19	10635.25	10/9	7286.27	8341.63
1973	1/11	1051.70	12/5	788.31	850.86	2003	12/31	10453.92	3/11	7524.06	10453.92
1974	3/13	891.66	12/6	577.60	616.24	2004	12/28	10854.54	10/25	9749.99	10783.01
1975	7/15	881.81	1/2	632.04	852.41	2005	3/4	10940.55	4/20	10012.36	10717.50
1976	9/21	1014.79	1/2	858.71	1004.65	2006	12/27	12510.57	1/20	10667.39	12463.15
1977	1/3	999.75	11/2	800.85	831.17	2007	10/9	14164.53	3/5	12050.41	13264.82
1978	9/8	907.74	2/28	742.12	805.01	2008	5/2	13058.20	11/20	7552.29	8776.39
1979	10/5	897.61	11/7	796.67	838.74	2009	12/30	10548.51	3/9	6547.05	10428.05
1980	11/20	1000.17	4/21	759.13	963.99	2010	12/29	11585.38	7/2	9686.48	11577.51
1981	4/27	1024.05	9/25	824.01	875.00	2011	4/29	12810.54	10/3	10655.30	12217.5
1982	12/27	1070.55	8/12	776.92	1046.54	2012	10/5	13610.15	6/4	12101.46	13104.14
1983	11/29	1287.20	1/3	1027.04	1258.64	2013	12/31	16576.66	1/8	13328.85	16576.66
1984	1/6	1286.64	7/24	1086.57	1211.57	2014	12/26	18053.71	2/3	15372.80	17823.07
1985	12/16	1553.10	1/4	1184.96	1546.67	2015	5/19	18312.39	8/25	15666.44	17425.03
1986	12/2	1955.57	1/22	1502.29	1895.95	2016	12/20	19974.62	2/11	15660.18	19762.60
1987	8/25	2722.42	10/19	1738.74	1938.83	2017	12/28	24837.51	1/19	19732.40	24719.22
1988	10/21	2183.50	1/20	1879.14	2168.57	2018	10/3	26828.39	12/24	21792.20	23327.46
1989	10/9	2791.41	1/3	2144.64	2753.20	2019	12/27	28645.26	1/3	22686.22	28538.44
1990	7/17	2999.75	10/11	2365.10	2633.66	2020	12/31	30606.48	3/23	18591.93	30606.48
1991	12/31	3168.83	1/9	2470.30	3168.83	2021	12/29	36488.63	1/29	29982.62	36338.30
1992	6/1	3413.21	10/9	3136.58	3301.11	2022	1/4	36799.65	9/30	28725.51	33147.25
1993	12/29	3794.33	1/20	3241.95	3754.09	2023*	1/13	34302.61	3/13	31819.14	At press time
1994	1/31	3978.36	4/4	3593.35	3834.44						

*Through May 26, 2023

S&P 500 ANNUAL HIGHS, LOWS, & CLOSES SINCE 1930

YEAR	HIGH DATE	HIGH CLOSE	LOW DATE	LOW CLOSE	YEAR CLOSE	YEAR	HIGH DATE	HIGH CLOSE	LOW DATE	LOW CLOSE	YEAR CLOSE
1930	4/10	25.92	12/16	14.44	15.34	1977	1/3	107.00	11/2	90.71	95.10
1931	2/24	18.17	12/17	7.72	8.12	1978	9/12	106.99	3/6	86.90	96.11
1932	9/7	9.31	6/1	4.40	6.89	1979	10/5	111.27	2/27	96.13	107.94
1933	7/18	12.20	2/27	5.53	10.10	1980	11/28	140.52	3/27	98.22	135.76
1934	2/6	11.82	7/26	8.36	9.50	1981	1/6	138.12	9/25	112.77	122.55
1935	11/19	13.46	3/14	8.06	13.43	1982	11/9	143.02	8/12	102.42	140.64
1936	11/9	17.69	1/2	13.40	17.18	1983	10/10	172.65	1/3	138.34	164.93
1937	3/6	18.68	11/24	10.17	10.55	1984	11/6	170.41	7/24	147.82	167.24
1938	11/9	13.79	3/31	8.50	13.21	1985	12/16	212.02	1/4	163.68	211.28
1939	1/4	13.23	4/8	10.18	12.49	1986	12/2	254.00	1/22	203.49	242.17
1940	1/3	12.77	6/10	8.99	10.58	1987	8/25	336.77	12/4	223.92	247.08
1941	1/10	10.86	12/29	8.37	8.69	1988	10/21	283.66	1/20	242.63	277.72
1942	12/31	9.77	4/28	7.47	9.77	1989	10/9	359.80	1/3	275.31	353.40
1943	7/14	12.64	1/2	9.84	11.67	1990	7/16	368.95	10/11	295.46	330.22
1944	12/16	13.29	2/7	11.56	13.28	1991	12/31	417.09	1/9	311.49	417.09
1945	12/10	17.68	1/23	13.21	17.36	1992	12/18	441.28	4/8	394.50	435.71
1946	5/29	19.25	10/9	14.12	15.30	1993	12/28	470.94	1/8	429.05	466.45
1947	2/8	16.20	5/17	13.71	15.30	1994	2/2	482.00	4/4	438.92	459.27
1948	6/15	17.06	2/14	13.84	15.20	1995	12/13	621.69	1/3	459.11	615.93
1949	12/30	16.79	6/13	13.55	16.76	1996	11/25	757.03	1/10	598.48	740.74
1950	12/29	20.43	1/14	16.65	20.41	1997	12/5	983.79	1/2	737.01	970.43
1951	10/15	23.85	1/3	20.69	23.77	1998	12/29	1241.81	1/9	927.69	1229.23
1952	12/30	26.59	2/20	23.09	26.57	1999	12/31	1469.25	1/14	1212.19	1469.25
1953	1/5	26.66	9/14	22.71	24.81	2000	3/24	1527.46	12/20	1264.74	1320.28
1954	12/31	35.98	1/11	24.80	35.98	2001	2/1	1373.47	9/21	965.80	1148.08
1955	11/14	46.41	1/17	34.58	45.48	2002	1/4	1172.51	10/9	776.76	879.82
1956	8/2	49.74	1/23	43.11	46.67	2003	12/31	1111.92	3/11	800.73	1111.92
1957	7/15	49.13	10/22	38.98	39.99	2004	12/30	1213.55	8/12	1063.23	1211.92
1958	12/31	55.21	1/2	40.33	55.21	2005	12/14	1272.74	4/20	1137.50	1248.29
1959	8/3	60.71	2/9	53.58	59.89	2006	12/15	1427.09	6/13	1223.69	1418.30
1960	1/5	60.39	10/25	52.30	58.11	2007	10/9	1565.15	3/5	1374.12	1468.36
1961	12/12	72.64	1/3	57.57	71.55	2008	1/2	1447.16	11/20	752.44	903.25
1962	1/3	71.13	6/26	52.32	63.10	2009	12/28	1127.78	3/9	676.53	1115.10
1963	12/31	75.02	1/2	62.69	75.02	2010	12/29	1259.78	7/2	1022.58	1257.64
1964	11/20	86.28	1/2	75.43	84.75	2011	4/29	1363.61	10/3	1099.23	1257.60
1965	11/15	92.63	6/28	81.60	92.43	2012	9/14	1465.77	1/3	1277.06	1426.19
1966	2/9	94.06	10/7	73.20	80.33	2013	12/31	1848.36	1/8	1457.15	1848.36
1967	9/25	97.59	1/3	80.38	96.47	2014	12/29	2090.57	2/3	1741.89	2058.90
1968	11/29	108.37	3/5	87.72	103.86	2015	5/21	2130.82	8/25	1867.61	2043.94
1969	5/14	106.16	12/17	89.20	92.06	2016	12/13	2271.72	2/11	1829.08	2238.83
1970	1/5	93.46	5/26	69.29	92.15	2017	12/18	2690.16	1/3	2257.83	2673.61
1971	4/28	104.77	11/23	90.16	102.09	2018	9/20	2930.75	12/24	2351.10	2506.85
1972	12/11	119.12	1/3	101.67	118.05	2019	12/27	3240.02	1/3	2447.89	3230.78
1973	1/11	120.24	12/5	92.16	97.55	2020	12/31	3756.07	3/23	2237.40	3756.07
1974	1/3	99.80	10/3	62.68	68.56	2021	12/29	4793.06	1/4	3700.65	4766.18
1975	7/15	95.61	1/8	70.04	90.19	2022	1/3	4796.56	10/12	3577.03	3839.50
1976	9/21	107.83	1/2	90.90	107.46	2023*	5/26	4205.23	1/5	3808.10	At press time

*Through May 26, 2023

153

NASDAQ ANNUAL HIGHS, LOWS, & CLOSES SINCE 1971

YEAR	HIGH DATE	HIGH CLOSE	LOW DATE	LOW CLOSE	YEAR CLOSE
1971	12/31	114.12	1/5	89.06	114.12
1972	12/8	135.15	1/3	113.65	133.73
1973	1/11	136.84	12/24	88.67	92.19
1974	3/15	96.53	10/3	54.87	59.82
1975	7/15	88.00	1/2	60.70	77.62
1976	12/31	97.88	1/2	78.06	97.88
1977	12/30	105.05	4/5	93.66	105.05
1978	9/13	139.25	1/11	99.09	117.98
1979	10/5	152.29	1/2	117.84	151.14
1980	11/28	208.15	3/27	124.09	202.34
1981	5/29	223.47	9/28	175.03	195.84
1982	12/8	240.70	8/13	159.14	232.41
1983	6/24	328.91	1/3	230.59	278.60
1984	1/6	287.90	7/25	225.30	247.35
1985	12/16	325.16	1/2	245.91	324.93
1986	7/3	411.16	1/9	323.01	349.33
1987	8/26	455.26	10/28	291.88	330.47
1988	7/5	396.11	1/12	331.97	381.38
1989	10/9	485.73	1/3	378.56	454.82
1990	7/16	469.60	10/16	325.44	373.84
1991	12/31	586.34	1/14	355.75	586.34
1992	12/31	676.95	6/26	547.84	676.95
1993	10/15	787.42	4/26	645.87	776.80
1994	3/18	803.93	6/24	693.79	751.96
1995	12/4	1069.79	1/3	743.58	1052.13
1996	12/9	1316.27	1/15	988.57	1291.03
1997	10/9	1745.85	4/2	1201.00	1570.35
1998	12/31	2192.69	10/8	1419.12	2192.69
1999	12/31	4069.31	1/4	2208.05	4069.31
2000	3/10	5048.62	12/20	2332.78	2470.52
2001	1/24	2859.15	9/21	1423.19	1950.40
2002	1/4	2059.38	10/9	1114.11	1335.51
2003	12/30	2009.88	3/11	1271.47	2003.37
2004	12/30	2178.34	8/12	1752.49	2175.44
2005	12/2	2273.37	4/28	1904.18	2205.32
2006	11/22	2465.98	7/21	2020.39	2415.29
2007	10/31	2859.12	3/5	2340.68	2652.28
2008	1/2	2609.63	11/20	1316.12	1577.03
2009	12/30	2291.28	3/9	1268.64	2269.15
2010	12/22	2671.48	7/2	2091.79	2652.87
2011	4/29	2873.54	10/3	2335.83	2605.15
2012	9/14	3183.95	1/4	2648.36	3019.51
2013	12/31	4176.59	1/8	3091.81	4176.59
2014	12/29	4806.91	2/3	3996.96	4736.05
2015	7/20	5218.86	8/25	4506.49	5007.41
2016	12/27	5487.44	2/11	4266.84	5383.12
2017	12/18	6994.76	1/3	5429.08	6903.39
2018	8/29	8109.69	12/24	6192.92	6635.28
2019	12/26	9022.39	1/3	6463.50	8972.60
2020	12/28	12899.42	3/23	6860.67	12888.28
2021	11/29	16057.44	3/8	12609.16	15644.97
2022	1/3	15832.80	12/28	10213.29	10466.48
2023*	5/26	12975.69	1/5	10305.24	At press time

*Through May 26, 2023

154

RUSSELL 1000 ANNUAL HIGHS, LOWS, & CLOSES SINCE 1979

YEAR	HIGH DATE	HIGH CLOSE	LOW DATE	LOW CLOSE	YEAR CLOSE	YEAR	HIGH DATE	HIGH CLOSE	LOW DATE	LOW CLOSE	YEAR CLOSE
1979	10/5	61.18	2/27	51.83	59.87	2002	3/19	618.74	10/9	410.52	466.18
1980	11/28	78.26	3/27	53.68	75.20	2003	12/31	594.56	3/11	425.31	594.56
1981	1/6	76.34	9/25	62.03	67.93	2004	12/30	651.76	8/13	566.06	650.99
1982	11/9	78.47	8/12	55.98	77.24	2005	12/14	692.09	4/20	613.37	679.42
1983	10/10	95.07	1/3	76.04	90.38	2006	12/15	775.08	6/13	665.81	770.08
1984	1/6	92.80	7/24	79.49	90.31	2007	10/9	852.32	3/5	749.85	799.82
1985	12/16	114.97	1/4	88.61	114.39	2008	1/2	788.62	11/20	402.91	487.77
1986	7/2	137.87	1/22	111.14	130.00	2009	12/28	619.22	3/9	367.55	612.01
1987	8/25	176.22	12/4	117.65	130.02	2010	12/29	698.11	7/2	562.58	696.90
1988	10/21	149.94	1/20	128.35	146.99	2011	4/29	758.45	10/3	604.42	693.36
1989	10/9	189.93	1/3	145.78	185.11	2012	9/14	809.01	1/4	703.72	789.90
1990	7/16	191.56	10/11	152.36	171.22	2013	12/31	1030.36	1/8	807.95	1030.36
1991	12/31	220.61	1/9	161.94	220.61	2014	12/29	1161.45	2/3	972.95	1144.37
1992	12/18	235.06	4/8	208.87	233.59	2015	5/21	1189.55	8/25	1042.77	1131.88
1993	10/15	252.77	1/8	229.91	250.71	2016	12/13	1260.06	2/11	1005.89	1241.66
1994	2/1	258.31	4/4	235.38	244.65	2017	12/18	1490.06	1/3	1252.11	1481.81
1995	12/13	331.18	1/3	244.41	328.89	2018	9/20	1624.28	12/24	1298.02	1384.26
1996	12/2	401.21	1/10	318.24	393.75	2019	12/26	1789.56	1/3	1351.87	1784.21
1997	12/5	519.72	4/11	389.03	513.79	2020	12/31	2120.87	3/23	1224.45	2120.87
1998	12/29	645.36	1/9	490.26	642.87	2021	12/27	2660.44	1/4	2089.72	2645.91
1999	12/31	767.97	2/9	632.53	767.97	2022	1/3	2660.78	10/12	1969.25	2105.90
2000	9/1	813.71	12/20	668.75	700.09	2023*	2/2	2305.00	1/5	2089.03	*At press time*
2001	1/30	727.35	9/21	507.98	604.94						

RUSSELL 2000 ANNUAL HIGHS, LOWS, & CLOSES SINCE 1979

YEAR	HIGH DATE	HIGH CLOSE	LOW DATE	LOW CLOSE	YEAR CLOSE	YEAR	HIGH DATE	HIGH CLOSE	LOW DATE	LOW CLOSE	YEAR CLOSE
1979	12/31	55.91	1/2	40.81	55.91	2002	4/16	522.95	10/9	327.04	383.09
1980	11/28	77.70	3/27	45.36	74.80	2003	12/30	565.47	3/12	345.94	556.91
1981	6/15	85.16	9/25	65.37	73.67	2004	12/28	654.57	8/12	517.10	651.57
1982	12/8	91.01	8/12	60.33	88.90	2005	12/2	690.57	4/28	575.02	673.22
1983	6/24	126.99	1/3	88.29	112.27	2006	12/27	797.73	7/21	671.94	787.66
1984	1/12	116.69	7/25	93.95	101.49	2007	7/13	855.77	11/26	735.07	766.03
1985	12/31	129.87	1/2	101.21	129.87	2008	6/5	763.27	11/20	385.31	499.45
1986	7/3	155.30	1/9	128.23	135.00	2009	12/24	634.07	3/9	343.26	625.39
1987	8/25	174.44	10/28	106.08	120.42	2010	12/27	792.35	2/8	586.49	783.65
1988	7/15	151.42	1/12	121.23	147.37	2011	4/29	865.29	10/3	609.49	740.92
1989	10/9	180.78	1/3	146.79	168.30	2012	9/14	864.70	6/4	737.24	849.35
1990	6/15	170.90	10/30	118.82	132.16	2013	12/31	1163.64	1/3	872.60	1163.64
1991	12/31	189.94	1/15	125.25	189.94	2014	12/29	1219.11	10/13	1049.30	1204.70
1992	12/31	221.01	7/8	185.81	221.01	2015	6/23	1295.80	9/29	1083.91	1135.89
1993	11/2	260.17	2/23	217.55	258.59	2016	12/9	1388.07	2/11	953.72	1357.13
1994	3/18	271.08	12/9	235.16	250.36	2017	12/28	1548.93	4/13	1345.24	1535.51
1995	9/14	316.12	1/30	246.56	315.97	2018	8/31	1740.75	12/24	1266.92	1348.56
1996	5/22	364.61	1/16	301.75	362.61	2019	12/24	1678.01	1/3	1330.83	1668.47
1997	10/13	465.21	4/25	335.85	437.02	2020	12/23	2007.10	3/18	991.16	1974.86
1998	4/21	491.41	10/8	310.28	421.96	2021	11/8	2442.74	1/4	1945.91	2245.31
1999	12/31	504.75	3/23	383.37	504.75	2022	1/3	2272.56	6/16	1649.84	1761.25
2000	3/9	606.05	12/20	443.80	483.53	2023*	2/2	2001.22	5/4	1718.81	*At press time*
2001	5/22	517.23	9/21	378.89	488.50						

*Through May 26, 2023

DOW JONES INDUSTRIALS MONTHLY PERCENT CHANGES SINCE 1950

	Jan	Feb	Mar	Apr	May	Jun	Jul	Aug	Sep	Oct	Nov	Dec	Year's Change
1950	0.8	0.8	1.3	4.0	4.2	-6.4	0.1	3.6	4.4	-0.6	1.2	3.4	17.6
1951	5.7	1.3	-1.6	4.5	-3.7	-2.8	6.3	4.8	0.3	-3.2	-0.4	3.0	14.4
1952	0.5	-3.9	3.6	-4.4	2.1	4.3	1.9	-1.6	-1.6	-0.5	5.4	2.9	8.4
1953	-0.7	-1.9	-1.5	-1.8	-0.9	-1.5	2.7	-5.1	1.1	4.5	2.0	-0.2	-3.8
1954	4.1	0.7	3.0	5.2	2.6	1.8	4.3	-3.5	7.3	-2.3	9.8	4.6	44.0
1955	1.1	0.7	-0.5	3.9	-0.2	6.2	3.2	0.5	-0.3	-2.5	6.2	1.1	20.8
1956	-3.6	2.7	5.8	0.8	-7.4	3.1	5.1	-3.0	-5.3	1.0	-1.5	5.6	2.3
1957	-4.1	-3.0	2.2	4.1	2.1	-0.3	1.0	-4.8	-5.8	-3.3	2.0	-3.2	-12.8
1958	3.3	-2.2	1.6	2.0	1.5	3.3	5.2	1.1	4.6	2.1	2.6	4.7	34.0
1959	1.8	1.6	-0.3	3.7	3.2	-0.03	4.9	-1.6	-4.9	2.4	1.9	3.1	16.4
1960	-8.4	1.2	-2.1	-2.4	4.0	2.4	-3.7	1.5	-7.3	0.04	2.9	3.1	-9.3
1961	5.2	2.1	2.2	0.3	2.7	-1.8	3.1	2.1	-2.6	0.4	2.5	1.3	18.7
1962	-4.3	1.1	-0.2	-5.9	-7.8	-8.5	6.5	1.9	-5.0	1.9	10.1	0.4	-10.8
1963	4.7	-2.9	3.0	5.2	1.3	-2.8	-1.6	4.9	0.5	3.1	-0.6	1.7	17.0
1964	2.9	1.9	1.6	-0.3	1.2	1.3	1.2	-0.3	4.4	-0.3	0.3	-0.1	14.6
1965	3.3	0.1	-1.6	3.7	-0.5	-5.4	1.6	1.3	4.2	3.2	-1.5	2.4	10.9
1966	1.5	-3.2	-2.8	1.0	-5.3	-1.6	-2.6	-7.0	-1.8	4.2	-1.9	-0.7	-18.9
1967	8.2	-1.2	3.2	3.6	-5.0	0.9	5.1	-0.3	2.8	-5.1	-0.4	3.3	15.2
1968	-5.5	-1.7	0.02	8.5	-1.4	-0.1	-1.6	1.5	4.4	1.8	3.4	-4.2	4.3
1969	0.2	-4.3	3.3	1.6	-1.3	-6.9	-6.6	2.6	-2.8	5.3	-5.1	-1.5	-15.2
1970	-7.0	4.5	1.0	-6.3	-4.8	-2.4	7.4	4.1	-0.5	-0.7	5.1	5.6	4.8
1971	3.5	1.2	2.9	4.1	-3.6	-1.8	-3.7	4.6	-1.2	-5.4	-0.9	7.1	6.1
1972	1.3	2.9	1.4	1.4	0.7	-3.3	-0.5	4.2	-1.1	0.2	6.6	0.2	14.6
1973	-2.1	-4.4	-0.4	-3.1	-2.2	-1.1	3.9	-4.2	6.7	1.0	-14.0	3.5	-16.6
1974	0.6	0.6	-1.6	-1.2	-4.1	0.03	-5.6	-10.4	-10.4	9.5	-7.0	-0.4	-27.6
1975	14.2	5.0	3.9	6.9	1.3	5.6	-5.4	0.5	-5.0	5.3	2.9	-1.0	38.3
1976	14.4	-0.3	2.8	-0.3	-2.2	2.8	-1.8	-1.1	1.7	-2.6	-1.8	6.1	17.9
1977	-5.0	-1.9	-1.8	0.8	-3.0	2.0	-2.9	-3.2	-1.7	-3.4	1.4	0.2	-17.3
1978	-7.4	-3.6	2.1	10.6	0.4	-2.6	5.3	1.7	-1.3	-8.5	0.8	0.7	-3.1
1979	4.2	-3.6	6.6	-0.8	-3.8	2.4	0.5	4.9	-1.0	-7.2	0.8	2.0	4.2
1980	4.4	-1.5	-9.0	4.0	4.1	2.0	7.8	-0.3	-0.02	-0.9	7.4	-3.0	14.9
1981	-1.7	2.9	3.0	-0.6	-0.6	-1.5	-2.5	-7.4	-3.6	0.3	4.3	-1.6	-9.2
1982	-0.4	-5.4	-0.2	3.1	-3.4	-0.9	-0.4	11.5	-0.6	10.7	4.8	0.7	19.6
1983	2.8	3.4	1.6	8.5	-2.1	1.8	-1.9	1.4	1.4	-0.6	4.1	-1.4	20.3
1984	-3.0	-5.4	0.9	0.5	-5.6	2.5	-1.5	9.8	-1.4	0.1	-1.5	1.9	-3.7
1985	6.2	-0.2	-1.3	-0.7	4.6	1.5	0.9	-1.0	-0.4	3.4	7.1	5.1	27.7
1986	1.6	8.8	6.4	-1.9	5.2	0.9	-6.2	6.9	-6.9	6.2	1.9	-1.0	22.6
1987	13.8	3.1	3.6	-0.8	0.2	5.5	6.3	3.5	-2.5	-23.2	-8.0	5.7	2.3
1988	1.0	5.8	-4.0	2.2	-0.1	5.4	-0.6	-4.6	4.0	1.7	-1.6	2.6	11.8

continued

DOW JONES INDUSTRIALS MONTHLY PERCENT CHANGES SINCE 1950 (continued)

	Jan	Feb	Mar	Apr	May	Jun	Jul	Aug	Sep	Oct	Nov	Dec	Year's Change
1989	8.0	-3.6	1.6	5.5	2.5	-1.6	9.0	2.9	-1.6	-1.8	2.3	1.7	27.0
1990	-5.9	1.4	3.0	-1.9	8.3	0.1	0.9	-10.0	-6.2	-0.4	4.8	2.9	-4.3
1991	3.9	5.3	1.1	-0.9	4.8	-4.0	4.1	0.6	-0.9	1.7	-5.7	9.5	20.3
1992	1.7	1.4	-1.0	3.8	1.1	-2.3	2.3	-4.0	0.4	-1.4	2.4	-0.1	4.2
1993	0.3	1.8	1.9	-0.2	2.9	-0.3	0.7	3.2	-2.6	3.5	0.1	1.9	13.7
1994	6.0	-3.7	-5.1	1.3	2.1	-3.5	3.8	4.0	-1.8	1.7	-4.3	2.5	2.1
1995	0.2	4.3	3.7	3.9	3.3	2.0	3.3	-2.1	3.9	-0.7	6.7	0.8	33.5
1996	5.4	1.7	1.9	-0.3	1.3	0.2	-2.2	1.6	4.7	2.5	8.2	-1.1	26.0
1997	5.7	0.9	-4.3	6.5	4.6	4.7	7.2	-7.3	4.2	-6.3	5.1	1.1	22.6
1998	-0.02	8.1	3.0	3.0	-1.8	0.6	-0.8	-15.1	4.0	9.6	6.1	0.7	16.1
1999	1.9	-0.6	5.2	10.2	-2.1	3.9	-2.9	1.6	-4.5	3.8	1.4	5.7	25.2
2000	-4.8	-7.4	7.8	-1.7	-2.0	-0.7	0.7	6.6	-5.0	3.0	-5.1	3.6	-6.2
2001	0.9	-3.6	-5.9	8.7	1.6	-3.8	0.2	-5.4	-11.1	2.6	8.6	1.7	-7.1
2002	-1.0	1.9	2.9	-4.4	-0.2	-6.9	-5.5	-0.8	-12.4	10.6	5.9	-6.2	-16.8
2003	-3.5	-2.0	1.3	6.1	4.4	1.5	2.8	2.0	-1.5	5.7	-0.2	6.9	25.3
2004	0.3	0.9	-2.1	-1.3	-0.4	2.4	-2.8	0.3	-0.9	-0.5	4.0	3.4	3.1
2005	-2.7	2.6	-2.4	-3.0	2.7	-1.8	3.6	-1.5	0.8	-1.2	3.5	-0.8	-0.6
2006	1.4	1.2	1.1	2.3	-1.7	-0.2	0.3	1.7	2.6	3.4	1.2	2.0	16.3
2007	1.3	-2.8	0.7	5.7	4.3	-1.6	-1.5	1.1	4.0	0.2	-4.0	-0.8	6.4
2008	-4.6	-3.0	-0.03	4.5	-1.4	-10.2	0.2	1.5	-6.0	-14.1	-5.3	-0.6	-33.8
2009	-8.8	-11.7	7.7	7.3	4.1	-0.6	8.6	3.5	2.3	0.005	6.5	0.8	18.8
2010	-3.5	2.6	5.1	1.4	-7.9	-3.6	7.1	-4.3	7.7	3.1	-1.0	5.2	11.0
2011	2.7	2.8	0.8	4.0	-1.9	-1.2	-2.2	-4.4	-6.0	9.5	0.8	1.4	5.5
2012	3.4	2.5	2.0	0.01	-6.2	3.9	1.0	0.6	2.6	-2.5	-0.5	0.6	7.3
2013	5.8	1.4	3.7	1.8	1.9	-1.4	4.0	-4.4	2.2	2.8	3.5	3.0	26.5
2014	-5.3	4.0	0.8	0.7	0.8	0.7	-1.6	3.2	-0.3	2.0	2.5	-0.03	7.5
2015	-3.7	5.6	-2.0	0.4	1.0	-2.2	0.4	-6.6	-1.5	8.5	0.3	-1.7	-2.2
2016	-5.5	0.3	7.1	0.5	0.1	0.8	2.8	-0.2	-0.5	-0.9	5.4	3.3	13.4
2017	0.5	4.8	-0.7	1.3	0.3	1.6	2.5	0.3	2.1	4.3	3.8	1.8	25.1
2018	5.8	-4.3	-3.7	0.2	1.0	-0.6	4.7	2.2	1.9	-5.1	1.7	-8.7	-5.6
2019	7.2	3.7	0.1	2.6	-6.7	7.2	1.0	-1.7	1.9	0.5	3.7	1.7	22.3
2020	-1.0	-10.1	-13.7	11.1	4.3	1.7	2.4	7.6	-2.3	-4.6	11.8	3.3	7.2
2021	-2.0	3.2	6.6	2.7	1.9	-0.1	1.3	1.2	-4.3	5.8	-3.7	5.4	18.7
2022	-3.3	-3.5	2.3	-4.9	0.04	-6.7	6.7	-4.1	-8.8	14.0	5.7	-4.2	-8.8
2023	2.8	-4.2	1.9	2.5									
TOTALS	67.7	3.7	70.4	143.1	-0.6	-18.0	97.3	-6.7	-60.1	57.3	127.5	110.4	
AVG.	0.9	0.1	1.0	1.9	-0.01	-0.2	1.3	-0.09	-0.8	0.8	1.7	1.5	
# Up	46	43	48	51	40	34	48	41	29	44	50	51	
# Down	28	31	26	23	33	39	25	32	44	29	23	22	

DOW JONES INDUSTRIALS MONTHLY POINT CHANGES SINCE 1950

	Jan	Feb	Mar	Apr	May	Jun	Jul	Aug	Sep	Oct	Nov	Dec	Year'a Change
1950	1.66	1.65	2.61	8.28	9.09	−14.31	0.29	7.47	9.49	−1.35	2.59	7.81	235.41
1951	13.42	3.22	−4.11	11.19	−9.48	−7.01	15.22	12.39	0.91	−8.81	−1.08	7.96	269.23
1952	1.46	−10.61	9.38	−11.83	5.31	11.32	5.30	−4.52	−4.43	−1.38	14.43	8.24	291.90
1953	−2.13	−5.50	−4.40	−5.12	−2.47	−4.02	7.12	−14.16	2.82	11.77	5.56	−0.47	280.90
1954	11.49	2.15	8.97	15.82	8.16	6.04	14.39	−12.12	24.66	−8.32	34.63	17.62	404.39
1955	4.44	3.04	−2.17	15.95	−0.79	26.52	14.47	2.33	−1.56	−11.75	28.39	5.14	488.40
1956	−17.66	12.91	28.14	4.33	−38.07	14.73	25.03	−15.77	−26.79	4.60	−7.07	26.69	499.47
1957	−20.31	−14.54	10.19	19.55	10.57	−1.64	5.23	−24.17	−28.05	−15.26	8.83	−14.18	435.69
1958	14.33	−10.10	6.84	9.10	6.84	15.48	24.81	5.64	23.46	11.13	14.24	26.19	583.65
1959	10.31	9.54	−1.79	22.04	20.04	−0.19	31.28	−10.47	−32.73	14.92	12.58	20.18	679.36
1960	−56.74	7.50	−13.53	−14.89	23.80	15.12	−23.89	9.26	−45.85	0.22	16.86	18.67	615.89
1961	32.31	13.88	14.55	2.08	18.01	−12.76	21.41	14.57	−18.73	2.71	17.68	9.54	731.14
1962	−31.14	8.05	−1.10	−41.62	−51.97	−52.08	36.65	11.25	−30.20	10.79	59.53	2.80	652.10
1963	30.75	−19.91	19.58	35.18	9.26	−20.08	−11.45	33.89	3.47	22.44	−4.71	12.43	762.95
1964	22.39	14.80	13.15	−2.52	9.79	10.94	9.60	−2.62	36.89	−2.29	2.35	−1.30	874.13
1965	28.73	0.62	−14.43	33.26	−4.27	−50.01	13.71	11.36	37.48	30.24	−14.11	22.55	969.26
1966	14.25	−31.62	−27.12	8.91	−49.61	−13.97	−22.72	−58.97	−14.19	32.85	−15.48	−5.90	785.69
1967	64.20	−10.52	26.61	31.07	−44.49	7.70	43.98	−2.95	25.37	−46.92	−3.93	29.30	905.11
1968	−49.64	−14.97	0.17	71.55	−13.22	−1.20	−14.80	13.01	39.78	16.60	32.69	−41.33	943.75
1969	2.30	−40.84	30.27	14.70	−12.62	−64.37	−57.72	21.25	−23.63	42.90	−43.69	−11.94	800.36
1970	−56.30	33.53	7.98	−49.50	−35.63	−16.91	50.59	30.46	−3.90	−5.07	38.48	44.83	838.92
1971	29.58	10.33	25.54	37.38	−33.94	−16.67	−32.71	39.64	−10.88	−48.19	−7.66	58.86	890.20
1972	11.97	25.96	12.57	13.47	6.55	−31.69	−4.29	38.99	−10.46	2.25	62.69	1.81	1020.02
1973	−21.00	−43.95	−4.06	−29.58	−20.02	−9.70	34.69	−38.83	59.53	9.48	−134.33	28.61	850.86
1974	4.69	4.98	−13.85	−9.93	−34.58	0.24	−44.98	−78.85	−70.71	57.65	−46.86	−2.42	616.24
1975	87.45	35.36	29.10	53.19	10.95	46.70	−47.48	3.83	−41.46	42.16	24.63	−8.26	852.41
1976	122.87	−2.67	26.84	−2.60	−21.62	27.55	−18.14	−10.90	16.45	−25.26	−17.71	57.43	1004.65
1977	−50.28	−17.95	−17.29	7.77	−28.24	17.64	−26.23	−28.58	−14.38	−28.76	11.35	1.47	831.17
1978	−61.25	−27.80	15.24	79.96	3.29	−21.66	43.32	14.55	−11.00	−73.37	6.58	5.98	805.01
1979	34.21	−30.40	53.36	−7.28	−32.57	19.65	4.44	41.21	−9.05	−62.88	6.65	16.39	838.74
1980	37.11	−12.71	−77.39	31.31	33.79	17.07	67.40	−2.73	−0.17	−7.93	68.85	−29.35	963.99
1981	−16.72	27.31	29.29	−6.12	−6.00	−14.87	−24.54	−70.87	−31.49	2.57	36.43	−13.98	875.00
1982	−3.90	−46.71	−1.62	25.59	−28.82	−7.61	−3.33	92.71	−5.06	95.47	47.56	7.26	1046.54
1983	29.16	36.92	17.41	96.17	−26.22	21.98	−22.74	16.94	16.97	−7.93	50.82	−17.38	1258.64
1984	−38.06	−65.95	10.26	5.86	−65.90	27.55	−17.12	109.10	−17.67	0.67	−18.44	22.63	1211.57
1985	75.20	−2.76	−17.23	−8.72	57.35	20.05	11.99	−13.44	−5.38	45.68	97.82	74.54	1546.67
1986	24.32	138.07	109.55	−34.63	92.73	16.01	−117.41	123.03	−130.76	110.23	36.42	−18.28	1895.95
1987	262.09	65.95	80.70	−18.33	5.21	126.96	153.54	90.88	−66.67	−602.75	−159.98	105.28	1938.83
1988	19.39	113.40	−83.56	44.27	−1.21	110.59	−12.98	−97.08	81.26	35.74	−34.14	54.06	2168.57

continued

158

DOW JONES INDUSTRIALS MONTHLY POINT CHANGES SINCE 1950 (continued)

	Jan	Feb	Mar	Apr	May	Jun	Jul	Aug	Sep	Oct	Nov	Dec	Year's Change
1989	173.75	-83.93	35.23	125.18	61.35	-40.09	220.60	76.61	-44.45	-47.74	61.19	46.93	2753.20
1990	-162.66	36.71	79.96	-50.45	219.90	4.03	24.51	-290.84	-161.88	-10.15	117.32	74.01	2633.66
1991	102.73	145.79	31.68	-25.99	139.63	-120.75	118.07	18.78	-26.83	52.33	-174.42	274.15	3168.83
1992	54.56	44.28	-32.20	123.65	37.76	-78.36	75.26	-136.43	14.31	-45.38	78.88	-4.05	3301.11
1993	8.92	60.78	64.30	-7.56	99.88	-11.35	23.39	111.78	-96.13	125.47	3.36	70.14	3754.09
1994	224.27	-146.34	-196.06	45.73	76.68	-133.41	139.54	148.92	-70.23	64.93	-168.89	95.21	3834.44
1995	9.42	167.19	146.64	163.58	143.87	90.96	152.37	-97.91	178.52	-33.60	319.01	42.63	5117.12
1996	278.18	90.32	101.52	-18.06	74.10	11.45	-125.72	87.30	265.96	147.21	492.32	-73.43	6448.27
1997	364.82	64.65	-294.26	425.51	322.05	341.75	549.82	-600.19	322.84	-503.18	381.05	85.12	7908.25
1998	-1.75	639.22	254.09	263.56	-163.42	52.07	-68.73	-1344.22	303.55	749.48	524.45	64.88	9181.43
1999	177.40	-52.25	479.58	1002.88	-229.30	411.06	-315.65	174.13	-492.33	392.91	147.95	619.31	11497.12
2000	-556.59	-812.22	793.61	-188.01	-211.58	-74.44	74.09	693.12	-564.18	320.22	-556.65	372.36	10786.85
2001	100.51	-392.08	-616.50	856.19	176.97	-409.54	20.41	-573.06	-1102.19	227.58	776.42	169.94	10021.50
2002	-101.50	186.13	297.81	-457.72	-20.97	-681.99	-506.67	-73.09	-1071.57	805.10	499.06	-554.46	8341.63
2003	-287.82	-162.73	101.05	487.96	370.17	135.18	248.36	182.02	-140.76	526.06	-18.66	671.46	10453.92
2004	34.15	95.85	-226.22	-132.13	-37.12	247.03	-295.77	34.21	-93.65	-52.80	400.55	354.99	10783.01
2005	-293.07	276.29	-262.47	-311.25	274.97	-192.51	365.94	-159.31	87.10	-128.63	365.80	-88.37	10717.50
2006	147.36	128.55	115.91	257.82	-198.83	-18.09	35.46	195.47	297.92	401.66	141.20	241.22	12463.15
2007	158.54	-353.06	85.72	708.56	564.73	-219.02	-196.63	145.75	537.89	34.38	-558.29	-106.90	13264.82
2008	-614.46	-383.97	-3.50	557.24	-181.81	-1288.31	28.01	165.53	-692.89	-1525.65	-495.97	-52.65	8776.39
2009	-775.53	-937.93	545.99	559.20	332.21	-53.33	724.61	324.67	216.00	0.45	632.11	83.21	10428.05
2010	-360.72	257.93	531.37	151.98	-871.98	-362.61	691.92	-451.22	773.33	330.44	-112.47	571.49	11577.51
2011	314.42	334.41	93.39	490.81	-240.75	-155.45	-271.10	-529.71	-700.15	1041.63	90.67	171.88	12217.56
2012	415.35	319.16	259.97	1.59	-820.18	486.64	128.59	82.16	346.29	-340.67	-70.88	78.56	13104.14
2013	756.44	193.91	524.05	261.26	275.77	-205.94	589.94	-689.23	319.36	416.08	540.66	490.25	16576.66
2014	-877.81	622.86	135.95	123.18	136.33	109.43	-263.30	535.15	-55.55	347.62	437.72	-5.17	17823.07
2015	-658.12	967.75	-356.58	64.40	170.16	-391.17	70.35	-1161.83	-244.03	1379.54	56.38	-294.89	17425.03
2016	-958.73	50.20	1168.59	88.55	13.56	142.79	502.25	-31.36	-92.73	-165.73	981.16	639.02	19762.60
2017	101.49	948.15	-149.02	277.29	68.14	340.98	541.49	56.98	456.99	972.15	895.11	446.87	24719.22
2018	1430.17	-1120.19	-926.09	60.04	252.69	-144.43	1143.78	549.63	493.49	-1342.55	422.70	-2211.00	23327.46
2019	1672.21	916.33	12.68	664.23	-1777.87	1784.92	264.31	-460.99	513.55	129.40	1005.18	487.03	28538.44
2020	-282.41	-2846.67	-3492.20	2428.56	1037.39	429.77	615.44	2001.73	-648.35	-1280.10	3137.04	967.84	30606.48
2021	-623.86	949.75	2049.18	893.30	654.60	-26.94	432.96	425.26	-1516.81	1975.64	-1335.84	1854.58	36338.30
2022	-1206.44	-1239.26	785.75	-1701.14	12.91	-2214.69	2069.70	-1334.70	-2784.92	4007.44	1856.82	-1442.52	33147.25
2023	938.79	-1429.34	617.45	824.01									
TOTALS	266.96	-2304.10	3061.02	9469.26	531.01	-2035.30	7939.53	-1668.16	-5749.19	8616.39	11101.49	4669.12	
# Up	46	43	48	51	40	34	48	41	29	44	50	51	
# Down	28	31	26	23	33	39	25	32	44	29	23	22	

159

DOW JONES INDUSTRIALS MONTHLY CLOSING PRICES SINCE 1950

	Jan	Feb	Mar	Apr	May	Jun	Jul	Aug	Sep	Oct	Nov	Dec
1950	201.79	203.44	206.05	214.33	223.42	209.11	209.40	216.87	226.36	225.01	227.60	235.41
1951	248.83	252.05	247.94	259.13	249.65	242.64	257.86	270.25	271.16	262.35	261.27	269.23
1952	270.69	260.08	269.46	257.63	262.94	274.26	279.56	275.04	270.61	269.23	283.66	291.90
1953	289.77	284.27	279.87	274.75	272.28	268.26	275.38	261.22	264.04	275.81	281.37	280.90
1954	292.39	294.54	303.51	319.33	327.49	333.53	347.92	335.80	360.46	352.14	386.77	404.39
1955	408.83	411.87	409.70	425.65	424.86	451.38	465.85	468.18	466.62	454.87	483.26	488.40
1956	470.74	483.65	511.79	516.12	478.05	492.78	517.81	502.04	475.25	479.85	472.78	499.47
1957	479.16	464.62	474.81	494.36	504.93	503.29	508.52	484.35	456.30	441.04	449.87	435.69
1958	450.02	439.92	446.76	455.86	462.70	478.18	502.99	508.63	532.09	543.22	557.46	583.65
1959	593.96	603.50	601.71	623.75	643.79	643.60	674.88	664.41	631.68	646.60	659.18	679.36
1960	622.62	630.12	616.59	601.70	625.50	640.62	616.73	625.99	580.14	580.36	597.22	615.89
1961	648.20	662.08	676.63	678.71	696.72	683.96	705.37	719.94	701.21	703.92	721.60	731.14
1962	700.00	708.05	706.95	665.33	613.36	561.28	597.93	609.18	578.98	589.77	649.30	652.10
1963	682.85	662.94	682.52	717.70	726.96	706.88	695.43	729.32	732.79	755.23	750.52	762.95
1964	785.34	800.14	813.29	810.77	820.56	831.50	841.10	838.48	875.37	873.08	875.43	874.13
1965	902.86	903.48	889.05	922.31	918.04	868.03	881.74	893.10	930.58	960.82	946.71	969.26
1966	983.51	951.89	924.77	933.68	884.07	870.10	847.38	788.41	774.22	807.07	791.59	785.69
1967	849.89	839.37	865.98	897.05	852.56	860.26	904.24	901.29	926.66	879.74	875.81	905.11
1968	855.47	840.50	840.67	912.22	899.00	897.80	883.00	896.01	935.79	952.39	985.08	943.75
1969	946.05	905.21	935.48	950.18	937.56	873.19	815.47	836.72	813.09	855.99	812.30	800.36
1970	744.06	777.59	785.57	736.07	700.44	683.53	734.12	764.58	760.68	755.61	794.09	838.92
1971	868.50	878.83	904.37	941.75	907.81	891.14	858.43	898.07	887.19	839.00	831.34	890.20
1972	902.17	928.13	940.70	954.17	960.72	929.03	924.74	963.73	953.27	955.52	1018.21	1020.02
1973	999.02	955.07	951.01	921.43	901.41	891.71	926.40	887.57	947.10	956.58	822.25	850.86
1974	855.55	860.53	846.68	836.75	802.17	802.41	757.43	678.58	607.87	665.52	618.66	616.24
1975	703.69	739.05	768.15	821.34	832.29	878.99	831.51	835.34	793.88	836.04	860.67	852.41
1976	975.28	972.61	999.45	996.85	975.23	1002.78	984.64	973.74	990.19	964.93	947.22	1004.65
1977	954.37	936.42	919.13	926.90	898.66	916.30	890.07	861.49	847.11	818.35	829.70	831.17
1978	769.92	742.12	757.36	837.32	840.61	818.95	862.27	876.82	865.82	792.45	799.03	805.01
1979	839.22	808.82	862.18	854.90	822.33	841.98	846.42	887.63	878.58	815.70	822.35	838.74
1980	875.85	863.14	785.75	817.06	850.85	867.92	935.32	932.59	932.42	924.49	993.34	963.99
1981	947.27	974.58	1003.87	997.75	991.75	976.88	952.34	881.47	849.98	852.55	888.98	875.00
1982	871.10	824.39	822.77	848.36	819.54	811.93	808.60	901.31	896.25	991.72	1039.28	1046.54
1983	1075.70	1112.62	1130.03	1226.20	1199.98	1221.96	1199.22	1216.16	1233.13	1225.20	1276.02	1258.64
1984	1220.58	1154.63	1164.89	1170.75	1104.85	1132.40	1115.28	1224.38	1206.71	1207.38	1188.94	1211.57
1985	1286.77	1284.01	1266.78	1258.06	1315.41	1335.46	1347.45	1334.01	1328.63	1374.31	1472.13	1546.67
1986	1570.99	1709.06	1818.61	1783.98	1876.71	1892.72	1775.31	1898.34	1767.58	1877.81	1914.23	1895.95

continued

	Jan	Feb	Mar	Apr	May	Jun	Jul	Aug	Sep	Oct	Nov	Dec
1987	2158.04	2223.99	2304.69	2286.36	2291.57	2418.53	2572.07	2662.95	2596.28	1993.53	1833.55	1938.83
1988	1958.22	2071.62	1988.06	2032.33	2031.12	2141.71	2128.73	2031.65	2112.91	2148.65	2114.51	2168.57
1989	2342.32	2258.39	2293.62	2418.80	2480.15	2440.06	2660.66	2737.27	2692.82	2645.08	2706.27	2753.20
1990	2590.54	2627.25	2707.21	2656.76	2876.66	2880.69	2905.20	2614.36	2452.48	2442.33	2559.65	2633.66
1991	2736.39	2882.18	2913.86	2887.87	3027.50	2906.75	3024.82	3043.60	3016.77	3069.10	2894.68	3168.83
1992	3223.39	3267.67	3235.47	3359.12	3396.88	3318.52	3393.78	3257.35	3271.66	3226.28	3305.16	3301.11
1993	3310.03	3370.81	3435.11	3427.55	3527.43	3516.08	3539.47	3651.25	3555.12	3680.59	3683.95	3754.09
1994	3978.36	3832.02	3635.96	3681.69	3758.37	3624.96	3764.50	3913.42	3843.19	3908.12	3739.23	3834.44
1995	3843.86	4011.05	4157.69	4321.27	4465.14	4556.10	4708.47	4610.56	4789.08	4755.48	5074.49	5117.12
1996	5395.30	5485.62	5587.14	5569.08	5643.18	5654.63	5528.91	5616.21	5882.17	6029.38	6521.70	6448.27
1997	6813.09	6877.74	6583.48	7008.99	7331.04	7672.79	8222.61	7622.42	7945.26	7442.08	7823.13	7908.25
1998	7906.50	8545.72	8799.81	9063.37	8899.95	8952.02	8883.29	7539.07	7842.62	8592.10	9116.55	9181.43
1999	9358.83	9306.58	9786.16	10789.04	10559.74	10970.80	10655.15	10829.28	10336.95	10729.86	10877.81	11497.12
2000	10940.53	10128.31	10921.92	10733.91	10522.33	10447.89	10521.98	11215.10	10650.92	10971.14	10414.49	10786.85
2001	10887.36	10495.28	9878.78	10734.97	10911.94	10502.40	10522.81	9949.75	8847.56	9075.14	9851.56	10021.50
2002	9920.00	10106.13	10403.94	9946.22	9925.25	9243.26	8736.59	8663.50	7591.93	8397.03	8896.09	8341.63
2003	8053.81	7891.08	7992.13	8480.09	8850.26	8985.44	9233.80	9415.82	9275.06	9801.12	9782.46	10453.92
2004	10488.07	10583.92	10357.70	10225.57	10188.45	10435.48	10139.71	10173.92	10080.27	10027.47	10428.02	10783.01
2005	10489.94	10766.23	10503.76	10192.51	10467.48	10274.97	10640.91	10481.60	10568.70	10440.07	10805.87	10717.50
2006	10864.86	10993.41	11109.32	11367.14	11168.31	11150.22	11185.68	11381.15	11679.07	12080.73	12221.93	12463.15
2007	12621.69	12268.63	12354.35	13062.91	13627.64	13408.62	13211.99	13357.74	13895.63	13930.01	13371.72	13264.82
2008	12650.36	12266.39	12262.89	12820.13	12638.32	11350.01	11378.02	11543.55	10850.66	9325.01	8829.04	8776.39
2009	8000.86	7062.93	7608.92	8168.12	8500.33	8447.00	9171.61	9496.28	9712.28	9712.73	10344.84	10428.05
2010	10067.33	10325.26	10856.63	11008.61	10136.63	9774.02	10465.94	10014.72	10788.05	11118.49	11006.02	11577.51
2011	11891.93	12226.34	12319.73	12810.54	12569.79	12414.34	12143.24	11613.53	10913.38	11955.01	12045.68	12217.56
2012	12632.91	12952.07	13212.04	13213.63	12393.45	12880.09	13008.68	13090.84	13437.13	13096.46	13025.58	13104.14
2013	13860.58	14054.49	14578.54	14839.80	15115.57	14909.60	15499.54	14810.31	15129.67	15545.75	16086.41	16576.66
2014	15698.85	16321.71	16457.66	16580.84	16717.17	16826.60	16563.30	17098.45	17042.90	17390.52	17828.24	17823.07
2015	17164.95	18132.70	17776.12	17840.52	18010.68	17619.51	17689.86	16528.03	16284.00	17663.54	17719.92	17425.03
2016	16466.30	16516.50	17685.09	17773.64	17787.20	17929.99	18432.24	18400.88	18308.15	18142.42	19123.58	19762.60
2017	19864.09	20812.24	20663.22	20940.51	21008.65	21349.63	21891.12	21948.10	22405.09	23377.24	24272.35	24719.22
2018	26149.39	25029.20	24103.11	24163.15	24415.84	24271.41	25415.19	25964.82	26458.31	25115.76	25538.46	23327.46
2019	24999.67	25916.00	25928.68	26592.91	24815.04	26599.96	26864.27	26403.28	26916.83	27046.23	28051.41	28538.44
2020	28256.03	25409.36	21917.16	24345.72	25383.11	25812.88	26428.32	28430.05	27781.70	26501.60	29638.64	30606.48
2021	29982.62	30932.37	32981.55	33874.85	34529.45	34502.51	34935.47	35360.73	33843.92	35819.56	34483.72	36338.30
2022	35131.86	33892.60	34678.35	32977.21	32990.12	30775.43	32845.13	31510.43	28725.51	32732.95	34589.77	33147.25
2023	34086.04	32656.70	33274.15	34098.16								

STANDARD & POOR'S 500 MONTHLY PERCENT CHANGES SINCE 1950

	Jan	Feb	Mar	Apr	May	Jun	Jul	Aug	Sep	Oct	Nov	Dec	Year's Change
1950	1.7	1.0	0.4	4.5	3.9	-5.8	0.8	3.3	5.6	0.4	-0.1	4.6	21.8
1951	6.1	0.6	-1.8	4.8	-4.1	-2.6	6.9	3.9	-0.1	-1.4	-0.3	3.9	16.5
1952	1.6	-3.6	4.8	-4.3	2.3	4.6	1.8	-1.5	-2.0	-0.1	4.6	3.5	11.8
1953	-0.7	-1.8	-2.4	-2.6	-0.3	-1.6	2.5	-5.8	0.1	5.1	0.9	0.2	-6.6
1954	5.1	0.3	3.0	4.9	3.3	0.1	5.7	-3.4	8.3	-1.9	8.1	5.1	45.0
1955	1.8	0.4	-0.5	3.8	-0.1	8.2	6.1	-0.8	1.1	-3.0	7.5	-0.1	26.4
1956	-3.6	3.5	6.9	-0.2	-6.6	3.9	5.2	-3.8	-4.5	0.5	-1.1	3.5	2.6
1957	-4.2	-3.3	2.0	3.7	3.7	-0.1	1.1	-5.6	-6.2	-3.2	1.6	-4.1	-14.3
1958	4.3	-2.1	3.1	3.2	1.5	2.6	4.3	1.2	4.8	2.5	2.2	5.2	38.1
1959	0.4	-0.02	0.1	3.9	1.9	-0.4	3.5	-1.5	-4.6	1.1	1.3	2.8	8.5
1960	-7.1	0.9	-1.4	-1.8	2.7	2.0	-2.5	2.6	-6.0	-0.2	4.0	4.6	-3.0
1961	6.3	2.7	2.6	0.4	1.9	-2.9	3.3	2.0	-2.0	2.8	3.9	0.3	23.1
1962	-3.8	1.6	-0.6	-6.2	-8.6	-8.2	6.4	1.5	-4.8	0.4	10.2	1.3	-11.8
1963	4.9	-2.9	3.5	4.9	1.4	-2.0	-0.3	4.9	-1.1	3.2	-1.1	2.4	18.9
1964	2.7	1.0	1.5	0.6	1.1	1.6	1.8	-1.6	2.9	0.8	-0.5	0.4	13.0
1965	3.3	-0.1	-1.5	3.4	-0.8	-4.9	1.3	2.3	3.2	2.7	-0.9	0.9	9.1
1966	0.5	-1.8	-2.2	2.1	-5.4	-1.6	-1.3	-7.8	-0.7	4.8	0.3	-0.1	-13.1
1967	7.8	0.2	3.9	4.2	-5.2	1.8	4.5	-1.2	3.3	-2.9	0.1	2.6	20.1
1968	-4.4	-3.1	0.9	8.2	1.1	0.9	-1.8	1.1	3.9	0.7	4.8	-4.2	7.7
1969	-0.8	-4.7	3.4	2.1	-0.2	-5.6	-6.0	4.0	-2.5	4.4	-3.5	-1.9	-11.4
1970	-7.6	5.3	0.1	-9.0	-6.1	-5.0	7.3	4.4	3.3	-1.1	4.7	5.7	0.1
1971	4.0	0.9	3.7	3.6	-4.2	0.1	-4.1	3.6	-0.7	-4.2	-0.3	8.6	10.8
1972	1.8	2.5	0.6	0.4	1.7	-2.2	0.2	3.4	-0.5	0.9	4.6	1.2	15.6
1973	-1.7	-3.7	-0.1	-4.1	-1.9	-0.7	3.8	-3.7	4.0	-0.1	-11.4	1.7	-17.4
1974	-1.0	-0.4	-2.3	-3.9	-3.4	-1.5	-7.8	-9.0	-11.9	16.3	-5.3	-2.0	-29.7
1975	12.3	6.0	2.2	4.7	4.4	4.4	-6.8	-2.1	-3.5	6.2	2.5	-1.2	31.5
1976	11.8	-1.1	3.1	-1.1	-1.4	4.1	-0.8	-0.5	2.3	-2.2	-0.8	5.2	19.1
1977	-5.1	-2.2	-1.4	0.02	-2.4	4.5	-1.6	-2.1	-0.2	-4.3	2.7	0.3	-11.5
1978	-6.2	-2.5	2.5	8.5	0.4	-1.8	5.4	2.6	-0.7	-9.2	1.7	1.5	1.1
1979	4.0	-3.7	5.5	0.2	-2.6	3.9	0.9	5.3	N/C	-6.9	4.3	1.7	12.3
1980	5.8	-0.4	-10.2	4.1	4.7	2.7	6.5	0.6	2.5	1.6	10.2	-3.4	25.8
1981	-4.6	1.3	3.6	-2.3	-0.2	-1.0	-0.2	-6.2	-5.4	4.9	3.7	-3.0	-9.7
1982	-1.8	-6.1	-1.0	4.0	-3.9	-2.0	-2.3	11.6	0.8	11.0	3.6	1.5	14.8
1983	3.3	1.9	3.3	7.5	-1.2	3.5	-3.3	1.1	1.0	-1.5	1.7	-0.9	17.3
1984	-0.9	-3.9	1.3	0.5	-5.9	1.7	-1.6	10.6	-0.3	-0.01	-1.5	2.2	1.4
1985	7.4	0.9	-0.3	-0.5	5.4	1.2	-0.5	-1.2	-3.5	4.3	6.5	4.5	26.3
1986	0.2	7.1	5.3	-1.4	5.0	1.4	-5.9	7.1	-8.5	5.5	2.1	-2.8	14.6
1987	13.2	3.7	2.6	-1.1	0.6	4.8	4.8	3.5	-2.4	-21.8	-8.5	7.3	2.0
1988	4.0	4.2	-3.3	0.9	0.3	4.3	-0.5	-3.9	4.0	2.6	-1.9	1.5	12.4

continued

	Jan	Feb	Mar	Apr	May	Jun	Jul	Aug	Sep	Oct	Nov	Dec	Year's Change
1989	7.1	−2.9	2.1	5.0	3.5	−0.8	8.8	1.6	−0.7	−2.5	1.7	2.1	27
1990	−6.9	0.9	2.4	−2.7	9.2	−0.9	−0.5	−9.4	−5.1	−0.7	6.0	2.5	−6.6
1991	4.2	6.7	2.2	0.03	3.9	−4.8	4.5	2.0	−1.9	1.2	−4.4	11.2	26.3
1992	−2.0	1.0	−2.2	2.8	0.1	−1.7	3.9	−2.4	0.9	0.2	3.0	1.0	4.5
1993	0.7	1.0	1.9	−2.5	2.3	0.1	−0.5	3.4	−1.0	1.9	−1.3	1.0	7.1
1994	3.3	−3.0	−4.6	1.2	1.2	−2.7	3.1	3.8	−2.7	2.1	−4.0	1.2	−1.5
1995	2.4	3.6	2.7	2.8	3.6	2.1	3.2	−0.03	4.0	−0.5	4.1	1.7	34.1
1996	3.3	0.7	0.8	1.3	2.3	0.2	−4.6	1.9	5.4	2.6	7.3	−2.2	20.3
1997	6.1	0.6	−4.3	5.8	5.9	4.3	7.8	−5.7	5.3	−3.4	4.5	1.6	31.0
1998	1.0	7.0	5.0	0.9	−1.9	3.9	−1.2	−14.6	6.2	8.0	5.9	5.6	26.7
1999	4.1	−3.2	3.9	3.8	−2.5	5.4	−3.2	−0.6	−2.9	6.3	1.9	5.8	19.5
2000	−5.1	−2.0	9.7	−3.1	−2.2	2.4	−1.6	6.1	−5.3	−0.5	−8.0	0.4	−10.1
2001	3.5	−9.2	−6.4	7.7	0.5	−2.5	−1.1	−6.4	−8.2	1.8	7.5	0.8	−13.0
2002	−1.6	−2.1	3.7	−6.1	−0.9	−7.2	−7.9	0.5	−11.0	8.6	5.7	−6.0	−23.4
2003	−2.7	−1.7	1.0	8.0	5.1	1.1	1.6	1.8	−1.2	5.5	0.7	5.1	26.4
2004	1.7	1.2	−1.6	−1.7	1.2	1.8	−3.4	0.2	0.9	1.4	3.9	3.2	9.0
2005	−2.5	1.9	−1.9	−2.0	3.0	−0.01	3.6	−1.1	0.7	−1.8	3.5	−0.1	3.0
2006	2.5	0.05	1.1	1.2	−3.1	0.01	0.5	2.1	2.5	3.2	1.6	1.3	13.6
2007	1.4	−2.2	1.0	4.3	3.3	−1.8	−3.2	1.3	3.6	1.5	−4.4	−0.9	3.5
2008	−6.1	−3.5	−0.6	4.8	1.1	−8.6	−1.0	1.2	−9.1	−16.9	−7.5	0.8	−38.5
2009	−8.6	−11.0	8.5	9.4	5.3	0.02	7.4	3.4	3.6	−2.0	5.7	1.8	23.5
2010	−3.7	2.9	5.9	1.5	−8.2	−5.4	6.9	−4.7	8.8	3.7	−0.2	6.5	12.8
2011	2.3	3.2	−0.1	2.8	−1.4	−1.8	−2.1	−5.7	−7.2	10.8	−0.5	0.9	−0.003
2012	4.4	4.1	3.1	−0.7	−6.3	4.0	1.3	2.0	2.4	−2.0	0.3	0.7	13.4
2013	5.0	1.1	3.6	1.8	2.1	−1.5	4.9	−3.1	3.0	4.5	2.8	2.4	29.6
2014	−3.6	4.3	0.7	0.6	2.1	1.9	−1.5	3.8	−1.6	2.3	2.5	−0.4	11.4
2015	−3.1	5.5	−1.7	0.9	1.0	−2.1	2.0	−6.3	−2.6	8.3	0.1	−1.8	−0.7
2016	−5.1	−0.4	6.6	0.3	1.5	0.1	3.6	−0.1	−0.1	−1.9	3.4	1.8	9.5
2017	1.8	3.7	−0.04	0.9	1.2	0.5	1.9	0.1	1.9	2.2	2.8	1.0	19.4
2018	5.6	−3.9	−2.7	0.3	2.2	0.5	3.6	3.0	0.4	−6.9	1.8	−9.2	−6.2
2019	7.9	3.0	1.8	3.9	−6.6	6.9	1.3	−1.8	1.7	2.0	3.4	2.9	28.9
2020	−0.2	−8.4	−12.5	12.7	4.5	1.8	5.5	7.0	−3.9	−2.8	10.8	3.7	16.3
2021	−1.1	2.6	4.2	5.2	0.5	2.2	2.3	2.9	−4.8	6.9	−0.8	4.4	26.9
2022	−5.3	− 3.1	3.6	−8.8	0.01	−8.4	9.1	−4.2	−9.3	8.0	5.4	−5.9	−19.4
2023	6.2	−2.6	3.5	1.5									
TOTALS	77.7	−5.6	81.3	114.5	16.3	1.4	91.8	0.9	−48.3	69.8	125.8	105.4	
AVG.	1.1	−0.08	1.1	1.5	0.2	0.02	1.3	0.01	−0.7	1.0	1.7	1.4	
# Up	44	40	48	53	44	40	43	40	32	44	50	54	
# Down	30	34	26	21	29	33	30	33	40	29	23	19	

STANDARD & POOR'S 500 MONTHLY CLOSING PRICES SINCE 1950

	Jan	Feb	Mar	Apr	May	Jun	Jul	Aug	Sep	Oct	Nov	Dec
1950	17.05	17.22	17.29	18.07	18.78	17.69	17.84	18.42	19.45	19.53	19.51	20.41
1951	21.66	21.80	21.40	22.43	21.52	20.96	22.40	23.28	23.26	22.94	22.88	23.77
1952	24.14	23.26	24.37	23.32	23.86	24.96	25.40	25.03	24.54	24.52	25.66	26.57
1953	26.38	25.90	25.29	24.62	24.54	24.14	24.75	23.32	23.35	24.54	24.76	24.81
1954	26.08	26.15	26.94	28.26	29.19	29.21	30.88	29.83	32.31	31.68	34.24	35.98
1955	36.63	36.76	36.58	37.96	37.91	41.03	43.52	43.18	43.67	42.34	45.51	45.48
1956	43.82	45.34	48.48	48.38	45.20	46.97	49.39	47.51	45.35	45.58	45.08	46.67
1957	44.72	43.26	44.11	45.74	47.43	47.37	47.91	45.22	42.42	41.06	41.72	39.99
1958	41.70	40.84	42.10	43.44	44.09	45.24	47.19	47.75	50.06	51.33	52.48	55.21
1959	55.42	55.41	55.44	57.59	58.68	58.47	60.51	59.60	56.88	57.52	58.28	59.89
1960	55.61	56.12	55.34	54.37	55.83	56.92	55.51	56.96	53.52	53.39	55.54	58.11
1961	61.78	63.44	65.06	65.31	66.56	64.64	66.76	68.07	66.73	68.62	71.32	71.55
1962	68.84	69.96	69.55	65.24	59.63	54.75	58.23	59.12	56.27	56.52	62.26	63.10
1963	66.20	64.29	66.57	69.80	70.80	69.37	69.13	72.50	71.70	74.01	73.23	75.02
1964	77.04	77.80	78.98	79.46	80.37	81.69	83.18	81.83	84.18	84.86	84.42	84.75
1965	87.56	87.43	86.16	89.11	88.42	84.12	85.25	87.17	89.96	92.42	91.61	92.43
1966	92.88	91.22	89.23	91.06	86.13	84.74	83.60	77.10	76.56	80.20	80.45	80.33
1967	86.61	86.78	90.20	94.01	89.08	90.64	94.75	93.64	96.71	93.90	94.00	96.47
1968	92.24	89.36	90.20	97.59	98.68	99.58	97.74	98.86	102.67	103.41	108.37	103.86
1969	103.01	98.13	101.51	103.69	103.46	97.71	91.83	95.51	93.12	97.24	93.81	92.06
1970	85.02	89.50	89.63	81.52	76.55	72.72	78.05	81.52	84.21	83.25	87.20	92.15
1971	95.88	96.75	100.31	103.95	99.63	99.70	95.58	99.03	98.34	94.23	93.99	102.09
1972	103.94	106.57	107.20	107.67	109.53	107.14	107.39	111.09	110.55	111.58	116.67	118.05
1973	116.03	111.68	111.52	106.97	104.95	104.26	108.22	104.25	108.43	108.29	95.96	97.55
1974	96.57	96.22	93.98	90.31	87.28	86.00	79.31	72.15	63.54	73.90	69.97	68.56
1975	76.98	81.59	83.36	87.30	91.15	95.19	88.75	86.88	83.87	89.04	91.24	90.19
1976	100.86	99.71	102.77	101.64	100.18	104.28	103.44	102.91	105.24	102.90	102.10	107.46
1977	102.03	99.82	98.42	98.44	96.12	100.48	98.85	96.77	96.53	92.34	94.83	95.10
1978	89.25	87.04	89.21	96.83	97.24	95.53	100.68	103.29	102.54	93.15	94.70	96.11
1979	99.93	96.28	101.59	101.76	99.08	102.91	103.81	109.32	109.32	101.82	106.16	107.94
1980	114.16	113.66	102.09	106.29	111.24	114.24	121.67	122.38	125.46	127.47	140.52	135.76
1981	129.55	131.27	136.00	132.81	132.59	131.21	130.92	122.79	116.18	121.89	126.35	122.55
1982	120.40	113.11	111.96	116.44	111.88	109.61	107.09	119.51	120.42	133.71	138.54	140.64
1983	145.30	148.06	152.96	164.42	162.39	168.11	162.56	164.40	166.07	163.55	166.40	164.93
1984	163.41	157.06	159.18	160.05	150.55	153.18	150.66	166.68	166.10	166.09	163.58	167.24
1985	179.63	181.18	180.66	179.83	189.55	191.85	190.92	188.63	182.08	189.82	202.17	211.28
1986	211.78	226.92	238.90	235.52	247.35	250.84	236.12	252.93	231.32	243.98	249.22	242.17

continued

	Jan	Feb	Mar	Apr	May	Jun	Jul	Aug	Sep	Oct	Nov	Dec
1987	274.08	284.20	291.70	288.36	290.10	304.00	318.66	329.80	321.83	251.79	230.30	247.08
1988	257.07	267.82	258.89	261.33	262.16	273.50	272.02	261.52	271.91	278.97	273.70	277.72
1989	297.47	288.86	294.87	309.64	320.52	317.98	346.08	351.45	349.15	340.36	345.99	353.40
1990	329.08	331.89	339.94	330.80	361.23	358.02	356.15	322.56	306.05	304.00	322.22	330.22
1991	343.93	367.07	375.22	375.35	389.83	371.16	387.81	395.43	387.86	392.46	375.22	417.09
1992	408.79	412.70	403.69	414.95	415.35	408.14	424.21	414.03	417.80	418.68	431.35	435.71
1993	438.78	443.38	451.67	440.19	450.19	450.53	448.13	463.56	458.93	467.83	461.79	466.45
1994	481.61	467.14	445.77	450.91	456.50	444.27	458.26	475.49	462.69	472.35	453.69	459.27
1995	470.42	487.39	500.71	514.71	533.40	544.75	562.06	561.88	584.41	581.50	605.37	615.93
1996	636.02	640.43	645.50	654.17	669.12	670.63	639.95	651.99	687.31	705.27	757.02	740.74
1997	786.16	790.82	757.12	801.34	848.28	885.14	954.29	899.47	947.28	914.62	955.40	970.43
1998	980.28	1049.34	1101.75	1111.75	1090.82	1133.84	1120.67	957.28	1017.01	1098.67	1163.63	1229.23
1999	1279.64	1238.33	1286.37	1335.18	1301.84	1372.71	1328.72	1320.41	1282.71	1362.93	1388.91	1469.25
2000	1394.46	1366.42	1498.58	1452.43	1420.60	1454.60	1430.83	1517.68	1436.51	1429.40	1314.95	1320.28
2001	1366.01	1239.94	1160.33	1249.46	1255.82	1224.42	1211.23	1133.58	1040.94	1059.78	1139.45	1148.08
2002	1130.20	1106.73	1147.39	1076.92	1067.14	989.82	911.62	916.07	815.28	885.76	936.31	879.82
2003	855.70	841.15	849.18	916.92	963.59	974.50	990.31	1008.01	995.97	1050.71	1058.20	1111.92
2004	1131.13	1144.94	1126.21	1107.30	1120.68	1140.84	1101.72	1104.24	1114.58	1130.20	1173.82	1211.92
2005	1181.27	1203.60	1180.59	1156.85	1191.50	1191.33	1234.18	1220.33	1228.81	1207.01	1249.48	1248.29
2006	1280.08	1280.66	1294.83	1310.61	1270.09	1270.20	1276.66	1303.82	1335.85	1377.94	1400.63	1418.30
2007	1438.24	1406.82	1420.86	1482.37	1530.62	1503.35	1455.27	1473.99	1526.75	1549.38	1481.14	1468.36
2008	1378.55	1330.63	1322.70	1385.59	1400.38	1280.00	1267.38	1282.83	1166.36	968.75	896.24	903.25
2009	825.88	735.09	797.87	872.81	919.14	919.32	987.48	1020.62	1057.08	1036.19	1095.63	1115.10
2010	1073.87	1104.49	1169.43	1186.69	1089.41	1030.71	1101.60	1049.33	1141.20	1183.26	1180.55	1257.64
2011	1286.12	1327.22	1325.83	1363.61	1345.20	1320.64	1292.28	1218.89	1131.42	1253.30	1246.96	1257.60
2012	1312.41	1365.68	1408.47	1397.91	1310.33	1362.16	1379.32	1406.58	1440.67	1412.16	1416.18	1426.19
2013	1498.11	1514.68	1569.19	1597.57	1630.74	1606.28	1685.73	1632.97	1681.55	1756.54	1805.81	1848.36
2014	1782.59	1859.45	1872.34	1883.95	1923.57	1960.23	1930.67	2003.37	1972.29	2018.05	2067.56	2058.90
2015	1994.99	2104.50	2067.89	2085.51	2107.39	2063.11	2103.84	1972.18	1920.03	2079.36	2080.41	2043.94
2016	1940.24	1932.23	2059.74	2065.30	2096.96	2098.86	2173.60	2170.95	2168.27	2126.15	2198.81	2238.83
2017	2278.87	2363.64	2362.72	2384.20	2411.80	2423.41	2470.30	2471.65	2519.36	2575.26	2647.58	2673.61
2018	2823.81	2713.83	2640.87	2648.05	2705.27	2718.37	2816.29	2901.52	2913.98	2711.74	2760.16	2506.85
2019	2704.10	2784.49	2834.40	2945.83	2752.06	2941.76	2980.38	2926.46	2976.74	3037.56	3140.98	3230.78
2020	3225.52	2954.22	2584.59	2912.43	3044.31	3100.29	3271.12	3500.31	3363.00	3269.96	3621.63	3756.07
2021	3714.24	3811.15	3972.89	4181.17	4204.11	4297.50	4395.26	4522.68	4307.54	4605.38	4567.00	4766.18
2022	4515.55	4373.94	4530.41	4131.93	4132.15	3785.38	4130.29	3955.00	3585.62	3871.98	4080.11	3839.50
2023	4076.60	3970.15	4109.31	4169.48								

NASDAQ COMPOSITE MONTHLY PERCENT CHANGES SINCE 1971

	Jan	Feb	Mar	Apr	May	Jun	Jul	Aug	Sep	Oct	Nov	Dec	Year's Change
1971	10.2	2.6	4.6	6.0	-3.6	-0.4	-2.3	3.0	0.6	-3.6	-1.1	9.8	27.4
1972	4.2	5.5	2.2	2.5	0.9	-1.8	-1.8	1.7	-0.3	0.5	2.1	0.6	17.2
1973	-4.0	-6.2	-2.4	-8.2	-4.8	-1.6	7.6	-3.5	6.0	-0.9	-15.1	-1.4	-31.1
1974	3.0	-0.6	-2.2	-5.9	-7.7	-5.3	-7.9	-10.9	-10.7	17.2	-3.5	-5.0	-35.1
1975	16.6	4.6	3.6	3.8	5.8	4.7	-4.4	-5.0	-5.9	3.6	2.4	-1.5	29.8
1976	12.1	3.7	0.4	-0.6	-2.3	2.6	1.1	-1.7	1.7	-1.0	0.9	7.4	26.1
1977	-2.4	-1.0	-0.5	1.4	0.1	4.3	0.9	-0.5	0.7	-3.3	5.8	1.8	7.3
1978	-4.0	0.6	4.7	8.5	4.4	0.05	5.0	6.9	-1.6	-16.4	3.2	2.9	12.3
1979	6.6	-2.6	7.5	1.6	-1.8	5.1	2.3	6.4	-0.3	-9.6	6.4	4.8	28.1
1980	7.0	-2.3	-17.1	6.9	7.5	4.9	8.9	5.7	3.4	2.7	8.0	-2.8	33.9
1981	-2.2	0.1	6.1	3.1	3.1	-3.5	-1.9	-7.5	-8.0	8.4	3.1	-2.7	-3.2
1982	-3.8	-4.8	-2.1	5.2	-3.3	-4.1	-2.3	6.2	5.6	13.3	9.3	0.04	18.7
1983	6.9	5.0	3.9	8.2	5.3	3.2	-4.6	-3.8	1.4	-7.4	4.1	-2.5	19.9
1984	-3.7	-5.9	-0.7	-1.3	-5.9	2.9	-4.2	10.9	-1.8	-1.2	-1.8	2.0	-11.2
1985	12.7	2.0	-1.7	0.5	3.6	1.9	1.7	-1.2	-5.8	4.4	7.3	3.5	31.4
1986	3.3	7.1	4.2	2.3	4.4	1.3	-8.4	3.1	-8.4	2.9	-0.3	-2.8	7.5
1987	12.2	8.4	1.2	-2.8	-0.3	2.0	2.4	4.6	-2.3	-27.2	-5.6	8.3	-5.4
1988	4.3	6.5	2.1	1.2	-2.3	6.6	-1.9	-2.8	3.0	-1.4	-2.9	2.7	15.4
1989	5.2	-0.4	1.8	5.1	4.4	-2.4	4.3	3.4	0.8	-3.7	0.1	-0.3	19.3
1990	-8.6	2.4	2.3	-3.6	9.3	0.7	-5.2	-13.0	-9.6	-4.3	8.9	4.1	-17.8
1991	10.8	9.4	6.5	0.5	4.4	-6.0	5.5	4.7	0.2	3.1	-3.5	11.9	56.8
1992	5.8	2.1	-4.7	-4.2	1.1	-3.7	3.1	-3.0	3.6	3.8	7.9	3.7	15.5
1993	2.9	-3.7	2.9	-4.2	5.9	0.5	0.1	5.4	2.7	2.2	-3.2	3.0	14.7
1994	3.0	-1.0	-6.2	-1.3	0.2	-4.0	2.3	6.0	-0.2	1.7	-3.5	0.2	-3.2
1995	0.4	5.1	3.0	3.3	2.4	8.0	7.3	1.9	2.3	-0.7	2.2	-0.7	39.9
1996	0.7	3.8	0.1	8.1	4.4	-4.7	-8.8	5.6	7.5	-0.4	5.8	-0.1	22.7
1997	6.9	-5.1	-6.7	3.2	11.1	3.0	10.5	-0.4	6.2	-5.5	0.4	-1.9	21.6
1998	3.1	9.3	3.7	1.8	-4.8	6.5	-1.2	-19.9	13.0	4.6	10.1	12.5	39.6
1999	14.3	-8.7	7.6	3.3	-2.8	8.7	-1.8	3.8	0.2	8.0	12.5	22.0	85.6

continued

Based on NASDAQ composite, prior to Feb. 5, 1971, based on National Quotation Bureau indices

	Jan	Feb	Mar	Apr	May	Jun	Jul	Aug	Sep	Oct	Nov	Dec	Year's Change
2000	-3.2	19.2	-2.6	-15.6	-11.9	16.6	-5.0	11.7	-12.7	-8.3	-22.9	-4.9	-39.3
2001	12.2	-22.4	-14.5	15.0	-0.3	2.4	-6.2	-10.9	-17.0	12.8	14.2	1.0	-21.1
2002	-0.8	-10.5	6.6	-8.5	-4.3	-9.4	-9.2	-1.0	-10.9	13.5	11.2	-9.7	-31.5
2003	-1.1	1.3	0.3	9.2	9.0	1.7	6.9	4.3	-1.3	8.1	1.5	2.2	50.0
2004	3.1	-1.8	-1.8	-3.7	3.5	3.1	-7.8	-2.6	3.2	4.1	6.2	3.7	8.6
2005	-5.2	-0.5	-2.6	-3.9	7.6	-0.5	6.2	-1.5	-0.02	-1.5	5.3	-1.2	1.4
2006	4.6	-1.1	2.6	-0.7	-6.2	-0.3	-3.7	4.4	3.4	4.8	2.7	-0.7	9.5
2007	2.0	-1.9	0.2	4.3	3.1	-0.05	-2.2	2.0	4.0	5.8	-6.9	-0.3	9.8
2008	-9.9	-5.0	0.3	5.9	4.6	-9.1	1.4	1.8	-11.6	-17.7	-10.8	2.7	-40.5
2009	-6.4	-6.7	10.9	12.3	3.3	3.4	7.8	1.5	5.6	-3.6	4.9	5.8	43.9
2010	-5.4	4.2	7.1	2.6	-8.3	-6.5	6.9	-6.2	12.0	5.9	-0.4	6.2	16.9
2011	1.8	3.0	-0.04	3.3	-1.3	-2.2	-0.6	-6.4	-6.4	11.1	-2.4	-0.6	-1.8
2012	8.0	5.4	4.2	-1.5	-7.2	3.8	0.2	4.3	1.6	-4.5	1.1	0.3	15.9
2013	4.1	0.6	3.4	1.9	3.8	-1.5	6.6	-1.0	5.1	3.9	3.6	2.9	38.3
2014	-1.7	5.0	-2.5	-2.0	3.1	3.9	-0.9	4.8	-1.9	3.1	3.5	-1.2	13.4
2015	-2.1	7.1	-1.3	0.8	2.6	-1.6	2.8	-6.9	-3.3	9.4	1.1	-2.0	5.7
2016	-7.9	-1.2	6.8	-1.9	3.6	-2.1	6.6	1.0	1.9	-2.3	2.6	1.1	7.5
2017	4.3	3.8	1.5	2.3	2.5	-0.9	3.4	1.3	1.0	3.6	2.2	0.4	28.2
2018	7.4	-1.9	-2.9	0.04	5.3	0.9	2.2	5.7	-0.8	-9.2	0.3	-9.5	-3.9
2019	9.7	3.4	2.6	4.7	-7.9	7.4	2.1	-2.6	0.5	3.7	4.5	3.5	35.2
2020	2.0	-6.4	-10.1	15.4	6.8	6.0	6.8	9.6	-5.2	-2.3	11.8	5.7	43.6
2021	1.4	0.9	0.4	5.4	-1.5	5.5	1.2	4.0	-5.3	7.3	0.3	0.7	21.4
2022	-9.0	-3.4	3.4	-13.3	-2.1	-8.7	12.3	-4.6	-10.5	3.9	4.4	-8.7	-33.1
2023	10.7	-1.1	6.7	0.04									
TOTALS	142.1	25.9	42.8	76.5	46.5	41.3	44.1	18.8	-44.6	41.4	98.0	76.9	
AVG.	2.7	0.5	0.8	1.4	0.9	0.8	0.8	0.4	-0.9	0.8	1.9	1.5	
# Up	35	28	34	35	31	29	30	29	27	29	37	31	
# Down	18	25	19	18	21	23	22	23	25	23	15	21	

Based on NASDAQ composite, prior to Feb. 5, 1971, based on National Quotation Bureau indices

NASDAQ COMPOSITE MONTHLY CLOSING PRICES SINCE 1971

	Jan	Feb	Mar	Apr	May	Jun	Jul	Aug	Sep	Oct	Nov	Dec
1971	98.77	101.34	105.97	112.30	108.25	107.80	105.27	108.42	109.03	105.10	103.97	114.12
1972	118.87	125.38	128.14	131.33	132.53	130.08	127.75	129.95	129.61	130.24	132.96	133.73
1973	128.40	120.41	117.46	107.85	102.64	100.98	108.64	104.87	111.20	110.17	93.51	92.19
1974	94.93	94.35	92.27	86.86	80.20	75.96	69.99	62.37	55.67	65.23	62.95	59.82
1975	69.78	73.00	75.66	78.54	83.10	87.02	83.19	79.01	74.33	76.99	78.80	77.62
1976	87.05	90.26	90.62	90.08	88.04	90.32	91.29	89.70	91.26	90.35	91.12	97.88
1977	95.54	94.57	94.13	95.48	95.59	99.73	100.65	100.10	100.85	97.52	103.15	105.05
1978	100.84	101.47	106.20	115.18	120.24	120.30	126.32	135.01	132.89	111.12	114.69	117.98
1979	125.82	122.56	131.76	133.82	131.42	138.13	141.33	150.44	149.98	135.53	144.26	151.14
1980	161.75	158.03	131.00	139.99	150.45	157.78	171.81	181.52	187.76	192.78	208.15	202.34
1981	197.81	198.01	210.18	216.74	223.47	215.75	211.63	195.75	180.03	195.24	201.37	195.84
1982	188.39	179.43	175.65	184.70	178.54	171.30	167.35	177.71	187.65	212.63	232.31	232.41
1983	248.35	260.67	270.80	293.06	308.73	318.70	303.96	292.42	296.65	274.55	285.67	278.60
1984	268.43	252.57	250.78	247.44	232.82	239.65	229.70	254.64	249.94	247.03	242.53	247.35
1985	278.70	284.17	279.20	280.56	290.80	296.20	301.29	297.71	280.33	292.54	313.95	324.93
1986	335.77	359.53	374.72	383.24	400.16	405.51	371.37	382.86	350.67	360.77	359.57	349.33
1987	392.06	424.97	430.05	417.81	416.54	424.67	434.93	454.97	444.29	323.30	305.16	330.47
1988	344.66	366.95	374.64	379.23	370.34	394.66	387.33	376.55	387.71	382.46	371.45	381.38
1989	401.30	399.71	406.73	427.55	446.17	435.29	453.84	469.33	472.92	455.63	456.09	454.82
1990	415.81	425.83	435.54	420.07	458.97	462.29	438.24	381.21	344.51	329.84	359.06	373.84
1991	414.20	453.05	482.30	484.72	506.11	475.92	502.04	525.68	526.88	542.98	523.90	586.34
1992	620.21	633.47	603.77	578.68	585.31	563.60	580.83	563.12	583.27	605.17	652.73	676.95
1993	696.34	670.77	690.13	661.42	700.53	703.95	704.70	742.84	762.78	779.26	754.39	776.80
1994	800.47	792.50	743.46	733.84	735.19	705.96	722.16	765.62	764.29	777.49	750.32	751.96
1995	755.20	793.73	817.21	843.98	864.58	933.45	1001.21	1020.11	1043.54	1036.06	1059.20	1052.13
1996	1059.79	1100.05	1101.40	1190.52	1243.43	1185.02	1080.59	1141.50	1226.92	1221.51	1292.61	1291.03
1997	1379.85	1309.00	1221.70	1260.76	1400.32	1442.07	1593.81	1587.32	1685.69	1593.61	1600.55	1570.35

continued

Based on NASDAQ composite, prior to Feb. 5, 1971, based on National Quotation Bureau indices

	Jan	Feb	Mar	Apr	May	Jun	Jul	Aug	Sep	Oct	Nov	Dec
1998	1619.36	1770.51	1835.68	1868.41	1778.87	1894.74	1872.39	1499.25	1693.84	1771.39	1949.54	2192.69
1999	2505.89	2288.03	2461.40	2542.85	2470.52	2686.12	2638.49	2739.35	2746.16	2966.43	3336.16	4069.31
2000	3940.35	4696.69	4572.83	3860.66	3400.91	3966.11	3766.99	4206.35	3672.82	3369.63	2597.93	2470.52
2001	2772.73	2151.83	1840.26	2116.24	2110.49	2160.54	2027.13	1805.43	1498.80	1690.20	1930.58	1950.40
2002	1934.03	1731.49	1845.35	1688.23	1615.73	1463.21	1328.26	1314.85	1172.06	1329.75	1478.78	1335.51
2003	1320.91	1337.52	1341.17	1464.31	1595.91	1622.80	1735.02	1810.45	1786.94	1932.21	1960.26	2003.37
2004	2066.15	2029.82	1994.22	1920.15	1986.74	2047.79	1887.36	1838.10	1896.84	1974.99	2096.81	2175.44
2005	2062.41	2051.72	1999.23	1921.65	2068.22	2056.96	2184.83	2152.09	2151.69	2120.30	2232.82	2205.32
2006	2305.82	2281.39	2339.79	2322.57	2178.88	2172.09	2091.47	2183.75	2258.43	2366.71	2431.77	2415.29
2007	2463.93	2416.15	2421.64	2525.09	2604.52	2603.23	2545.57	2596.36	2701.50	2859.12	2660.96	2652.28
2008	2389.86	2271.48	2279.10	2412.80	2522.66	2292.98	2325.55	2367.52	2091.88	1720.95	1535.57	1577.03
2009	1476.42	1377.84	1528.59	1717.30	1774.33	1835.04	1978.50	2009.06	2122.42	2045.11	2144.60	2269.15
2010	2147.35	2238.26	2397.96	2461.19	2257.04	2109.24	2254.70	2114.03	2368.62	2507.41	2498.23	2652.87
2011	2700.08	2782.27	2781.07	2873.54	2835.30	2773.52	2756.38	2579.46	2415.40	2684.41	2620.34	2605.15
2012	2813.84	2966.89	3091.57	3046.36	2827.34	2935.05	2939.52	3066.96	3116.23	2977.23	3010.24	3019.51
2013	3142.13	3160.19	3267.52	3328.79	3455.91	3403.25	3626.37	3589.87	3771.48	3919.71	4059.89	4176.59
2014	4103.88	4308.12	4198.99	4114.56	4242.62	4408.18	4369.77	4580.27	4493.39	4630.74	4791.63	4736.05
2015	4635.24	4963.53	4900.88	4941.42	5070.03	4986.87	5128.28	4776.51	4620.16	5053.75	5108.67	5007.41
2016	4613.95	4557.95	4869.85	4775.36	4948.05	4842.67	5162.13	5213.22	5312.00	5189.13	5323.68	5383.12
2017	5614.79	5825.44	5911.74	6047.61	6198.52	6140.42	6348.12	6428.66	6495.96	6727.67	6873.97	6903.39
2018	7411.48	7273.01	7063.44	7066.27	7442.12	7510.30	7671.79	8109.54	8046.35	7305.90	7330.54	6635.28
2019	7281.74	7532.53	7729.32	8095.39	7453.15	8006.24	8175.42	7962.88	7999.34	8292.36	8665.47	8972.60
2020	9150.94	8567.37	7700.10	8889.55	9489.87	10058.77	10745.27	11775.46	11167.51	10911.59	12198.74	12888.28
2021	13070.69	13192.35	13246.87	13962.68	13748.74	14503.95	14672.68	15259.24	14448.58	15498.39	15537.69	15644.97
2022	14239.88	13751.40	14220.52	12334.64	12081.39	11028.74	12390.69	11816.20	10575.62	10988.15	11468.00	10466.48
2023	11584.55	11455.54	12221.91	12226.58								

Based on NASDAQ composite, prior to Feb. 5, 1971, based on National Quotation Bureau indices

	Jan	Feb	Mar	Apr	May	Jun	Jul	Aug	Sep	Oct	Nov	Dec	Year
1979	4.2	−3.5	6.0	0.3	−2.2	4.3	1.1	5.6	0.02	−7.1	5.1	2.1	16.1
1980	5.9	−0.5	−11.5	4.6	5.0	3.2	6.4	1.1	2.6	1.8	10.1	−3.9	25.6
1981	−4.6	1.0	3.8	−1.9	0.2	−1.2	−0.1	−6.2	−6.4	5.4	4.0	−3.3	−9.7
1982	−2.7	−5.9	−1.3	3.9	−3.6	−2.6	−2.3	11.3	1.2	11.3	4.0	1.3	13.7
1983	3.2	2.1	3.2	7.1	−0.2	3.7	−3.2	0.5	1.3	−2.4	2.0	−1.2	17.0
1984	−1.9	−4.4	1.1	0.3	−5.9	2.1	−1.8	10.8	−0.2	−0.1	−1.4	2.2	−0.1
1985	7.8	1.1	−0.4	−0.3	5.4	1.6	−0.8	−1.0	−3.9	4.5	6.5	4.1	26.7
1986	0.9	7.2	5.1	−1.3	5.0	1.4	−5.9	6.8	−8.5	5.1	1.4	−3.0	13.6
1987	12.7	4.0	1.9	−1.8	0.4	4.5	4.2	3.8	−2.4	−21.9	−8.0	7.2	0.02
1988	4.3	4.4	−2.9	0.7	0.2	4.8	−0.9	−3.3	3.9	2.0	−2.0	1.7	13.1
1989	6.8	−2.5	2.0	4.9	3.8	−0.8	8.2	1.7	−0.5	−2.8	1.5	1.8	25.9
1990	−7.4	1.2	2.2	−2.8	8.9	−0.7	−1.1	−9.6	−5.3	−0.8	6.4	2.7	−7.5
1991	4.5	6.9	2.5	−0.1	3.8	−4.7	4.6	2.2	−1.5	1.4	−4.1	11.2	28.8
1992	−1.4	0.9	−2.4	2.3	0.3	−1.9	4.1	−2.5	1.0	0.7	3.5	1.4	5.9
1993	0.7	0.6	2.2	−2.8	2.4	0.4	−0.4	3.5	−0.5	1.2	−1.7	1.6	7.3
1994	2.9	−2.9	−4.5	1.1	1.0	−2.9	3.1	3.9	−2.6	1.7	−3.9	1.2	−2.4
1995	2.4	3.8	2.3	2.5	3.5	2.4	3.7	0.5	3.9	−0.6	4.2	1.4	34.4
1996	3.1	1.1	0.7	1.4	2.1	−0.1	−4.9	2.5	5.5	2.1	7.1	−1.8	19.7
1997	5.8	0.2	−4.6	5.3	6.2	4.0	8.0	−4.9	5.4	−3.4	4.2	1.9	30.5
1998	0.6	7.0	4.9	0.9	−2.3	3.6	−1.3	−15.1	6.5	7.8	6.1	6.2	25.1
1999	3.5	−3.3	3.7	4.2	−2.3	5.1	−3.2	−1.0	−2.8	6.5	2.5	6.0	19.5
2000	−4.2	−0.4	8.9	−3.3	−2.7	2.5	−1.8	7.4	−4.8	−1.2	−9.3	1.1	−8.8
2001	3.2	−9.5	−6.7	8.0	0.5	−2.4	−1.4	−6.2	−8.6	2.0	7.5	0.9	−13.6
2002	−1.4	−2.1	4.0	−5.8	−1.0	−7.5	−7.5	0.3	−10.9	8.1	5.7	−5.8	−22.9
2003	−2.5	−1.7	0.9	7.9	5.5	1.2	1.8	1.9	−1.2	5.7	1.0	4.6	27.5
2004	1.8	1.2	−1.5	−1.9	1.3	1.7	−3.6	0.3	1.1	1.5	4.1	3.5	9.5
2005	−2.6	2.0	−1.7	−2.0	3.4	0.3	3.8	−1.1	0.8	−1.9	3.5	0.01	4.4
2006	2.7	0.01	1.3	1.1	−3.2	0.003	0.1	2.2	2.3	3.3	1.9	1.1	13.3
2007	1.8	−1.9	0.9	4.1	3.4	−2.0	−3.2	1.2	3.7	1.6	−4.5	−0.8	3.9
2008	−6.1	−3.3	−0.8	5.0	1.6	−8.5	−1.3	1.2	−9.7	−17.6	−7.9	1.3	−39.0
2009	−8.3	−10.7	8.5	10.0	5.3	0.1	7.5	3.4	3.9	−2.3	5.6	2.3	25.5
2010	−3.7	3.1	6.0	1.8	−8.1	−5.7	6.8	−4.7	9.0	3.8	0.1	6.5	13.9
2011	2.3	3.3	0.1	2.9	−1.3	−1.9	−2.3	−6.0	−7.6	11.1	−0.5	0.7	−0.5
2012	4.8	4.1	3.0	−0.7	−6.4	3.7	1.1	2.2	2.4	−1.8	0.5	0.8	13.9
2013	5.3	1.1	3.7	1.7	2.0	−1.5	5.2	−3.0	3.3	4.3	2.6	2.5	30.4
2014	−3.3	4.5	0.5	0.4	2.1	2.1	−1.7	3.9	−1.9	2.3	2.4	−0.4	11.1
2015	−2.8	5.5	−1.4	0.6	1.1	−2.0	1.8	−6.2	−2.9	8.0	0.1	−2.0	−1.1
2016	−5.5	−0.3	6.8	0.4	1.5	0.1	3.7	−0.1	−0.1	−2.1	3.7	1.7	9.7
2017	1.9	3.6	−0.1	0.9	1.0	0.5	1.9	0.1	2.0	2.2	2.8	1.0	19.3
2018	5.4	−3.9	−2.4	0.2	2.3	0.5	3.3	3.2	0.2	−7.2	1.8	−9.3	−6.6
2019	8.2	3.2	1.6	3.9	−6.6	6.9	1.4	−2.0	1.6	2.0	3.6	2.7	28.9
2020	−0.01	−8.3	−13.4	13.1	5.1	2.1	5.7	7.2	−3.8	−2.5	11.6	4.1	18.9
2021	−0.9	2.8	3.7	5.3	0.3	2.4	2.0	2.8	−4.7	6.9	−1.5	3.9	24.8
2022	−5.7	−2.9	3.2	−9.0	−0.3	−8.5	9.2	−4.0	−9.4	7.9	5.2	−5.9	−20.4
2023	6.6	−2.5	3.0	1.1									
TOTALS	48.3	5.4	42.1	74.2	38.5	10.3	50.0	14.6	−38.6	46.5	87.5	55.3	
AVG.	1.1	0.1	0.9	1.6	0.9	0.2	1.1	0.3	−0.9	1.1	2.0	1.3	
# Up	27	26	30	32	30	27	24	27	21	28	33	33	
# Down	18	19	15	13	14	17	20	17	23	16	11	11	

	Jan	Feb	Mar	Apr	May	Jun	Jul	Aug	Sep	Oct	Nov	Dec
1979	53.76	51.88	54.97	55.15	53.92	56.25	56.86	60.04	60.05	55.78	58.65	59.87
1980	63.40	63.07	55.79	58.38	61.31	63.27	67.30	68.05	69.84	71.08	78.26	75.20
1981	71.75	72.49	75.21	73.77	73.90	73.01	72.92	68.42	64.06	67.54	70.23	67.93
1982	66.12	62.21	61.43	63.85	61.53	59.92	58.54	65.14	65.89	73.34	76.28	77.24
1983	79.75	81.45	84.06	90.04	89.89	93.18	90.18	90.65	91.85	89.69	91.50	90.38
1984	88.69	84.76	85.73	86.00	80.94	82.61	81.13	89.87	89.67	89.62	88.36	90.31
1985	97.31	98.38	98.03	97.72	103.02	104.65	103.78	102.76	98.75	103.16	109.91	114.39
1986	115.39	123.71	130.07	128.44	134.82	136.75	128.74	137.43	125.70	132.11	133.97	130.00
1987	146.48	152.29	155.20	152.39	152.94	159.84	166.57	172.95	168.83	131.89	121.28	130.02
1988	135.55	141.54	137.45	138.37	138.66	145.31	143.99	139.26	144.68	147.55	144.59	146.99
1989	156.93	152.98	155.99	163.63	169.85	168.49	182.27	185.33	184.40	179.17	181.85	185.11
1990	171.44	173.43	177.28	172.32	187.66	186.29	184.32	166.69	157.83	156.62	166.69	171.22
1991	179.00	191.34	196.15	195.94	203.32	193.78	202.67	207.18	204.02	206.96	198.46	220.61
1992	217.52	219.50	214.29	219.13	219.71	215.60	224.37	218.86	221.15	222.65	230.44	233.59
1993	235.25	236.67	241.80	235.13	240.80	241.78	240.78	249.20	247.95	250.97	246.70	250.71
1994	258.08	250.52	239.19	241.71	244.13	237.11	244.44	254.04	247.49	251.62	241.82	244.65
1995	250.52	260.08	266.11	272.81	282.48	289.29	299.98	301.40	313.28	311.37	324.36	328.89
1996	338.97	342.56	345.01	349.84	357.35	357.10	339.44	347.79	366.77	374.38	401.05	393.75
1997	416.77	417.46	398.19	419.15	445.06	462.95	499.89	475.33	500.78	483.86	504.25	513.79
1998	517.02	553.14	580.31	585.46	572.16	592.57	584.97	496.66	529.11	570.63	605.31	642.87
1999	665.64	643.67	667.49	695.25	679.10	713.61	690.51	683.27	663.83	707.19	724.66	767.97
2000	736.08	733.04	797.99	771.58	750.98	769.68	755.57	811.17	772.60	763.06	692.40	700.09
2001	722.55	654.25	610.36	658.90	662.39	646.64	637.43	597.67	546.46	557.29	599.32	604.94
2002	596.66	583.88	607.35	572.04	566.18	523.72	484.39	486.08	433.22	468.51	495.00	466.18
2003	454.30	446.37	450.35	486.09	512.92	518.94	528.53	538.40	532.15	562.51	568.32	594.56
2004	605.21	612.58	603.42	591.83	599.40	609.31	587.21	589.09	595.66	604.51	629.26	650.99
2005	633.99	646.93	635.78	623.32	644.28	645.92	670.26	663.13	668.53	656.09	679.35	679.42
2006	697.79	697.83	706.74	714.37	691.78	691.80	692.59	707.55	723.48	747.30	761.43	770.08
2007	784.11	768.92	775.97	807.82	835.14	818.17	792.11	801.22	830.59	844.20	806.44	799.82
2008	750.97	726.42	720.32	756.03	768.28	703.22	694.07	702.17	634.08	522.47	481.43	487.77
2009	447.32	399.61	433.67	476.84	501.95	502.27	539.88	558.21	579.97	566.50	598.41	612.01
2010	589.41	607.45	643.79	655.06	601.79	567.37	606.09	577.68	629.78	653.57	654.24	696.90
2011	712.97	736.24	737.07	758.45	748.75	734.48	717.77	674.79	623.45	692.41	688.77	693.36
2012	726.33	756.42	778.92	773.50	724.12	750.61	758.60	775.07	793.74	779.35	783.37	789.90
2013	831.74	840.97	872.11	886.89	904.44	890.67	937.16	909.28	939.50	979.68	1004.97	1030.36
2014	996.48	1041.36	1046.42	1050.20	1071.96	1094.59	1075.60	1117.71	1096.43	1121.98	1148.90	1144.37
2015	1111.85	1173.46	1156.95	1164.03	1176.67	1152.64	1173.55	1100.51	1068.46	1153.55	1154.66	1131.88
2016	1069.78	1066.58	1138.84	1143.76	1160.95	1161.57	1204.43	1203.05	1202.25	1177.22	1220.68	1241.66
2017	1265.35	1311.34	1310.06	1322.44	1336.18	1343.52	1368.57	1369.61	1396.90	1427.43	1467.42	1481.81
2018	1561.66	1501.23	1464.87	1468.28	1502.31	1509.96	1560.36	1610.70	1614.54	1498.65	1525.56	1384.26
2019	1498.36	1545.73	1570.23	1631.87	1524.42	1629.02	1652.40	1618.61	1644.18	1677.08	1736.85	1784.21
2020	1784.03	1635.21	1416.49	1601.82	1682.75	1717.47	1815.99	1946.15	1872.70	1825.67	2037.36	2120.87
2021	2101.36	2159.32	2238.17	2356.67	2364.53	2421.14	2469.17	2537.31	2418.16	2583.83	2545.78	2645.91
2022	2494.64	2422.79	2501.29	2276.45	2269.07	2075.96	2267.10	2176.45	1972.29	2128.36	2239.12	2105.90
2023	2244.91	2187.75	2253.36	2279.16								

RUSSELL 2000 INDEX MONTHLY PERCENT CHANGES SINCE 1979

	Jan	Feb	Mar	Apr	May	Jun	Jul	Aug	Sep	Oct	Nov	Dec	Year
1979	9.0	–3.2	9.7	2.3	–1.8	5.3	2.9	7.8	–0.7	–11.3	8.1	6.6	38.0
1980	8.2	–2.1	–18.5	6.0	8.0	4.0	11.0	6.5	2.9	3.9	7.0	–3.7	33.8
1981	–0.6	0.3	7.7	2.5	3.0	–2.5	–2.6	–8.0	–8.6	8.2	2.8	–2.0	–1.5
1982	–3.7	–5.3	–1.5	5.1	–3.2	–4.0	–1.7	7.5	3.6	14.1	8.8	1.1	20.7
1983	7.5	6.0	2.5	7.2	7.0	4.4	–3.0	–4.0	1.6	–7.0	5.0	–2.1	26.3
1984	–1.8	–5.9	0.4	–0.7	–5.4	2.6	–5.0	11.5	–1.0	–2.0	–2.9	1.4	–9.6
1985	13.1	2.4	–2.2	–1.4	3.4	1.0	2.7	–1.2	–6.2	3.6	6.8	4.2	28.0
1986	1.5	7.0	4.7	1.4	3.3	–0.2	–9.5	3.0	–6.3	3.9	–0.5	–3.1	4.0
1987	11.5	8.2	2.4	–3.0	–0.5	2.3	2.8	2.9	–2.0	–30.8	–5.5	7.8	–10.8
1988	4.0	8.7	4.4	2.0	–2.5	7.0	–0.9	–2.8	2.3	–1.2	–3.6	3.8	22.4
1989	4.4	0.5	2.2	4.3	4.2	–2.4	4.2	2.1	0.01	–6.0	0.4	0.1	14.2
1990	–8.9	2.9	3.7	–3.4	6.8	0.1	–4.5	–13.6	–9.2	–6.2	7.3	3.7	–21.5
1991	9.1	11.0	6.9	–0.2	4.5	–6.0	3.1	3.7	0.6	2.7	–4.7	7.7	43.7
1992	8.0	2.9	–3.5	–3.7	1.2	–5.0	3.2	–3.1	2.2	3.1	7.5	3.4	16.4
1993	3.2	–2.5	3.1	–2.8	4.3	0.5	1.3	4.1	2.7	2.5	–3.4	3.3	17.0
1994	3.1	–0.4	–5.4	0.6	–1.3	–3.6	1.6	5.4	–0.5	–0.4	–4.2	2.5	–3.2
1995	–1.4	3.9	1.6	2.1	1.5	5.0	5.7	1.9	1.7	–4.6	4.2	2.4	26.2
1996	–0.2	3.0	1.8	5.3	3.9	–4.2	–8.8	5.7	3.7	–1.7	4.0	2.4	14.8
1997	1.9	–2.5	–4.9	0.1	11.0	4.1	4.6	2.2	7.2	–4.5	–0.8	1.7	20.5
1998	–1.6	7.4	4.1	0.5	–5.4	0.2	–8.2	–19.5	7.6	4.0	5.2	6.1	–3.4
1999	1.2	–8.2	1.4	8.8	1.4	4.3	–2.8	–3.8	–0.1	0.3	5.9	11.2	19.6
2000	–1.7	16.4	–6.7	–6.1	–5.9	8.6	–3.2	7.4	–3.1	–4.5	–10.4	8.4	–4.2
2001	5.1	–6.7	–5.0	7.7	2.3	3.3	–5.4	–3.3	–13.6	5.8	7.6	6.0	1.0
2002	–1.1	–2.8	7.9	0.8	–4.5	–5.1	–15.2	–0.4	–7.3	3.1	8.8	–5.7	–21.6
2003	–2.9	–3.1	1.1	9.4	10.6	1.7	6.2	4.5	–2.0	8.3	3.5	1.9	45.4
2004	4.3	0.8	0.8	–5.2	1.5	4.1	–6.8	–0.6	4.6	1.9	8.6	2.8	17.0
2005	–4.2	1.6	–3.0	–5.8	6.4	3.7	6.3	–1.9	0.2	–3.2	4.7	–0.6	3.3
2006	8.9	–0.3	4.7	–0.1	–5.7	0.5	–3.3	2.9	0.7	5.7	2.5	0.2	17.0
2007	1.6	–0.9	0.9	1.7	4.0	–1.6	–6.9	2.2	1.6	2.8	–7.3	–0.2	–2.7
2008	–6.9	–3.8	0.3	4.1	4.5	–7.8	3.6	3.5	–8.1	–20.9	–12.0	5.6	–34.8
2009	–11.2	–12.3	8.7	15.3	2.9	1.3	9.5	2.8	5.6	–6.9	3.0	7.9	25.2
2010	–3.7	4.4	8.0	5.6	–7.7	–7.9	6.8	–7.5	12.3	4.0	3.4	7.8	25.3
2011	–0.3	5.4	2.4	2.6	–2.0	–2.5	–3.7	–8.8	–11.4	15.0	–0.5	0.5	–5.5
2012	7.0	2.3	2.4	–1.6	–6.7	4.8	–1.4	3.2	3.1	–2.2	0.4	3.3	14.6
2013	6.2	1.0	4.4	–0.4	3.9	–0.7	6.9	–3.3	6.2	2.5	3.9	1.8	37.0
2014	–2.8	4.6	–0.8	–3.9	0.7	5.2	–6.1	4.8	–6.2	6.5	–0.02	2.7	3.5
2015	–3.3	5.8	1.6	–2.6	2.2	0.6	–1.2	–6.4	–5.1	5.6	3.1	–5.2	–5.7
2016	–8.8	–0.1	7.8	1.5	2.1	–0.2	5.9	1.6	0.9	–4.8	11.0	2.6	19.5
2017	0.3	1.8	–0.1	1.0	–2.2	3.3	0.7	–1.4	6.1	0.8	2.8	–0.6	13.1
2018	2.6	–4.0	1.1	0.8	5.9	0.6	1.7	4.2	–2.5	–10.9	1.4	–12.0	–12.2
2019	11.2	5.1	–2.3	3.3	–7.9	6.9	0.5	–5.1	1.9	2.6	4.0	2.7	23.7
2020	–3.3	–8.5	–21.9	13.7	6.4	3.4	2.7	5.5	–3.5	2.0	18.3	8.5	18.4
2021	5.0	6.1	0.9	2.1	0.1	1.8	–3.6	2.1	–3.1	4.2	–4.3	2.1	13.7
2022	–9.7	1.0	1.1	–10.0	–0.003	–8.4	10.4	–2.2	–9.7	10.9	2.2	–6.6	–21.6
2023	9.7	–1.8	–5.0	–1.9									
TOTALS	69.5	46.1	29.9	65.0	54.3	28.5	0.5	12.1	–30.9	–1.1	102.1	92.4	
AVG.	1.5	1.0	0.7	1.4	1.2	0.6	0.01	0.3	–0.7	–0.03	2.3	2.1	
# Up	25	26	31	28	28	28	23	25	23	26	30	33	
# Down	20	19	14	17	16	16	21	19	21	18	14	11	

172

RUSSELL 2000 INDEX MONTHLY CLOSING PRICES SINCE 1979

	Jan	Feb	Mar	Apr	May	Jun	Jul	Aug	Sep	Oct	Nov	Dec
1979	44.18	42.78	46.94	48.00	47.13	49.62	51.08	55.05	54.68	48.51	52.43	55.91
1980	60.50	59.22	48.27	51.18	55.26	57.47	63.81	67.97	69.94	72.64	77.70	74.80
1981	74.33	74.52	80.25	82.25	84.72	82.56	80.41	73.94	67.55	73.06	75.14	73.67
1982	70.96	67.21	66.21	69.59	67.39	64.67	63.59	68.38	70.84	80.86	87.96	88.90
1983	95.53	101.23	103.77	111.20	118.94	124.17	120.43	115.60	117.43	109.17	114.66	112.27
1984	110.21	103.72	104.10	103.34	97.75	100.30	95.25	106.21	105.17	103.07	100.11	101.49
1985	114.77	117.54	114.92	113.35	117.26	118.38	121.56	120.10	112.65	116.73	124.62	129.87
1986	131.78	141.00	147.63	149.66	154.61	154.23	139.65	143.83	134.73	139.95	139.26	135.00
1987	150.48	162.84	166.79	161.82	161.02	164.75	169.42	174.25	170.81	118.26	111.70	120.42
1988	125.24	136.10	142.15	145.01	141.37	151.30	149.89	145.74	149.08	147.25	142.01	147.37
1989	153.84	154.56	157.89	164.68	171.53	167.42	174.50	178.20	178.21	167.47	168.17	168.30
1990	153.27	157.72	163.63	158.09	168.91	169.04	161.51	139.52	126.70	118.83	127.50	132.16
1991	144.17	160.00	171.01	170.61	178.34	167.61	172.76	179.11	180.16	185.00	176.37	189.94
1992	205.16	211.15	203.69	196.25	198.52	188.64	194.74	188.79	192.92	198.90	213.81	221.01
1993	228.10	222.41	229.21	222.68	232.19	233.35	236.46	246.19	252.95	259.18	250.41	258.59
1994	266.52	265.53	251.06	252.55	249.28	240.29	244.06	257.32	256.12	255.02	244.25	250.36
1995	246.85	256.57	260.77	266.17	270.25	283.63	299.72	305.31	310.38	296.25	308.58	315.97
1996	315.38	324.93	330.77	348.28	361.85	346.61	316.00	333.88	346.39	340.57	354.11	362.61
1997	369.45	360.05	342.56	343.00	380.76	396.37	414.48	423.43	453.82	433.26	429.92	437.02
1998	430.05	461.83	480.68	482.89	456.62	457.39	419.75	337.95	363.59	378.16	397.75	421.96
1999	427.22	392.26	397.63	432.81	438.68	457.68	444.77	427.83	427.30	428.64	454.08	504.75
2000	496.23	577.71	539.09	506.25	476.18	517.23	500.64	537.89	521.37	497.68	445.94	483.53
2001	508.34	474.37	450.53	485.32	496.50	512.64	484.78	468.56	404.87	428.17	460.78	488.50
2002	483.10	469.36	506.46	510.67	487.47	462.64	392.42	390.96	362.27	373.50	406.35	383.09
2003	372.17	360.52	364.54	398.68	441.00	448.37	476.02	497.42	487.68	528.22	546.51	556.91
2004	580.76	585.56	590.31	559.80	568.28	591.52	551.29	547.93	572.94	583.79	633.77	651.57
2005	624.02	634.06	615.07	579.38	616.71	639.66	679.75	666.51	667.80	646.61	677.29	673.22
2006	733.20	730.64	765.14	764.54	721.01	724.67	700.56	720.53	725.59	766.84	786.12	787.66
2007	800.34	793.30	800.71	814.57	847.19	833.69	776.13	792.86	805.45	828.02	767.77	766.03
2008	713.30	686.18	687.97	716.18	748.28	689.66	714.52	739.50	679.58	537.52	473.14	499.45
2009	443.53	389.02	422.75	487.56	501.58	508.28	556.71	572.07	604.28	562.77	579.73	625.39
2010	602.04	628.56	678.64	716.60	661.61	609.49	650.89	602.06	676.14	703.35	727.01	783.65
2011	781.25	823.45	843.55	865.29	848.30	827.43	797.03	726.81	644.16	741.06	737.42	740.92
2012	792.82	810.94	830.30	816.88	761.82	798.49	786.94	812.09	837.45	818.73	821.92	849.35
2013	902.09	911.11	951.54	947.46	984.14	977.48	1045.26	1010.90	1073.79	1100.15	1142.89	1163.64
2014	1130.88	1183.03	1173.04	1126.86	1134.50	1192.96	1120.07	1174.35	1101.68	1173.51	1173.23	1204.70
2015	1165.39	1233.37	1252.77	1220.13	1246.53	1253.95	1238.68	1159.45	1100.69	1161.86	1198.11	1135.89
2016	1035.38	1033.90	1114.03	1130.84	1154.79	1151.92	1219.94	1239.91	1251.65	1191.39	1322.34	1357.13
2017	1361.82	1386.68	1385.92	1400.43	1370.21	1415.36	1425.14	1405.28	1490.86	1502.77	1544.14	1535.51
2018	1574.98	1512.45	1529.43	1541.88	1633.61	1643.07	1670.80	1740.75	1696.57	1511.41	1533.27	1348.56
2019	1499.42	1575.55	1539.74	1591.21	1465.49	1566.57	1574.61	1494.84	1523.37	1562.45	1624.50	1668.47
2020	1614.06	1476.43	1153.10	1310.66	1394.04	1441.37	1480.43	1561.88	1507.69	1538.48	1819.82	1974.86
2021	2073.64	2201.05	2220.52	2266.45	2268.97	2310.55	2226.25	2273.77	2204.37	2297.19	2198.91	2245.31
2022	2028.45	2048.09	2070.13	1864.10	1864.04	1707.99	1885.23	1844.12	1664.72	1846.86	1886.58	1761.25
2023	1931.95	1896.99	1802.48	1768.99								

173

10 <u>BEST</u> DAYS BY PERCENT AND POINT

	BY PERCENT CHANGE				BY POINT CHANGE		
DAY	CLOSE	PNT CHANGE	% CHANGE	DAY	CLOSE	PNT CHANGE	% CHANGE
DJIA 1901 to 1949							
3/15/33	62.10	8.26	15.3	10/30/29	258.47	28.40	12.3
10/6/31	99.34	12.86	14.9	11/14/29	217.28	18.59	9.4
10/30/29	258.47	28.40	12.3	10/5/29	341.36	16.19	5.0
9/21/32	75.16	7.67	11.4	10/31/29	273.51	15.04	5.8
8/3/32	58.22	5.06	9.5	10/6/31	99.34	12.86	14.9
2/11/32	78.60	6.80	9.5	11/15/29	228.73	11.45	5.3
11/14/29	217.28	18.59	9.4	6/19/30	228.97	10.13	4.6
12/18/31	80.69	6.90	9.4	9/5/39	148.12	10.03	7.3
2/13/32	85.82	7.22	9.2	11/22/28	290.34	9.81	3.5
5/6/32	59.01	4.91	9.1	10/1/30	214.14	9.24	4.5
DJIA 1950 to MAY 26, 2023							
3/24/2020	20704.91	2112.98	11.4	3/24/2020	20704.91	2112.98	11.4
10/13/2008	9387.61	936.42	11.1	3/13/2020	23185.62	1985.00	9.4
10/28/2008	9065.12	889.35	10.9	4/6/2020	22679.99	1627.46	7.7
10/21/1987	2027.85	186.84	10.2	3/26/2020	22552.17	1351.62	6.4
3/13/2020	23185.62	1985.00	9.4	3/2/2020	26703.32	1293.96	5.1
4/6/2020	22679.99	1627.46	7.7	11/10/2022	33715.37	1201.43	3.7
3/23/2009	7775.86	497.48	6.8	3/4/2020	27090.86	1173.45	4.5
11/13/2008	8835.25	552.59	6.7	3/10/2020	25018.16	1167.14	4.9
11/21/2008	8046.42	494.13	6.5	12/26/2018	22878.45	1086.25	5.0
3/26/2020	22552.17	1351.62	6.4	3/17/2020	21237.38	1048.86	5.2
S&P 500 1930 to MAY 26, 2023							
3/15/1933	6.81	0.97	16.6	3/13/2020	2711.02	230.38	9.3
10/6/1931	9.91	1.09	12.4	3/24/2020	2447.33	209.93	9.4
9/21/1932	8.52	0.90	11.8	11/10/2022	3956.37	207.80	5.5
10/13/2008	1003.35	104.13	11.6	4/6/2020	2663.68	175.03	7.0
10/28/2008	940.51	91.59	10.8	3/26/2020	2630.07	154.51	6.2
2/16/1935	10.00	0.94	10.4	3/17/2020	2529.19	143.06	6.0
8/17/1935	11.70	1.08	10.2	3/2/2020	3090.23	136.01	4.6
3/16/1935	9.05	0.82	10.0	3/10/2020	2882.23	135.67	4.9
9/12/1938	12.06	1.06	9.6	3/4/2020	3130.12	126.75	4.2
9/5/1939	12.64	1.11	9.6	5/4/2020	4300.17	124.69	3.0
NASDAQ 1971 to MAY 26, 2023							
1/3/2001	2616.69	324.83	14.2	11/10/2022	11114.15	760.98	7.4
10/13/2008	1844.25	194.74	11.8	3/13/2020	7874.88	673.08	9.4
12/5/2000	2889.80	274.05	10.5	3/24/2020	7417.86	557.19	8.1
10/28/2008	1649.47	143.57	9.5	4/6/2020	7913.24	540.16	7.3
3/13/2020	7874.88	673.08	9.4	3/16/2022	13436.55	487.93	3.8
4/5/2001	1785.00	146.20	8.9	11/30/2022	11468.00	484.22	4.4
3/24/2020	7417.86	557.19	8.1	7/27/2022	12032.42	469.85	4.1
4/18/2001	2079.44	156.22	8.1	1/31/2022	14239.88	469.31	3.4
5/30/2000	3459.48	254.37	7.9	3/9/2021	13073.82	464.66	3.7
10/13/2000	3316.77	242.09	7.9	12/7/2021	15686.92	461.77	3.0
RUSSELL 1000 1979 to MAY 26, 2023							
10/13/2008	542.98	56.75	11.7	3/13/2020	1488.04	123.38	9.0
10/28/2008	503.74	47.68	10.5	11/10/2022	2173.72	117.45	5.7
3/24/2020	1340.32	115.87	9.5	3/24/2020	1340.32	115.87	9.5
3/13/2020	1488.04	123.38	9.0	4/6/2020	1455.56	96.55	7.1
10/21/1987	135.85	11.15	8.9	3/26/2020	1442.70	83.87	6.2
4/6/2020	1455.56	96.55	7.1	3/17/2020	1381.49	74.98	5.7
3/23/2009	446.90	29.36	7.0	3/10/2020	1588.36	73.59	4.9
11/13/2008	489.83	31.99	7.0	3/2/2020	1708.13	72.92	4.5
11/24/2008	456.14	28.26	6.6	3/4/2020	1729.80	68.44	4.1
3/10/2009	391.01	23.46	6.4	5/4/2020	2368.74	67.67	2.9
RUSSELL 2000 1979 to MAY 26, 2023							
3/24/2020	1096.54	94.14	9.4	11/10/2022	1867.93	107.53	6.1
10/13/2008	570.89	48.41	9.3	3/24/2020	1096.54	94.14	9.4
11/13/2008	491.23	38.43	8.5	3/13/2020	1210.13	87.20	7.8
3/23/2009	433.72	33.61	8.4	4/6/2020	1138.78	86.73	8.2
4/6/2020	1138.78	86.73	8.2	1/6/2021	2057.92	78.81	4.0
3/13/2020	1210.13	87.20	7.8	5/18/2020	1333.69	76.70	6.1
10/21/1987	130.65	9.26	7.6	3/1/2021	2275.32	74.27	3.4
10/28/2008	482.55	34.15	7.6	3/26/2020	1180.32	69.95	6.3
11/24/2008	436.80	30.26	7.4	3/17/2020	1106.51	69.09	6.7
3/10/2009	367.75	24.49	7.1	3/19/2020	1058.75	67.59	6.8

10 <u>WORST</u> DAYS BY PERCENT AND POINT

	BY PERCENT CHANGE				BY POINT CHANGE		
DAY	CLOSE	PNT CHANGE	% CHANGE	DAY	CLOSE	PNT CHANGE	% CHANGE
			DJIA 1901 to 1949				
10/28/1929	260.64	–38.33	–12.8	10/28/1929	260.64	–38.33	–12.8
10/29/1929	230.07	–30.57	–11.7	10/29/1929	230.07	–30.57	–11.7
11/6/1929	232.13	–25.55	–9.9	11/6/1929	232.13	–25.55	–9.9
8/12/1932	63.11	–5.79	–8.4	10/23/1929	305.85	–20.66	–6.3
3/14/1907	55.84	–5.05	–8.3	11/11/1929	220.39	–16.14	–6.8
7/21/1933	88.71	–7.55	–7.8	11/4/1929	257.68	–15.83	–5.8
10/18/1937	125.73	–10.57	–7.8	12/12/1929	243.14	–15.30	–5.9
2/1/1917	88.52	–6.91	–7.2	10/3/1929	329.95	–14.55	–4.2
10/5/1932	66.07	–5.09	–7.2	6/16/1930	230.05	–14.20	–5.8
9/24/1931	107.79	–8.20	–7.1	8/9/1929	337.99	–14.11	–4.0
			DJIA 1950 to MAY 26, 2023				
10/19/1987	1738.74	–508.00	–22.6	3/16/2020	20188.52	–2997.10	–12.9
3/16/2020	20188.52	–2997.10	–12.9	3/12/2020	21200.62	–2352.60	–10.0
3/12/2020	21200.62	–2352.60	–10.0	3/9/2020	23851.02	–2013.76	–7.8
10/26/1987	1793.93	–156.83	–8.0	6/11/2020	25128.17	–1861.82	–6.9
10/15/2008	8577.91	–733.08	–7.9	3/11/2020	23553.22	–1464.94	–5.9
3/9/2020	23851.02	–2013.76	–7.8	3/18/2020	19898.92	–1338.46	–6.3
12/1/2008	8149.09	–679.95	–7.7	9/13/2022	31104.97	–1276.37	–3.9
10/9/2008	8579.19	–678.91	–7.3	2/27/2020	25766.64	–1190.95	–4.4
10/27/1997	7161.15	–554.26	–7.2	2/5/2018	24345.75	–1175.21	–4.6
9/17/2001	8920.70	–684.81	–7.1	5/18/2022	31490.07	–1164.52	–3.6
			S&P 500 1930 to MAY 26, 2023				
10/19/1987	224.84	–57.86	–20.5	3/16/2020	2386.13	–324.89	–12.0
3/16/2020	2386.13	–324.89	–12.0	3/12/2020	2480.64	–260.74	–9.5
3/18/1935	8.14	–0.91	–10.1	3/9/2020	2746.56	–225.81	–7.6
4/16/1935	8.22	–0.91	–10.0	6/11/2020	3002.10	–188.04	–5.9
9/3/1946	15.00	–1.65	–9.9	9/13/2022	3932.69	–177.72	–4.3
3/12/2020	2480.64	–260.74	–9.5	5/18/2022	3923.68	–165.17	–4.0
10/18/1937	10.76	–1.10	–9.3	4/29/2022	4131.93	–155.57	–3.6
10/15/2008	907.84	–90.17	–9.0	5/5/2022	4146.87	–153.30	–3.6
12/1/2008	816.21	–80.03	–8.9	6/13/2022	3749.63	–151.23	–3.9
7/20/1933	10.57	–1.03	–8.9	8/26/2022	4057.66	–141.46	–3.4
			NASDAQ 1971 to MAY 26, 2023				
3/16/2020	6904.59	–970.29	–12.3	3/16/2020	6904.59	–970.29	–12.3
10/19/1987	360.21	–46.12	–11.4	3/12/2020	7201.80	–750.25	–9.4
4/14/2000	3321.29	–355.49	–9.7	5/5/2002	12317.69	–647.17	–5.0
3/12/2020	7201.80	–750.25	–9.4	9/13/2022	11633.57	–632.84	–5.2
9/29/2008	1983.73	–199.61	–9.1	3/9/2020	7950.68	–624.94	–7.3
10/26/1987	298.90	–29.55	–9.0	9/3/2020	11458.10	–598.34	–5.0
10/20/1987	327.79	–32.42	–9.0	5/18/2022	11418.15	–566.37	–4.7
12/1/2008	1398.07	–137.50	–9.0	2/3/2022	13878.82	–538.73	–3.7
8/31/1998	1499.25	–140.43	–8.6	4/29/2022	12334.64	–536.89	–4.2
10/15/2008	1628.33	–150.68	–8.5	6/13/2022	10809.23	–530.79	–4.7
			RUSSELL 1000 1979 to MAY 26, 2023				
10/19/1987	121.04	–28.40	–19.0	3/16/2020	1306.51	–181.53	–12.2
3/16/2020	1306.51	–181.53	–12.2	3/12/2020	1364.66	–144.34	–9.6
3/12/2020	1364.66	–144.34	–9.6	3/9/2020	1514.77	–127.21	–7.8
10/15/2008	489.71	–49.11	–9.1	6/11/2020	1660.70	–104.50	–5.9
12/1/2008	437.75	–43.68	–9.1	9/13/2022	2167.18	–97.21	–4.3
9/29/2008	602.34	–57.35	–8.7	5/18/2022	2154.00	–90.51	–4.0
10/26/1987	119.45	–10.74	–8.3	5/5/2022	2281.85	–86.89	–3.7
3/9/2020	1514.77	–127.21	–7.8	6/13/2022	2057.56	–86.45	–4.0
10/9/2008	492.13	–40.05	–7.5	4/29/2022	2276.45	–85.24	–3.6
8/8/2011	617.28	–45.56	–6.9	3/11/2020	1509.00	–79.36	–5.0
			RUSSELL 2000 1979 to MAY 26, 2023				
3/16/2020	1037.42	–172.71	–14.3	3/16/2020	1037.42	–172.71	–14.3
10/19/1987	133.60	–19.14	–12.5	3/12/2020	1122.93	–141.37	–11.2
12/1/2008	417.07	–56.07	–11.9	3/9/2020	1313.44	–135.78	–9.4
3/12/2020	1122.93	–141.37	–11.2	3/18/2020	991.16	–115.35	–10.4
3/18/2020	991.16	–115.35	–10.4	6/11/2020	1356.22	–111.17	–7.6
10/15/2008	502.11	–52.54	–9.5	3/11/2020	1264.30	–86.60	–6.4
3/9/2020	1313.44	–135.78	–9.4	6/13/2022	1714.60	–85.68	–4.8
10/26/1987	110.33	–11.26	–9.3	11/26/2021	2245.94	–85.52	–3.7
10/20/1987	121.39	–12.21	–9.1	2/25/2021	2200.17	–84.21	–3.7
8/8/2011	650.96	–63.67	–8.9	6/16/2022	1649.84	–81.30	–4.7

10 BEST WEEKS BY PERCENT AND POINT

	BY PERCENT CHANGE				BY POINT CHANGE		
WEEK ENDS	CLOSE	PNT CHANGE	% CHANGE	WEEK ENDS	CLOSE	PNT CHANGE	% CHANGE
DJIA 1901 to 1949							
8/6/1932	66.56	12.30	22.7	12/7/1929	263.46	24.51	10.3
6/25/1938	131.94	18.71	16.5	6/25/1938	131.94	18.71	16.5
2/13/1932	85.82	11.37	15.3	6/27/1931	156.93	17.97	12.9
4/22/1933	72.24	9.36	14.9	11/22/1929	245.74	17.01	7.4
10/10/1931	105.61	12.84	13.8	8/17/1929	360.70	15.86	4.6
7/30/1932	54.26	6.42	13.4	12/22/1928	285.94	15.22	5.6
6/27/1931	156.93	17.97	12.9	8/24/1929	375.44	14.74	4.1
9/24/1932	74.83	8.39	12.6	2/21/1929	310.06	14.21	4.8
8/27/1932	75.61	8.43	12.6	5/10/1930	272.01	13.70	5.3
3/18/1933	60.56	6.72	12.5	11/15/1930	186.68	13.54	7.8
DJIA 1950 to MAY 26, 2023							
3/27/2020	21636.78	2462.80	12.8	4/9/2020	23719.37	2666.84	12.7
4/9/2020	23719.37	2666.84	12.7	3/27/2020	21636.78	2462.80	12.8
10/11/1974	658.17	73.61	12.6	5/27/2022	33212.96	1951.06	6.2
10/31/2008	9325.01	946.06	11.3	11/6/2020	28323.40	1821.80	6.9
8/20/1982	869.29	81.24	10.3	3/18/2022	34754.93	1810.74	5.5
11/28/2008	8829.04	782.62	9.7	10/28/2022	32861.80	1779.24	5.7
3/13/2009	7223.98	597.04	9.0	6/5/2020	27110.98	1727.87	6.8
10/8/1982	986.85	79.11	8.7	6/24/2022	31500.68	1611.90	5.4
3/21/2003	8521.97	662.26	8.4	10/21/2022	31082.56	1447.73	4.9
8/3/1984	1202.08	87.46	7.9	12/10/2021	35970.99	1390.91	4.0
S&P 500 1930 to MAY 26, 2023							
8/6/1932	7.22	1.12	18.4	4/9/2020	2789.82	301.17	12.1
6/25/1938	11.39	1.72	17.8	3/18/2022	4463.12	258.81	6.2
7/30/1932	6.10	0.89	17.1	5/27/2022	4158.24	256.88	6.6
4/22/1933	7.75	1.09	16.4	11/6/2020	3509.44	239.48	7.3
10/11/1974	71.14	8.80	14.1	6/24/2022	3911.74	236.90	6.5
2/13/1932	8.80	1.08	14.0	3/27/2020	2541.47	236.55	10.3
9/24/1932	8.52	1.02	13.6	11/11/2022	3992.93	222.38	5.9
10/10/1931	10.64	1.27	13.6	12/10/2021	4712.02	173.59	3.8
8/27/1932	8.57	1.01	13.4	2/5/2021	3886.83	172.59	4.7
3/18/1933	6.61	0.77	13.2	10/21/2022	3752.75	169.68	4.7
NASDAQ 1971 to MAY 26, 2023							
6/2/2000	3813.38	608.27	19.0	3/18/2022	13893.84	1050.03	8.2
4/12/2001	1961.43	241.07	14.0	11/6/2020	11895.23	983.64	9.0
11/28/2008	1535.57	151.22	10.9	11/11/2022	11323.33	848.08	8.1
10/31/2008	1720.95	168.92	10.9	6/24/2022	11607.62	809.27	7.5
3/13/2009	1431.50	137.65	10.6	2/5/2021	13856.30	785.61	6.0
4/9/2020	8153.58	780.50	10.6	4/9/2020	8153.58	780.50	10.6
4/20/2001	2163.41	201.98	10.3	5/27/2022	12131.13	776.51	6.8
12/8/2000	2917.43	272.14	10.3	3/27/2020	7502.38	622.86	9.1
4/20/2000	3643.88	322.59	9.7	6/2/2000	3813.38	608.27	19.0
10/11/1974	60.42	5.26	9.5	7/29/2022	12390.69	556.58	4.7
RUSSELL 1000 1979 to MAY 26, 2023							
4/9/2020	1530.05	171.04	12.6	4/9/2020	1530.05	171.04	12.6
11/28/2008	481.43	53.55	12.5	3/18/2022	2466.14	146.57	6.3
10/31/2008	522.47	50.94	10.8	5/27/2022	2285.42	140.71	6.6
3/13/2009	411.10	39.88	10.7	11/6/2020	1962.60	136.93	7.5
3/27/2020	1394.65	133.96	10.6	3/27/2020	1394.65	133.96	10.6
8/20/1982	61.51	4.83	8.5	6/24/2022	2149.71	132.36	6.6
6/2/2000	785.02	57.93	8.0	11/11/2022	2195.85	125.55	6.1
9/28/2001	546.46	38.48	7.6	2/5/2021	2204.27	102.91	4.9
10/16/1998	546.09	38.45	7.6	12/10/2021	2615.38	92.35	3.7
8/3/1984	87.43	6.13	7.5	10/21/2022	2061.13	91.75	4.7
RUSSELL 2000 1979 to MAY 26, 2023							
4/9/2020	1246.73	194.68	18.5	4/9/2020	1246.73	194.68	18.5
11/28/2008	473.14	66.60	16.4	3/12/2021	2352.79	160.58	7.3
10/31/2008	537.52	66.40	14.1	2/5/2021	2233.33	159.69	7.7
6/2/2000	513.03	55.66	12.2	11/5/2021	2437.08	139.89	6.1
3/13/2009	393.09	42.04	12.0	11/11/2016	1282.38	118.94	10.2
3/27/2020	1131.99	118.10	11.7	3/27/2020	1131.99	118.10	11.7
12/2/2011	735.02	68.86	10.3	1/8/2021	2091.66	116.80	5.9
11/11/2016	1282.38	118.94	10.2	5/27/2022	1887.90	114.63	6.5
10/14/2011	712.46	56.25	8.6	6/5/2020	1507.15	113.11	8.1
6/5/2020	1507.15	113.11	8.1	8/27/2021	2277.15	109.55	5.1

10 WORST WEEKS BY PERCENT AND POINT

	BY PERCENT CHANGE				BY POINT CHANGE		
WEEK ENDS	CLOSE	PNT CHANGE	% CHANGE	WEEK ENDS	CLOSE	PNT CHANGE	% CHANGE
DJIA 1901 to 1949							
7/22/1933	88.42	−17.68	−16.7	11/8/1929	236.53	−36.98	−13.5
5/18/1940	122.43	−22.42	−15.5	12/8/1928	257.33	−33.47	−11.5
10/8/1932	61.17	−10.92	−15.2	6/21/1930	215.30	−28.95	−11.9
10/3/1931	92.77	−14.59	−13.6	10/19/1929	323.87	−28.82	−8.2
11/8/1929	236.53	−36.98	−13.5	5/3/1930	258.31	−27.15	−9.5
9/17/1932	66.44	−10.10	−13.2	10/31/1929	273.51	−25.46	−8.5
10/21/1933	83.64	−11.95	−12.5	10/26/1929	298.97	−24.90	−7.7
12/12/1931	78.93	−11.21	−12.4	5/18/1940	122.43	−22.42	−15.5
5/8/1915	62.77	−8.74	−12.2	2/8/1929	301.53	−18.23	−5.7
6/21/1930	215.30	−28.95	−11.9	10/11/1930	193.05	−18.05	−8.6
DJIA 1950 to MAY 26, 2023							
10/10/2008	8451.19	−1874.19	−18.2	3/20/2020	19173.98	−4011.64	−17.3
3/20/2020	19173.98	−4011.64	−17.3	2/28/2020	25409.36	−3583.05	−12.4
9/21/2001	8235.81	−1369.70	−14.3	3/13/2020	23185.62	−2679.16	−10.4
10/23/1987	1950.76	−295.98	−13.2	10/10/2008	8451.19	−1874.19	−18.2
2/28/2020	25409.36	−3583.05	−12.4	10/30/2020	26501.60	−1833.97	−6.5
3/13/2020	23185.62	−2679.16	−10.4	12/21/2018	22445.37	−1655.14	−6.9
10/16/1987	2246.74	−235.47	−9.5	1/21/2022	31392.79	−1646.44	−4.6
10/13/1989	2569.26	−216.26	−7.8	6/10/2022	31392.79	−1506.91	−4.6
3/16/2001	9823.41	−821.21	−7.7	6/12/2020	25605.54	−1505.44	−5.6
7/19/2002	8019.26	−665.27	−7.7	6/17/2022	29888.78	−1504.01	−4.8
S&P 500 1930 to MAY 26, 2023							
7/22/1933	9.71	−2.20	−18.5	3/20/2020	2304.92	−406.10	−15.0
10/10/2008	899.22	−200.01	−18.2	2/28/2020	2954.22	−383.53	−11.5
5/18/1940	9.75	−2.05	−17.4	1/21/2022	4397.94	−264.91	−5.7
10/8/1932	6.77	−1.38	−16.9	3/13/2020	2711.02	−261.35	−8.8
3/20/2020	2304.92	−406.10	−15.0	6/17/2022	3674.84	−226.02	−5.8
9/17/1932	7.50	−1.28	−14.6	6/10/2022	3900.86	−207.68	−5.1
10/21/1933	8.57	−1.31	−13.3	10/10/2008	899.22	−200.01	−18.2
10/3/1931	9.37	−1.36	−12.7	10/30/2020	3269.96	−195.43	−5.6
10/23/1987	248.22	−34.48	−12.2	9/16/2022	3873.33	−194.03	−4.8
12/12/1931	8.20	−1.13	−12.1	3/10/2023	3861.59	−184.05	−4.6
NASDAQ 1971 to MAY 26, 2023							
4/14/2000	3321.29	−1125.16	−25.3	4/14/2000	3321.29	−1125.16	−25.3
10/23/1987	328.45	−77.88	−19.2	1/21/2022	13768.92	−1124.83	−7.6
9/21/2001	1423.19	−272.19	−16.1	2/28/2020	8567.37	−1009.22	−10.5
10/10/2008	1649.51	−297.88	−15.3	3/20/2020	6879.52	−995.36	−12.6
3/20/2020	6879.52	−995.36	−12.6	1/7/2022	14935.90	−709.07	−4.5
11/10/2000	3028.99	−422.59	−12.2	3/13/2020	7874.88	−700.74	−8.2
10/3/2008	1947.39	−235.95	−10.8	2/26/2021	13192.35	−682.11	−4.9
7/28/2000	3663.00	−431.45	−10.5	6/10/2022	11340.02	−672.71	−5.6
2/28/2020	8567.37	−1009.22	−10.5	9/16/2022	11448.40	−663.91	−5.5
10/24/2008	1552.03	−159.26	−9.3	10/30/2020	10911.59	−636.69	−5.5
RUSSELL 1000 1979 to MAY 26, 2023							
10/10/2008	486.23	−108.31	−18.2	3/20/2020	1260.69	−227.35	−15.3
3/20/2020	1260.69	−227.35	−15.3	2/28/2020	1635.21	−214.22	−11.6
10/23/1987	130.19	−19.25	−12.9	3/13/2020	1488.04	−153.94	−9.4
9/21/2001	507.98	−67.59	−11.7	1/21/2022	2427.56	−149.96	−5.8
2/28/2020	1635.21	−214.22	−11.6	6/17/2022	2017.35	−126.66	−5.9
4/14/2000	715.20	−90.39	−11.2	6/10/2022	2144.01	−114.51	−5.1
10/3/2008	594.54	−65.15	−9.9	10/30/2020	1825.67	−110.60	−5.7
3/13/2020	1488.04	−153.94	−9.4	3/10/2023	2120.53	−109.44	−4.9
10/16/1987	149.44	−14.42	−8.8	10/10/2008	486.23	−108.31	−18.2
11/21/2008	427.88	−41.15	−8.8	9/16/2022	2132.17	−108.31	−4.8
RUSSELL 2000 1979 to MAY 26, 2023							
10/23/1987	121.59	−31.15	−20.4	3/13/2020	1210.13	−239.09	−16.5
3/13/2020	1210.13	−239.09	−16.5	2/28/2020	1476.43	−202.18	−12.0
4/14/2000	453.72	−89.27	−16.4	3/20/2020	1013.89	−196.24	−16.2
3/20/2020	1013.89	−196.24	−16.2	1/21/2022	1987.92	−174.54	−8.1
10/10/2008	522.48	−96.92	−15.7	3/10/2023	1772.70	−155.56	−8.1
9/21/2001	378.89	−61.84	−14.0	6/17/2022	1665.69	−134.59	−7.5
10/3/2008	619.40	−85.39	−12.1	6/12/2020	1387.68	−119.47	−7.9
2/28/2020	1476.43	−202.18	−12.0	12/21/2018	1292.09	−118.72	−8.4
11/21/2008	406.54	−49.98	−11.0	9/23/2022	1679.59	−118.60	−6.6
10/24/2008	471.12	−55.31	−10.5	7/16/2021	2163.24	−116.76	−5.1

10 **BEST** MONTHS BY PERCENT AND POINT

	BY PERCENT CHANGE				BY POINT CHANGE		
MONTH	CLOSE	PNT CHANGE	% CHANGE	MONTH	CLOSE	PNT CHANGE	% CHANGE
DJIA 1901 to 1949							
Apr-1933	77.66	22.26	40.2	Nov-1928	293.38	41.22	16.3
Aug-1932	73.16	18.90	34.8	Jun-1929	333.79	36.38	12.2
Jul-1932	54.26	11.42	26.7	Aug-1929	380.33	32.63	9.4
Jun-1938	133.88	26.14	24.3	Jun-1938	133.88	26.14	24.3
Apr-1915	71.78	10.95	18.0	Aug-1928	240.41	24.41	11.3
Jun-1931	150.18	21.72	16.9	Apr-1933	77.66	22.26	40.2
Nov-1928	293.38	41.22	16.3	Feb-1931	189.66	22.11	13.2
Nov-1904	52.76	6.59	14.3	Jun-1931	150.18	21.72	16.9
May-1919	105.50	12.62	13.6	Aug-1932	73.16	18.90	34.8
Sep-1939	152.54	18.13	13.5	Jan-1930	267.14	18.66	7.5
DJIA 1950 to APRIL 2023							
Jan-1976	975.28	122.87	14.4	Oct-2022	32732.95	4007.44	14.0
Jan-1975	703.69	87.45	14.2	Nov-2020	29638.64	3137.04	11.8
Oct-2022	32732.95	4007.44	14.0	Apr-2020	24345.72	2428.56	11.1
Jan-1987	2158.04	262.09	13.8	Jul-2022	32845.13	2069.70	6.7
Nov-2020	29638.64	3137.04	11.8	Mar-2021	32981.55	2049.18	6.6
Aug-1982	901.31	92.71	11.5	Aug-2020	28430.05	2001.73	7.6
Apr-2020	24345.72	2428.56	11.1	Oct-2021	35819.56	1975.64	5.8
Oct-1982	991.72	95.47	10.7	Nov-2022	34589.77	1856.82	5.7
Oct-2002	8397.03	805.10	10.6	Dec-2021	36338.30	1854.58	5.4
Apr-1978	837.32	79.96	10.6	Jun-2019	26599.96	1784.92	7.2
S&P 500 1930 to APRIL 2023							
Apr-1933	8.32	2.47	42.2	Nov-2020	3621.63	351.67	10.8
Jul-1932	6.10	1.67	37.7	Jul-2022	4130.29	344.91	9.1
Aug-1932	8.39	2.29	37.5	Apr-2020	2912.43	327.84	12.7
Jun-1938	11.56	2.29	24.7	Oct-2021	4605.38	297.84	6.9
Sep-1939	13.02	1.84	16.5	Oct-2022	3871.98	286.36	8.0
Oct-1974	73.90	10.36	16.3	Jan-2023	4076.60	237.10	6.2
May-1933	9.64	1.32	15.9	Aug-2020	3500.31	229.19	7.0
Apr-1938	9.70	1.20	14.1	Apr-2021	4181.17	208.28	5.2
Jun-1931	14.83	1.81	13.9	Nov-2022	4080.11	208.13	5.4
Jan-1987	274.08	31.91	13.2	Dec-2021	4766.18	199.18	4.4
NASDAQ 1971 to APRIL 2023							
Dec-1999	4069.31	733.15	22.0	Jul-2022	12390.69	1361.95	12.4
Feb-2000	4696.69	756.34	19.2	Nov-2020	12198.74	1287.15	11.8
Oct-1974	65.23	9.56	17.2	Apr-2020	8889.55	1189.45	15.5
Jan-1975	69.78	9.96	16.7	Jan-2023	11584.55	1118.07	10.7
Jun-2000	3966.11	565.20	16.6	Oct-2021	15498.39	1049.81	7.3
Apr-2020	8889.55	1189.45	15.5	Aug-2020	11775.46	1030.19	9.6
Apr-2001	2116.24	275.98	15.0	Mar-2023	12221.91	766.37	6.7
Jan-1999	2505.89	313.20	14.3	Feb-2000	4696.69	756.34	19.2
Nov-2001	1930.58	240.38	14.2	Jun-2021	14503.95	755.21	5.5
Oct-2002	1329.75	157.69	13.5	Dec-1999	4069.31	733.15	22.0
RUSSELL 1000 1979 to APRIL 2023							
Apr-2020	1601.82	185.33	13.1	Nov-2020	2037.36	211.69	11.6
Jan-1987	146.48	16.48	12.7	Jul-2022	2267.10	191.14	9.2
Nov-2020	2037.36	211.69	11.6	Apr-2020	1601.82	185.33	13.1
Oct-1982	73.34	7.45	11.3	Oct-2021	2583.83	165.67	6.9
Aug-1982	65.14	6.60	11.3	Oct-2022	2128.36	156.07	7.9
Dec-1991	220.61	22.15	11.2	Jan-2023	2244.91	139.01	6.6
Oct-2011	692.41	68.96	11.1	Aug-2020	1946.15	130.16	7.2
Aug-1984	89.87	8.74	10.8	Apr-2021	2356.67	118.50	5.3
Nov-1980	78.26	7.18	10.1	Jan-2019	1498.36	114.10	8.2
Apr-2009	476.84	43.17	10.0	Nov-2022	2239.12	110.76	5.2
RUSSELL 2000 1979 to APRIL 2023							
Nov-2020	1819.82	281.34	18.3	Nov-2020	1819.82	281.34	18.3
Feb-2000	577.71	81.48	16.4	Oct-2022	1846.86	182.14	10.9
Apr-2009	487.56	64.81	15.3	Jul-2022	1885.23	177.24	10.4
Oct-2011	741.06	96.90	15.0	Jan-2023	1931.95	170.70	9.7
Oct-1982	80.86	10.02	14.1	Apr-2020	1310.66	157.56	13.7
Apr-2020	1310.66	157.56	13.7	Dec-2020	1974.86	155.04	8.5
Jan-1985	114.77	13.28	13.1	Jan-2019	1499.42	150.86	11.2
Sep-2010	676.14	74.08	12.3	Nov-2016	1322.34	130.95	11.0
Aug-1984	106.21	10.96	11.5	Feb-2021	2201.05	127.41	6.1
Jan-1987	150.48	15.48	11.5	Jun-2019	1566.57	101.08	6.9

10 <u>WORST</u> MONTHS BY PERCENT AND POINT

	BY PERCENT CHANGE				BY POINT CHANGE		
MONTH	CLOSE	PNT CHANGE	% CHANGE	MONTH	CLOSE	PNT CHANGE	% CHANGE
DJIA 1901 to 1949							
Sep-1931	96.61	−42.80	−30.7	Oct-1929	273.51	−69.94	−20.4
Mar-1938	98.95	−30.69	−23.7	Jun-1930	226.34	−48.73	−17.7
Apr-1932	56.11	−17.17	−23.4	Sep-1931	96.61	−42.80	−30.7
May-1940	116.22	−32.21	−21.7	Sep-1929	343.45	−36.88	−9.7
Oct-1929	273.51	−69.94	−20.4	Sep-1930	204.90	−35.52	−14.8
May-1932	44.74	−11.37	−20.3	Nov-1929	238.95	−34.56	−12.6
Jun-1930	226.34	−48.73	−17.7	May-1940	116.22	−32.21	−21.7
Dec-1931	77.90	−15.97	−17.0	Mar-1938	98.95	−30.69	−23.7
Feb-1933	51.39	−9.51	−15.6	Sep-1937	154.57	−22.84	−12.9
May-1931	128.46	−22.73	−15.0	May-1931	128.46	−22.73	−15.0
DJIA 1950 to APRIL 2023							
Oct-1987	1993.53	−602.75	−23.2	Mar-2020	21917.16	−3492.20	−13.7
Aug-1998	7539.07	−1344.22	−15.1	Feb-2020	25409.36	−2846.67	−10.1
Oct-2008	9325.01	−1525.65	−14.1	Sep-2022	28725.51	−2784.92	−8.8
Nov-1973	822.25	−134.33	−14.0	Jun-2022	30775.43	−2214.69	−6.7
Mar-2020	21917.16	−3492.20	−13.7	Dec-2018	23327.46	−2211.00	−8.7
Sep-2002	7591.93	−1071.57	−12.4	May-2019	24815.04	−1777.87	−6.7
Feb-2009	7062.93	−937.93	−11.7	Apr-2022	32977.21	−1701.14	−4.9
Sep-2001	8847.56	−1102.19	−11.1	Oct-2008	9325.01	−1525.65	−14.1
Sep-1974	607.87	−70.71	−10.4	Sep-2021	33843.92	−1516.81	−4.3
Aug-1974	678.58	−78.85	−10.4	Dec-2022	33147.25	−1442.52	−4.2
S&P 500 1930 to APRIL 2023							
Sep-1931	9.71	−4.15	−29.9	Apr-2022	4131.93	−398.48	−8.8
Mar-1938	8.50	−2.84	−25.0	Mar-2020	2584.59	−369.63	−12.5
May-1940	9.27	−2.92	−24.0	Sep-2022	3585.62	−369.38	−9.3
May-1932	4.47	−1.36	−23.3	Jun-2022	3785.38	−346.77	−8.4
Oct-1987	251.79	−70.04	−21.8	Feb-2020	2954.22	−271.30	−8.4
Apr-1932	5.83	−1.48	−20.2	Dec-2018	2506.85	−253.31	−9.2
Feb-1933	5.66	−1.28	−18.4	Jan-2022	4515.55	−250.63	−5.3
Oct-2008	968.75	−197.61	−16.9	Dec-2022	3839.50	−240.61	−5.9
Jun-1930	20.46	−4.03	−16.5	Sep-2021	4307.54	−215.14	−4.8
Aug-1998	957.28	−163.39	−14.6	Oct-2018	2711.74	−202.24	−6.9
NASDAQ 1971 to APRIL 2023							
Oct-1987	323.30	−120.99	−27.2	Apr-2022	12334.64	−1885.88	−13.3
Nov-2000	2597.93	−771.70	−22.9	Jan-2022	14239.88	−1405.09	−9.0
Feb-2001	2151.83	−620.90	−22.4	Sep-2022	10575.62	−1240.58	−10.5
Aug-1998	1499.25	−373.14	−19.9	Jun-2022	11028.74	−1052.65	−8.7
Oct-2008	1720.95	−370.93	−17.7	Dec-2022	10466.48	−1001.52	−8.7
Mar-1980	131.00	−27.03	−17.1	Mar-2020	7700.10	−867.27	−10.1
Sep-2001	1498.80	−306.63	−17.0	Sep-2021	14448.58	−810.66	−5.3
Oct-1978	111.12	−21.77	−16.4	Nov-2000	2597.93	−771.70	−22.9
Apr-2000	3860.66	−712.17	−15.6	Oct-2018	7305.90	−740.45	−9.2
Nov-1973	93.51	−16.66	−15.1	Apr-2000	3860.66	−712.17	−15.6
RUSSELL 1000 1979 to APRIL 2023							
Oct-1987	131.89	−36.94	−21.9	Apr-2022	2276.45	−224.84	−9.0
Oct-2008	522.47	−111.61	−17.6	Mar-2020	1416.49	−218.72	−13.4
Aug-1998	496.66	−88.31	−15.1	Sep-2022	1972.29	−204.16	−9.4
Mar-2020	1416.49	−218.72	−13.4	Jun-2022	2075.96	−193.11	−8.5
Mar-1980	55.79	−7.28	−11.5	Jan-2022	2494.64	−151.27	−5.7
Sep-2002	433.22	−52.86	−10.9	Feb-2020	1635.21	−148.82	−8.3
Feb-2009	399.61	−47.71	−10.7	Dec-2018	1384.26	−141.30	−9.3
Sep-2008	634.08	−68.09	−9.7	Dec-2022	2105.90	−133.22	−5.9
Aug-1990	166.69	−17.63	−9.6	Sep-2021	2418.16	−119.15	−4.7
Feb-2001	654.25	−68.30	−9.5	Oct-2018	1498.65	−115.89	−7.2
RUSSELL 2000 1979 to APRIL 2023							
Oct-1987	118.26	−52.55	−30.8	Mar-2020	1153.10	−323.33	−21.9
Mar-2020	1153.10	−323.33	−21.9	Jan-2022	2028.45	−216.86	−9.7
Oct-2008	537.52	−142.06	−20.9	Apr-2022	1864.10	−206.03	−10.0
Aug-1998	337.95	−81.80	−19.5	Oct-2018	1511.41	−185.16	−10.9
Mar-1980	48.27	−10.95	−18.5	Dec-2018	1348.56	−184.71	−12.0
Jul-2002	392.42	−70.22	−15.2	Sep-2022	1664.72	−179.40	−9.7
Aug-1990	139.52	−21.99	−13.6	Jun-2022	1707.99	−156.05	−8.4
Sep-2001	404.87	−63.69	−13.6	Oct-2008	537.52	−142.06	−20.9
Feb-2009	389.02	−54.51	−12.3	Feb-2020	1476.43	−137.63	−8.5
Dec-2018	1348.56	−184.71	−12.0	May-2019	1465.49	−125.72	−7.9

179

10 BEST QUARTERS BY PERCENT AND POINT

BY PERCENT CHANGE				BY POINT CHANGE			
QUARTER	CLOSE	PNT CHANGE	% CHANGE	QUARTER	CLOSE	PNT CHANGE	% CHANGE
DJIA 1901 to 1949							
Jun-1933	98.14	42.74	77.1	Dec-1928	300.00	60.57	25.3
Sep-1932	71.56	28.72	67.0	Jun-1933	98.14	42.74	77.1
Jun-1938	133.88	34.93	35.3	Mar-1930	286.10	37.62	15.1
Sep-1915	90.58	20.52	29.3	Jun-1938	133.88	34.93	35.3
Dec-1928	300.00	60.57	25.3	Sep-1927	197.59	31.36	18.9
Dec-1904	50.99	8.80	20.9	Sep-1928	239.43	28.88	13.7
Jun-1919	106.98	18.13	20.4	Sep-1932	71.56	28.72	67.0
Sep-1927	197.59	31.36	18.9	Jun-1929	333.79	24.94	8.1
Dec-1905	70.47	10.47	17.4	Sep-1939	152.54	21.91	16.8
Jun-1935	118.21	17.40	17.3	Sep-1915	90.58	20.52	29.3
DJIA 1950 to MARCH 2023							
Mar-1975	768.15	151.91	24.7	Dec-2022	33147.25	4421.74	15.4
Mar-1987	2304.69	408.74	21.6	Jun-2020	25812.88	3895.72	17.8
Jun-2020	25812.88	3895.72	17.8	Dec-2020	30606.48	2824.78	10.2
Mar-1986	1818.61	271.94	17.6	Mar-2019	25928.68	2601.22	11.2
Mar-1976	999.45	147.04	17.3	Dec-2021	36338.30	2494.38	7.4
Dec-1998	9181.43	1338.81	17.1	Mar-2021	32981.55	2375.07	7.8
Dec-1982	1046.54	150.29	16.8	Dec-2017	24719.22	2314.13	10.3
Jun-1997	7672.79	1089.31	16.6	Sep-2018	26458.31	2186.90	9.0
Dec-1985	1546.67	218.04	16.4	Sep-2020	27781.70	1968.82	7.6
Dec-2022	33147.25	4421.74	15.4	Dec-2019	28538.44	1621.61	6.0
S&P 500 1930 to MARCH 2023							
Jun-1933	10.91	5.06	86.5	Jun-2020	3100.29	515.70	20.0
Sep-1932	8.08	3.65	82.4	Dec-2021	4766.18	458.64	10.7
Jun-1938	11.56	3.06	36.0	Dec-2020	3756.07	393.07	11.7
Mar-1975	83.36	14.80	21.6	Mar-2019	2834.40	327.55	13.1
Dec-1998	1229.23	212.22	20.9	Jun-2021	4297.50	324.61	8.2
Jun-1935	10.23	1.76	20.8	Mar-2023	4109.31	269.81	7.0
Mar-1987	291.70	49.53	20.5	Sep-2020	3363.00	262.71	8.5
Jun-2020	3100.29	515.70	20.0	Dec-2019	3230.78	254.04	8.5
Sep-1939	13.02	2.16	19.9	Dec-2022	3839.50	253.88	7.1
Mar-1943	11.58	1.81	18.5	Mar-2021	3972.89	216.82	5.8
NASDAQ 1971 to MARCH 2023							
Dec-1999	4069.31	1323.15	48.2	Jun-2020	10058.77	2358.67	30.6
Jun-2020	10058.77	2358.67	30.6	Mar-2023	12221.91	1755.43	16.8
Dec-2001	1950.40	451.60	30.1	Dec-2020	12888.28	1720.77	15.4
Dec-1998	2192.69	498.85	29.5	Dec-1999	4069.31	1323.15	48.2
Mar-1991	482.30	108.46	29.0	Jun-2021	14503.95	1257.08	9.5
Mar-1975	75.66	15.84	26.5	Dec-2021	15644.97	1196.39	8.3
Dec-1982	232.41	44.76	23.9	Sep-2020	11167.51	1108.74	11.0
Mar-1987	430.05	80.72	23.1	Mar-2019	7729.32	1094.04	16.5
Jun-2003	1622.80	281.63	21.0	Dec-2019	8972.60	973.26	12.2
Jun-1980	157.78	26.78	20.4	Sep-2018	8046.35	536.05	7.1
RUSSELL 1000 1979 to MARCH 2023							
Dec-1998	642.87	113.76	21.5	Jun-2020	1717.47	300.98	21.3
Jun-2020	1717.47	300.98	21.3	Dec-2020	2120.87	248.17	13.3
Mar-1987	155.20	25.20	19.4	Dec-2021	2645.91	227.75	9.4
Dec-1982	77.24	11.35	17.2	Mar-2019	1570.23	185.97	13.4
Jun-1997	462.95	64.76	16.3	Jun-2021	2421.14	182.97	8.2
Dec-1985	114.39	15.64	15.8	Sep-2020	1872.70	155.23	9.0
Jun-2009	502.27	68.60	15.8	Mar-2023	2253.36	147.46	7.0
Dec-1999	767.97	104.14	15.7	Dec-2019	1784.21	140.03	8.5
Sep-2009	579.97	77.70	15.5	Dec-2022	2105.90	133.61	6.8
Jun-2003	518.94	68.59	15.2	Mar-2021	2238.17	117.30	5.5
RUSSELL 2000 1979 to MARCH 2023							
Dec-2020	1974.86	467.17	31.0	Dec-2020	1974.86	467.17	31.0
Mar-1991	171.01	38.85	29.4	Jun-2020	1441.37	288.27	25.0
Dec-1982	88.90	18.06	25.5	Mar-2021	2220.52	245.66	12.4
Jun-2020	1441.37	288.27	25.0	Mar-2019	1539.74	191.18	14.2
Mar-1987	166.79	31.79	23.6	Dec-2019	1668.47	145.10	9.5
Jun-2003	448.37	83.83	23.0	Jun-2018	1643.07	113.64	7.4
Sep-1980	69.94	12.47	21.7	Dec-2010	783.65	107.51	15.9
Dec-2001	488.50	83.63	20.7	Dec-2016	1357.13	105.48	8.4
Jun-2009	508.28	85.53	20.2	Dec-2014	1204.70	103.02	9.4
Jun-1983	124.17	20.40	19.7	Mar-2013	951.54	102.19	12.0

10 <u>WORST</u> QUARTERS BY PERCENT AND POINT

	BY PERCENT CHANGE				BY POINT CHANGE		
QUARTER	CLOSE	PNT CHANGE	% CHANGE	QUARTER	CLOSE	PNT CHANGE	% CHANGE
DJIA 1901 to 1949							
Jun-1932	42.84	–30.44	–41.5	Dec-1929	248.48	–94.97	–27.7
Sep-1931	96.61	–53.57	–35.7	Jun-1930	226.34	–59.76	–20.9
Dec-1929	248.48	–94.97	–27.7	Sep-1931	96.61	–53.57	–35.7
Sep-1903	33.55	–9.73	–22.5	Dec-1930	164.58	–40.32	–19.7
Dec-1937	120.85	–33.72	–21.8	Dec-1937	120.85	–33.72	–21.8
Jun-1930	226.34	–59.76	–20.9	Sep-1946	172.42	–33.20	–16.1
Dec-1930	164.58	–40.32	–19.7	Jun-1932	42.84	–30.44	–41.5
Dec-1931	77.90	–18.71	–19.4	Jun-1940	121.87	–26.08	–17.6
Mar-1938	98.95	–21.90	–18.1	Mar-1939	131.84	–22.92	–14.8
Jun-1940	121.87	–26.08	–17.6	Jun-1931	150.18	–22.18	–12.9
DJIA 1950 to MARCH 2023							
Dec-1987	1938.83	–657.45	–25.3	Mar-2020	21917.16	–6621.28	–23.2
Sep-1974	607.87	–194.54	–24.2	Jun-2022	30775.43	–3902.92	–11.3
Mar-2020	21917.16	–6621.28	–23.2	Dec-2018	23327.46	–3130.85	–11.8
Jun-1962	561.28	–145.67	–20.6	Dec-2008	8776.39	–2074.27	–19.1
Dec-2008	8776.39	–2074.27	–19.1	Sep-2002	28725.51	–2049.92	–6.7
Sep-2002	7591.93	–1651.33	–17.9	Mar-2022	34678.35	–1659.95	–4.6
Sep-2001	8847.56	–1654.84	–15.8	Sep-2001	8847.56	–1654.84	–15.8
Sep-1990	2452.48	–428.21	–14.9	Sep-2002	7591.93	–1651.33	–17.9
Mar-2009	7608.92	–1167.47	–13.3	Sep-2011	10913.38	–1500.96	–12.1
Sep-1981	849.98	–126.90	–13.0	Sep-2015	16284.00	–1335.51	–7.6
S&P 500 1930 to MARCH 2023							
Jun-1932	4.43	–2.88	–39.4	Jun-2022	3785.38	–745.03	–16.4
Sep-1931	9.71	–5.12	–34.5	Mar-2020	2584.59	–646.19	–20.0
Sep-1974	63.54	–22.46	–26.1	Dec-2018	2506.85	–407.13	–14.0
Dec-1937	10.55	–3.21	–23.3	Dec-2008	903.25	–263.11	–22.6
Dec-1987	247.08	–74.75	–23.2	Mar-2022	4530.41	–235.77	–4.9
Dec-2008	903.25	–263.11	–22.6	Sep-2022	3585.62	–199.76	–5.3
Jun-1962	54.75	–14.80	–21.3	Sep-2011	1131.42	–189.22	–14.3
Mar-2020	2584.59	–646.19	–20.0	Sep-2001	1040.94	–183.48	–15.0
Mar-1938	8.50	–2.05	–19.4	Sep-2002	815.28	–174.54	–17.6
Jun-1970	72.72	–16.91	–18.9	Mar-2001	1160.33	–159.95	–12.1
NASDAQ 1971 to MARCH 2023							
Dec-2000	2470.52	–1202.30	–32.7	Jun-2022	11028.74	–3191.78	–22.4
Sep-2001	1498.80	–661.74	–30.6	Mar-2022	14220.52	–1424.45	–9.1
Sep-1974	55.67	–20.29	–26.7	Dec-2018	6635.28	–1411.07	–17.5
Dec-1987	330.47	–113.82	–25.6	Mar-2020	7700.10	–1272.50	–14.2
Mar-2001	1840.26	–630.26	–25.5	Dec-2000	2470.52	–1202.30	–32.7
Sep-1990	344.51	–117.78	–25.5	Sep-2001	1498.80	–661.74	–30.6
Dec-2008	1577.03	–514.85	–24.6	Mar-2001	1840.26	–630.26	–25.5
Jun-2022	11028.74	–3191.78	–22.4	Jun-2000	3966.11	–606.72	–13.3
Jun-2002	1463.21	–382.14	–20.7	Dec-2008	1577.03	–514.85	–24.6
Sep-2002	1172.06	–291.15	–19.9	Sep-2022	10575.62	–453.12	–4.1
RUSSELL 1000 1979 to MARCH 2023							
Dec-2008	487.77	–146.31	–23.1	Jun-2022	2075.96	–425.33	–17.0
Dec-1987	130.02	–38.81	–23.0	Mar-2020	1416.49	–367.72	–20.6
Mar-2020	1416.49	–367.72	–20.6	Dec-2018	1384.26	–230.28	–14.3
Sep-2002	433.22	–90.50	–17.3	Dec-2008	487.77	–146.31	–23.1
Jun-2022	2075.96	–425.33	–17.0	Mar-2022	2501.29	–144.62	–5.5
Sep-2001	546.46	–100.18	–15.5	Sep-2011	623.45	–111.03	–15.1
Sep-1990	157.83	–28.46	–15.3	Sep-2022	1972.29	–103.67	–5.0
Sep-2011	623.45	–111.03	–15.1	Sep-2001	546.46	–100.18	–15.5
Dec-2018	1384.26	–230.28	–14.3	Sep-2002	433.22	–90.50	–17.3
Jun-2002	523.72	–83.63	–13.8	Mar-2001	610.36	–89.73	–12.8
RUSSELL 2000 1979 to MARCH 2023							
Mar-2020	1153.10	–515.37	–30.9	Mar-2020	1153.10	–515.37	–30.9
Dec-1987	120.42	–50.39	–29.5	Jun-2022	1707.99	–362.14	–17.5
Dec-2008	499.45	–180.13	–26.5	Dec-2018	1348.56	–348.01	–20.5
Sep-1990	126.70	–42.34	–25.0	Sep-2011	644.16	–183.27	–22.1
Sep-2011	644.16	–183.27	–22.1	Dec-2008	499.45	–180.13	–26.5
Sep-2002	362.27	–100.37	–21.7	Mar-2022	2070.13	–175.18	–7.8
Sep-2001	404.87	–107.77	–21.0	Sep-2015	1100.69	–153.26	–12.2
Dec-2018	1348.56	–348.01	–20.5	Sep-2001	404.87	–107.77	–21.0
Sep-1998	363.59	–93.80	–20.5	Sep-2021	2204.37	–106.18	–4.6
Sep-1981	67.55	–15.01	–18.2	Sep-2002	362.27	–100.37	–21.7

10 **BEST** YEARS BY PERCENT AND POINT

	BY PERCENT CHANGE				BY POINT CHANGE		
YEAR	CLOSE	PNT CHANGE	% CHANGE	YEAR	CLOSE	PNT CHANGE	% CHANGE
DJIA 1901 to 1949							
1915	99.15	44.57	81.7	1928	300.00	97.60	48.2
1933	99.90	39.97	66.7	1927	202.40	45.20	28.8
1928	300.00	97.60	48.2	1915	99.15	44.57	81.7
1908	63.11	20.07	46.6	1945	192.91	40.59	26.6
1904	50.99	15.01	41.7	1935	144.13	40.09	38.5
1935	144.13	40.09	38.5	1933	99.90	39.97	66.7
1905	70.47	19.48	38.2	1925	156.66	36.15	30.0
1919	107.23	25.03	30.5	1936	179.90	35.77	24.8
1925	156.66	36.15	30.0	1938	154.76	33.91	28.1
1927	202.40	45.20	28.8	1919	107.23	25.03	30.5
DJIA 1950 TO 2022							
1954	404.39	123.49	44.0	2019	28538.44	5210.98	22.3
1975	852.41	236.17	38.3	2017	24719.22	4956.62	25.1
1958	583.65	147.96	34.0	2013	16576.66	3472.52	26.5
1995	5117.12	1282.68	33.5	2016	19762.60	2337.57	13.4
1985	1546.67	335.10	27.7	1999	11497.12	2315.69	25.2
1989	2753.20	584.63	27.0	2003	10453.92	2112.29	25.3
2013	16576.66	3472.52	26.5	2020	30606.48	2068.04	7.3
1996	6448.27	1331.15	26.0	2006	12463.15	1745.65	16.3
2003	10453.92	2112.29	25.3	2009	10428.05	1651.66	18.8
1999	11497.12	2315.69	25.2	1997	7908.25	1459.98	22.6
S&P 500 1930 TO 2022							
1933	10.10	3.21	46.6	2019	3230.78	723.93	28.9
1954	35.98	11.17	45.0	2020	3756.07	525.29	16.3
1935	13.43	3.93	41.4	2017	2673.61	434.78	19.4
1958	55.21	15.22	38.1	2013	1848.36	422.17	29.6
1995	615.93	156.66	34.1	1998	1229.23	258.80	26.7
1975	90.19	21.63	31.5	1999	1469.25	240.02	19.5
1997	970.43	229.69	31.0	2003	1111.92	232.10	26.4
1945	17.36	4.08	30.7	1997	970.43	229.69	31.0
2013	1848.36	422.17	29.6	2009	1115.10	211.85	23.5
2019	3230.78	723.93	28.9	2014	2058.90	210.54	11.4
NASDAQ 1971 TO 2022							
1999	4069.31	1876.62	85.6	2020	12888.28	3915.68	43.6
1991	586.34	212.50	56.8	2019	8972.60	2337.32	35.2
2003	2003.37	667.86	50.0	1999	4069.31	1876.62	85.6
2009	2269.15	692.12	43.9	2017	6903.39	1520.27	28.2
2020	12888.28	3915.68	43.6	2013	4176.59	1157.08	38.3
1995	1052.13	300.17	39.9	2009	2269.15	692.12	43.9
1998	2192.69	622.34	39.6	2003	2003.37	667.86	50.0
2013	4176.59	1157.08	38.3	1998	2192.69	622.34	39.6
2019	8972.60	2337.32	35.2	2014	4736.05	559.46	13.4
1980	202.34	51.20	33.9	2012	3019.51	414.36	15.9
RUSSELL 1000 1979 TO 2022							
1995	328.89	84.24	34.4	2019	1784.21	399.95	28.9
1997	513.79	120.04	30.5	2020	2120.87	336.66	18.9
2013	1030.36	240.46	30.4	2013	1030.36	240.46	30.4
2019	1784.21	399.95	28.9	2017	1481.81	240.15	19.3
1991	220.61	49.39	28.9	1998	642.87	129.08	25.1
2003	594.56	128.38	27.5	2003	594.56	128.38	27.5
1985	114.39	24.08	26.7	1999	767.97	125.10	19.5
1989	185.11	38.12	25.9	2009	612.01	124.24	25.5
1980	75.20	15.33	25.6	1997	513.79	120.04	30.5
2009	612.01	124.24	25.5	2014	1144.37	114.01	11.1
RUSSELL 2000 1979 TO 2022							
2003	556.91	173.82	45.4	2019	1668.47	319.91	23.7
1991	189.94	57.78	43.7	2013	1163.64	314.29	37.0
1979	55.91	15.39	38.0	2020	1974.86	306.39	18.4
2013	1163.64	314.29	37.0	2016	1357.13	221.24	19.5
1980	74.80	18.89	33.8	2017	1535.51	178.38	13.1
1985	129.87	28.38	28.0	2003	556.91	173.82	45.4
1983	112.27	23.37	26.3	2010	783.65	158.26	25.3
1995	315.97	65.61	26.2	2009	625.39	125.94	25.2
2010	783.65	158.26	25.3	2006	787.66	114.44	17.0
2009	625.39	125.94	25.2	2012	849.35	108.43	14.6

10 <u>WORST</u> YEARS BY PERCENT AND POINT

	BY PERCENT CHANGE				BY POINT CHANGE		
YEAR	CLOSE	PNT CHANGE	% CHANGE	YEAR	CLOSE	PNT CHANGE	% CHANGE

DJIA 1901 to 1949

YEAR	CLOSE	PNT CHANGE	% CHANGE	YEAR	CLOSE	PNT CHANGE	% CHANGE
1931	77.90	−86.68	−52.7	1931	77.90	−86.68	−52.7
1907	43.04	−26.08	−37.7	1930	164.58	−83.90	−33.8
1930	164.58	−83.90	−33.8	1937	120.85	−59.05	−32.8
1920	71.95	−35.28	−32.9	1929	248.48	−51.52	−17.2
1937	120.85	−59.05	−32.8	1920	71.95	−35.28	−32.9
1903	35.98	−11.12	−23.6	1907	43.04	−26.08	−37.7
1932	59.93	−17.97	−23.1	1917	74.38	−20.62	−21.7
1917	74.38	−20.62	−21.7	1941	110.96	−20.17	−15.4
1910	59.60	−12.96	−17.9	1940	131.13	−19.11	−12.7
1929	248.48	−51.52	−17.2	1932	59.93	−17.97	−23.1

DJIA 1950 TO 2022

YEAR	CLOSE	PNT CHANGE	% CHANGE	YEAR	CLOSE	PNT CHANGE	% CHANGE
2008	8776.39	−4488.43	−33.8	2008	8776.39	−4488.43	−33.8
1974	616.24	−234.62	−27.6	2022	33147.25	−3191.05	−8.8
1966	785.69	−183.57	−18.9	2002	8341.63	−1679.87	−16.8
1977	831.17	−173.48	−17.3	2018	23327.46	−1391.76	−5.6
2002	8341.63	−1679.87	−16.8	2001	10021.50	−765.35	−7.1
1973	850.86	−169.16	−16.6	2000	10786.85	−710.27	−6.2
1969	800.36	−143.39	−15.2	2015	17425.03	−398.04	−2.2
1957	435.69	−63.78	−12.8	1974	616.24	−234.62	−27.6
1962	652.10	−79.04	−10.8	1966	785.69	−183.57	−18.9
1960	615.89	−63.47	−9.3	1977	831.17	−173.48	−17.3

S&P 500 1930 TO 2022

YEAR	CLOSE	PNT CHANGE	% CHANGE	YEAR	CLOSE	PNT CHANGE	% CHANGE
1931	8.12	−7.22	−47.1	2022	3839.50	−926.68	−19.4
1937	10.55	−6.63	−38.6	2008	903.25	−565.11	−38.5
2008	903.25	−565.11	−38.5	2002	879.82	−268.26	−23.4
1974	68.56	−28.99	−29.7	2001	1148.08	−172.20	−13.0
1930	15.34	−6.11	−28.5	2018	2506.85	−166.76	−6.2
2002	879.82	−268.26	−23.4	2000	1320.28	−148.97	−10.1
2022	3839.50	−926.68	−19.4	1974	68.56	−28.99	−29.7
1941	8.69	−1.89	−17.9	1990	330.22	−23.18	−6.6
1973	97.55	−20.50	−17.4	1973	97.55	−20.50	−17.4
1940	10.58	−1.91	−15.3	2015	2043.94	−14.96	−0.7

NASDAQ 1971 TO 2022

YEAR	CLOSE	PNT CHANGE	% CHANGE	YEAR	CLOSE	PNT CHANGE	% CHANGE
2008	1577.03	−1075.25	−40.5	2022	10466.48	−5178.49	−33.1
2000	2470.52	−1598.79	−39.3	2000	2470.52	−1598.79	−39.3
1974	59.82	−32.37	−35.1	2008	1577.03	−1075.25	−40.5
2022	10466.48	−5178.49	−33.1	2002	1335.51	−614.89	−31.5
2002	1335.51	−614.89	−31.5	2001	1950.40	−520.12	−21.1
1973	92.19	−41.54	−31.1	2018	6635.28	−268.11	−3.9
2001	1950.40	−520.12	−21.1	1990	373.84	−80.98	−17.8
1990	373.84	−80.98	−17.8	2011	2605.15	−47.72	−1.8
1984	247.35	−31.25	−11.2	1973	92.19	−41.54	−31.1
1987	330.47	−18.86	−5.4	1974	59.82	−32.37	−35.1

RUSSELL 1000 1979 TO 2022

YEAR	CLOSE	PNT CHANGE	% CHANGE	YEAR	CLOSE	PNT CHANGE	% CHANGE
2008	487.77	−312.05	−39.0	2022	2105.90	−540.01	−20.4
2002	466.18	−138.76	−22.9	2008	487.77	−312.05	−39.0
2022	2105.90	−540.01	−20.4	2002	466.18	−138.76	−22.9
2001	604.94	−95.15	−13.6	2018	1384.26	−97.55	−6.6
1981	67.93	−7.27	−9.7	2001	604.94	−95.15	−13.6
2000	700.09	−67.88	−8.8	2000	700.09	−67.88	−8.8
1990	171.22	−13.89	−7.5	1990	171.22	−13.89	−7.5
2018	1384.26	−97.55	−6.6	2015	1131.88	−12.49	−1.1
1994	244.65	−6.06	−2.4	1981	67.93	−7.27	−9.7
2015	1131.88	−12.49	−1.1	1994	244.65	−6.06	−2.4

RUSSELL 2000 1979 TO 2022

YEAR	CLOSE	PNT CHANGE	% CHANGE	YEAR	CLOSE	PNT CHANGE	% CHANGE
2008	499.45	−266.58	−34.8	2022	1761.25	−484.06	−21.6
2002	383.09	−105.41	−21.6	2008	499.45	−266.58	−34.8
2022	1761.25	−484.06	−21.6	2018	1348.56	−186.95	−12.2
1990	132.16	−36.14	−21.5	2002	383.09	−105.41	−21.6
2018	1348.56	−186.95	−12.2	2015	1135.89	−68.81	−5.7
1987	120.42	−14.58	−10.8	2011	740.92	−42.73	−5.5
1984	101.49	−10.78	−9.6	1990	132.16	−36.14	−21.5
2015	1135.89	−68.81	−5.7	2007	766.03	−21.63	−2.7
2011	740.92	−42.73	−5.5	2000	483.53	−21.22	−4.2
2000	483.53	−21.22	−4.2	1998	421.96	−15.06	−3.4

STRATEGY PLANNING AND RECORD SECTION

CONTENTS

These forms are available at our website, www.stocktradersalmanac.com under "Forms" located at the bottom of the homepage.

PORTFOLIO AT START OF 2024

DATE ACQUIRED	NO. OF SHARES	SECURITY	PRICE	TOTAL COST	PAPER PROFITS	PAPER LOSSES

ADDITIONAL PURCHASES

DATE ACQUIRED	NO. OF SHARES	SECURITY	PRICE	TOTAL COST	REASON FOR PURCHASE PRIME OBJECTIVE, ETC.

ADDITIONAL PURCHASES

DATE ACQUIRED	NO. OF SHARES	SECURITY	PRICE	TOTAL COST	REASON FOR PURCHASE PRIME OBJECTIVE, ETC.

SHORT-TERM TRANSACTIONS

Pages 188–191 can accompany next year's income tax return (Schedule D). Enter transactions as completed to avoid last-minute pressures.

NO. OF SHARES	SECURITY	DATE ACQUIRED	DATE SOLD	SALE PRICE	COST	LOSS	GAIN

TOTALS:
Carry over to next page

188

SHORT-TERM TRANSACTIONS (continued)

NO. OF SHARES	SECURITY	DATE ACQUIRED	DATE SOLD	SALE PRICE	COST	LOSS	GAIN

TOTALS:

LONG-TERM TRANSACTIONS

Pages 188–191 can accompany next year's income tax return (Schedule D). Enter transactions as completed to avoid last-minute pressures.

NO. OF SHARES	SECURITY	DATE ACQUIRED	DATE SOLD	SALE PRICE	COST	LOSS	GAIN

TOTALS: Carry over to next page

190

LONG-TERM TRANSACTIONS *(continued)*

NO. OF SHARES	SECURITY	DATE ACQUIRED	DATE SOLD	SALE PRICE	COST	LOSS	GAIN

TOTALS:

191

INTEREST/DIVIDENDS RECEIVED DURING 2024

SHARES	STOCK/BOND	FIRST QUARTER		SECOND QUARTER		THIRD QUARTER		FOURTH QUARTER	
		$		$		$		$	

BROKERAGE ACCOUNT DATA 2024

	MARGIN INTEREST	TRANSFER TAXES	CAPITAL ADDED	CAPITAL WITHDRAWN
JAN				
FEB				
MAR				
APR				
MAY				
JUN				
JUL				
AUG				
SEP				
OCT				
NOV				
DEC				

WEEKLY PORTFOLIO PRICE RECORD 2024 (FIRST HALF)

Place purchase price above stock name and weekly closes below.

STOCKS Week Ending	1	2	3	4	5	6	7	8	9	10
5										
12										
19										
26										
2										
9										
16										
23										
1										
8										
15										
22										
29										
5										
12										
19										
26										
3										
10										
17										
24										
31										
7										
14										
21										
28										

WEEKLY PORTFOLIO PRICE RECORD 2024 (SECOND HALF)

Place purchase price above stock name and weekly closes below.

STOCKS										
Week Ending	1	2	3	4	5	6	7	8	9	10

JULY

	1	2	3	4	5	6	7	8	9	10
5										
12										
19										
26										

AUGUST

2										
9										
16										
23										
30										

SEPTEMBER

6										
13										
20										
27										

OCTOBER

4										
11										
18										
25										

NOVEMBER

1										
8										
15										
22										
29										

DECEMBER

6										
13										
20										
27										

WEEKLY INDICATOR DATA 2024 (FIRST HALF)

Week Ending	Dow Jones Industrial Average	Net Change for Week	Net Change on Friday	Net Change Next Monday	S&P or NASDAQ	NYSE Ad-vances	NYSE De-clines	New Highs	New Lows	CBOE Put/Call Ratio	90-Day Treas. Rate	Moody's AAA Rate
5												
12												
19												
26												
2												
9												
16												
23												
1												
8												
15												
22												
29												
5												
12												
19												
26												
3												
10												
17												
24												
31												
7												
14												
21												
28												

WEEKLY INDICATOR DATA 2024 (SECOND HALF)

Week Ending	Dow Jones Industrial Average	Net Change for Week	Net Change on Friday	Net Change Next Monday	S&P or NASDAQ	NYSE Advances	NYSE Declines	New Highs	New Lows	CBOE Put/Call Ratio	90-Day Treas. Rate	Moody's AAA Rate
JULY												
5												
12												
19												
26												
AUGUST												
2												
9												
16												
23												
30												
SEPTEMBER												
6												
13												
20												
27												
OCTOBER												
4												
11												
18												
25												
NOVEMBER												
1												
8												
15												
22												
29												
DECEMBER												
6												
13												
20												
27												

MONTHLY INDICATOR DATA 2024

	DJIA% Last 3 + 1st 2 Days	DJIA% 9th to 11th Trading Days	DJIA% Change Rest of Month	DJIA% Change Whole Month	% Change Your Stocks	Gross Domestic Product	Prime Rate	Trade Deficit $ Billion	CPI % Change	% Unem- ployment Rate
JAN										
FEB										
MAR										
APR										
MAY										
JUN										
JUL										
AUG										
SEP										
OCT										
NOV										
DEC										

INSTRUCTIONS:

Weekly Indicator Data (pages 195-196). Keeping data on several indicators may give you a better feel of the market. In addition to the closing Dow and its net change for the week, post the net change for Friday's Dow and also the following Monday's. A series of "down Fridays" followed by "down Mondays" often precedes a downswing (see page 78). Tracking either the S&P or NASDAQ composite, and advances and declines, will help prevent the Dow from misleading you. New highs and lows and put/call ratios (www.cboe.com) are also useful indicators. Many of these weekly figures appear in weekend papers or *Barron's* (https://www.barrons.com/market-data/market-lab). Data for the 90-day Treasury Rate and 30-year Treasury Rate are quite important for tracking short- and long-term interest rates. These figures are available from:

https://fred.stlouisfed.org/

Monthly Indicator Data. The purpose of the first three columns is to enable you to track the market's bullish bias near the end, beginning and middle of the month, which has been shifting lately (see pages 86, 147 and 148). Market direction, performance of your stocks, gross domestic product, prime rate, trade deficit, Consumer Price Index, and unemployment rate are worthwhile indicators to follow. Or, readers may wish to gauge other data.

PORTFOLIO AT END OF 2024

DATE ACQUIRED	NO. OF SHARES	SECURITY	PRICE	TOTAL COST	PAPER PROFITS	PAPER LOSSES

IF YOU DON'T PROFIT FROM YOUR INVESTMENT MISTAKES, SOMEONE ELSE WILL

No matter how much we may deny it, almost every successful person on Wall Street pays a great deal of attention to trading suggestions—especially when they come from "the right sources."

One of the hardest things to learn is to distinguish between good tips and bad ones. Usually, the best tips have a logical reason behind them, which accompanies the tip. Poor tips usually have no reason to support them.

The important thing to remember is that the market discounts. It does not review, it does not reflect. The Street's real interest in "tips," inside information, buying and selling suggestions and everything else of this kind emanates from a desire to find out just what the market has on hand to discount. The process of finding out involves separating the wheat from the chaff—and there is plenty of chaff.

HOW TO MAKE USE OF STOCK "TIPS"

- The source should be **reliable**. (By listing all "tips" and suggestions on a Performance Record of Recommendations, such as the form below, and then periodically evaluating the outcomes, you will soon know the "batting average" of your sources.)

- The story should make sense. Would the merger violate antitrust laws? Are there too many computers on the market already? How many years will it take to become profitable?

- The stock should not have had a recent sharp run-up. Otherwise, the story may already be discounted, and confirmation or denial in the press would most likely be accompanied by a sell-off in the stock.

PERFORMANCE RECORD OF RECOMMENDATIONS

STOCK RECOMMENDED	BY WHOM	DATE	PRICE	REASON FOR RECOMMENDATION	SUBSEQUENT ACTION OF STOCK

INDIVIDUAL RETIREMENT ACCOUNTS: MOST AWESOME INVESTMENT INCENTIVE EVER DEVISED

MAX IRA INVESTMENTS OF $6,500* A YEAR COMPOUNDED AT VARIOUS INTEREST RATES OF RETURN FOR DIFFERENT PERIODS

Annual Rate	5 Yrs	10 Yrs	15 Yrs	20 Yrs	25 Yrs	30 Yrs	35 Yrs	40 Yrs	45 Yrs	50 Yrs
1%	$33,488	$68,684	$105,676	$144,555	$185,417	$228,363	$273,500	$320,939	$370,798	$423,201
2%	34,503	72,597	114,655	161,092	212,361	268,966	331,463	400,465	476,649	560,761
3%	35,545	76,751	124,520	179,897	244,095	318,517	404,794	504,811	620,759	755,175
4%	36,614	81,161	135,359	201,300	281,526	379,134	497,889	642,372	818,159	1,032,029
5%	37,712	85,844	147,274	225,675	325,737	453,445	616,436	824,458	1,089,954	1,428,800
6%	38,840	90,816	160,371	253,453	378,016	544,711	767,786	1,066,310	1,465,803	2,000,414
7%	39,996	96,093	174,772	285,124	439,897	656,975	961,437	1,388,462	1,987,386	2,827,409
8%	41,184	101,696	190,608	321,249	513,204	795,248	1,209,664	1,818,577	2,713,269	4,027,866
9%	42,402	107,642	208,022	362,469	600,106	965,739	1,528,311	2,393,897	3,725,709	5,774,867
10%	43,651	113,953	227,173	409,516	703,181	1,176,132	1,937,824	3,164,537	5,140,170	8,321,946
11%	44,934	120,649	248,235	463,223	825,492	1,435,936	2,464,569	4,197,875	7,118,597	12,040,184
12%	46,249	127,755	271,396	524,542	970,671	1,756,902	3,142,510	5,584,426	9,887,915	17,472,133
13%	47,598	135,293	296,866	594,554	1,143,026	2,153,548	4,015,371	7,445,658	13,765,739	25,410,080
14%	48,981	143,289	324,872	674,495	1,347,663	2,643,791	5,139,374	9,944,406	19,196,085	37,009,403
15%	50,399	151,770	355,664	765,766	1,590,628	3,249,720	6,586,747	13,298,700	26,798,835	53,952,429
16%	51,854	160,764	389,513	869,963	1,879,074	3,998,550	8,450,176	17,800,110	37,438,165	78,684,792
17%	53,345	170,300	426,718	988,900	2,221,457	4,923,774	10,848,464	23,838,039	52,317,005	114,755,660
18%	54,873	180,408	467,604	1,124,637	2,627,769	6,066,571	13,933,718	31,931,844	73,107,196	167,306,428
19%	56,439	191,123	512,526	1,279,508	3,109,799	7,477,519	17,900,443	42,773,227	102,128,486	243,771,126
20%	58,044	202,478	561,874	1,456,166	3,681,452	9,218,676	22,997,061	57,282,091	142,594,218	354,878,088

* At Press Time - 2024 Contribution Limit will be indexed to inflation

G. M. LOEB'S "BATTLE PLAN" FOR INVESTMENT SURVIVAL

LIFE IS CHANGE: Nothing can ever be the same a minute from now as it was a minute ago. Everything you own is changing in price and value. You can find that last price of an active security on the stock ticker, but you cannot find the next price anywhere. The value of your money is changing. Even the value of your home is changing, though no one walks in front of it with a sandwich board consistently posting the changes.

RECOGNIZE CHANGE: Your basic objective should be to profit from change. The art of investing is being able to recognize change and to adjust investment goals accordingly.

WRITE THINGS DOWN: You will score more investment success and avoid more investment failures if you write things down. Very few investors have the drive and inclination to do this.

KEEP A CHECKLIST: If you aim to improve your investment results, get into the habit of keeping a checklist on every issue you consider buying. Before making a commitment, it will pay you to write down the answers to at least some of the basic questions—How much am I investing in this company? How much do I think I can make? How much do I have to risk? How long do I expect to take to reach my goal?

HAVE A SINGLE RULING REASON: Above all, writing things down is the best way to find "the ruling reason." When all is said and done, there is invariably a single reason that stands out above all others, why a particular security transaction can be expected to show a profit. All too often, many relatively unimportant statistics are allowed to obscure this single important point.

Any one of a dozen factors may be the point of a particular purchase or sale. It could be a technical reason—an increase in earnings or dividend not yet discounted in the market price—a change of management—a promising new product—an expected improvement in the market's valuation of earnings—or many others. But, in any given case, one of these factors will almost certainly be more important than all the rest put together.

CLOSING OUT A COMMITMENT: If you have a loss, the solution is automatic, provided you decide what to do at the time you buy. Otherwise, the question divides itself into two parts. Are we in a bull or bear market? Few of us really know until it is too late. For the sake of the record, if you think it is a bear market, just put that consideration first and sell as much as your conviction suggests and your nature allows.

If you think it is a bull market, or at least a market where some stocks move up, some mark time and only a few decline, do not sell unless:

✓ You see a bear market ahead.
✓ You see trouble for a particular company in which you own shares.
✓ Time and circumstances have turned up a new and seemingly far better buy than the issue you like least in your list.
✓ Your shares stop going up and start going down.

A subsidiary question is, which stock to sell first? Two further observations may help:

✓ Do not sell solely because you think a stock is "overvalued."
✓ If you want to sell some of your stocks and not all, in most cases it is better to go against your emotional inclinations and sell first the issues with losses, small profits or none at all, the weakest, the most disappointing and so on.

Mr. Loeb is the author of *The Battle for Investment Survival*, John Wiley & Sons.

G. M. LOEB'S INVESTMENT SURVIVAL CHECKLIST

OBJECTIVES AND RISKS

Security		Price	Shares	Date

"Ruling reason" for commitment	Amount of commitment $_____
	% of my investment capital _____%

Price objective	Est. time to achieve it	I will risk _____ points	Which would be $_____

TECHNICAL POSITION

Price action of stock:	Dow Jones Industrial Average
❏ Hitting new highs ❏ In a trading range	
❏ Pausing in an uptrend ❏ Moving up from low ground	Trend of market
❏ Acting stronger than market ❏ _____	

SELECTED YARDSTICKS

	Price Range		Earnings Per Share Actual or Projected	Price/Earnings Ratio Actual or Projected
	High	Low		
Current year				
Previous year				

Merger possibilities	Years for earnings to double in past
Comment on future	Years for market price to double in past

PERIODIC RECHECKS

Date	Stock Price	DJIA	Comment	Action taken, if any

COMPLETED TRANSACTIONS

Date closed	Period of time held	Profit or loss

Reason for profit or loss

NOTES

NOTES